TELEVISION BRANDCASTING

WITHDRAWN

Television Brandcasting examines U.S. television's utility as a medium for branded storytelling. It investigates the current and historical role that television content, promotion, and hybrids of the two have played in disseminating brand messaging and influencing consumer decision-making. Juxtaposing the current period of transition with that of the 1950s–1960s, Jennifer Gillan outlines how in each era new technologies unsettled entrenched business models, an emergent viewing platform threatened to undermine an established one, and content providers worried over the behavior of once-dependable audiences. The anxieties led to storytelling, promotion, and advertising experiments, including the *Disneyland* series, embedded rock music videos in *Ozzie & Harriet*, credit sequence brand integration, *Modern Family*'s parent company promotion episodes, second screen initiatives, and social TV experiments. Offering contemporary and classic examples from the American Broadcasting Company, Disney Channel, ABC Family, and Showtime, alongside series such as *Bewitched*, *Leave It to Beaver*, *Laverne & Shirley*, and *Pretty Little Liars*, individual chapters focus on brandcasting at the level of the television series, network schedule, "Blu-ray/DVD/Digital" combo pack, promotional short, cause marketing campaign, and across social media.

In this follow-up to her successful previous book, *Television and New Media: Must-Click TV*, Gillan provides vital insights into television's role in the expansion of a brand-centric U.S. culture.

Jennifer Gillan is Professor of English and Media Studies at Bentley University. She is the author of *Television and New Media: Must-Click TV* (Routledge 2010). Gillan's articles have appeared in *Cinema Journal, American Literature, Arizona Quarterly, Duke Journal of Gender Law & Policy, Columbia Journal of Gender & Law, African American Review, American Drama*, and *Mosaic*. She has co-edited four award-winning literature anthologies—*Unsettling America, Identity Lessons*, and *Growing Up Ethnic in America* from Penguin Books, and *Italian American Writers on* ... ...ersity Press.

TELEVISION BRANDCASTING

The Return of the Content–Promotion Hybrid

Jennifer Gillan

Routledge
Taylor & Francis Group

NEW YORK AND LONDON

First published 2015
by Routledge
711 Third Avenue, New York, NY 10017

and by Routledge
2 Park Square, Milton Park, Abingdon, Oxon OX14 4RN

Routledge is an imprint of the Taylor & Francis Group, an informa business

© 2015 Taylor & Francis

The right of Jennifer Gillan to be identified as author of this work has been asserted by her in accordance with sections 77 and 78 of the Copyright, Designs and Patents Act 1988.

Library of Congress Cataloging-in-Publication Data

Gillan, Jennifer.
    Television brandcasting : the return of the content-promotion hybrid / Jennifer Gillan.
        pages cm
    Includes bibliographical references and index.
    1. Television broadcasting—United States. 2. Branding (Marketing)—United States. 3. Television broadcasting—Technological innovations—United States. 4. Convergence (Telecommunication) I. Title.
    HE8700.8.G55   2015
    384.55068'8—dc23   2014024842

ISBN: 978-0-415-84121-4 (hbk)
ISBN: 978-0-415-84122-1 (pbk)
ISBN: 978-0-203-76656-9 (ebk)

Typeset in Bembo
by Apex CoVantage, LLC

Printed and bound in the United States of America by Publishers Graphics, LLC on sustainably sourced paper.

CONTENTS

Illustrations   *ix*
Schedules   *xiii*
Acknowledgments   *xv*

Introduction: Television Brandcasting   1
0.1   Return of the Content–Promotion Hybrid   3
0.2   Viewers and Their Networks of Friends   4
0.3   Television Endorsements and the Call-to-Affiliation   8
0.4   Studying Promotion, Paratexts, and "Total
        Merchandising"   12
0.5   Chapter Summaries   19

1   Broadcasting Series and Sponsors   32
      1.1   Branding the Modern Family: 1950s and Now   32
      1.2   Sponsored Credit Sequences   35
      1.3   Dramatized Advertisements   38
      1.4   Danny Thomas, Dodge, and Ethnic Strivers   39
      1.5   Star Sitcoms: Lucy, Desi, and Danny . . . and MacMurray?   42
      1.6   The Nelsons as America's Favorite Endorsers   49
      1.7   Showcasing Consumer Aspirations   54
      1.8   Buying and Being American from the Andersons to
               the Goldbergs   61
      1.9   Suburban Strivers, *Modern Family*, and *The Middle*   65
      1.10   Re-contextualizing Sponsored Sitcoms of the 1950s   71

2 Narrowcasting Schedules and Stars   86
   2.1 Narrowcast Broadcasting   86
   2.2 Showtime's "Bleak Comedy" Schedule Pairs   87
   2.3 From Premium to Broadcast Channel Brands   92
   2.4 ABC as Middlecaster   95
   2.5 *Ozzie & Harriet* and the Peer-ent   97
   2.6 The Rock 'n' Roll Era Arrives on ABC   100
   2.7 *My Three Sons* and the Generational Accord Sitcom
      Cycle   106
   2.8 Wally, Ward, and Eddie Haskell on *Leave It to Beaver*   110
   2.9 From Bobby Soxer to Beach Bunny on *Donna Reed*   114
   2.10 Rock 'n' Roll (& Lose Control) on *Patty Duke* and
      Gidget   117
   2.11 *That* Kind of Girl on *That Girl* and *Bewitched*   123
   2.12 ABC's *Thursday's Girls* Schedule Promotions   127
   2.13 Family Fridays and Tween Tuesdays   132
   2.14 ABC's Mid-1970s Ratings Dominance   134
   2.15 From *TGIF* to Disney Channel's Friendship Economy   138

3 Cable Brandcasting and Disney Channel's Company Voice   149
   3.1 Disney Channel as Brandcaster   149
   3.2 Disney Channel: A Premium/Basic Cable Hybrid   152
   3.3 Brandcasting Through Myth Stories   156
   3.4 The Obstinate Optimist and "In-Betweener" Content   159
   3.5 Brandcasters and Boutique Content-about-Content
      Firms   162
   3.6 Disney's Sunny Outlook on Stardom: YouTube
      to Hollywood   165
   3.7 Brand Managing Themselves: Miley Cyrus and
      The Jonas Brothers   169
   3.8 From BFF Sitcoms to Disney's *Friends for Change*   172
   3.9 *Friends for Change* Music Videos   178
   3.10 Purchaser Citizens and Parent Company Sustainability   181

4 Disney Studios' Brand Management on TV and
   Blu-ray/DVD   191
   4.1 Parent Company Brandcasting   191
   4.2 Disney Brand Management Films? *Saving Mr. Banks*
      and *Frozen*   193
   4.3 Authorizing Walt Disney   199
   4.4 Interpretive Frames on Blu-ray/DVD   200

4.5	Hosted Lead-ins and Studio History as Creative Nonfiction	206
4.6	Coca-Cola and Custom Character-Based Commercials	211
4.7	Television "Trailerizing" and *The Parent Trap*	214
4.8	Disney Channel's Decision Engines	223
4.9	Disney Parks on *Modern Family* and *The Middle*	228

Epilogue: Twitter Multitasking, *Mad*-vertising, and Sustainable TV — 245

E.1	Disney *Re-Micks*	245
E.2	Complementary Storytelling: The Influence of the *Lost* Model	249
E.3	Must-Tweet TV: #*Pretty Little Liars*	253
E.4	From "*Mad*-vertising" *Mad Men* to Mad Predictions	259

Index — 269

ILLUSTRATIONS

0.1	Welch's *Mickey Mouse* clubhouse "giveaway."	7
0.2	*Mickey Mouse Club*'s promotional paratexts of 1955.	17
1.1	*Act like a parent talk like a peer* on *Modern Family*.	33
1.2	Danny Thomas for American Tobacco Company on *Make Room for Daddy*.	40
1.3	Danny Thomas as Dodge's ethnic striver in the *Make Room for Daddy* credits.	41
1.4	Movie star Fred MacMurray and domestic ambivalence on *My Three Sons*.	46
1.5	Donna Stone's gender role ambivalence on *The Donna Reed Show*.	48
1.6	A dramatized advertisement for Quaker Oats on *Ozzie & Harriet*.	51
1.7	Teen appeal elements of *My Three Sons* and *Ozzie & Harriet*.	53
1.8	Kodak's endorsement of the Nelsons and their lifestyle.	55
1.9	Demographic appeals in early 1960s marketing of sitcom families.	57
1.10	Flirting with Kodak on *Ozzie & Harriet*.	59
1.11	"Irrepressible Ricky" teases his father Ozzie in front of Hotpoint's new range.	61
1.12	In *The Middle*, the Hecks embody "driving happiness" in a borrowed car.	70
2.1	A dramatized schedule promotion for Showtime's pairing of its hit series *Weeds* with newcomer *The Big C*.	88
2.2	Pop idols and their admiring fans, on *Ozzie & Harriet* and Disney Channel's "Make a Wave" music video.	102

2.3   1950s meta-commentary on television as a brandcasting platform.   104

2.4   Ricky Nelson performs on *Ozzie & Harriet* in a new televisual form: the embedded music video.   105

2.5   Bub, the all-male family's caregiver on *My Three Sons*, serves breakfast using a turntable to showcase Hunt's condiments.   109

2.6   Later seasons of *Leave It to Beaver* showcase Ward Cleaver's Plymouth.   113

2.7   Mary Stone, good 1950s mini-mommy in *The Donna Reed Show*, evolves into a rock-'n'-roll-era teen looking beyond the staid suburbs.   115

2.8   Mary Stone's resort wear registers the beginning of Shelley Fabares' move from sitcom daughter to Elvis' leading lady.   116

2.9   Steve Douglas, peer-ent, plays with Robbie's band in *My Three Sons*; Patty Duke sings with the Shindogs on her self-titled sitcom.   119

2.10 Costuming and shot composition position Gidget as the "new girl" of 1965 and the middle ground between female types.   122

2.11 Class and ethnic conflicts on *Bewitched* and *Make Room for Daddy*.   126

2.12 The ABC's *Thursday's Girls* schedule line-up promotion signaled a move away from sexy girl sitcoms to screwball sitcoms with tween appeal.   129

2.13 Costuming and musical taste signal the difference between blond, suburban Sam and her dark-haired and dangerous alter ego Serena.   131

2.14 Shirley shares her "obstinate optimist" advice with her best friend Laverne.   136

3.1   Phineas activates the "It's On!" Disney Channel brand campaign and amusement pier music video.   151

3.2   Ross Lynch on *Disney 365*, a short that promotes "all things Disney."   154

3.3   Riverstreet Productions created an American Dream-themed profile of a representative obstinate optimist for Disney's *The Time I . . .* short series.   161

3.4   Brandcasting on *Austin & Ally* and *The Coppertop Flop*.   164

3.5   *Friends for Change* and Disney Channel star trios and short videos.   176

4.1   In the hosted lead-in to *Walt Disney Presents*, Walt reminds viewers about earlier Disney output.   193

4.2   Walt Disney explains how stereophonic sound enhances
        storytelling in *Sleeping Beauty*.   202
4.3   The framing and shot composition implies an equivalence
        between Walt Disney and Jules Verne, the author of *20,000*
        Leagues Under the Sea.   204
4.4   "Operation Undersea," the first behind-the-scenes
        television feature, "captures" Kirk Douglas and Peter
        Lorre as they goof around on set.   205
4.5   Brand evolution in Walt Disney's 1954 and 1964
        lead-ins to *Alice in Wonderland*.   210
4.6   Disney leveraged Coca-Cola's *One Hour in Wonderland*
        special to familiarize viewers with the voice actor for
        Disney's animated *Alice in Wonderland*.   212
4.7   Brands like Ipana deepened their connection with
        The Mickey Mouse Club and its tween audience by
        offering gifts and special offers.   213
4.8   Disney's cohost Tinker Bell appears during the lead-in
        to the episode P.L. Travers supposedly watched during
        her 1961 visit.   216
4.9   *The Mickey Mouse Club* promoted albums for
        Annette Funicello.   218
4.10   Rocky and CeCe are Best Friend Brandcasters.   220
4.11   *Shake It Up*'s Zendaya (Rocky) and Bella (CeCe)
        appear "as themselves" goofing around in a short series
        filmed in Germany.   222
4.12   *Leo Little's Big Show*, a faux vodcasting series,
        creatively showcases Disney's signature Blu-ray/DVD
        combo pack format.   224
4.13   Three actors who play stepsiblings on a Disney Channel
        sitcom enjoy the Mad Tea Party Ride.   227
4.14   Manny Delgado-Pritchett is at Disneyland riding
        Dumbo the Flying Elephant with his mother Gloria.   229
4.15   In a *Modern Family* episode, Jay puts a comfy Minnie
        Mouse plush shoe on the aching foot of his grateful
        wife Gloria.   230
4.16   On *Modern Family*, Mitchell Pritchett gets trapped
        in his daughter Lily's princess castle two months
        prior to the release of *Tangled*.   231
4.17   "Hecking Up" a *Disney Memories* photo opportunity during
        a free trip to Walt Disney World Resort on *The Middle*.   233
E.1   The opening sequence for *Disney's Re-Micks* registers
        the long history of Disney circulating its legacy brands
        among different platforms.   247

SCHEDULES

2.1 *Weeds* acts as lead-in for new series on Showtime. 89
2.2 An overview of the different kinds of programming airing alongside
     The Adventures of Ozzie & Harriet. 98
2.3 Teen-inclusive schedules on ABC from 1960–65. 106
2.4 The schedule parings for ABC's *Bewitched*. 128
2.5 Tween Fridays on ABC reflected a narrowcasting streak already
     in place in 1970. 133
2.6 Tween Tuesdays enabled ABC to reach its first #1 network
     finish in the three-way ratings race. 135
2.7 ABC's sitcom successes on Tween Tuesdays during the run
     of *Happy Days*. 137
E.1 The ABC schedule grid for the series run of *Lost*. 251

ACKNOWLEDGMENTS

This project began because of the generosity of the UCLA Film and Television Archive and the International Radio and Television Society Foundation Faculty Fellowship to the Disney Impact Summit on Disney Channels Worldwide. I extend special thanks to IRTS President Joyce Tudryn, Disney's Bob Mendez, and Frank Gonzalez at Disney's Talent Development and Diversity, whose department made the funding for the event possible. As I did most of the research at UCLA, I am indebted to Mark Quigley, who ordered DVD transfers of the original versions of *Ozzie & Harriet*, *The Mickey Mouse Club*, *Disneyland*, and *My Three Sons* for me. I always enjoyed hearing his insights on midcentury television, and was eager to see what new content he had unearthed for me. I cannot say enough about how indispensible Mark is to the archive's Research and Study Center and how much he helped this project develop. I am also grateful for the support from the UCLA Film & Television Archive Research Stipend, the Television Academy of Arts & Sciences Foundation faculty fellowship, and the National Association of Television Production Executives Educational Foundation. Special thanks to coordinators Nancy Robinson, Nikki Kaffee, and Greg Pitts.

As I kept falling down research rabbit holes, I must extend my apologies as well as thanks to Erica Wetter, my editor at Routledge. She encouraged me from the beginnings of this project, ushered it through production, and did it all with good cheer, great patience, and a skilled hand. The ever-efficient Simon Jacobs made his best efforts to keep the trains running, and was probably amazed at the ways I derailed them. I am grateful to him for his hard work and extreme patience. The whole team at Routledge has been wonderful and I thank them for all their efforts on behalf of this book. I also thank the reviewers along the way for their thinking and feedback. I developed my ideas on sustainable television in relation to my preparations for a keynote speech for "Das ist Fernsehen!" ("This Is

Television!") in Regensburg, Germany. I want to thank Judith Keilbach at Utrecht University for the invitation and the good conversation. I continued to develop my ideas in relation to a public lecture and visit to the Freie Universität Berlin. I had the great pleasure of conversations with my host, Thomas Morsch, and his research cohort investigating "Aesthetic Experience and the Dissolution of Artistic Limits" through the Collaborative Research Centre. I thank them for the opportunity to share and discuss preliminary ideas. Closer to home, Tom Doherty was always willing to hear about *Television Brandcasting* and show support for the project. His role as respondent to a public lecture I gave very early in the writing of the sections on sponsored 1950s television was especially valuable. Over the past year, I enjoyed talking paratexts at conferences with Paul Grainge, Jonathan Gray, Cathy Johnson, Taylor Nygaard, Melanie Kohnen, Myles McNutt, and Louisa Stein. I thank the insightful audience members at previous conferences, especially at the Society for Cinema and Media Studies annual meetings. In addition to great conversation, especially about the sidekick girls of the 1960s, Lindsay Giggey generously shared her work on Connie Stevens, which is mentioned here in Chapter 2. I look forward to reading her ABC/Warner Brothers book one day.

Bentley University has been very generous in its support of this project with a faculty fellowship from the Valente Center for Arts & Sciences and grants from the Dean's Office and the Faculty Affairs Committee. Thanks to Dan Everett, Vicki Lafarge, Juliet Gainsborough, Chris Beneke, Linda McJannet, Wiley Davi, Anna Siomopoulos, and the English and Media Studies Department grants committees. For support plus extreme patience with my need to go into hiding to finish this book, I want to single out Wiley Davi and Kathy Sheehan. For 2013–14, I was lucky to have my courses filled with many repeat customers. These students made the process of the final stages of reworking my ideas so much easier because the class discussions were a pleasure to lead, even when they always led back to *True Detective*. I formulated some early ideas about Ozzie Nelson for the chapter, "From Ozzie Nelson to Ozzy Osbourne: the Genesis and Development of the Reality (Star) Sitcom," in *Understanding Reality Television* (Routledge 2004). I want to thank the editors, Su Holmes and Deborah Jermyn, for the opportunity. While I do no more than mention *Veronica Mars* in this book, I want to express my thanks to Louisa Stein and Sharon Marie Ross for publishing, "Fashion Sleuths and Aerie Girls: *Veronica Mars*' Fan Forums and Network Strategies of Fan Address," in *Teen Television* (McFarland 2008). The chapter's focus on channel branding and series-related Television Without Pity fan forums started me thinking about connected viewing in the television industry more generally. An earlier iteration of my thoughts on Kodak sponsorship and *Mad*-vertising began in "Kodak, Jack and Coke: Advertising and *Mad*-vertising on *Mad Men*," in *Analyzing Mad Men: Critical Essays on the Series*, ed. Scott Stoddart (McFarland 2011). Some of the ideas from the *Saving Mr. Banks* section of Chapter 4 come from a review essay I wrote on the film for *Journal of American History* 101, no. 1 (June 2014).

Through several trips to UCLA and at USC, I unearthed a fascinating array of material, most of which I could not use in this book. As a librarian's daughter, I enjoyed the process, even if my editorial team did not enjoy the delays. I am sure my dad would have been proud had he lived to see the finished book, and he would have agreed that just one more research trip couldn't hurt. For her incredible patience and belief in this project, I am grateful to Maria Mazziotti Gillan. I could not have completed the book without her encouragement and her obstinate optimism. Every day I wish I were more my mother's daughter. This book would literally not exist without her, as I began my interest in 1950s television while looking for poems and stories for our multicultural literature anthologies over a decade ago. I also thank her for powering though many a sophomoric television sitcom. I enjoyed sharing old television episodes with her again and with anyone who would watch them. To Devil Duck, thank you for all the image optimization and help with production even when it was so fully outside the job description. This book is infinitely better for all your help. Others deserve mention for their support and patience, including the Jennifers, Annamaria, Nicky, Alex, Debbie, Rachel, and Rebecca. Lucille Ponte showed remarkable wisdom at an important moment, and changed this project and my life for the better. I only wish I could be as a good an advisor and friend as she is.

Sometimes topics evolve perfectly haphazardly, expunging nagging doubts, utterly compelling kooky investigations, elaborations. I know where I was when this project began. I know where I was when I finished it. The unexpected tangents in the middle, especially those of Thanksgiving 2012, gave me the greatest joy. I will never look at the covers of some TV on DVD cases the same way again. Atticus, I will cherish the time you told me that *Leave It to Beaver* was "The Best. Show. Ever," although I suspect when you grow up you will revise that opinion. To Indigo, my little Elsa, I will remember fondly our Disney film marathons and your attempts to get me up to speed about plucky princesses and pixies. Finally, the singular force motivating this book is Stephen, a man of everlasting patience, unwavering love and support, and a refreshingly sassy sense of humor for Boston (by way of Texas, I suspect). I cannot imagine that I would have actually finished this book without the keen analytical insights, design expertise, and the technical support from my little bit of MIT in my own living room. For keeping me both focused and distracted in just the right balance, especially in the seventh inning stretch plus double overtime, I am forever grateful. Finally, to Walter for coming into our lives at the precise moment I should have been finishing the final chapter. Now that this book is done, the future is yours and ours.

INTRODUCTION

Television Brandcasting

With the proliferation of tablets and smart phones, television is not required for "watching television" today. Yet, the economic model of most of U.S. television still depends on the ability of television channels, especially the broadcast networks, to promise audience attention to 30-second-spot advertisers. New modes of reception, distribution, and exhibition cause a great deal of anxiety for commercially supported television networks, although advertisers can be mollified by deals that expand messaging across platforms or customize it for new devices (like iPads). The dramatic changes have prompted a revival of 1950s-style branded entertainment in which sponsor messaging is integrated into off-TV interfaces or into specific content elements, segments, or special episodes.

1950s television made "Happy Hotpoint" appliances synonymous with the Nelson family of *The Adventures of Ozzie & Harriet*. *The George Burns and Gracie Allen Show* is forever entwined with the star couple's stockpile of Carnation Condensed Milk (the *milk from contented cows*). Television still trafficked in jingles with Texaco gas station attendants singing, "We're the men of Texaco, We work from Maine to Mexico" and Bucky Beaver reminding kids to "Brusha, Brusha, Brusha" with Ipana toothpaste. The song and dance routines by the men of Texaco were integrated into *Texaco Star Theater* with program host Milton Berle often joining in. Bucky Beaver appeared only in the breaks between *The Mickey Mouse Club* segments, running as the now standard spot advertising on commercially financed U.S. broadcast networks. Yet, the Ipana commercials, like those with the Cheerios Kid, Mickey Mouse and friends for American Motors, and the *Peter Pan* characters for Derby Food's Peter Pan Peanut Butter, felt continuous with the late afternoon show because animators on the Disney lot created the character spots and adult Mouseketeer Jimmie Dodd wrote the jingle for Ipana.[1]

In the 2000s, broadcast television networks began returning to a more seamless style of dramatized advertising and brand integration. The directors of FOX's *24* offered multiple angles on the Ford SUV driven by main character and counterterrorism agent Jack Bauer (Kiefer Sutherland), or showed him using the GPS system or some other marketable feature.[2] The shots paralleled the images in *24*/Ford dramatized advertisements and content–promotion hybrids running in the story breaks and encouraging recall of the fact that this popular show was made possible by Ford's sponsorship. The character appeared in Sprint minisodes for mobile phones. These mobisodes made it clear that Jack had a Sprint mobile messaging plan on his ever-present smart phone. Viewers could even sign up to receive text messages from the character. Bing, an Internet search engine competitor of Google, employed similar strategies but stamped its sponsorship on a whole slate of series airing on the CW "netlet." The Bing logo and graphic would briefly replace the CW channel bug and link to a text box with messages about off-TV content. Bing even produced some customized content–promotion hybrids during the *Bing is for Doing* campaign. These shorts blurred the line between entertainment and promotion, between self-promotion and cause advocacy. They entwined Bing's company voice messaging with "Social Shorts" about the involvement of CW actors in social media-enabled advocacy campaigns. Of course, these multitasking content–promotion hybrids also acted as promotion for the stars, the series, and CW as a channel brand.

Television Brandcasting examines U.S. television's utility as a medium for branded storytelling. It investigates the current and historical role that television content, promotion, and hybrids of the two have played in disseminating brand messaging and influencing consumer decision-making. Juxtaposing the current period of transition with that of the 1950s–60s, this book outlines how in each era new technologies unsettled entrenched business models; an emergent viewing platform threatened to undermine an established one; and content providers worried over the behavior of once-dependable audiences (to fill theater seats in the early 1950s and to watch on-air TV today). The anxieties led to storytelling, promotion, and advertising experiments, including ABC's *Disneyland/Walt Disney Presents* series, *The Mickey Mouse Club*, embedded rock music videos in *Ozzie & Harriet*, credit sequence brand integration, *Modern Family*'s parent company promotion episodes, second screen initiatives, and social TV experiments. Offering contemporary and classic examples from American Broadcasting Company, Disney Channel, ABC Family, and Showtime, individual chapters focus on brandcasting at the level of the television series, network schedule, the "Blu-ray/DVD/Digital" combo pack, the promotional short, the cause marketing campaign, and social media space. While providing an account of the industry utility of each approach, the chapters also identify and define key terms. As a whole, the book locates precedent-setting programming, scheduling, and promotion that have contemporary parallels to demonstrate that many strategies that seem like millennial developments have much earlier origins. The comparative frame also calls attention to ways in which today's media platforms and devices have enabled new kinds of brandcasting. The book provides vital insights into television's role in the troubling expansion of a brand-centric U.S. culture. It also illuminates why some industry stakeholders succeed and others fail to circulate their preferred brand identities and engage target audiences when they leverage television as a brandcasting platform.

0.1   Return of the Content–Promotion Hybrid

The return of the content–promotion hybrid was precipitated by a larger change in the U.S. television industry, now characterized by a fragmented audience with access not only to hundreds of channels, but also to alternate platforms through which to access television content as well as the other forms of entertainment competing for market share. A comparison of Nielsen's ratings for current sitcom "hits," for example, with those from earlier periods charts steep declines. Immensely popular 1970s sitcoms *All in the Family* and *M*A*S*H*,[3] for example, aired on CBS during a period designated by television studies as the heyday of the "classic network era."[4] As the only available programming outlets, CBS, ABC, and NBC could create a distribution bottleneck.[5] Attracted to the ratings that the Big Three network oligopoly could generate,[6] advertisers would eagerly purchase 30-second spots to run in the magazine-style flow between story segments. In this era advertisers had confidence that many viewers were exposed to their commercials, in part because television was watched on televisions without remote controls. Changing the channel during commercial breaks required going over to the set and turning the dial. Of course, the commercials mostly played at the same time on all three broadcast channels. Avoiding them probably required leaving the room, but that meant a well-timed return because there was no rewinding or fast forwarding of live television. Such features are recent innovations on cable systems, as are the digital platforms and the DVRs that enable watching outside the scheduled time slot or at least on a slight delay (to skip through the commercials and still finish by the end of the time slot).

While viewers of on-air television today have several means of skipping advertising, those who access television from alternate content delivery platforms often find advertising that can't be skipped. In the case of network-affiliated media players, companies can make multiplatform advertising deals so that messaging travels with series as they move across the network's branded interfaces on off-TV platforms. Advertising, along with some degree of studio or channel brand identification, is also part of the model of content aggregators like Hulu. Brand integration appeals to advertisers in an ad-skipping era because the messaging becomes unskippable no matter what the distribution platform. The need for embedded messaging helps explain the turn back to 1950s branded entertainment strategies, particularly the proliferation of content–promotion hybrids.

Of course, just as branding, advertising, and content can flow across platforms, so can commentary on it. One-way communication structures the classic network era's traditional push model, one in which companies control the platforms and the schedules on which they release content and desired self-representations to consumers. The pull model responds to the fact that television viewers and web/mobile users can access desired content on their own schedules, talk back to producers, and circulate brand commentary (some of it undesirable). Companies must now engage potential consumers in the places that they congregate (e.g., on social networking sites) and try to influence their entertainment choices and their recommendations to others.

0.2 Viewers and Their Networks of Friends

As smart phones become more prevalent and social media platforms and utilities multiply, so does the power of "viewsers."[7] These World Wide Web-savvy television viewers who are also mobile device users have become valuable not only as audiences and potential consumers, but also as brand advocates who can offer public displays of brand affiliation and affection.[8] On countless web message boards, social networking spaces, individual blogs and micro-blogging communities, viewers can circulate endorsements of television series and stars, entertainment content, and consumer products. These endorsements by "viewsers" (hereafter just simplified to "viewers") have the capacity to spread rapidly among wider and wider social networks. Twitter micro-bloggers can tweet instant feedback to their followers and Facebook has amassed a nearly one-billion-strong network of word-of-mouse commentators and potential marketers.

Facebook became the recommendation platform of choice when its Like button was externalized in 2010 as part of its new Open Graph infrastructure. This change enabled its trademark thumbs up symbol to morph into a web-pervasive form of endorsement of products and their producers, of lifestyles and their representatives. Users could now click the thumbs up symbol anywhere on the web to register and broadcast the kinds of products, services, and brands they liked. Consumers see these "Likes" in social terms as signifiers of their lifestyle choices and utilize them as building blocks for their social identities. Brand managers and the corporations and entities they represent view these Likes in economic terms as signifiers of their reach and as contributors to brand building and promotion. Looking for a return on monetary rather than emotional investment, television divisions have been working hard to translate social interactivity into economic value. They try to do so by entwining viewers' emotional connections and experiences with brand connections and experiences.

Out of the externalization of Facebook's Like function grew "the Like economy," which Carolin Gerlitz and Anne Helmond describe as a "data-intensive, performative infrastructure" that "enables the simultaneous *materialization, measurement, and multiplication* of . . . a combination of users' affective investments and social relations." This infrastructure, they argue, makes possible "the connection between social interactivity and economic value."[9] Likes have become particularly important to the U.S. television industry because they function as a way to move beyond measuring who in general is watching a series to identifying precisely the viewers who are engaged by it or engaging with it. The tallying of Likes is an imprecise metric, but then so is the infamously inaccurate Nielsen Company's rating/share measurement system. Although they currently remain the "coin of the realm," Nielsen's ratings are now supplemented by various new media metrics. Television networks and program producers rely on click-through data from the web and even strive to accumulate as many Likes as possible to contextualize their on-air numbers.

Recognizing the power of these Likes, the search engine Bing joined forces with Facebook for a 2011 campaign, *Bing and decide . . . with your friends.* Bing, the self-described "decision engine," promised to go beyond the basic enabling of a web search by offering advice on how to interpret the results. To enhance this brand claim, Bing partnered with Facebook because its interface pivots on the concept of friending and making recommendations to friends. Originally, Facebook represented the virtual mapping of networks of actual friends and acquaintances, but, as explained above, it soon expanded to include the ability to "friend and recommend" through its feature that allows users to identify themselves by lists of Likes. They would include songs, films, television programs, books, fashions, and particular brands within those categories and others. Working with Facebook enabled Bing to tap into these Like lists and deliver its search results in relation to the number of the user's Facebook friends who formally Liked the items returned by the search. Bing later settled on the tagline, *Search Goes Social*, to bolster the promise that Bing would use your friends' endorsements to customize your search. This would expand your search results exponentially. The claim was reinforced by the visuals in Bing commercials used to support the categories *here's what you know* (not much) *here's what your friends know* (a great deal). This social media partnership affirmed faith in two standard market research findings: that consumer decisions are rarely made independently and that they are more likely to be made upon the advice of friends. It also made clear that those with Facebook accounts were becoming an army of uncompensated (and often unknowing) brandcasters, especially when the site auto-generated "sponsored stories" in the form of endorsements linked to the pictures of those who merely clicked-to-Like a product.

Such features on new media platforms and devices now work in tandem with the television platform to facilitate instantaneous circulation of brand recommendations. As of this writing, Facebook enables a particularly effective way to circulate viewers' intentional or unintentional content endorsements among their social networks. With the rapid pace of change, Facebook may well be displaced by some other social networking utility. At present, however, Facebook's fan pages still encourage users to follow the activities and Like lists of their favorite television characters, television stars, and sometimes even production workers. Television producers and networks actively court new media-savvy viewers on such pages and reward them through exclusive content and extensions of story worlds. These pages are part of the more widespread attempt by companies to exploit the information gathered through social networking sites. Networks of friends, music playlists, and Like lists become the basis for targeted advertising and speculative profit. The data that is mined from tracking our interests, affiliations, and habits can be sold or it can be used to send customized recommendations and advertising to our Facebook friends.

With the pace of new media change and the scrutiny resulting from its May 2012 Initial Public Offering, Facebook could implode spectacularly or slowly slip from its position as the predominant social-networking utility. If either happens (or perhaps when), television channels and their advertisers will find other ways to address viewers as "friends making recommendations to friends" and to leverage new forms of social networking and peer-to-peer marketing. Ever since the "pal" elbowed past the professional advice giver in the 1950s commercials, the peer recommendation has remained a valued commodity in television promotion and advertising.

Although the terminology is new, it has been a long-standing television practice "to friend" viewers and to recommend products and lifestyles to them. It could be done explicitly in an advertising bumper at the end of an episode or in a dramatized advertisement integrated into the series flow, or conveyed implicitly through costuming and other elements of the mise-en-scène of a series. This book analyzes and historicizes the "friend and recommend" paradigm and U.S. television's role in constructing and reimagining television stars as close friends of viewers and as spokespeople for corporations that want to represent themselves as friendly entities rather than uncaring monoliths. In the 1950s, a corporation would purchase a block of advertising time on a network schedule and use it to sponsor a program to circulate company voice messaging. It might do so through a dramatized advertisement attached to the credits or running as interstitial content in breaks between the episode segments. Such corporations controlled the schedule either through sponsored narrative programs (Philip Morris for *I Love Lucy*) or "time franchises" in which they offered musical variety acts (*The Dinah Shore Chevy Show*) or anthology series that had rotating drama content (*General Electric Theater*).[10] The hosts or the lead actors usually had prior Hollywood credentials, even if only in B-movies or as nightclub acts. The embedded product pitched within such programming called attention to the star's status, while the comic situations affirmed their positions as typical people "just like you and me." In all of these cases, the intention was to use the television time to associate the corporation with an appealing personality and a set of values. The logic here was that if viewers "bought in" to the brand claims or felt connected to the television personalities, they would be more likely to buy or recommend company products.

The star-helmed situation comedy format provided an even better vehicle through which to utilize the "recommended to you by a [famous] friend" dynamic. The series could depict products in use within a fantasy lifestyle. Direct-from-the-star recommendations evolved into endorsements for the products associated with a "modern and convenient," leisure-oriented, suburban lifestyle

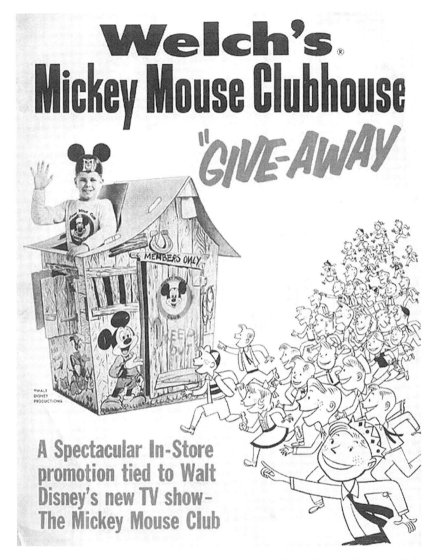

FIGURE 0.1   In this promotional card related to a Welch's clubhouse "giveaway" the image of the kids rushing to acquire anything related to *The Mickey Mouse Club* captures the program's appeal for sponsoring companies.

(equipped with new appliances, electronics, and packaged foods). I address this point in Chapter 1's analysis of the branded credit sequences and integrated commercials within *The Adventures of Ozzie & Harriet, Make Room for Daddy/The Danny Thomas Show,* and *My Three Sons,* and in sitcoms such as *I Love Lucy, The Goldbergs,* and *Leave It to Beaver.* I compare them to product integration and dramatization strategies used in today's ABC sitcoms, *Modern Family* and *The Middle*.

0.3 Television Endorsements and the Call-to-Affiliation

Throughout *Television Brandcasting* I argue that the television industry's endorsement structure is most effective when its calls-to-action coincide with such calls-to-affiliation, that is, when customers feel as if their actual values and interests or their aspirations align with their recommenders'. To explore how this value transfer works, I rely on a variety of branding theories, particularly those of Douglas Holt. He contends that brand equity accrues through the *identity value* that consumers associate with a brand's stories. His theory contrasts with the mind share model in which brand equity is the brand essence "lodged in consumers' minds" or the viral model in which brand equity stems from a brand's ability to become "entrenched among the most influential and fashionable people." Holt counters that brands only act "as vessels for self-expression" when they "are imbued with stories that consumers find valuable in constructing their identities." When they make use of such myths, individual consumers "forge tight emotional connections" to brands. Yet, brands only become icons if they tell stories that help the public at large manage identity crises and desires, and Holt says, they "earn their keep by creating mythic resolutions to societal contradictions."[11]

Although he doesn't support his branding theories with analysis of any series, Holt describes television as the optimal "channel for delivering powerful myths." *Television Brandcasting* builds on Holt's observation and details how U.S. television functions as a medium for branded storytelling. This book begins with the assumption that all programming elements on network and basic cable television in the U.S. are part of the promotional surround for advertising and company voice messaging. Analyzing the promotional surround in which television series are embedded can bring to light the cultural aspirations and anxieties exploited in order to attract audiences to series, platforms, and associated advertisers. I concentrate on programming that registers mutually reinforcing textual and commercial goals or, in Holt's terms, that offers *identity value* and brand value. I look at audience address strategies in which calls-to-action double as calls-to-affiliation through their reliance on myths that appeal to viewers and serve industry needs.

The way that *The Adventures of Ozzie & Harriet* (American Broadcasting Company, 1952–66) builds Kodak into its credits sequences[12] provides a good example of how content–promotion hybrids were central to the endorsement structure of midcentury sitcoms. The Kodak messaging and the representation of the Nelsons both in the episodes and in the branded credited sequences and interstitials are connected through the following myth story. Spending leisure time together forges bonds between the generations and creates memories worth preserving in pictures. Taking pictures with high quality Kodak film and cameras makes them perfect for long-term preservation. Archiving those pictures helps families (and particularly mothers like Harriet) demonstrate to others the health of the inter-generational bond and reminds individual family members of that bond if they want to reaffirm its strength. Simply put, Kodak turns ordinary family moments into memories that people can preserve as part of their family heritage. This parallels the way that *Ozzie & Harriet* episodes turn ordinary intergenerational interactions and activities into moments worth televising. Viewers are called to identify with other families (or individual family members) who believe in the value of nuclear family togetherness, particularly through shared leisure-time pursuits.[13] In the Nelsons' dramatized advertisements for Kodak, this call-to-affiliation is linked to a call-to-action to visit a local retailer to buy Kodak film or the latest Kodak cameras. Beyond appearances in the pitches made by the Nelsons as a unit, there are individual peer-to-peer pitches: to leisure-oriented suburbanites; to the archivists of the families' *good times together*; to teens; and to the young girls who had transformed Ricky Nelson into a teen idol.

In addition to his innovations in this kind of branded entertainment, producer Ozzie Nelson pioneered the embedded music video, recognizing that the call-to-action in *Ozzie & Harriet* could be to buy his son's singles and albums at a local record store. To support this call-to-action, Ozzie Nelson, the producer, leverages Ozzie, his television father character, for a more subtle level of "peer-to peer" audience address. He presents himself as a "peer-ent," a parent who advocates for rather than chafes against his children's points of view. While Chapter 1 looks at *Modern Family*'s Phil Dunphy as a more ambivalent representation of the peer-ent type, I argue that Ozzie Nelson's embrace of the role is inflected by generational changes that his sitcom depicts as positive. In addition to supporting the leisure-oriented aspirations of his sons, Ozzie rejects the generational discord narrative and uses the depiction of Ricky to help de-stigmatize rock 'n' roll music and the teen rock musician or listener.[14] Of course, Ricky had plenty of appeal for the younger generation. The sitcom turned him into a teen idol with Billboard-charting singles and several albums. Chapter 2 explores how other ABC series copycatted the approach for sitcom stars such as Shelley Fabares of *The Donna Reed Show*, albeit with much less success. I also explore leveraging of the fame of Ricky Nelson and later Shelley Fabares to build schedules around blocks of programs with teen characters. This led as well to a cycle of what I call "generational accord" programs, including sitcoms such as *My Three Sons* and *Gidget*, in which parents took on the role of empathetic "peer-ents" attempting to understand the behaviors of their rock 'n' roll generational teens.

While some of these sitcoms maintained a sponsored by relationship with a particular brand (e.g., Chevrolet's *My Three Sons*), the transition was already underway to the magazine-style flow of random commercials we associate with "classic network era" television advertising. When advertisers lost faith in this model in the era of ad-skipping DVRs, there was a return to the *Ozzie & Harriet–Kodak* strategy of entwining series and sponsor messaging. Today, we see season premiere episodes take on an explicit single sponsorship model, but more often products become part of the lifestyle on display through product-related characterization, as was the case with the use of Apple iPad's on both ABC and Disney Channel sitcoms in 2010:

- characterization: depicting Phil on ABC's *Modern Family* as an early adopter and as a peer-ent who uses the same Apple devices his teen daughter uses
- single episodes: fleshing out Phil's characterization in an episode about the desirability of a release-day iPad tablet. The same situation is a source of comic characterization on Disney Channel sitcom *Austin & Ally*
- series structure: utilizing the iPad's touch screen interface in the credits sequence of Disney Channel's *A.N.T. Farm*
- cultural messaging: naturalizing the iPad as a necessity for high achievement in the Advanced Natural Talents program depicted in *A.N.T. Farm* and as a necessity for overachiever Brick Heck in ABC's *The Middle* even though the family struggles to pay basic bills.

It is important to note that ABC and Disney Channel are owned by The Walt Disney Company, which means the similar messaging points to the channels' connection within a media company's channel portfolio. In the case of the iPad examples, when these episodes aired Disney's largest shareholder was Apple's Steve Jobs, so there was self-interest in the brand's appearance. As is typical in such circumstances, there are not any documented monetary arrangements.

Beyond such instances of branded characterizations, this book analyzes a variety of types of more explicit hybrid content, including:

- branded credit sequences
- dramatized advertising in the form of shorts starring series actors who maintain some consistency of persona with their in-series characters
- dramatized channel branding (also with actor/characters)
- short-form storytelling integrated with promotional paratexts (e.g., movie trailers, sneak peeks, interviews)
- customized and hosted lead-ins and lead-outs framing such fare
- content–promotion hybrids that blur the lines between education or cause advocacy and storytelling.

I argue that these kinds of content–promotion hybrids construct and maintain a network or studio brand and encourage viewers to identify with its output and recommend it to others. In the close analyses of specific episodes, I examine the interplay of thematics or characterization with some promotional element, such as a branded credit sequence or a dramatized advertisement. I concentrate mostly on sitcoms because of their industry utility, especially in relation to their versatility for schedule pairings and for syndication (which often utilizes episodes stripped in marathon format across an evening's schedule, or at least pairing of episodes).

Through its comparative analyses *Television Brandcasting* details the differences between early peer-to-peer forms of marketing and the current new-media-enabled strategies for audience address, advertising, programming, and promotion. I start with the obvious, but often overlooked, fact that television programs are not simply entertainment products in their own right because they always also function as platforms for promoting other entertainment content, consumer products, and brands, whether those of stars, sponsors, advertisers, networks, studios, or media conglomerates. In this way, television programs are simultaneously creative texts and industry products. As such, their signature elements (like thematics and characterizations) cannot be accounted for entirely by close textual analysis. They need to be considered within the context of the industry producing them. I place programming back into the frameworks from which it is too often detached. To examine specific television programming, I consider it alongside the industrial logic behind program thematics, set design, scheduling, promotion, and content repurposing for other platforms.

As a means of focus, I consider the variety of short-form, content–promotion hybrids that act as stand-alone entertainment and double as channel branding, advertainment, or institutional advertising (company voice messaging). I also bring attention to new categories to study, including branded credits sequences, dramatized advertising and relevant pods of commercials linked directly to series thematics, product integration character arcs, and studio identity integration and placement on new distribution platforms such as Walt Disney's signature Blu-ray/DVD combo packs. In my attention to these promotional elements, I align myself with John Caldwell, Jonathan Gray, Paul Grainge, and Catherine Johnson, arguing that promotional content is not merely appended to a program, but is central to its mode of address. To evaluate that address, I pay particular attention to the way television programmers, producers, promoters, sponsors, and advertisers leverage television properties, timeslots, scheduling grids, and Blu-ray/DVD/Digital releases as brandcasting platforms from which to circulate a set of core values to potential customers and brand advocates.

All of this brandcasting is always conflicted and often contested, because as much as it tries to pre-create meaning, it cannot predetermine it.[15] The amount of promotional surround associated with today's U.S. television industry indicates just how desperately all these stakeholders want to shape the "context of consumption," a phrase Adam Arvidsson uses to denote, "the significance that commodities acquired in the minds of consumers."[16] This attempted control continues on other platforms and through social media utilities. Some recent scholars have assessed the modifications of established industry practices in relation to these and other emerging distribution and engagement platforms. They have not considered how television networks and entertainment companies approach content distribution through these platforms as communicative opportunities, or how they use them to circulate their company voice messaging.

The Walt Disney Company is most often the lens through which this book focuses its commentary on the current practices and historical origins of the brand-intensive environment of U.S. television. Its strategies merit in-depth analysis as Disney has been committed to a brand-centric approach to television and the platform's potential as a cross-company promotional space since its first-regularly scheduled 1950s programming. Close examination also reveals that many of millennial modifications to long-standing industry practices have their roots in the partnership between the midcentury Walt Disney Studio and ABC. The network broadcast Disney Studio's primetime anthology series, initially titled *Disneyland*, its late afternoon narrowcast series, *The Mickey Mouse Club*, and its primetime serial, *Zorro*.[17] ABC is now owned by Disney and is just one of several channels in the Disney–ABC Television Group. The group includes ABC Family, a cable channel narrowcast to 12- to 24-year olds (with emphasis on females), Disney Channel, the U.S. channel spectrum's only brandcaster, and its two "spinoff" channels, Disney XD (microcast to tween boys) and Disney Junior (microcast to toddlers and their caretakers). As a media conglomerate, The Walt Disney Company can now spread its self-promotion across its channel portfolio and, as Chapter 4 details, utilize its signature Blu-ray/DVD combo pack along with web and mobile outlets to brandcast itself.

0.4 Studying Promotion, Paratexts, and "Total Merchandising"

The turn toward branding has been studied by several key scholars in television studies. My examination of television's content–promotion hybrids and more general promotional surround draws on the field-defining work of Caldwell, who brought attention to channel identifiers ("idents") and promotion in *Televisuality* and expanded upon that earlier work in *Production Culture* and later book chapters. In *Show Sold Separately: Promos, Spoilers and Other Media Paratexts*, Gray offered the first book-length study to pay "closer attention to the frames that surround television viewing" and to treat promotional elements as texts in their own right. Building on his foundational work, I look at content-about-content shorts not only as texts to be analyzed, but also as expressions of industry logic.

My work has been influenced by Philip Napoli and Joseph Turow, among others, who have closely analyzed the audience marketplace and the role of "capturing audience attention." As Napoli argues, "media institutions define audiences in particular ways, using analytical tools and perspectives that reflect their needs and interests."[18] With this theory in mind, I consider how television programming and scheduling decisions in each era reflect the ways that the desired audience is defined within particular institutional frameworks and specific channel branding goals and studio messaging needs. I borrow from Holt, Cameron, Adam Arvidsson, Celia Lury, Liz Moor, and other branding theorists to talk about the way brands' storytelling is inflected by the cultural concerns of their historical moments.

In his book *Brand Hollywood*, Grainge analyzed how the evolution of the logos for Hollywood studios conveyed their changing self-representations. He has recently segued into an analysis of television channel idents and other brand-related ephemeral media. Grainge has partnered with Catherine Johnson to assess the implications for the proliferation of interstitial content in relation to channel branding. They look at the idents and interstitials of the British public broadcasters to consider the ways that they address viewers through arresting aural and visual design. Grainge and Johnson are particularly interested in the production culture and output of Red Bee Media, a U.K.-based boutique design company that is part of what Grainge calls an emerging "promotional screen industry." An interview related to this new work is included in Grainge's anthology, *Ephemeral Media: Transitory Screen Culture from Television to YouTube*.

In her book *Branding Television*, Johnson offers in-depth commentary on British channel strategies and provides analyses of U.S. strategies as counterpoints. This structure results from the difficulty of studying on-air channel branding when not residing in the country. Despite the fact that television series travel internationally and are produced by transnational media conglomerates, the experience of watching television on television and on officially supported platforms, typically only available within their country of production, is a surprisingly national one. With this in mind, I focused only on the U.S. television industry's approaches to channel branding in my book, *Television and New Media: Must-Click TV*. Confronting the same logistical problem that Johnson had in locating copies of the ephemeral promotional content of on-air television in another country, I remain focused in *Television Brandcasting* on the brand-saturated context of U.S. culture, but I move beyond the contemporary historical parameters that both Johnson and I set in our books. Historical material on midcentury Disney programming could be unearthed in the UCLA Film and Television Archive and in university library special collections, but it proved impossible in the time frame of this book's production to consider fully how Disney maintains a consistency today across Disney Channels Worldwide. Disney launched this international channel portfolio as means for preventing the brand detachment that occurs when programs travel internationally. Through its 100 branded channels and channel feeds, The Walt Disney Company could assure consistency of its programming so that its content always appears alongside other Disney content or alongside approved acquired series or international co-productions. Although I assumed it would also freely circulate its content-about-content shorts as it does in the U.S., it turns out that Disney has less control over the promotional surround of its international channels. There is very little of the interstitial content that Disney uses on the U.S. channel to pre-create meaning for its signature sitcoms and movies. Although I could only analyze some European versions of Disney Channel, I learned that in those markets they varied greatly in the promotions because of each nation's different regulations governing promotions. It would be fascinating to investigate what happens in terms of promotional surround in Asian and Latin American markets as well, but such local observation and analysis was not possible for this study. Of course, the fact of having a dedicated channel in so many international markets that only plays Disney-approved programming still is a major contributor to consistency across Disney Channels Worldwide. With its strong international portfolio in mind, Disney must develop sitcoms that can travel well internationally and speak not just to Americans, but to a global cohort of tweens willing to identify with the same aspirations and anxieties. To do so, Disney Channel naturalizes the value of global tween culture oriented toward a neoliberal worldview (in which brandcasting yourself is the optimal form of self-expression). It does not accommodate local children's culture or make room for an alternate set of values. Instead, it functions as the promotional arm of The Walt Disney Company and as such spreads company voice messaging in 169 countries and 35 languages, thereby consolidating the media giant's global influence.

On-air scheduling, the topic of Chapter 2, is also a necessarily national analysis, but I build on John Ellis' important work on U.K. strategies. For his contribution to Grainge's *Ephemeral Media* collection, Ellis also looks briefly at U.K. channel identifiers and other interstitial content. Likely because they were not yet such a prominent feature of British broadcasting channels, Ellis does not focus on those elements in his earlier article, "Scheduling: the Last Creative Act in Television" (2000). He offers a paradigm for studying series within the context of the national schedules into which they are slotted and the schedules with which they compete. As the first to address this completely overlooked area of analysis in television studies, Ellis lays the foundation for future study of scheduling grids and practices, and calls for others to follow his lead. I do so in my analysis of American scheduling grids. I start Chapter 2 with a focus on Showtime's schedule-pairings as channel branding. The bulk of the chapter analyzes what ABC's scheduling in the mid-1950s to the early 1970s can tell us about the movement toward channel branding and self-promotion as well as narrowcasting through scheduling decisions.

Gray's "Television Pre-views and the Meaning of Hype" provides the vocabulary through which to discuss promotional elements that frame television texts. They serve as paratexts, which, as Gray defines them, are the "texts before the text" that try to pre-create its meaning for viewers. Throughout this book, I use Gray's iteration of the term paratext and rely on his insights about how paratexts function to discuss how particular content–promotion hybrids attempt to pre-create meaning for forthcoming media works. While Gray looks at paratexts attached to particular texts, I broaden the scope to look at how content-about-content shorts on Disney Channel, for example, become a form of channel branding beyond their immediate role in relation to a specific forthcoming sitcom or movie.

My focus on Disney television more generally distinguishes my book from most work on The Walt Disney Company or Disney Studios. The majority of accounts concentrate on Disney's A-level animation and its breakout features like *Mary Poppins*. In doing so, they overlook the studio firsts in the midcentury period when the studio released its first live-action comedy, its first live-action family adventure, its first tween girl-helmed comedy, its first "clean teen" picture, and its first young adult comedy. Chapter 4 considers how Disney offers its position as "first in the field" as one of several lenses through which it asks to be read by viewers of its classic films screened on its ABC anthology series (1954–61) or on Disney's signature DVD multi packs and Blu-ray/DVD combo packs. In this chapter my focus is still on television in that I am most interested in the lead-ins to trailers that were aired as part of Disney television series and then repurposed on Disney's home media releases. One of the lead-ins even finds its way into *Saving Mr. Banks*, a 2013 feature film whose brand management function I deconstruct alongside that of *Frozen*, Disney's billion-dollar animated blockbuster. The comparative analysis of the public perception of these films in relation to Disney Studio's branding is a way into a larger discussion of brandcasting at the level of a studio with a television platform it uses for circulating desired brand messaging.

Within this discussion, I look closely at the hosted lead-ins to trailers airing on the 1950s television series produced by Disney. I am interested as well in a comparison of how this midcentury content was then repurposed in the 2000s on Disney's signature Blu-ray/DVD/Digital multiplatform combo packs. I argue that the comparison of midcentury and millennial Disney Studios brand management strategies is necessary to demonstrate that many strategies that seem like recent innovations are really evolutions of early Disney television practices. For the political economic view of the evolution of The Walt Disney Company as a media conglomerate, every scholar owes a debt to Janet Wasko. In *Understanding Disney*, she offers a detailed account of the history of the rise of Disney as a media conglomerate and the skill with which it expanded and interconnected its operations. Wasko adds to the body of scholarship that considers the implications of the troubling fact that a small group of companies control global media culture and circulation. This scholarship has fully detailed the expansion of Disney and other U.S.-based media companies into global media conglomerates. As this process of media concentration has been so ably studied by Wasko and others, I turn to the related questions about the business strategies through which this occurs at The Walt Disney Company.

My focus on Disney's use of peer-to-peer audience address in its television programming also distinguishes my work from the other studies that consider Disney television as a promotional platform. In his often-cited *Disneyland* chapter from his book *Hollywood TV*, Christopher Anderson addresses the role that Disney Studio's television programs played in the company's self-promotion. In *Disney TV*, a condensed case study volume in Wayne State's TV Milestones series, J. P. Telotte fleshes out Anderson's insights about Disney's use of television as a promotional platform. As my account below suggests, my work is differentiated from theirs in its scope, thematic focus, and its attention to aspects of

Disney's multiplatform audience address that are outside the parameters of their studies or developed after their studies were published.

Anderson's historical account of the origins of Disney television production has been enormously influential in television studies. His chapter on *Disneyland* reads the program and the theme park in terms of the book's larger examination of the initial relationship between Hollywood studios and the new broadcast television platform. Anderson ends the chapter with the claim that *Disneyland* promoted the consumption of other kinds of Disney entertainment and experiences. In his provocative final comments on "total merchandising," Anderson claims that viewers of *Disneyland* are "propelled by a centrifugal force" from television outward because the program drew their attention to the television platform "only to disperse it outward, toward other Disney products." Anderson is most interested in theme park promotion, but he also addresses the program's role in film promotion. Telotte then provides ample evidence for such assertions about the promotional function of the 1950s anthology series. Through excellent, concise treatments of the various other iterations of the anthology series in this short volume, Telotte contributes many important insights about the changes from ABC's *Disneyland* to *Walt Disney Presents* to NBC's *Walt Disney's Wonderful World of Color* and beyond. He also looks in detail at *Davy Crockett* and more briefly at the other anthology program serials and the stand-alone serial *Zorro*.

Anderson and Telotte do not mention the important role that television exposure played in the launch of an in-house recording division, or the crucial role of the in-house magazine (1955–9) in encouraging viewers/consumers to follow the television actors across all available platforms. Given my focus on Disney Channel, I find *The Mickey Mouse Club* quite significant in the way its young stars played a pivotal role in motivating viewers of the television series not only to don the mouse ears, but also to go out and buy records, comics, books, magazines, and movie tickets as well as a wealth of tie-in merchandising (e.g., record players and guitars). They also pitched sponsor products (e.g., toothpaste and cereal) featured in the customized spots produced by a studio affiliate. The Mouseketeers appeared in hosted lead-ins to studio film trailers as well as to television serials like *Spin and Marty*, which played an important role in establishing what I call the studio's Tween Bs. The studio released these live-action films in theaters, starting with *The Shaggy Dog* in 1959, a surprise hit with Fred MacMurray and several actors from *Spin and Marty*.

Considering the midcentury lead-ins in order and looking at archival studio documents reveals that the synchronization of the studio's television episodes with the features release schedule allowed Disney to create a good deal of hype that it could then reinforce through its new in-house magazine and recording division. Because many of the young stars were hyped to the point that they were emerging as brands in their own right, the stars associated with *The Mickey Mouse Club* played a big role in propelling viewers outwards to movie theaters,

FIGURE 0.2 *The Mickey Mouse Club* created iconic brand signifiers, a generational cohort, and a brandcasting platform for Disney Studios, stars, sponsors and licensees.

live events, the record store, and the local store for various tie-in products manufactured by studio licensees. (See Figure 0.1 earlier in the chapter).

Disney television's early use of a peer-to-peer endorsement structure to promote the serials and films of this earlier era is very relevant to my analysis in

Chapter 3 of the current peer-to-peer address that structures Disney Channel short-form programming. I am especially interested in the consistency in both eras of representing the studio's young actors as an ensemble of friends sharing their enthusiasm for upcoming Disney releases (when they are really paid endorsers). There have not yet been any studies of the architecture of the entire output of Disney Channel or its many ways of packaging promotion as entertainment in its own right. It is especially important to look at the role of Disney television within The Walt Disney Company after 2004, which is the year Disney Channel began its first rebrand (its second was in 2007), launching Disney Channels Worldwide as it exists today. Recall that *Hannah Montana*, the sitcom that was truly seen around the world on Disney Channels Worldwide, began its run in 2006 and concluded in 2010.

As suggested by the Disney examples already offered, a significant reason for looking at current programming juxtaposed with the programming airing prior to the entrenchment of the classic three-network system in the 1970s is that several of ABC's earlier series established paradigms that have been resurrected. The reemergence of those paradigms is evident in an examination of current brandcasting strategies. Through this book's analyses my general purpose is to construct a more complex history of strategies that we think of as unique to the current television industry or simply as a byproduct of new media's impact on classic network era practices.

Of course, the biggest difference today is the three-tier structure of the U.S. industry and the important distinctions among premium subscription channels, basic cable channels, and broadcast networks, especially in relation to what kind of content and messaging typically appears on series in each tier. In an off-television environment where many series exist as stand-alone brands for purchase, the important impact of a series' home channel on content and even thematics often gets forgotten. As I discuss in the Epilogue, it is necessary to detail how these distinctions shape programming because those who access series via an alternate distribution method do not typically recognize these differences and judge content as if it is produced on an equal playing field. More troubling for promotional departments is that these new content delivery platforms detach content from the channel's original promotional surround.

The Walt Disney Company, and therefore Disney Channel, ABC Family, and the ABC network, has been a leader in preventing such brand detachment because it has always understood the need to partner with new platforms on which viewers seek out content. Its ability to manage and later leverage the viewer behavior facilitated by social media was certainly enabled by the company's relationship with Steve Jobs. As already noted, Jobs was The Walt Disney Company's largest shareholder because the Apple CEO owned Pixar animation, which Disney acquired in 2006.[19] As a result, Disney experimented with iTunes distribution starting in 2005 and with a 2010 iPad application that Apple and Nielsen conceptualized to encourage and measure the engagement of viewers.

Disney recognized such experiments as necessary adjustments to the realities of the new mediasphere,[20] particularly the changes in viewer practices and the modified financing, distribution, marketing, and branding models with which millennial television industry developments are associated.

0.5   Chapter Summaries

Focused on brandcasting at the episode and series level, Chapter 1 establishes the existence of direct and indirect forms of peer-to-peer recommendations in the first decades of U.S. television. This chapter compares today's strategies to those in 1953–63. Framed with analyses of *Modern Family* and *The Middle*, it demonstrates that product integration strategies they employ have much earlier origins in 1950s TV. In sitcoms such as *Leave It to Beaver*, *I Love Lucy*, *Make Room for Daddy/The Danny Thomas Show*, and *My Three Sons* these recommendations involve the integration of a product, a product demonstration, or a product pitch into an episode or its credits sequence. These sitcoms are also emblematic of ABC's embrace of the teen-inclusive family sitcom and the generational accord sitcom subgenre, one in which ABC has specialized since it aired *The Adventures of Ozzie & Harriet* (1952–66). As a producer, Ozzie Nelson combined different generational appeals in the dramatized advertisements and other content–promotion hybrid forms he incorporated into his sitcom. He not only made sponsor products part of storylines about a new kind of "peer-ent type," but he also showed products in use in situations that felt like forms of endorsement. In addition to setting the standard for content–promotion hybrids Nelson also innovated the embedded music video to showcase son Ricky's rock 'n' roll talents. He was the first of many producers to understand that television could function as a highly effective platform for promoting potential Billboard Top 100 singles, particularly to those 9- to 14-year-olds marketers now call tweens.

While this kind of branded entertainment model was displaced during the entrenchment of the Big Three network oligopoly in the 1970s and 1980s, it has returned in the current era of multichannel competition, mass audience fragmentation, and increased viewer control over where and when to access television content. No longer the only platform for television programming, the broadcast networks have to make deals with advertisers to offset declining ratings and the diminished reach of the on-air commercial.

Brandcasting might also be part of the strategy of an individual channel through its scheduling of an identifiable grouping of series (by subgenre, format, or thematic cycle). To support this point, Chapter 2 looks first at Showtime's female-helmed "bleak comedies" of the late 2000s and then positions them as a counterpoint to ABC's 1960s and 1970s "generational accord" sitcoms that followed the wake of *Ozzie & Harriet*. To begin, it analyzes a schedule dramatization that reveals how Showtime used *Weeds* as a promotional platform through which to launch new bleak comedies. Eventually, the premium cable channel had amassed a very clear brand through a series cycle of female-helmed half-hours. As a premium channel is technically a generalist channel, this narrowcast branding struck some commentators as problematic, even though the so-called "ladies with problems" series were bringing home lead actress Emmys. Whatever its flaws, the formula enabled Showtime to be recognized as a legitimate competitor to HBO.

This parallels ABC's position in the 1960s and 1970s with its competitor CBS. Airing series cycles representing the era's "peer-ents," "think youngs," teens, and "new girls" gave ABC a narrowcast inflection, enabling it to reach the top of Nielsen's ratings by 1976–7. The cultural concerns embedded within ABC series dismissed as either simple family comedies or escapist fantasy become more overt when considered in terms of their schedule pairings. ABC series considered include *Bewitched*, *That Girl*, *The Partridge Family*, *Patty Duke*, *Gidget*, *My Three Sons*, and *Laverne & Shirley*.

Through close analysis of scheduling grids, this chapter examines what scheduling can tells us about channel branding and differentiation through scheduling decisions. It builds on John Ellis's commentary about the speculation (and, more often than not, speculative failures) inherent in scheduling and demographic targeting. Ellis contends that scheduling is in need of deeper analysis in television studies if we are to understand how networks imagined themselves and the viewers that they hoped to attract and then deliver to advertisers.

Chapter 3 focuses on Disney Channel, which is distinct on the U.S. channel spectrum because it can focus all of its attention on brandcasting and generate enthusiasm and sometimes content for other Disney divisions.[21] Disney's ownership of this basic cable channel enables it to fill the flow between episodes with a variety of brandcasting forms. Of particular interest are the content-about-content shorts that circulate Walt Disney's company voice messaging, while serving series and channel branding needs.

In addition to looking closely at these signature shorts, the chapter considers the brandcasting function of Disney Channel's recent stars-in-the-making sitcom cycle. The main characters are brandcasters, entrepreneurial individuals who make the most of their access to social media platforms and networks to showcase talents and build an audience for themselves with the hopes of someday becoming marketable brands. My reading of the emergence of this sitcom cycle is informed by the commentary of Sarah Banet-Weiser, Roopali Mukherjee, Richard Sennett, Laurie Ouellette, and James Hay, among others, who have examined the emergence of a problematic enterprising and self-actualizing worker paradigm.[22] I turn to Holt and Cameron's branding theories to support my claim that the gap between the ideology of neoliberal entrepreneurialism and the actual state of jobs and behavior of corporations has produced an enormous "demand for new myths" to manage and "shore up the nation's cultural contradictions," to use Holt's phrasing.[23] The brandcaster is what Holt would call a "populist type" that emerges in response to anxieties. In this case, the brandcaster surfaces at a time of doubt about the feasibility of upward mobility, especially through the fabled work ethic paradigm in which steady hard work within a bureaucracy and loyal service is supposed to result in the steady accrual of rewards. It looks at Disney Channel's brandcasters in its recent cycle of stars-in-the-making sitcoms and original movies, through which Disney deconstructs the star-making process at the same time as it constructs a platform from which to promote the latest performer to be groomed for multiplatform stardom across several Disney divisions. The core of the chapter looks at the effacement of the more self-interested aspects of brandcasting through a series of corporate social responsibility shorts.

This chapter demonstrates that friendship on Disney Channel goes beyond buddy pairings in promotions and programs. Friendship is integral to the channel's economic structure (the friends of Disney Channel sponsorship paradigm) and its company voice messaging. The channel's multiplatform invitations to viewers to participate make it feel as if they are in peer-to-peer relationships with Disney Channel's *circle of stars* and in a network of other Disney Channel viewers. To examine this dynamic, the last section of the chapter looks closely at *Disney's Friends for Change* campaign, a tween "empowerment initiative" linked to green causes supported by The Walt Disney Company. Viewers could pledge to be a friend for change or submit video evidence of their leadership in *Friends for Change* initiatives in their local communities. Representative viewers were also featured in channel shorts showcasing personal talents, hobbies, histories, or experiences (*The Time I . . ., Who I Am,* and *Make Your Mark*). To create *Friends for Change* and most of its content-about-content shorts, Disney quietly hired some boutique production houses. At the heart of this chapter is an argument about how the slate of short-form content designed by these specialists enables Disney to shape perceptions without resorting to overt messaging. Analysis of representative shorts brings to light the cultural aspirations and anxieties on which their producers draw in order to engage audiences and generate subjectivities that affirm a specific interpretation of the roles of Walt Disney and the millennial generation.

Chapter 4 examines television brandcasting strategies of film studios through the lens of Disney's 1950s television programming and the repurposing of that television programming on Disney's recent Blu-ray/DVDs. Blu-ray and DVD were new distribution platforms for the 2000s, which enabled the site of promotion to be simultaneous with the site of exhibition because they delivered special features (and brand messaging) to consumers already committed to watching the films. While the "making ofs" included on these multi-disc sets are interesting as brandcasting in their own right, they also point to 1950s brandcasting at Disney Studios. This is because many of the content-about-content features are taken, at least in part, from the "Uncle Walt" or Mousekeeter hosted lead-ins from 1950s Disney television programs. Indicative of the circularity of Disney brandcasting, these home media releases and forthcoming films are then promoted via content-about-content short-form series airing on Disney Channel.

The chapter offers some commentary on episodes of *Disneyland/Walt Disney Presents*, which aired on ABC from 1954–61. Initially, the program promoted the launch of a new destination (Disneyland, the theme park), and then Disney used the series to generate awareness about new rides and sections of the park. This series function has been analyzed capably by Anderson and Telotte, so I turn instead to how the series helped entrench the studio's brand identity as it was embodied in Walt Disney himself as he appeared in hosted lead-ins to the studio's theatrical releases. In addition to considering how segments of these hosted lead-ins were repurposed in brand-centric ways on Disney's home media releases, I also analyze how Blu-ray/DVDs were promoted through *Leo Little's Big Show* online and on Disney Channel.

The chapter ends with some analysis of episodes of *Disney 365*, a Disneyland-set short form series, and Disney parks-themed episodes of *The Middle* and *Modern Family*, looking at them all as forms of parent company brand management. The chapter begins with a comparison of Disney's successful brand management strategies in relation to 2013's *Frozen* and its Disney Channel programming. It details why it is inaccurate to call the feature film *Saving Mr. Banks* a recent attempt to control the desired self-representation of Walt Disney, the man and the studio. In contrast, it looks at how and when the studio actually does skillfully assert that control, using Disney's midcentury television programs and its millennial Blu-ray/DVD combo packs as case studies.

Also moving the discussion off television, the Epilogue considers the use of social media and websites both for brandcasting and for driving social media users to tune-in to television programming. Approaching new media as a challenge rather than as competition, smart producers have found ways to leverage to their advantage new viewer practices, including uploading, downloading, and streaming video and audio; two-screen viewing; or posting, tweeting, texting, and blogging about media texts. To exemplify this point I look at the use of Twitter for ABC Family's *Pretty Little Liars*, but I also provide context through an overview of some the earlier strategies leveraged by the producers of ABC's *Lost*. To bring the discussion back to sponsorship, I look briefly at the inventive on-air attention strategies for *Mad Men* and the role they played in recommending sponsors' brands and in circulating AMC's revamped channel brand. Finally, the Epilogue addresses the changing role of television series as stand-alone brands delivered on demand through subscription providers on cable and via off-television platforms.

★★★

In *Television Brandcasting*, I join other authors who have begun to assess the impact of new content distribution and exhibition platforms (e.g., web, DVD, social media utilities, and mobile interfaces) on established television industry practices. I move beyond earlier work through my consideration of how television networks and entertainment companies approach content distribution though the different platforms as new communicative opportunities through which to circulate their company voice messaging and brand their content. As this book demonstrates, these forms of communication have some surprising parallels in industry practices from the 1950s and 1960s. At the most general level, I intend *Television Brandcasting* to make a case for taking this and earlier forms of promotional surround seriously as sites of study. Doing so requires us to look at elements of the on-air and off-TV promotional surround as creative texts and as sensitive registers of the industry logic and brand messaging goals of the various stakeholders involved in production and circulation of content. I hope the book also sheds light on the interactions among advertisers, networks, and studios and offers fresh perspectives on the ways in which these various stakeholders try and often fail to circulate desired brand identities. Within the often-overlooked industry practices and programming analyzed throughout this study, I illustrate the ways in which television content is framed differently when it is distributed in different ways. This perspective opens the field for future studies of how such practices evolve or are abandoned in response to whatever new distribution platforms and interfaces emerge in the coming years.

Notes

1 *The Adventures of Ozzie & Harriet* (ABC, 1952–66); *I Love Lucy* (CBS, 1951–7), and *The George Burns and Gracie Allen Show* (CBS, 1950–8). Milton Berle's television show was initially called *Texaco Star Theater* when it ran on NBC from 1948–53. Jimmie Dodd was the MC and "adult Mouseketeer" from 1955–8 on *The Mickey Mouse Club*.
2 *24* ran on FOX from 2001–10.
3 *All in the Family* (CBS, January 1971–April 1979) and *M*A*S*H* (CBS, 1972–83).
4 Hilmes 2008, 218. Hilmes dates the classic three-network system from 1965–85, although there is always slippage in such date ranges. I focus on how the 1960s was still more of an era of transition prior to the entrenchment of practices in the 1970s.
5 In the 1960s the networks had taken ownership interests in production and often controlled syndication rights. The FCC was concerned with the power the networks had amassed and tried to undermine it through the Financial Interest and Syndication Rules (Fin-Syn), which prevented profit participation in future shows. The rules said that a network could not produce and distribute content. Networks had to purchase content from "independent producers," who were sometimes affiliated with independent production companies, but often with the television production company of a major Hollywood studio, such as Twentieth Century Fox and Warner Brothers. Fin-Syn was not renewed in 1995, at which point there began a concentration of ownership between networks and production companies.
6 See Hilmes 2008, 218, for a discussion of the networks' concentration of program ownership and scheduling control. The Big Three oligopoly refers to CBS, NBC, and ABC. Entering the network space in the 1980s, FOX did not program more than 15 hours a week and so the FCC did not consider it a full-service network. FOX has benefited from this questionable categorization, as it was then not subject to the financing and syndication rules. The loophole was not necessary for long as Fin-Syn was not renewed in 1995 and all the networks could then produce, distribute, and syndicate content. The regulatory changes that came in the wake of the Reagan-era deregulation also allowed for all the mergers and acquisitions that led to the formation of the giant, diversified media conglomerates.

7 The word "viewser" is used by Greg Roach, "Into the Vortex," *New Scientist*, September 23, 1995, 30–3.

8 Social utilities like Facebook and Twitter have also made possible a more direct relationship of viewers with series stars and creators. More than ever before, stars and now even some production workers, are expected to position themselves as viewers' friends.

9 Gerlitz and Helmond 2011.

10 *The Dinah Shore Chevy Show* (NBC, 1956–63); *General Electric Theater* (CBS, 1953–62).

11 Holt 2004, 3, 95, 3, 9, 73, 96.

12 Eastman Kodak started as *Ozzie & Harriet*'s sponsor in the fall of 1956. This resulted in more scenes outside and a photo shoot in Hawaii in 1959. As a producer, Ozzie Nelson proved particularly skilled at subliminal advertising. See Nelson 1973, 256, 266–7, 241–2. Although accommodating to sponsors, Nelson had a contract giving him complete control without sponsor interference. On July 14, 1949, Sonny Werblin and MCA brokered the Nelsons a non-cancellable 10-year package deal with ABC. As Ricky and David were 9 and 12 at the time, they had the option to leave the show at any time. To test out the family's screen appeal prior to moving the show to television in 1952, Nelson arranged for them to do a tester film for Universal, *Here Come the Nelsons*. It costarred Rock Hudson. See, Nelson 1973, 210, 212–13.

13 Paradoxically, this togetherness first requires a separation from the extended family. At the time, many Americans, especially those from lower-class levels and ethnic backgrounds, were seeing a move to the suburbs as a way to Americanize. It is a mistake to assume that *Ozzie & Harriet* only appealed to others of the same ethnic background or class level as the Nelsons. There is an aspirational element to television watching in this era. In *Ozzie* (1973) Nelson recounts a story about a native Hawaiian woman's attraction to the show and his conversation with her assimilated daughter during the Kodak photo shoot of 1959 (267). In my discussion of these issues in Chapter 1, I draw on Hartley's claim that we should not underestimate the appeal of "suburbanality," especially for those who have not yet achieved suburban status or are the first generation to do so. Hartley (1999, 199) describes the suburban everyday depicted on television as "a condition of stability, visibility and competence to which we aspired . . . our uniqueness was experienced as tragedy, others' sameness as happiness."

14 Nelson 1973, 251–3. Ricky had his biggest hits in summer 1960.

15 Gray 2008 says paratexts are the "texts before the text" that try to pre-create its meanings in the minds of viewers before they see it.

16 Arvidsson 2005, 244.

17 *Zorro* (ABC, 1957–9), *The Mickey Mouse Club* (1955–9), *Disneyland* (ABC 1954–8), *Walt Disney Presents* (ABC 1958–61), *Walt Disney's Wonderful World of Color* (NBC 1961–9, with various title changes thereafter).

18 Napoli 2003, 3–4.

19 Pixar and Marvel Entertainment (the latter acquired in 2009), both run as semi-autonomous studios. Their releases are heavily promoted in Disney Channel shorts and the films are rerun on Disney Channel and ABC Family.

20 The phrase is John Hartley's from *Popular Reality: Journalism, Modernity, Popular Culture* (London, UK: Arnold, 1996).

21 The ESPN channel group is a separate entity and is not part of the Disney–ABC Television Group. ESPN's position inside The Walt Disney Company is reflected in the fact that Disney XD, microcast to tween males, does have an X-Games flavor to some of its programming and promotions. Disney XD also has had a few promotainment crossovers with ESPN. The book does not focus on A&E Networks (which includes

Lifetime) as the Disney–ABC Television Group only manages an equity interest. For a discussion of some ways in which the Disney brand is affirmed and undercut on the channel, see Elana Levine, "Fractured Fairytales and Fragmented Markets: Disney's Weddings of a Lifetime and the Cultural Politics of Media Conglomeration," *Television and New Media* 6, no. 1 (February 2005): 71–88.

22 Banet-Weiser, "Free Self-Esteem Tools?" 2012, 53.

23 Holt 2004, 5–9.

Bibliography

Aaker, David. "Beyond Functional Benefits." *Marketing News*, September 30, 2009: 23.

Aaker, David and Enrich Joachimsthaler. "The Brand Relationship Spectrum: The Key to the Brand Architecture Challenge." *California Management Review* 42, no. 4 (Summer 2000): 8–23.

Anderson, Christopher. *Hollywood TV: The Studio System in the Fifties*. Austin, TX: University of Texas Press, 1994.

Anderson, Chris. "The Long Tail." *Wired* 12, no. 10, October 2004. Available: www.wired.com/wired/archive/12.10/tail_pr.html.

Aronczyk, Melissa and Devon Powers, eds., *Blowing Up the Brand: Critical Perspectives on Promotional Culture*. New York, NY: Peter Lang, 2010.

Arvidsson, Adam. "Brands: A Critical Perspective." *Journal of Consumer Culture* 52, no. 2 (2005): 235–58.

Bagdikian, Ben. *The New Media Monopoly*, Boston, MA: Beacon Press, 2004.

Banet-Weiser, Sarah. *Authentic™: The Politics of Ambivalence in a Brand Culture*. New York, NY: New York University Press, 2012.

——. "'Free Self-Esteem Tools?': Brand Culture, Gender, and the Dove Real Beauty Campaign." In Mukherjee and Banet-Weiser 2012, 39–56.

——. *Kids Rule!: Nickelodeon and Consumer Citizenship*. Durham, NC: Duke University Press, 2007.

Barnouw, Erik. *The Sponsor: Notes on a Modern Potentate*. New York, NY: Oxford University Press, 1979.

Baughman, James L. *Same Time, Same Station: Creating American Television, 1948–1961*. Baltimore, MD: The John Hopkins University Press, 2007.

Bennett, James and Tom Brown, eds. *Film and Television After DVD*. London, UK: Routledge, 2008.

Bird, Jr., William L. *"Better Living": Advertising, Media, and the New Vocabulary of Business Leadership*. Evanston, IL: Northwestern University Press, 1999.

Boddy, William. *Fifties Television: The Industry and its Critics*. Urbana and Chicago, IL: University of Illinois Press, 1993.

——. "Interactive Television and Advertising Form in Contemporary U.S. Television." In Spigel and Olsson 2004, 113–32.

——. "New Media as Old Media: Television." In Harries, 2002, 242–53.

——. *New Media and Popular Imagination: Launching Radio, Television, and Digital Media in the United States*. Oxford, UK: Oxford University Press, 2004.

Bodroghkozy, Aniko. *Groove Tube: Sixties Television and the Youth Rebellion*. Durham, NC: Duke University Press, 2001.

Bolter, Jay David and Richard Grusin. *Remediation: Understanding New Media*. Cambridge, MA: MIT Press, 1999.

Boyd, Dana. "Why Youth Heart Social Network Sites: The Role of Networked Publics in Teenage Social Life." In *Youth, Identity, and Digital Media*, ed. David Buckingham, 119–42. Cambridge, MA: MIT Press, 2008.

Brooks, Tim and Earle Marsh. *The Complete Directory to Primetime Network and Cable TV Shows: 1946–Present*. 8th edition. New York, NY: Ballantine, 2003.

Brown, Stephen, Robert V. Kozinets, and John F. Sherry Jr. "Teaching Old Brands New Tricks: Retro Branding and the Revival of Brand Meaning." *Journal of Marketing* 67, no. 3 (2003): 19–33.

Brunsdon, Charlotte. "What Is the 'Television' of Television Studies." In *Television: The Critical View*. 7th edition. ed. Horace Newcomb, 609–28. New York, NY: Oxford University Press, 2006.

Buckley, Peter. "Exploiting the Implicit." *Campaign*, November 16, 2012, 6–12.

Caldwell, John Thornton. "Convergence Television: Aggregating Form and Repurposing Content in the Culture of Conglomeration." In Spigel and Olsson 2004, 41–74.

——. "Critical Industrial Practice: Branding, Repurposing, and the Migratory Patterns of Industrial Texts." *Television & New Media* 7, no. 2 (May 2006): 99–134.

——. *Production Culture: Industrial Reflexivity and Critical Practice in Film and Television*. Durham, NC: Duke University Press, 2008.

——. *Televisuality: Style, Crisis, and Authority in American Television*. New Brunswick, NJ: Rutgers University Press, 1995.

——. "Welcome to the Viral Future of Cinema (Television)." *Cinema Journal* 45, no. 1 (Fall 2006): 90–7.

Castleman, Harry and Walter J. Podrazik. *Harry and Wally's Favorite TV Shows*. New York, NY: Prentice Hall, 1989.

——. *The TV Schedule Book*. New York, NY: McGraw-Hill, 1984.

Caves, Richard E. *Creative Industries: Contracts between Art and Commerce*. Cambridge, MA: Harvard University Press, 2000.

Cohen, Lizabeth. *A Consumer's Republic: The Politics of Mass Consumption in Postwar America*. New York, NY: Vintage/Random House, 2003.

Coontz, Stephanie. *The Way We Never Were: American Families and the Nostalgia Trap*. New York, NY: Basic Books, 1992.

Corner, John. *Critical Ideas in Television Studies*. Oxford, UK: Oxford University Press, 1999.

Davis, Aeron. *Promotional Cultures: The Rise and Spread of Advertising, Public Relations, Marketing and Branding*. Cambridge, UK: Polity Press, 2013.

Dawson, Max. "Television Abridged: Ephemeral Texts, Monumental Seriality and TV-Digital Media Convergence." In Grainge 2011, 37–56.

Deery, June. "Reality TV as Advertainment." *Popular Communication* 2, no. 1 (2004): 1–19.

Denis, Christopher Paul and Michael Denis. *Favorite Families of TV*. New York, NY: Citadel Press, 1992.

Dennis, Saul. "Brands Begin by Believing." *Promo Magazine* (June 2004): 121.

Deuze, Mark. "Convergence Culture in the Creative Industries." *International Journal of Cultural Studies* 10, no. 2 (2007): 243–63.

——. *Media Work*. Cambridge, UK: Polity, 2007.

Donaton, Scott. *Madison and Vine: Why the Entertainment and Advertising Industries Must Converge to Survive*. New York, NY: McGraw Hill, 2005.

Doty, Alexander. "The Cabinet of Lucy Ricardo: Lucille Ball's Star Image." *Cinema Journal* 29, no. 4 (Summer 1990): 11.

Douglas, Susan J. *Where the Girls Are: Growing Up Female with the Mass Media*. New York, NY: Times, 1995.

Dyer, Richard. *Stars*. London, UK: BFI Publishing, 1986.

Ellis, John. "Interstitials: How the 'Bits in Between' Define the Programmes." In Grainge 2011, 59–69.

——. "Scheduling: the Last Creative Act in Television?" *Media, Culture and Society* 22, no. 1 (2000): 25–38.

——. *Seeing Things: Television in the Age of Uncertainty*, London, UK: I.B. Tauris, 2000.

——. *Visible Fictions: Television, Cinema, Video*, Revised ed. New York, NY: Routledge, 1992.

Fiske, John. "The Cultural Economy of Fandom." In *The Adoring Audience: Fan Culture and Popular Culture*, ed. Lisa A. Lewis, 30–49. London, UK: Routledge, 1992.

——. "Cultural Studies and Television." *Channels of Discourse, Reassembled: Television and Contemporary Criticism*, 2nd edition, ed. Robert C. Allen. Chapel Hill, NC: University of North Carolina Press, 1992.

——. *Television Culture*. London, UK: Routledge, 1989.

Frank, Thomas. *The Conquest of Cool: Business Culture, Counterculture, and the Rise of Hip Consumerism*. Chicago, IL: University of Chicago Press, 1997.

Friedberg, Anne. "The Virtual Window." In Thornburn and Jenkins 2004, 337–53.

Gaines, Jane. "Costume and Narrative: How Dress Tells the Woman's Story." In *Fabrications: Costume and the Female Body*, eds. Jane Gaines and Charlotte Herzog, 180–211. New York, NY: Routledge, 1990.

Gerlitz, Carolin and Anne Helmond, "The Like Economy: Social Web in Transition." Conference Presentation at *MiT7: Unstable Platforms*. May 14, 2011.

Gertner, Jon. "Our Ratings, Ourselves." *New York Times Magazine*. April 10, 2005: 34.

Gillan, Jennifer. "From Ozzie Nelson to Ozzy Osbourne: The Genesis and Development of the Reality (Star) Sitcom." In *Understanding Reality Television*, eds. Su Holmes and Deborah Jermyn, 54–70. London: Routledge, 2004.

——. "Kodak, Jack and Coke: Advertising and *Mad*-vertising on *Mad Men*." In *Analyzing Mad Men: Critical Essays on the Series*, ed. Scott F. Stoddart, 95–116. Jefferson, NC and London, UK: McFarland, 2011.

——. *Television and New Media: Must-Click TV*. New York, NY: Routledge, 2010.

Gitelman, Lisa. *Always Already New: Media, History and the Data of Culture*. Cambridge, MA: MIT Press, 2006.

Gitlin, Todd. *Inside Prime Time*. New York, NY: Routledge, 1985.

Gobé, Marc. *Brandjam: Humanizing Brands Through Emotional Design*. New York, NY: Allworth Press, 2007.

Gomery, Douglas. *A History of Broadcasting in the United States*. London, UK: Blackwell, 2008.

——. "Talent Raids and Package Deals: NBC Loses Its Leadership in the 1950s." In Hilmes 2007, 153–68.

Grainge, Paul. *Brand Hollywood: Selling Entertainment in a Global Media Age*. New York, NY: Routledge, 2008.

——, ed. *Ephemeral Media: Transitory Screen Culture from Television to YouTube*. London, UK: BFI Publishing, 2011.

——. "TV Promotion and Broadcast Design: An Interview with Charlie Mawer, Red Bee Media." In Grainge 2011, 87–101.

Gray, Jonathan. *Show Sold Separately: Promos, Spoilers, and Other Media Paratexts*. New York, NY: New York University Press, 2010.

——. "Television Pre-views and the Meaning of Hype." *International Journal of Cultural Studies* 11, no. 1 (2008): 33–49.

Gwenllian-Jones, Sara and Roberta E. Pearson, eds. *Cult Television*. Minneapolis, MN: Minnesota University Press, 2004.

Halberstam, David. *The Fifties*. New York, NY: Villard, 1993.

Harries, Dan, ed. *The New Media Book*. London, UK: BFI Publishing, 2002.

——. "Watching the Internet." In Harries 2002. 171–82.

Hartley, John. *Creative Industries*. Malden, MA: Blackwell, 2005.

——. *The Uses of Television*. New York, NY: Routledge, 1999.

Havens, Timothy. *Global Television Marketplace*. London, UK: BFI Publishing, 2006.

Herman, Edward S. and Robert W. McChesney. *The Global Media: The New Missionaries of Global Capitalism*. London, UK: Cassell, 1997.

Hesmondhalgh, David. *The Cultural Industries*. Thousand Oaks, CA: Sage, 2002.

Hilmes, Michele. *Hollywood and Broadcasting: From Radio to Cable*. Urbana, IL: University of Illinois Press, 1990.

——, ed. *NBC: America's Network*. Berkeley, CA: University of California Press, 2007.

——. *Only Connect: A Cultural History of Broadcasting in the US*, 2nd edition. Belmont, CA: Wadsworth, 2008.

Holt, Douglas B. *How Brands Become Icons: Principles of Cultural Branding*. Boston, MA: Harvard Business School Press, 2004.

Holt, Douglas B. and Douglas Cameron. *Cultural Strategy: Using Innovative Ideologies to Build Breakthrough Brands*. Oxford, UK: Oxford University Press, 2010.

Holt, Jennifer. "The Age of Conglomerates or How Six Companies Ate the New Hollywood." In *Media Ownership: Research and Regulation*, ed. Ronald Rice, 103–30. Cresskill, NJ: Hampton, 2007.

——. "Vertical Vision: Deregulation, Industrial Economy and Prime-time Design." In Jancovich and Lyons 2003, 11–31.

Holt, Jennifer and Alisa Perren, eds. *Media Industries: History, Theory, and Method*. Malden, MA: Wiley-Blackwell, 2009.

Holt, Jennifer and Kevin Sanson, eds. *Connected Viewing: Selling, Streaming, and Sharing Media in the Digital Age*. New York, NY: Routledge, 2013.

Jancovich, Mark and James Lyons, eds. *Quality Popular Television*. London, UK: BFI Publishing, 2003.

Jenkins, Henry. *Convergence Culture: Where Old and New Media Collide*. New York, NY: New York University Press, 2006.

——. "Interactive Audiences?" In Harries 2002, 157–70.

——. "The Poachers and the Stormtroopers: Cultural Convergence in the Digital Age." Spring 1998. Available: http://web.mit.edu/21fms/People/henry3/pub/stormtroopers.htm.

——. "Quentin Tarantino's *Star Wars*? Digital Cinema, Media Convergence, and Participatory Culture." In Thornburn and Jenkins 2004, 281–311.

Jenkins, Henry and David Thornburn, eds. *Democracy and New Media*. Cambridge, MA: MIT Press, 2003.

Jenkins, Henry, Sam Ford, and Joshua Green. *Spreadable Media: Creating Value and Meaning in a Networked Culture*. New York, NY: New York University, 2013.

Johnson, Catherine. *Branding Television*. New York, NY: Routledge, 2012.

——. "Tele-branding in TVIII: the Network as Brand and the Programme as Brand." *New Review of Film and Television Studies* 5, no. 1 (2007): 5–24.

Johnson, Derek. "Inviting Audiences In: The Spatial Reorganization of Production and Consumption in 'TV III.'" *New Review of Film and Television Studies* 5, no.1 (April 2007): 61–80.

——. *Media Franchising: Creative License and Collaboration in the Culture Industries*. New York, NY: New York University Press, 2013.

Johnson, Victoria E. *Heartland TV: Primetime Television and the Struggle for U.S. Identity*. New York, NY: New York University Press, 2008.

Jones, Gerard. *Honey, I'm Home! Sitcoms: Selling the American Dream*. New York, NY: Grove Weidenfeld, 1992.

Kompare, Derek. *Rerun Nation: How Repeats Invented American Television*. New York, NY: Routledge, 2005.

Kozinets, Robert V. "E-tribalized Marketing?: The Strategic Implications of Virtual Communities of Consumption." *European Management Journal* 17, no. 3 (June 1999): 252–64.

——. "How Online Communities Are Growing in Power." *Financial Times*, November 9, 1998.

Kunz, William. *Culture Conglomerates: Consolidation in the Motion Picture and Television Industries*. Lanham, MD: Rowman and Littlefield, 1997.

Landay, Lori. *I Love Lucy*. Detroit, MI: Wayne State University Press, 2010.

Leibman, Nina C. *Living Room Lectures: The Fifties Family in Film & Television*. Austin, TX: University of Texas Press, 1995.

Lotz, Amanda. "How to Spend $9.3 Billion in Three Days: Examining the Upfront Buying Process in the Production of US Television Culture." *Media, Culture and Society* 29, no.4 (2007): 549–67.

——. *The Television Will Be Revolutionized*. New York, NY: New York University Press, 2007.

Lury, Celia. *Brands: The Logos of the Global Economy*. New York, NY: Routledge 2004.

"Madison Ave.'s Program Taboos." *Variety*, October 26, 1960.

Magder, Ted. "The End of TV 101: Reality Programs, Formats, and the New Business of Television." In Murray and Ouellette 2004, 137–56.

Manovich, Lev. *The Language of New Media*. Cambridge, MA: MIT Press, 2001.

Marling, Karal Ann. *As Seen On TV: The Visual of Everyday Life in the 1950s*. Cambridge, MA: Harvard University Press, 1994.

Mayer, Vicki, John Thornton Caldwell, and Miranda J. Banks, eds. *Production Studies: Cultural Studies of Media Industries*. New York, NY: Routledge, 2009.

McAllister, Matthew. *The Commercialization of American Culture: New Advertising, Control, and Democracy*. Thousand Oaks, CA: Sage, 1996. "

——. Television Advertising as Textual and Economic Systems." In *A Companion to Television*, ed. Janet Wasko, 217–37. Oxford, UK: Wiley Blackwell Publishing, 2005.

McCarthy, Anna. *Citizen Machine: Governing By Television in 1950s America*. Durham, NC: Duke University Press, 2009.

McCracken, Grant. *Culture and Consumption II: Markets, Meaning, and Brand Management*. Bloomington, IN: Indiana University Press, 2005.

McDonald, Paul. *The Star System: Hollywood's Production of Popular Identities*. London, UK: Wallflower, 2000.

McKee, Alan. "How to Tell the Difference between Production and Consumption: A Case Study in Doctor Who Fandom." In Gwenllian-Jones and Pearson 2004, 167–85.

McLean, Adrienne. *Being Rita Hayworth: Labor, Identity, and Hollywood Stardom*. New Brunswick, NJ: Rutgers University Press, 2004.

Meehan, Eileen. *Why Television is Not Our Fault: Television Programming, Viewers, and Who's Really in Control*. Lanham, MD: Rowman and Littlefield, 2005.

———. "Why We Don't Count: The Commodity Audience." In *Logics of Television: Essays in Cultural Criticism*, ed. Patricia Mellencamp, 117–37. Bloomington, IN: Indiana University Press, 1990.

Moor, Liz. *The Rise of Brands*. New York, NY: Oxford University Press, 2007.

Mukherjee, Roopali and Sarah Banet-Weiser, eds. *Commodity Activism: Cultural Resistance in Neoliberal Times*. New York, NY: New York University Press, 2012.

Mullen, Megan. *Television in the Multichannel Age*. Oxford, UK: Blackwell, 2007.

Murray, Simone. "Brand Loyalties: Rethinking Content within Global Corporate Media." *Media, Culture, Society* 27, no. 3 (2005): 415–35.

Murray, Susan. *Hitch Your Antenna to the Stars: Early Television and Broadcast Stardom*. New York, NY: Routledge, 2005.

Murray, Susan and Laurie Ouellette, eds. *Reality TV: Remaking Television Culture*. New York, NY: New York University Press, 2004.

Napoli, Philip M. *Audience Economics: Media Institutions and the Audience Marketplace*. New York, NY: Columbia University Press, 2003.

Negra, Diane. "Re-Made for Television: Hedy Lamarr's Post-War Star Textuality." In *Small Screens, Big Ideas: Television in the 1950s*, ed. Janet Thumim, 105–17. London, UK: I.B. Tauris, 2002.

Nelson, Ozzie. *Ozzie*. New York, NY: Prentice Hall, 1973.

Oswald, Laura R. *Marketing Semiotics: Signs, Strategies, and Brand Value*. Oxford, UK: Oxford University Press, 2012.

Ouellette, Laurie and James Hay, *Better Living Through Reality TV: Television and Post-Welfare Citizenship*. Malden, MA: Blackwell, 2008.

Parks, Lisa. "Flexible Microcasting: Gender, Generation, and Television-Internet Convergence." In Spigel and Olsson 2004, 133–62.

"Performer or Pitchman?" *Variety*, November 11, 1953: 31.

Samuel, Lawrence R. *Brought to You By: Postwar Television Advertising and The American Dream*. Austin, TX: University of Texas Press, 2001.

Schatz, Thomas. "Desilu, I Love Lucy, and the Rise of Network TV." In *Making Television: Authorship and the Production Process*, eds. Robert J. Thompson and Gary Burns, 117–35. New York, NY: Praeger, 1990.

———. "The New Hollywood." In *Film Theory Goes to the Movies*, eds. Jim Collins, Hilary Radner, and Ava Preacher Collins, 8–36. London, UK: Routledge, 1993.

Sconce, Jeffrey. "What If? Charting Television's New Textual Boundaries." In Spigel and Olsson 2004, 93–112.

Sella, Marshall. "The Remote Controllers." *New York Times Magazine*, October 20, 2002. 68+.

Sengupta, Somini. "So Much for Sharing His 'Like.'" *The New York Times*, June 1, 2012, A1.

Shattuc, Jane M. "Television Production: Who Makes American TV?" In *A Companion to Television*, ed. Janet Wasko, 142–54. Oxford, UK: Blackwell, 2005.

Shrum, L.J. *The Psychology of Entertainment Media: Blurring the Lines Between Entertainment and Persuasion*. New York, NY: Routledge, 2012.

Spigel, Lynn. *Make Room for TV: Television and the Family Ideal in Postwar America*. Chicago, IL: University of Chicago Press, 1992.

Spigel, Lynn and Jan Olsson, eds. *Television After TV: Essays on a Medium in Transition*. Durham, NC: Duke University Press, 2004.

Taylor, Ella. *Prime Time Families: Television Culture in Postwar America*. Berkeley, CA: University of California, 1989.

Telotte, J.P. *Disney TV*. Detroit, MI: Wayne State University Press, 2004.

Thornburn, David and Henry Jenkins, eds. *Rethinking Media Change: The Aesthetics of Transition*, Cambridge, MA: MIT Press 2004.

Tryon, Chuck. *Reinventing Cinema: Movies in the Age of Media Convergence*. New Brunswick, NJ: Rutgers University Press, 2010.

Turow, Joseph. *Breaking Up America: Advertisers and the New Media World*. Chicago, IL: University of Chicago Press, 1997.

——. *Niche Envy: Marketing Discrimination in the Digital Age*. Cambridge, MA: MIT Press, 2006.

Ulin, Jeffery C. *The Business of Media Distribution: Monetizing Film, TV, and Video Content in an Online World*. 2nd edition. New York, NY: Focal Press, 2014.

Uricchio, William. "Historicizing Media in Transition." In Thornburn and Jenkins 2004, 23–38.

——. "Old Media and New Media: Television." In Harries 2002, 219–30.

van Dijck, José. *The Culture of Connectivity: A Critical History of Social Media*. Oxford, UK: Oxford University Press, 2013.

Vogel, Harold. *Entertainment Industry Economics: A Guide for Financial Analysts*. 7th edition. New York, NY: Cambridge University Press, 2007.

Wasko, Janet. *Understanding Disney: The Manufacture of Fantasy*. Malden, MA: Polity Press, 2001.

Wernick, Andrew. *Promotional Culture: Advertising, Ideology, and Symbolic Expression*. London, UK: Sage, 1991.

Williams, Raymond. *Television, Technology and Cultural Forms*. London, UK: Fontana, 1974.

Wyatt, Justin. *High Concept: Movies and Marketing in Hollywood*. Austin, TX: University of Texas Press, 1994.

1

BROADCASTING SERIES AND SPONSORS

1.1 Branding the Modern Family: 1950s and Now

After it premiered on the American Broadcasting Company (ABC) in September 2009, *Modern Family* was quickly declared a game changer, especially because the family sitcom as a subgenre had gone missing and was presumed dead. Some of the praise for the writing team's skill at telling interlocking stories about three families within a larger extended family was tempered after "Game Changer" (1.19) aired in 2010. The episode has been critiqued for being a program-length commercial. At its center is a product integration story arc about the desire of forty-something suburban "doofus dad" Phil Dunphy to acquire an iPad on the day Apple released the tablets. The comedy comes from the fact that it is also Phil's birthday, which gives the early adopter great joy and then becomes the situation that delays Phil's gratification until the end of the episode. The comic mishaps begin after his wife Claire decides that she should be the one to wait in the pre-dawn line at Apple store. The episode ends with Phil's loving tribute to his iPad, the perfect endorsement for Apple's new tablet. While Kevin Sandler has written a compelling analysis of the product integration dynamics of the episode, I want to consider the related issue of how the product integration functions as a form of character differentiation of Phil as "the early adopter" willing to try out new tech devices and later trade in barely worn-in products for even newer models. Phil is emblematic of an audience desired by advertisers. He is part of what I call the "think young" consumer cohort, an adult who uses his acquisition of the latest trendy tech devices to signal his youthful self-perception. The "think youngs" have been targeted by advertisers at least since Pepsi coined its 1961 tagline *for those who think young*. As part of this consumer cohort, Phil is an adult who consumes like an adolescent because he desires to be seen as much younger than the age listed on his driver's license.

Modern Family also introduces the related concept of the peer-ent, a term Phil uses to describe himself and his *act like a parent, talk like a peer* parenting philosophy. The writers use the line, like many in the series, for some good-natured fun at Phil's expense, particularly for his desire to be an honorary member of the millennial generation. In consumer terms, Phil is a character who is more embraced than mocked. *Modern Family* favorably represents him as an early adopter and, thus, flatters those who see themselves as part of this consumer group. By categorizing Phil as a "think young," we can modify his motto into *earn like a parent, and spend like a teen*, thereby, drawing attention to the general validation in U.S. consumer culture of the "think young" worldview.

A sequence in "The Incident" (1.4) connected to Phil's initial coinage of the term "peer-ent" captures how he is both the peer-ent whose parenting tips are gently mocked and the "think young" consumer type whose spending habits are validated by the sitcom and its corporate underwriters. Two discontinuous beats establish that Phil and his eldest daughter Haley use the same MacBook style laptops, visually signaling their mutual belonging in the "think young" consumer cohort. Phil's youthful self-conception prompts him to decide to have a talk with Haley about her frustration with Claire's rules. Before doing so, Phil explains in direct address to the camera in the series' pseudo-documentary insert sequences that the secret to his closeness with his kids is his peer-enting philosophy: *act like a parent, talk like a peer*. After a cross cut from the faux interview insert, a shot frames Phil as he is about to enter Haley's room where she sits up on the bed with her open laptop. The cross cut returns to the direct address sequence in which Phil explains that he learned peer-enting from his dad, who initiated father-son talks with, "What's up sweathog?" The reference is to *Welcome Back, Kotter*,

FIGURE 1.1   *Act like a parent talk like a peer* counsels *Modern Family*'s Phil Dunphy, but his "peer-enting" is not working on his teen daughter Haley.

ABC's late-1970s tween-inclusive sitcom with an emphasis on the peer-enting style of a Jewish high school teacher.[1] Striking what he clearly thinks of as a "chillaxed" pose, Phil enters Haley's room and flips her desk chair around so he can sit on it backwards. Casually leaning forward, he suggests to Haley that they should talk to each other, "like a couple of friends kicking it in a juice bar." The comic beat comes from Haley's confused interjection, "What's a juice bar?" Phil begrudgingly modifies his statement, "Okay . . . a malt shop . . . whatever." Still, he believes she is accepting him as a peer until she ignores him to answer a cell phone call and then tells her friend she isn't doing anything important, "just talking to some dork I met in a malt shop." The reaction shot of Phil is one of many that gently pokes fun at him. Yet, such sequences encourage empathy for Phil mixed in with the laughter at his humorous miscalculations. His goofiness is also tempered by the conservative dynamics of the series, which imply that he is ultimately a good dad and an even better provider who can support a stay-at-home wife and three children, seemingly with plenty of time to spend with his three kids and money to spend on himself and them.

Phil Dunphy's characterization is definitely of a 21st-century "think young" peer-ent, but an earlier iteration of the type existed in the 1950s in the sitcom persona of Ozzie Nelson. In accounts of 1950s culture, Ozzie Nelson is more typically described as the *Father Knows Best*-style father and icon of conservative containment culture.[2] I argue against such characterizations, and demonstrate that Ozzie's television persona embodied the original "think young." As producer, director, and writer of *The Adventures of Ozzie & Harriet* (ABC 1952–66), Nelson leveraged the brandcasting potential of the then young medium of television. The former big band leader and his "girl singer" wife Harriet starred in this sitcom with their two sons, David and Ricky. For the purposes of this chapter, I want to focus on how Ozzie Nelson turned his whole family and then each individual member into brand representatives not only of "The Nelsons," but also of Hotpoint, Coca-Cola, Kodak, and a host of other corporate underwriters of the sitcom. The ways in which Nelson innovated the integration of brands into the story space over the series' fourteen-year run on ABC is instructive, not only for how sponsorship worked in 1950s sitcoms, but also for how current strategies have their origins in Nelson's early experiments in the use of the new medium as a brandcasting platform.

Starting with *Ozzie & Harriet* as a case study, this chapter explores the brandcasting that occurred at the series level in the 1950s and early 1960s through corporate underwriting of some of the costs of television programming. The chapter ends with an analysis of product integration on ABC's *The Middle*, to demonstrate that branded entertainment of the present is not a millennial development. Rather, it is a return to the dramatized advertisements and sponsor entwinements pioneered by Ozzie Nelson and other 1950s television producers working in the single and alternating sponsorship financing models.

One of the reasons why *Modern Family* offers product integration modes of characterization is that the rules of the game of broadcast advertising have changed dramatically. In what television scholars call "the classic network era," sitcoms garnered the kind of high ratings which networks could leverage to convince advertisers to pay a premium to put their products in front of all those "eyeballs." In this system, networks staged upfront presentations at which they would pre-sell the projected audience attention to the 30-second commercial spots that played in story breaks as part of "magazine concept" advertising (a.k.a. participating advertising). Although many factors contributed to the decline of the effectiveness of the 30-second spot, and hence of broadcast advertising, it is easy to point to the invention and then broad adoption of DVRs, among other timeshifting technologies, and the availability of placeshifting devices such as iPad tablets. Whatever the exact mixture of complex factors leading to this broadcast ratings decline, American companies who had been buying time on broadcast television were worried about the effectiveness of traditional spot advertising. Networks began to offset their anxieties with various kinds of branded entertainment deals.

I detailed some of the recent deals in my earlier book, *Television and New Media: Must-Click TV*. I looked at the creative product integration strategies on NBC series including *30 Rock* and *The Office*.[3] In *Television Brandcasting* I am more interested in demonstrating that these strategies only *seem* new because they are a departure from classic network-era strategies. They are actually a *return* to the content–promotion hybrid strategies utilized in midcentury American television programming.

Later in this chapter, I consider the dramatized advertisements that were essential parts of the 1950s corporate sponsorship of programming on the era's new media platform: broadcast television. At the time, television's function as an advertising platform for corporate products and a circulation platform for corporate self-representations was evident because television personalities of all kinds openly endorsed products. Sitcoms played a particularly important role in this process, not only because sitcom sets could double as product showcases, but also because the stars could stand in or outside of their television homes and recommend particular brands to viewers whom they would directly address as friends in content–promotion hybrids airing after the credits or in a break in the story.

1.2   Sponsored Credit Sequences

The credit sequences of several midcentury series establish a now common consumerist and aspirational representation of the American family on television. In them, images of families posed as if for official portraits are entwined with product endorsement: the all-male family of *My Three Sons* for Hunt's Ketchup and Chevrolet, the nuclear family of *Leave It to Beaver* for Plymouth and Ralston-Purina, the mother knows best family of *The Donna Reed Show* for Campbell's Soup and Singer Sewing machines, and, most significantly, "America's Favorite Family" from *The Adventures of Ozzie & Harriet* for Coca-Cola and Kodak. The Nelsons were definitely the sponsors' favorite family as they had willingly entwined their television personas with the suburban family messaging of several corporations starting with Hotpoint, a General Electric division. As series producer, Ozzie Nelson integrated Coca-Cola into scenes set at his television family's backyard cookouts and teen parties, and shot a variety of dramatized advertisements for Kodak. One of the more significant ones featured Harriet Nelson as a trusted advisor to new suburbanites to whom she recommends the practice of home videography as a way to both preserve memories of family fun and togetherness and to promote a desired self-representation. Before turning to an analysis of *Ozzie & Harriet*'s precedent-setting sponsor entwinements and an evaluation of those strategies over the sitcom's 14-year run, I first establish how industrial time (e.g., commercial and promotion spots) is blocked off, segmented, and sold in the U.S. television industry. I then consider why star sitcoms were so effective at conveying consumer advice to viewers. Finally, I discuss why "typical American," suburban sitcoms became the preferred sponsor-vehicle by the end of the 1950s.

Branding, not entertainment, is the main imperative of television as an industry. In the classic network era, broadcast television typically employed participating sponsorship, or magazine concept advertising (a variety of spots and sponsors), making branded entertainment of the 2000s (e.g., Ford's *24* and Maybelline's *Lipstick Jungle*) and product integration deals (e.g., Hiro and Ando's Nissan Versa on *Heroes*) seem new. Yet, these sponsor strategies actually are some of the oldest in the U.S. TV industry. Corporate sponsors shaped the look of 1950s television schedules, often exerting pressure on networks and producers to offer them programming that provided an appropriate context in which to place or integrate their products.[4] By the mid-1950s, sponsors including Chevrolet, Pontiac, Johnson & Johnson, Scott Paper, Ralston Purina, Nabisco, Polaroid, and Kodak concluded that one of the ideal spaces in which to locate products was in the fictional worlds of the U.S. television families that had the means to trade in old products (particularly barely broken-in cars and appliances) for new ones.[5] The cultural history of the standardization of the representation of the television family has been addressed by scholars, but not always in the context of the history of U.S. television industry practices. A better understanding of the industrial meaning of time on U.S. television helps to explain why certain kinds of series dominate the schedule, how the television industry sells time to sponsors, and what programming features motivate them to buy it.

William Bird, Susan Murray, Anna McCarthy, and Christopher Anderson, among other scholars, have offered some interesting accounts of how in the earliest days of U.S. television DuPont, US Steel, and General Electric, among other major corporate sponsors, put their stamp of ownership on TV programming. One simple form was to put a sponsor name in the title of a program that advertising agencies created for a corporate sponsor and for which they bought a desirable time slot on a network's schedule.[6] The long list of time franchises included Prudential Star Theater; Magnavox Theater; Colgate Comedy Hour; Kraft Television Theater; Lux Video Theater; Texaco Star Theater; Westinghouse Summer Theater; Buick Action Theater; Ford Television Theater; The Oldsmobile Show; The Plymouth Show; and The Chevrolet Show.

The proliferation of such time franchises demonstrates that it is inaccurate to claim that sitcoms dominated the U.S. schedule in the 1950s, but they did appeal to corporations who were using television to advertise small ticket products that came in cans, bottles, or boxes. When companies sponsored sitcom families, they reaped the benefits of entwining their products with the lives of continuing characters, often played by actors who were already established household names: George Burns and Gracie Allen (Carnation), Ozzie and Harriet Nelson (Quaker Oats), or Lucille Ball, Desi Arnaz, and Danny Thomas (American Tobacco Company). These performers had also already created radio program personas calculated for selling goods.

As Susan Murray has shown, the aforementioned anthology and variety shows were hosted by already-established radio stars who were self-reflexive about sponsor plugs within their programs. In contrast, the sponsors of suburban set sitcoms tried to make their product placement barely noticeable. Products were integrated into the everyday activities in which the characters engaged during the story segments, or the representative images included in the credits sequences. John Caldwell describes the story segments that come before commercials as, "Visual turf upon which stations erect promotional signs." He reminds us that "Television mise-en-scène is far from sacred or inviolable ground." Although talking specifically about station IDs keyed or burned into films that the broadcast networks pay to air, Caldwell gestures to a more general argument about the stamps of ownership within the space of television programs. As Caldwell says, "One cannot imagine this sort of stamp of ownership being allowed in other artforms—the signature of the purchaser rather than the maker stamped directly on the artform."[7] Today, various stamps of ownership have proliferated. They appear in the credits, in between the story segments, during the story segments at the bottom or in the corners of the screen. Channel bugs identifying the channel or its affiliated web or mobile sites remain on screen during story segments. The omnipresence of these overlaid "stamps of ownership" is a recent phenomenon, especially the intrusive use of channel bugs. All of these strategies are made possible by the preference of today's networks for what Caldwell calls videographic style that he traces to the early days of CNN and MTV. Yet the practice of program financers stamping ownership on television series in various ways can be traced to the early television industry.

Caldwell's comments provide a springboard to a discussion of the ways that sponsors stamped their seal of ownership on programs by transforming credit sequences into promotion for their corporate images or products. As the discussion later in this chapter demonstrates, *The Adventures of Ozzie & Harriet* became the proving ground in the early 1950s for such strategies, leading to the perceived desirability of sponsoring sitcoms about a white, middle-class, heteronormative nuclear family living in a two-story house in the suburbs. Although *Ozzie & Harriet* came to television in 1952, the bulk of the suburban sitcoms about nuclear families safely ensconced in suburban homes laden with new, time-saving appliances and the latest consumer goods did not begin their runs until the late 1950s.[8]

1.3 Dramatized Advertisements

When it sponsored *Leave It to Beaver* from 1959–63, Ralston Purina put its official stamp on a dramatization inserted into the end credits, which seem to be more often the ones on which main sponsors stamp their ownership. The dramatized advertisement is set in a suburban kitchen where Beaver is helping feed a dog a bowl of Ralston Purina's specially formulated dog food. The premise is that Beaver is going to be the dog sitter for teacher Miss Landers. In another dramatization Beaver attends a doggie birthday party thrown by his best friend Whitey. Upon receiving the dog chow from Beaver, Whitey says, "Purina is the best present Murphy got." Murphy lives up to the "eager eater" description in the narrative, and Beaver gets to add the "and how" emphasis to the tagline: *Purina Dog Chow, and how!* Such Ralston Purina dramatizations offered new suburbanites the advice that today's privileged pets should be provided with products designed especially for their needs because pets should be treated as family members.

The dramatized advertisements feature such advice, registering the 1950s elevation of national advice givers—often television personas—over the family and neighborhood advisors that many new suburbanites had left behind in the city. Thomas Hine contends that "the normality to which" recently arrived suburbanites "were trying to adhere was something entirely new—a way of life in which standards were set not by families and neighbors but by new kinds of authorities whose message came by television, magazines and the backs of boxes." Hine explains that in the new suburbs, "[p]eople were physically separated, out on their own in a new muddy and unfinished landscape, but they were also linked as never before through advertising, television, and magazines." Corporations began to act as substitute families and advice givers; these "[a]uthorities and experts" took the place of familial or local advisors and "served as national parents, telling young people separated from their families and thrown into unfamiliar contexts how to deal with their problems, raise their children, take care of their house and yard, dress, entertain and enjoy themselves."[9] Sponsors were telling viewers to listen to a new set of "trusted advisors," the official spokespeople who played "America's family" and neighbors on television. Television was one of the new sources for information on unfamiliar activities and behavior, and that advice was reiterated in magazines such as *Good Housekeeping* through its advertisements, like the one in which the Nelsons appeared in 1954 for Listerine. The copy read: *Got a sore throat? Ozzie and Harriet know what to do—Ricky and David gargle with it.*

The *Ozzie & Harriet* example suggests that content–promotion hybrids were especially effective when the spokespeople were hybrid types in the form of stars playing fictionalized versions of their lives. The 1950s schedule had many star sitcoms in which former B-movie stars like Lucille Ball and moderately famous nightclub performers were transformed into sitcom personas who bore some resemblance to the stars playing the roles. Ball's husband Desi Arnaz and their friend Danny Thomas, for instance, retained their careers as nightclub entertainers, which enabled some episodes or sequences of *I Love Lucy* and *Make Room for Daddy*, respectively, to be set in nightclubs. Overall, much more time was spent inside the characters' apartments than in the venues associated with the swanky nightclub and supper club circuit of New York.

1.4   Danny Thomas, Dodge, and Ethnic Strivers

In *Make Room for Daddy*, Danny Thomas's sitcom counterpart Danny Williams shares Thomas's career as a touring nightclub singer/comic who is home so infrequently that his children have to be reminded to "make room for daddy" when he returns.[10] Thomas's sitcom borrows this kind of actual detail from his offstage life experience, although his actual wife and children do not appear in the program. In the dramatization inserted at the end of each episode, Danny appears with his first TV wife Margaret (Jean Hagen) to endorse Pall Mall, Lucky Strike, and Herbert Taretyon cigarettes. The elegantly dressed couple has been smoking the American Tobacco Company brands as they wait to retrieve his formal coat and her mink stole from the nightclub coat check. Danny had made it big in an entertainment industry profession and so the dramatized pitches from his dressing room make sense. Those he does with his television wife from the faux nightclub cloakroom get a bit fuzzier, as Danny Williams is the entertainment, not a nightclub patron.

This fuzziness does point to how Danny's appeal comes from a combination of his status as the already-arrived American Dreamer and the American Striver. *Make Room for Daddy*'s "Your Dependable Dodge Dealer" advertising played on that duality. A Dodge spot preceded the opening credits. One from 1955 showed the cars in motion on the open road (rather than on New York City streets), as the announcer exclaims: *It's Dodge for '55: Flashing Ahead in Style, in Value, in Performance! Yes, it's the flair fashion Dodge for '55.* The end credits sometimes were preceded by a Dodge pitch set in Williams' luxury apartment and featuring Margaret and Danny sitting at his grand piano atop of which sits a child's die-cast Dodge. Sometimes the end credits included dramatized advertising as well, such as the one in which the family eagerly piles into the Dodge convertible parked in front of house.

These branded credits associate Danny with the already-achieved American Dream. They are obviously intended to showcase the new model Dodge convertible and the visual storytelling of the spots is consistent with the general characterization of the Danny Williams persona in the years the series aired on ABC and was titled *Make Room For Daddy* (1953–6). The sequence captures the bounce in Danny's step as he runs down to his Dodge parked outside his luxury apartment building. With a big smile plastered on his face, Danny is filled with obvious energy and enthusiasm. Danny's enthusiastic demeanor and his lively gait signal his positioning as an "ethnic striver" and the car symbolizes his already achieved social mobility. Danny becomes the aspirational ideal for all other strivers in the

FIGURE 1.2 Danny Thomas' direct endorsements of American Tobacco Company from the glamorous nightclub set of *Make Room for Daddy* are at odds with his scrappy in-series persona (upper). Thomas sits at his character's grand piano and promotes Dodge from the sitcom's luxury apartment set (lower).

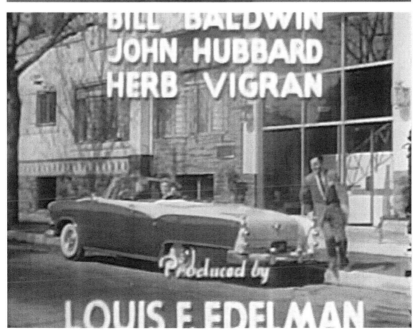

FIGURE 1.3 Danny Thomas is an ethnic striver, one who is *flashing ahead in style* with his new model Dodge convertible for '55.

audience. Williams/Thomas is the star living the extraordinary lifestyle, while still remaining a generous and humble ordinary guy. Danny is also an early exemplar of the obstinate optimist, a person who not only believes in dreams coming true, but in seeing the best in people. He helps all sorts of "up-and-coming" acts and embraces the "paying it forward" philosophy.

It made practical sense that Danny's Dodge only appeared in the credits as location shots were rare at the time and likely beyond the budget. In a story sense, however, Danny would have had little use for such a car in New York City or as part of his more itinerant lifestyle. As already noted, the title references the fact that Danny Williams is only home for short stints between gigs as a touring nightclub performer and his local Manhattan gig as the featured act at The Copa Club. The series also gives Margaret Williams a show-business mother and lingering hostility about the fact that she was absent so much that Margaret was mostly raised by relatives. The back story helps to explain why Margaret is often the one who wants to adopt what she perceives of as more normative upper-middle-class behavior. In the 1955 episode, "The Children's Governess" (2.19), she even hires a snobbish governess to teach them all proper English and to stay with the children instead of their maternal grandmother. Danny is caught in the middle of these battles whenever he is home (see Figure 2.11 in the next chapter). He is represented as the more grounded one in the relationship, never wishing to forget or deny his atypical family background (born to Lebanese immigrants), his barely assimilated relatives (his Uncle Tonoose), or his modest beginnings. Danny is loud and assertive and makes for a stark contrast to the staid and proper governess.

Make Room for Daddy calls attention to the problems caused by the gap between Danny's attainment of a high rung on the social class ladder and his acceptance by those already occupying that social class. Danny has conflicts with the other residents of his upscale building, for example, and sometimes chafes against the "suburban father" ideologies he is supposed to adopt despite the fact that they are at odds with his entertainment-industry lifestyle and the values instilled in him during his modest upbringing in an urban, ethnic community. Its overt racial and social class dynamics makes Thomas's series distinct from *I Love Lucy*, which used ethnicity as a source of humor, but did not tend to show ethnic conflicts or class conflicts in the way Danny Thomas did.

1.5 Star Sitcoms: Lucy, Desi, and Danny . . . and MacMurray?

The slippage between Danny Williams the loud-mouthed television persona we see in many episodes and Danny Thomas the soft-spoken and elegant star in the sponsor dramatizations set in The Copa Club are similar to the television persona/Hollywood star hybridity of the dramatizations airing at the end of *I Love Lucy* during the years in which Philip Morris was its sponsor. In contrast to these dramatized advertisements, the sitcom episodes themselves placed less emphasis on the glamour of Manhattan nightclub culture and more on domestic interactions between Lucy and Ricky, or between the same sex pairings (pitting Lucy and best friend Ethel Mertz against Ricky and Fred Mertz in "double couple" sitcom scenarios).

While retaining her real life position as wife of a Cuban bandleader and B-movie star, Lucille Ball reimagined herself as both a screwball best friend to Ethel and a stardom-obsessed housewife. While the characterization supposedly strips her of any vestiges of her 1940s glamour girl past, there are elements of that star image that surface during episodes and disrupt series logic and her characterization. At the same time, the in-series "star-in-the-making" storyline about Ricky Ricardo makes him representative of the "best of both worlds"—having close friends and star acquaintances.[11] It is also reflective of the popular narrative about how stars yearn for the pleasures of an ordinary life and cherish their pre-stardom friendships for keeping them grounded.

These dynamics point to how star sitcoms worked to distance the television personas from the star status of the actors who played them. To borrow Richard Dyer's famous formulation, their "star as ordinary/star as special" hybridity was also essential to their success as television's friend-recommenders of brands and lifestyles. Star-helmed sitcoms are especially important in this regard because they attempt to establish credibility and authenticity by blurring the line been actor and persona. Star sitcoms, especially those featuring real-life family members, tap into the fascination with ordinary people achieving a high level of success without sacrificing personal relationships, a mythology that was increasingly part of the Hollywood version of the American Dream. Before series stars can become advice givers, the stars have to be introduced as the kind of people with whom viewers would want to be friends. Sitcom stars who share the same first names with their characters become representative of the contemporary ideal of remaining ordinary (and grounded), while reaching an extraordinary level of public visibility. Lucille Ball is also just Lucy, whose antics could be enjoyed every Monday night in America's living room. Star sitcom personas provide evidence of the general likeability of stars, positioning them as the kinds of friends that viewers would want to have, and from whom they would be willing to take advice.

When they shared the same corporate underwriter, both *I Love Lucy* and *Make Room for Daddy* concluded with their main characters/actors directly addressing viewers as friends to whom they recommend American Tobacco Company brands. As already noted, their costuming references Manhattan nightclub culture and relies on the blurring of the lines between the television personalities and their personas. The elegant formalwear makes them look more like stars, but their familiarity makes them feel like the ordinary people depicted each week on the sitcoms.[12]

Technically, the aura associated with stars makes them seem strikingly out of place on television, according to Denise Mann and Diane Negra. The dynamic is complicated when a B-level Hollywood star takes on a starring role in a television series. The star image can break through and disrupt the governing series structure or characterizations. Episodes of *I Love Lucy* sometimes register the disruption caused by Ball's residual glamour. Disruptions often occur when her costume creates a disconnect because of her television persona's supposed ordinariness, and are doubly disruptive when an elegantly dressed Lucy is depicted smoking in a sophisticated way. In these moments Lucille Ball seems out of place in the Ricardos' modest living room. Negra argues that over time the external life of stars bubbles up within their series in which they are supposed to be representative of "viewers like you." Yet, they can also be representative of the promise that many ordinary people have "yet-to-be-discovered" star quality or talents that will eventually be noticed. *I Love Lucy* follows this series trajectory. In the first season Lucy appears in a supposedly typical living situation as a New York City housewife. Yet her marriage to a Cuban bandleader places her near celebrity, and slowly the celebrity world encroaches more on their daily lives. One season is spent in Los Angeles and another on a European tour. Even in the New York episodes, the narrative emphasis is often on Lucy's assumption that she is an undiscovered talent. The more glamorous Lucille Ball is the one on display in the dramatized advertising. When Lucy/Lucille and Ricky/Desi address the audience directly in American Tobacco Company integrated commercials that ran at the end of each episode, they appear elegant as the real couple might star in publicity photographs. Their duality makes their advice to their at-home viewers/friends to choose Philip Morris cigarettes all the more compelling.

Ball and Arnaz further encouraged their reception as hybrid types by building many episodes of *The Lucy–Desi Comedy Hour*, the series that replaced *I Love Lucy*, around star sitcom guest stars. In this way Lucy/Lucille and Ricky/Desi represent the best of both worlds in that they know famous people, but are ordinary people too. Guests on *The Lucy–Desi Comedy Hour* included Danny Thomas (appearing "in persona" with his television family) and Ida Lupino and Howard Duff (who played a version of "themselves" in a star sitcom called *Mr. Adams and Eve*). Television stars also appeared as themselves with their real spouses, as was the case with Fred MacMurray and wife June Haver. The aggregate result of these *Lucy–Desi Comedy Hour* episodes was to make it seem as if they were all a group of friends.

Although *My Three Sons* (ABC 1960–5; CBS 1965–72), was not a star sitcom, Fred MacMurray was prone to Dyer's "star as ordinary/star as special" disruptions as he tried to occupy the character of Steve Douglas. MacMurray had an ongoing film career in family films that complemented his sitcom persona, but it was his previous Hollywood career in romantic lead roles that were at odds with the television persona. The ongoing and "residual film stardom" of Fred MacMurray sometimes created ruptures in Steve Douglas, his *My Three Sons* television persona.[13] MacMurray's television persona is both a representative suburbanite and not representative at all given that he is an often-traveling aerospace engineer and widower whose three boys (an almost tween, an almost teen, and an almost eighteen-year-old) are being cared for by their maternal grandfather

"Bub." William Frawley (Fred Mertz in *I Love Lucy*) plays Bub as a proudly Irish American working-class scrappy tough guy with a sensitive side. Previously, Frawley played alongside MacMurray as his character's manager in *The Princess Comes Across*. In the 1936 film MacMurray plays King Mantel, a rakish bandleader and the film's romantic lead opposite Carole Lombard. The vestiges of this star image stay just below the surface of Steve Douglas, but Fred MacMurray, 1930s and 1940s leading man, completely displaces Steve Douglas in some scenes in the episode "Lady Engineer" (1.7).

Unlike the playboy bachelor uncle type already common on television by 1960, Steve does his real romancing off screen and mostly he's just shown leaving for dates. "Lady Engineer" is different as much for the screen time allotted to the romance as well as the profile of the woman. Joan "J. M." Johnson is an astronomer who captivates Steve when they both do consulting work for an aeronautical firm. It is a rare episode in which the first nineteen minutes develop their budding romantic relationship. In those scenes MacMurray looks less like Steve and more like one of the romantic heroes from his earlier film career. The slippage into Fred MacMurray movie star is evident when he passionately embraces Joan in the car. In the shot sequence shadows play across their faces as they might in film noir, raising some of the contradictory gender expectations of the era. Steve clearly wants to have a sexual relationship with Joan, which he could easily carry on during his frequent business trips. As if he might want more than that, Steve invites her over for dinner at "the Douglas Den of Disaster." When she does not even respond, she seems to be saying that she knows that her career prevents her from fitting into his domestic life and he knows that he cannot add a layer of complexity to his already uneasy balance of business trips and family time.

Steve seems more interested in a long-term relationship than she does because she is the one who would be expected to give up her career. She chooses it over Steve when she takes an earlier flight rather than accept a ride from him to the airport. In a scene on the plane, she is juxtaposed with a woman prattling on about her family members and explaining that she was so worried they could not handle everyday domestic tasks without her that she had to cut her vacation short and fly home. "J. M." looks mostly bored, but slightly wistful about what might have been with the Douglas family, or whatever family she might have had if she had followed a traditional life path. Undercutting some of the domestic fantasy, the woman's unconvincing monologue about the joys of domestic life are cross cut with moments from Steve's domestic life. It is the next morning and Steve realizes that Joan took off without saying goodbye. He does not know that she did call and leave a message with his nine-year-old son because he drew a picture of an airplane on the paper, partially obscuring the message. One cross cut places him on the Douglas' service porch where Steve has half his body buried in a broken washing machine. Chip keeps clanging the lid open and closed without regard to the impact on Steve's ears. After enduring the noise and dislodging several

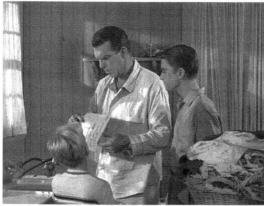

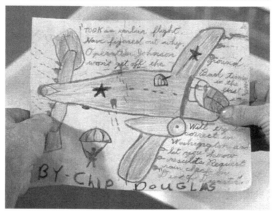

FIGURE 1.4 Fred MacMurray, 1930s leading man, disrupts his series persona on *My Three Sons* (upper). Suburban widower handyman Steve Douglas thinks wistfully of the romantic encounter that could have been with a "Lady Engineer." Tim Considine, MacMurray's *Shaggy Dog* costar, plays eldest son Mike (middle). Steve is torn between escaping and embracing domesticity, as represented by the illustrated phone message drawn by his youngest son Chip (lower).

items, including Chip's skate key, Steve declares the machine fixed again. Bub, as the family homemaker who pestered Steve into fixing the machine earlier that morning, marvels that Steve managed to do it and save them the repair charges. Older son Mike comes to inspect the work and delivers the misplaced phone message illustrated by Chip's cute airplane drawing (see Figure 1.4). Steve's facial expressions suggest that he is both charmed by his son's drawing and wistful for his missed chances with Joan. The episode does not resolve Steve's ambivalence (or Joan's for that matter) about priorities and competing demands related to personal, professional, and sexual desires. His wistful expression at the thought of Joan suggests that he is not foreclosing such a relationship in the future. At the very least he is tempted. Temptation returns in season two in "The Girls Next Door" (2.18) when four stewardesses move next to the Douglases. At first, Steve is frustrated with them because they block his driveway, but Mike and Robbie find a way to become friends and the two "families" have a neighborly gathering at which one of the women piques Steve's interest (as "luck" would have it, they are differently aged women).

Some of this "road not taken" messaging and the contradictory desire for individual mobility and family stability is captured in the sponsorships for *My Three Sons*. On a simple level, "Lady Engineer" and several other episodes have scenes set on or at least shots of American Airlines jets, and Steve is associated with airplanes of various kinds as an aeronautics engineer. While Steve always comes home again, his eldest son does move to New York City for good, suggesting the ways that the messages encoded in the era's advertisements might encourage the dissolution of the close-knit suburban family dynamic they are supposedly endorsing.

"Lady Engineer" points to the way that the early seasons of *My Three Sons* opened ruptures and technically contained them by the fact that the characters choose not to pursue activities which are at odds with the expectations of a typical conservative suburbanite of the early 1960s. The episodes often end on an ambivalent note. While it makes more sense for Steve as a commuter to flirt with taking on a more rebellious gender role than staid family man, it is surprising to note that even Donna Stone of *The Donna Reed Show*[14] has such moments of gender rebellion as well. Her wistful look in 1963's "A Woman's Place"(5.17) comes after she has flirted with running for town council, chosen to drop out, and then after returning to what looks like an unfulfilling role as the family maid and manager, looks at a leftover campaign flag with longing. The episode ends on that note and Donna's final look parallels Steve's right before we see the American Airlines jet fly off into the clouds, taking all the possibilities J. M. Johnson represented with it.

These details highlight how suburban-set sitcoms of the early 1960s are not as anxiety-free as they are assumed to be and often embrace impossibly contradictory values. Some of the branded credit sequences associated with *My Three Sons*' sponsor Chevrolet (1960–5) capture this ambivalence about mobility and security, albeit in a veiled way. As we have seen, the potential of "going on the

FIGURE 1.5 In a 1963 episode of *The Donna Reed Show*, Donna Stone is ambivalent about her decision to give up her town council election campaign to stay home with her family.

road" and rejecting suburbia is already an issue dramatized in some episodes. The characters do sometimes struggle against their desire for more excitement and adventure (perhaps to *See the USA in Your Chevrolet*).

As an all-male family sitcom, *My Three Sons* makes a good platform for promoting Chevrolets to single men as well as to suburban families. The demographics are kept open-ended by the fact that none of the sitcom characters appear in the credits. While the opening credits are animated, the end credits are comprised of what might as well be driverless cars on the new, empty highways. Choppy editing connects tracking shots of different cars traveling along various roads and highways through match on action shots, which also serve to convey a clear distinction between models and between different kinds of roads. Driving is emphasized over arriving as if to reinforce the message—*See the USA in Your Chevrolet*.

These Chevy-sponsored *My Three Sons* credits imply that America is on the move, which fits the content of the story segments, as Steve is an upper-middle-class commuter who travels both locally and nationally. Steve's various Chevrolets appear often in episodes, usually as his mode of commuting to his office or the airport for business trips. He is an ideal Chevrolet spokesperson as he does see more of the USA than most television suburbanites.

1.6   The Nelsons as America's Favorite Endorsers

When he created *The Adventures of Ozzie & Harriet*, former Big Band orchestra leader Ozzie Nelson found a way to be a good brandcasting platform for sponsors and to avoid the residual star image complications even though his costar was his real wife Harriet, whom Ozzie had met when she became the glamour girl singer for his 1930s Big Band orchestra. In creating their sitcom personas, Nelson dropped any star connection and refashioned the Nelsons as ordinary suburbanites rather than a family of performers. In doing so, he foreclosed the possibility of Big Band era guest stars because he seemed to be banking less on star appeal than on generational appeal (the new suburban generation and later the new youth culture as embodied by son and future teen heartthrob Ricky Nelson). It helped that Ozzie and Harriet had already created a successful radio act, which was oriented toward bantering between songs and conveyed a comic rather than a glamorous tone. They were still Hollywood stars, with the original credits even depicting the outside of their actual home in Beverly Hills. Yet the Ozzie and Harriet who appeared alongside sons David and Ricky on ABC television had no overt connection to the film and television industry. In fact, they had no connection to any industry at all as Ozzie's job remained unnamed even though he came home late afternoons in a suit. More often episodes were set during the weekend or evening leisure time.

Neither Ozzie nor Harriet performed in the series. After he became aware that youngest son Ricky was becoming a brand in his own right, Ozzie did begin to integrate Ricky's music into episodes or segue from a story segment into an interstitial that played like an early form of music video. As I mention in Chapter 2, Rick eventually becomes a representative of rock 'n' roll youth culture, both as a musician and later as "Rick Nelson, Dean of Drop-Ins" on ABC's summer of love music miniseries *Malibu U.* (July 21–September 1, 1967). As part of television's Nelson family, however, Ricky remained a representative, upper-middle-class suburbanite who eventually goes to college and works after classes as an assistant at the law firm where older brother David has his first job.[15]

As would be the case in the ordinary suburban family sitcoms that followed in its wake, the focus on the pleasures of a consumer-oriented suburban lifestyle with an emphasis on family time made *Ozzie & Harriet* an ideal platform from which to advertise appliances as well as small-ticket domestic goods. Ozzie Nelson produced the series, which gave him the opportunity to perfect the integrated commercial as a televisual form. Dressed in the same country club casual clothes they wore within the series, members of the Nelson family told the new suburbanites or those aspiring to that status in their *The Adventures of Ozzie & Harriet* audience first about Hotpoint appliances and later about Quaker Oats breakfast mixes and Kodak cameras. Eventually, the Nelson sons addressed fellow teens directly from the malt shop counter to recommend the refreshing taste of

Coca-Cola. Bottles of Coca-Cola were integrated into episodes as well, serving as a more implicit recommendation. Such integrated advertising enables brand consistency, a consistency enabled by Ozzie acting as series producer and star.

1950s sitcoms typically included integrated advertising, often in the form of embedded segments with the actors staying in character and speaking from some in-story world space. This dynamic made the segments feel less like a break in the action or in characterization even though they were pitches for sponsors' products. At some point, the television stars looked directly into the camera and endorsed products, although the pitch came after some live-action dramatization consistent with the story world. The stars would demonstrate the product in use, often in both the product integration segments and the dramatized advertisements

This dynamic can be illustrated through an analysis of the dramatized advertisements included as part of an episode of *The Adventures of Ozzie & Harriet* when Quaker Oats Company sponsored the star sitcom. In one scenario Ozzie was supposed to be making breakfast in bed for Harriet. David and Ricky come to the kitchen to help. Ozzie mixes up some pancake batter in a special shaker (shown on offer from the company in Harriet's earlier pitch for the brand). They have chosen buttermilk, but there were other varieties in the closet. This availability is indicative of how goods can be part of a broadcast product category, but can also be representative of narrowcasting (via different flavors, packaging styles, or quantities intended to appeal to a range of consumer tastes or needs).

After dramatizing how easy the mix makes the process, Ozzie and his sons are shown settled in the dining room finishing stacks of light and fluffy pancakes. Suddenly, Ozzie remembers he is supposed to be surprising Harriet. The final shot is of Harriet, sitting up in bed enjoying her pancake breakfast. She pauses to offer the direct pitch to the camera. As one would expect of 1950s advertising, the sequence leaves unmarked the whiteness of the family and racial history of Aunt Jemima, a brand and a cultural icon that has been studied extensively.[16] Perhaps this under-attention to the controversial brand is intentional, as the Aunt Jemima boxes (three kinds for different consumer taste preferences) are only shown in a fleeting shot of the open cupboard.

In any case, more attention is paid to the Quaker Oats parent company than to the specific brand packaging. Episodes that include such dramatized advertising have credits sequences that begin with Quaker Oats' signature Q occupying the full screen. Then the Q is filled with a picture of the family gathered at the dining room table for a meal. Each individual, starting with Ozzie, also appears cameo-style inside the Q. In such a custom credits bumper, an announcer intones the name of sponsoring company and series title and the actors remain quiet, relying only on a powerful visual entwinement of sponsor and series brands. While some actual episodes trouble the reputation of Ozzie and Harriet as the representative suburban couple, the still photographs and print advertising they did for sponsors still circulate today (more than actual episodes do). This material has helped

FIGURE 1.6 In a dramatized advertisement for Quaker Oats, Ozzie plans to serve Harriet pancakes in bed, but forgets and eats them with his sons (upper). The credits begin with Quaker Oats' signature Q in full screen, and then the Q frames images of the Nelson family as a unit and as individuals (lower).

entrench the popular association of the Nelsons with the effacement of diversity beneath stock images of idealized Anglo-American television families.

During its many seasons *Ozzie & Harriet* featured product endorsement segments. They would play like sponsored credits sequences because the family would gather as if for a cast photograph and the same shot would be repeated with an overlay of the name of the sponsoring company. For the American Dairy Association each member of the Nelson family simply gathered around a kitchen table and drank a glass of milk. As the announcer intoned the sponsor name, it would appear as an overlay on a shot of the whole Nelson family. No slogan was offered, but the subsequent dramatization associated milk drinking with increased "vitality," something the image of the Nelsons conveyed. In one dramatization during the 1962 episode "The Apartment," Harriet brings out milk in a cooler for Ricky's party. The teens dance to rock 'n' roll records. Ozzie looks at them and says, "Boy those kids sure have a lot of vitality," to which Harriet responds, "No wonder, they all drink milk." Then Harriet tells the audience, "Be sure to keep an extra supply of milk on hand for the weekend." The focus in these dramatizations is on milk as a beverage for all occasions, which seems much less logical than when Harriet serves Coca-Cola to guests. One dramatized advertisement for Coca-Cola seemed like part of an episode because the scenario was a backyard barbeque with the neighbors. After Ozzie bungles the guests' steak orders, Harriet makes up for it by handing out individual bottles of Coca-Cola. The lingering last shot is of Ricky Nelson enjoying a long drink. The broadcast–narrowcast combination approach is evident in the narrowcast address enfolded into the generalized broadcast address.

Ozzie Nelson achieved an even more demographically diverse appeal in "David's Golf Story," a 1961 episode in which the Coca-Cola product integration is quite seamless. First, Harriet comes to the living room with a tray filled with Coca-Cola bottles. Ricky then takes them from her and carries them, a very effective shot because of Ricky's fully established teen heartthrob status at this point. In a later shot Ozzie and Harriet are positioned as peers as well as parents because they are shown sipping their Cokes as eagerly as their sons and their friends. Later sequences show David alone at school in the school newspaper office where a coworker hands him a bottle of Coca-Cola from a well-stocked refrigerator. She and David then spend a few minutes chatting and drinking the soda. Later, Ricky is shown in the malt shop with a young kid and they drink Cokes as well.

During this era, Pepsi took the opportunity to challenge Coke through a demographic emphasis on *The Pepsi Generation*. Coca-Cola stuck with the Nelsons as spokespersons until 1961 and tried, *Zing! What a feeling with Coke*, but Pepsi's demographic appeal to *those who think young* better represented the changing times.[17] To meet the Pepsi challenge, Coca-Cola tried to appeal to Ricky Nelson's teen fans. In one spot, as the radio in the malt shop plays the new jingle, "Only Coca-Cola gives you *that refreshing new feeling*," Ricky sips a Coke and says,

FIGURE 1.7 On *My Three Sons*, Steve is a peer-ent like Harriet and Ozzie, supporting his son's lifestyle choices and his rock 'n' roll aspirations (upper). Harriet and Ricky Nelson in a product integration scene for Coca-Cola (lower).

"Isn't that new song for Coca-Cola great." David arrives and concurs. "Yeah, it's great," he says as he tries to order his own Coke from the counterman, who is too busy singing along to serve him. In the "hard sell" spot, there is just a close-up of Ricky enjoying a Coke as the announcer says, "For *that refreshing new feeling*, do as Ricky Nelson does." Then the teen idol looks into the camera and says, "Have a Coke!" By 1963 Coca-Cola had dumped the Nelsons and was spending 80 percent of its $33 million ad budget on television.[18] Before it settled on its successful *Things go better with Coke* tagline "Coca-Cola advertising floundered, searching for a unifying theme," Mark Pendergrast notes, whereas "Pepsi's efforts to identify with the dynamic youth market appeared more effective."[19]

1.7 Showcasing Consumer Aspirations

While the Coca-Cola dramatizations were effective, Kodak sponsorship is better remembered because it specialized in brandcasting at the credits level, which made the entwinement of brand and family more effective. The Kodak credits have become permanently associated with the Nelsons in part because the more posed Kodak images have continued to circulate as if they are representative family portraits of The Nelsons. In reality, they were just sponsor images attached to the sitcom credits sequence. The credits and the related dramatized advertising discussed below are indicative of how a sponsor's needs impact series dynamics. In these seasons Nelson had his family head outside more often and increased on-location scenes to showcase the sharpness of Kodak film and its environmentally precise film types.

Through its ten years of sponsorship, Kodak indelibly linked picture-taking and home movie-making with the Nelsons' leisure-oriented suburban lifestyle. While leisure time would be a luxury for the real-life Nelsons, always-working, wealthy Hollywood celebrities, ABC's Nelsons took countless pictures and movies of all the leisure activities in which they were engaging. Proclaiming before each broadcast, "Eastman Kodak Company is happy to bring you America's Favorite Family," Kodak outfitted the Nelsons in each variation of the opening credits sequence with Kodak cameras and products and declared, "They enjoy happy times together. Like most of us they know that *good times are picture times*."

The opening of the Kodak-era episodes became a sponsored credits sequence when the brand name Eastman Kodak Company was inserted as an overlay on a shot of the Nelsons' closed front door. To achieve this effect the initial medium shot of the front door was followed by a repeated shot, this time with the Eastman Kodak Company overlay. The brand name was removed for the subsequent shot sequence. The door opened and Ozzie exited, Harriet came next, followed by oldest son David, and then Ricky, each one pausing to pose in front of the door. One of the sons would be wearing a Kodak camera on a strap around his neck. Both were attractive spokespersons. Ricky was already established as a teen singing sensation and both boys had begun to have roles in feature films. The final

FIGURE 1.8 Kodak stamps its sponsorship on the Nelsons' front door and on their family portrait. The overly posed photo from the *Ozzie & Harriet* credits sequence does not capture how informal the family relations are within the series itself.

shot was of the family on the front lawn, the formality of their stance and the fact that this kind of posed shot tends to circulate as an official cast photograph may help to explain why people associate the Nelsons with an overly formal and idealized family in the *Father Knows Best*-mold. Although a family character-ized by more informal relations than the photograph suggests, the Nelsons are embodiments of the era's idealization of typical Americans: they are a heteronor-mative, Anglo American, upper-middle-class, nuclear family living in a colonial house in an upscale suburb. The price points of the cameras for sale indicate that the pitches are targeting upper-middle-class consumers, although the sequences could also make those who could not currently afford the purchase orient them-selves toward a plan for some future acquisition. In contrast to the posed shots of the Nelsons in the credits, the more candid shots within the dramatized adver-tisements show the parents and children to have a very relaxed manner with each other and an almost peer-to-peer equality. These family dynamics and specific likeable aspects of their personalities are more effectively utilized in the longer form dramatized advertisements.

Beyond the memorable Kodak credits, the Nelsons appeared in extended dra-matizations for Kodak products. They link a call-to-affiliation with the Nelsons to a call-to-action to visit a local retailer to buy Kodak film or the latest Kodak cameras to preserve or even encourage picture-worthy family leisure time. Yet, the sponsor's store cutouts of the Nelsons also indicate how each individual fam-ily member represented a demographic category and a potential for narrowcast-ing. This duality is evident in two Kodak dramatized advertisements.

Those dramatizations point to the power of the hybrid endorsement structure of *Ozzie & Harriet* in which two or more family members and then one alone would offer a combination of direct pitches and demonstrations of products in use. As Ricky's extratextual celebrity grew after he rocketed to the top of the charts as a teen idol in the music industry, he was often featured in the solo ele-ments of the dramatizations. They typify the powerful combination of "from our family to yours" pitches made by the television family as a unit and individual peer-to-peer pitches by each family member. In one dramatization Ozzie and Harriet are pitching Kodak cameras as holiday gifts, but then each makes a sepa-rate appeal to audience members who might feel affinity for Ozzie or Harriet in relation to gender, personality, or some other appeal.

The sitcom's early characterizations of Ozzie as bumbler and Harriet as the ever capable and patient household manager were so well known in the 1950s, for instance, that they were the unspoken foundation of the implied joke in one drama-tized advertisement for Kodak. Harriet is telling the audience to consider planning ahead for the holidays and buying cameras. Ozzie interrupts to advise men to buy their wives cameras as gifts, which they could then "borrow." The dramatization aligns with the sitcom's tendency to poke fun at Ozzie's self-interested behavior.

After Ricky became a teen idol, Ozzie Nelson replaced his Ozzie-the-self-interested bumbler persona with Ozzie-the-peer-ent, and the duality of the pitch

FIGURE 1.9   A camera store cutout of the Nelson family for Kodak is juxtaposed with an image of the demographically diverse all–male family on *My Three Sons*. The shot appears in the sponsored credits sequence, which also includes stamps of ownership by Chevrolet or Hunt's, the sitcom's alternate sponsor.

then featured David playing the competent family member indulging the Ozzie character. This new relationship is evident in a second dramatized advertisement in which Ozzie gives David and Ricky advice on how to charm girls by taking their pictures. In the demonstration portion Ricky tests out this theory and has great success with a girl who is clearly charmed enough by him to listen to his long explanation of how the new Kodak camera works. The product demonstration is, of course, central to the sponsor pitch and it takes place outdoors, as more scenes do in the years when Kodak sponsored the series. The initial conversation Ozzie has with David and Ricky happens in the Nelson home and puts on display important character dynamics: Ozzie positions himself more as a peer than a moral authority and his sons, especially David, are quite indulgent of their father, and seem to understand how important it is to him to feel like their peer (even if they really perceive him as too old to be one).

This family dynamic is much more modern than the common perception of 1950s family sitcoms as depictions of authoritative parent–child relations. Ozzie shares similarities to Phil Dunphy from *Modern Family* in that he is more liked than respected. Both men clearly love their children and demonstrate a desire to be emotionally connected to them, which the kids indulge, but less out of feeling the same desire for closeness than because they feel empathy for their fathers' attempts to "think young." Indeed, Ozzie is the forerunner of the cross-generational, "think young" cultural type, even though the concept would not be fleshed out until the Pepsi campaigns of the 1960s. While the midcentury U.S. is often thought of in terms of generational differences and tensions, "The Pepsi Generation" campaigns made generational connection a matter of feeling and more about consumption than age. As the next chapter will show, it is smart to convey a hybrid broadcast–narrowcast impression about a brand as it expands its potential reach.

As Ricky's generational appeal grew, his star status began to create an excess in the series, especially when "Ricky Nelson, teen idol" seemed to be on screen in the music videos. It is important to note that Ricky had been put forth as a star character in the series from the start. In early seasons, he was introduced as "the irrepressible Ricky" and Ozzie Nelson often gave Ricky the best jokes. In his most skilled uses of television as a brandcasting platform, Nelson managed to develop his tween son's "irrepressible Ricky" brand and the Ozzie Nelson "bumbling dad" persona in sequences that took place in front of the appliances supplied by Hotpoint, an early corporate sponsor.

Nelson was especially accommodating to Hotpoint. He explains in his autobiography how he blocked the series so that many scenes took place in the kitchen. In some scenes dialogue exchanges took place in front of appliances. Even more scenes were set in the dining area, which was connected to the kitchen through the open doorway and the open shutters of the pass through from dining area into kitchen. These openings gave a clear view of the appliances. In the Hotpoint seasons (and continuing in the Quaker Oats years), Nelson transformed the kitchen

FIGURE 1.10 Rick Nelson flirts with the help of a Kodak camera (upper). Ozzie "the peer-ent" gives his sons advice about flirting with a pretty girl by taking her picture (lower).

set into a branded space in which labor-saving devices and products (ranges, washer-dryers, dryers, and box mixes) could be yoked to ideologies about family leisure time and consumer-enabled modes of happiness. For the promotion of its new "push button ranges," one tagline was *Hotpoint changes your viewpoint . . . automatically!* The advertisements implied that "living electrically" gave people better dispositions. During early seasons, the Nelsons sat atop the Hotpoint logo in the credits sequence bumpers, as Lynn Spigel (1992) has detailed. Hotpoint also stood out as it had two memorable embodiments of its "Happy Hotpoint" character, one animated and one played by Mary Tyler Moore circa 1955. While she appeared as a dancing elf in segments that seemed more like standalone spots, other spots with animated versions of the Nelsons felt more continuous with the segments featuring Hotpoint's animated mascot.

The Nelsons' association with the chirpy Happy Hotpoint jingle might help to explain their current position as iconic signifiers of the blandly happy family like the one represented in the 1998 film *Pleasantville*. Close attention to actual episodes reveals that the family members were more sassy than sedate in the Hotpoint seasons when the credits ended with the introduction of "irrepressible Ricky" and the story segments put on display Harriet's punchy repartee, in a style left over from her 1940s radio persona. These personality dynamics are certainly evident in 1952's "The Pills." It is an episode that is indicative of the way that Nelson blocked scenes so that key beats of a big joke played out in front of the appliances. The premise is that Ozzie's pants are too tight and he is having a hard time moving in them. He has to bend over because he is too proud to let Harriet pick up something he dropped. As Ozzie bends over, Ricky stands behind him and tears a piece of paper down the middle so that Ozzie thinks that his pants have split. Harriet tries not to laugh and Ozzie tries not to get too irritated. The entire sequence provides lingering shots of the push-button range, and during some key dialogue cues, Ricky leans his hand on it, establishing a visual connection to the Hotpoint model. This episode demonstrates how Nelson established precedents for effective ways to use the physical space of an episode just as he had done when he leveraged the sitcom's credits sequence as a platform for promoting other brands.

Analysis of many *Ozzie & Harriet* episodes reveals the continuing impact of corporate sponsor needs on set design and shot sequences. Ozzie or other characters enter through the back door, so they can then stand in front of the washer dryer set or head right over toward the range. Sometimes the blocking emphasized the refrigerator and, depending on the alternate sponsor, it would have enough Coca-Cola or milk for each family member to sit down and drink a glass.

A suite of appliances became a new consumer aspiration and television played a part in putting the newest model on display. The hope was that exposure to what was available would lead directly to purchase. The announcer reminded viewers to go visit their local dealers for a closer look. In the dramatized advertisements one of the Nelsons would directly address viewers with a pitch and also would

FIGURE 1.11   "Irrepressible Ricky" starts out as a tween who teases his father Ozzie. Harriet tries not to laugh as the scene plays out in front of Hotpoint's push-button range.

prompt them to head to a local dealer to check out the latest models. Often, these dramatized advertisements positioned the brand as an education platform, teaching people about the benefits of automatic dishwashers, for example, or the benefits of convenience foods such as packages of pre-mixed ingredients. In this way, these dramatized advertisements played a role in normalizing behaviors that have since become commonplace (e.g., using paper towels instead of cloth towels in *Father Knows Best*, sponsored by Scott Paper; heating up canned soup instead of making it from scratch on Campbell's *The Donna Reed Show*). The dramatized advertisements indicate that such content was intended to enhance brand awareness and to motivate the target audience to adopt specific consumer behaviors.

1.8   Buying and Being American from the Andersons to the Goldbergs

As noted at the outset of this chapter, by the late 1950s the networks were targeting new, young suburbanites who were presumed to be in particular need of advice as to how to navigate this new world in which they found themselves. With consumer products to sell and an advice paradigm through which they intended to do it, advertisers were increasingly more interested in sitcoms that represented the pleasures of married life and happy suburban togetherness, rather than series in which the tensions of married life or gender or ethnic issues played a central role. Although dressed in the casual wear allowed in a suburban country club, rather than the formalwear required of a New York nightclub, characters in these suburban sitcoms still represented an upper-middle-class lifestyle unavailable to the majority of viewers. This distance points to the aspirational relationship typical viewers often had to the lifestyles on display on television.

As a good portion of the viewing public fell outside the class and ethnic parameters such sitcoms established, one goal of such program sponsorships was to nurture future brand advocates among the baby boomer generation. Product integration or dramatized advertisements could instill in some viewers the aspiration to one day purchase products. In any case, we should not lose sight of the appeal of this normativity for those who did not fit the decade's definition of the typical American. Writers such as Gary Soto, Maria Mazziotti Gillan, Lan Samantha Chang, and Susan Cheever have remarked upon their fascination with the unattainable typical American worlds on display in 1950s and 1960s television programming. Reflecting on the continuing appeal of programming that represents mundane middle-class worlds, John Hartley writes that we should not underestimate the lure of "suburbanality," especially for those who have not yet achieved suburban status or are the first generation to do so. Indeed, they could be included in the "think young" consumer cohort of the later 1950s and early 1960s. We can generalize the term "think youngs," to refer to consumers whose worldviews were different from that of their parents. Think youngs could be first-generation suburbanites, baby boomer teens and tweens, or even the "born here" Americans of immigrant heritage who take on a different, typically more "youthful," attitude, lifestyle, or spending habit than those of their parents. This expanded understanding of the target market allows for inclusion of those privileged viewers who looked like the Andersons or could afford to consume like them, as well those who aspired to do so in the future.

Of course, it was in the best interest of sponsors promoting domestic goods to convey the message that the *Father Knows Best-type* family was the new normal. Eventually such families proved quite appealing for parent companies such as P&G, which manufactured an array of brands and a variety of small ticket products. Scott Paper sponsored *Father Knows Best* (1954–60)[20] for a time and when it did the Anderson's kitchen set featured two paper towel dispensers in an era when most people still used cloth towels. Sylvania gave *Father Knows Best* its seal of approval when in 1954 it bestowed on it the "Sylvania Award for Outstanding Family Entertainment." Advertising agencies cited Jane Wyatt (playing good suburban wife Margaret Anderson in *Father Knows Best*) and Donna Reed (aka Donna Stone, the mother who knows best) as representatives of the types of people with whom they wanted their products associated. In 1958, a Campbell's Soup Company executive personally chose *The Donna Reed Show* and even kept it on the air despite its low-rated first season because Donna and the Stones received his stamp of approval. Fortunately, the ratings picked up and it lasted eight seasons, ending in 1966.[21] Yet it is *Father Knows Best* that has the patriarchal nuclear family structure and the authoritative parenting most associated with today's memory of the 1950s television family. The Andersons of *Father Knows Best* are also representative of the normative 1950s family in terms of racial and social class parameters. They are a generationally upper-middle-class, white, Anglo-Saxon Protestant family, independent of and isolated from extended family (and they do not interact with many neighbors). They do not have any connections, current or former, to urban, ethnic, or class-conscious fraternal organizations, the kind to which working-class city workers Ralph Kramden and Ed Norton of *The Honeymooners* belonged or with which Irish American Michael Francis "Bub" O'Casey maintains ties in *My Three Sons*. Suburbanites were not expected to belong to groups or organizations connected to their personal identities, specific skills/professions, or ethnicities. Instead they were supposed to conform to a common set of country-club-approved leisure activities, menu choices, and social interactions.

In an era when all communal activity and ethnic ties were considered suspect, Americans were encouraged to substitute brand loyalty for family and class loyalty. The change from ethnic, working-class, and interdependent extended families and urban neighborhoods to ethnically unmarked, middle-class, isolated, and independent nuclear family units represented a move from public-to private-sphere concerns. By the later 1950s the urban, ethnic sitcom had mostly been replaced. Viewers were encouraged to model themselves on suburban characters who spent very little time outside their single-family colonials and who sought private and familial solutions to their problems. While unions and fraternal orders sought to speak for their members as a class, 1950s Americans were being encouraged to speak for themselves as individuals through their personal and familial consumer choices. It was a lesson learned by the Goldbergs from the 1950s sitcom of the same name.

A correspondence was being established in this era of assimilation between buying and being American, an ideology at the heart of the corporate-sponsored suburban sitcom. This correspondence is evident in the final 1955–6 season of *The Goldbergs*, which arrived on TV in 1949 as a slice-of-life in the Bronx sitcom, but was forced into a suburban sitcom format by the end of its run. The original urban ethnic sitcom version had been adapted from the radio show that series star and producer Gertrude Berg had created in 1929 and kept on air until 1945.[22] The earlier urban seasons offered moments of a systematic class critique, especially in famously class-oriented episodes such 1949's "The New Landlord," in which Molly organizes some collective action in her Bronx apartment building and threatens a rent strike. In contrast, one of the final season's suburban episodes included a segment about getting a family picture taken at a studio. It is one of the first things the Goldbergs do when they arrive in Haverville, but only because they get a free coupon to do so. The Bronx Goldbergs categorize the photography session as an unnecessary luxury on which they feel they should not waste money. The Haverville Goldbergs learn in the episode that such expenditures should be thought of as family necessities, and once they do, they gleefully spend money on reprints to mail to their now far-away family members. This message was also the one Harriet Nelson conveyed in Kodak dramatizations.

Of course, Gertrude Berg's sitcom had always been about assimilation, with the emphasis on "The Rise of the Goldbergs" (the original title of the radio show) and their life in the bourgeois Bronx apartment in which they lived after moving up from the Lower East Side. It was then a sponsor-friendly message with which Maxwell House coffee wanted to be associated. In the early 1950s Sanka sales rose 57 percent with the overtly Jewish Molly Goldberg praising it from the windowsill of her Bronx apartment.[23] By the middle of the decade sponsors felt that it was safest given the newly expanded national reach of U.S. television programming to choose their spokespeople from the unambiguously white and suburban families of the new WASP sitcoms.

During the Haverville season, *The Goldbergs* did not always stay "on message" about the desirability of the new suburban lifestyle.[24] There were often slippages between the urban world of the Goldbergs to which viewers had been accustomed and these new Goldbergs who lived in a Long Island suburb.[25] Their clear preference for the ethnic, extended family and neighbors-as-family dynamics they left behind in the Bronx unsettled the typical messaging of the suburb-set sitcom: that the suburban, middle-class, nuclear family with a breadwinner–homemaker couple at its center is the most desirable family formation.[26]

The episodes in the final season of *The Goldbergs* (sometimes called *Molly*) also do not necessarily confirm the desirability of the suburban lifestyle because, despite their contrived happy endings, they have moments depicting just how much Molly misses the involved neighborliness of her old home.[27] Clearly, the isolated suburbs and the *Father Knows Best* family formation that supposedly typified it had a detrimental rather than a beneficial effect on Molly, who looks increasingly miserable over the course of the season before the sponsors and network put her out of her misery.

George Lipsitz, in his foundational work on early television's ethnic sitcoms, argues for the necessity of studying programs such as *The Goldbergs* and *Mama* (1949–57) because they can offer us "important insight into how Americans explained drastic changes [of the urban to suburban migration] to themselves and others."[28] Looking at those same shows in relation to industrial TV time, we can see how the U.S. television industry and its sponsors have provided Americans with the preferred rhetoric and interpretative paradigms through which to explain those changes in specific ways.[29] The industry has also transformed selected sitcoms into time capsules through their rerun practices, allowing successive generations of Americans to view them as artifacts of a lost time rather than as carefully chosen brand representatives of what Derek Kompare calls America's "Television Heritage" shaped by industry rerun and re-release practices.

It is surprising to discover that *The Adventures of Ozzie & Harriet* was on television alongside *The Goldbergs*, which was still on the air when *Father Knows Best* premiered in 1954. After the 1955–6 season in which the Goldbergs tried to conform to the Anderson ideal by moving to a suburb called Haverville, the show was canceled and never resurfaced in rerun packages. These shows overlapped in industrial TV time, but the Goldbergs were not invited to the TVLand block party marathons in the late 1980s and early 90s. That absence contributes to the misperception that the two kinds of family formations they represented did not coexist in America, likely because that actuality is at odds with the deeply ingrained assumption that all families in the 1950s resembled the Andersons of *Father Knows Best*.

1.9 Suburban Strivers, *Modern Family*, and *The Middle*

It might be surprising to learn that Danny Thomas' more ethnic-focused sitcom stayed on the air from 1953 to 1964. Recall the original *Make Room for Daddy* focused on situations related to an entertainer father unable to contain the anxieties that his showbiz life and lengthy absences produced for his wife, tween son, and teen daughter. After a contract dispute resulted in Jean Hagen's departure in 1956, the ABC sitcom was retooled with Danny as a widower and renamed *The Danny Thomas Show*. Danny eventually marries Kathy, a nurse to his son and the widowed mother of a spunky five-year-old named Linda. The show still had plenty of ethnic jokes that Danny made at his own expense, and ethnicity was also addressed through Kathy, whose Irish American heritage was often foregrounded. When *The Danny Thomas Show* moved to CBS in 1957, it took over the old *I Love Lucy* timeslot, where it achieved very high ratings. Despite the ethnic emphasis maintained in *The Danny Thomas Show* into the 1960s, and the possibility of reading the 1960s supernatural sitcoms like *Bewitched* as offering displaced, mixed marriage storylines, the overtly ethnic and urban sitcoms as well as the working class sitcoms of the early 1950s disappeared as companies chose to sponsor suburban sitcoms about "unmarked" white, middle-class Americans. This change also reflected that televisions were now in more homes across the nation after technology enabled more extensive broadcast reach and better picture quality.

Danny Thomas was now associated not with Dodge, but with small ticket household items because the CBS sponsor was General Foods, the maker of Jell-O, Maxwell House, and Post Cereals.[30] For similar reasons, the alternate sponsor of *My Three Sons* was Hunt's, makers of catsup and other condiments. Pontiac also joined Chevrolet from 1963–5 in sponsoring *My Three Sons*. Given that car sponsorships make more sense for such suburban-set sitcoms, it's not surprising that sponsors' cars appeared in the driveways of a variety of other suburban commuters such as Ward Cleaver of *Leave It to Beaver*.

On the surface it would seem that Ward Cleaver and his car purchases in *Leave It to Beaver* would have little in common with those of Danny Williams. Yet,

Ward is subtly connected to an aspirational consumption dynamic. Some early episodes reveal that Ward is still an upwardly mobile American. The fact that Ward has new Plymouth Fury models in 1959, 1960, and 1963 goes beyond the terms of the sponsorship deal with Chrysler. His trade-in behavior registers the "annual model year change in cars," which David Halberstam says automakers "designed to make car owners restless with the cars they owned and eager for new products."[31] The car is still "a vehicle for myth," as Andrew Wernick would say, because it is associated with Ward's upward mobility. He was born on a farm, attends state college, and becomes a white-collar businessman. He marries up in social class, buys one house and trades up to a larger one, and buys new cars. Unlike the work-oriented farm lifestyle in which he grew up, Ward enjoys the leisure time his white-collar work both allows and affords. Yet, he is somewhat ambivalent about consumer culture, as represented by his wife, as is evident in episodes such as "Beaver's Sweater" (2.31).

It is intriguing to note that Ward Cleaver was not shown commuting in the car. The emphasis in the story is most often on what happens after work and on weekends. In the later seasons, there are more family outings in the car, and a representative family outing becomes the dramatization for the 1961 credits. The family sedan references the new suburban leisure activity—the Sunday Drive. Perhaps June is the planner of such outings as she comes out of the front door first and stops and poses, picnic basket in hand (in the way the Nelsons do in the Kodak credits). The rest of the Cleavers exit in age order, pose and then all head over to the driveway to get into the car. It is a new 1961 Plymouth Fury, a model chosen as part of a product placement deal. In the Plymouth seasons, Ward backs the car down the driveway as Beaver and Wally look out of the back window and smile into the camera (see Figure 2.6 for an image of the car). We assume they are happy to be heading off to enjoy leisure activities. In a few episodes, we do see the car in motion, but not for Ward's daily commute because it is never narrativized

To meet the needs of series sponsor Plymouth, Ward Cleaver is transformed into a spender, but actual episodes show him to be a saver. It is surprising to learn from viewing *Leave It to Beaver* that even the supposedly conflict-free WASP families on television at this time had anxieties about the embrace of consumer culture. Ward Cleaver's ideas about consumer and familial behavior are in conflict at times with June's. She was born into an upper-middle-class family, which seems to have a more Victorian view of class divisions, judging by the behavior of relatives who come to visit. A college graduate, June embraces the behavior of a suburban spender. A rural striver, Ward was born on a farm in the country and has an orientation toward making do with what he has and saving for the future. He represents upward mobility achieved through education as an engineer and military service in the Seabees (the United States Navy Construction Battalion). Now an established white-collar suburbanite, Ward struggles to adjust to the competitive neighborliness at odds with the mutual aid he describes as marking his rural upbringing.

The tension between Ward the saver and June the spender is more problematic because it exists within the supposedly conflict-free family itself.[32] The tension reflects how sponsors who were buying TV time hoped to influence consumers to accept the concept of buying on time, to change, that is, their Depression-era (or rural or immigrant) ideas about debt and spending. Suburbanites were told to let go of the adages about "living within one's means," "saving for a rainy day," and sacrificing personal luxuries in order to be able to pay outright for family necessities. Just as the World War II-era Ward Cleaver did his duty by serving in the military, postwar Ward needed to do his patriotic duty and contribute to the new consumer economy.[33]

Although it has more of a downward mobility in the Midwest theme, ABC's *The Middle* (2009–present) depicts a similar spender versus saver dynamic between Mike Heck and his wife Frankie. The sitcom shares the Wednesday night schedule with *Modern Family*, which features different kinds of consumers across the three branches of the sitcom's extended family. The Dunphys are a consumer-oriented nuclear family of five, easily linked to advertising and product integration for the family sedans, minivans, portable tech devices, and upscale chain eateries associated with middle-class to upper-middle-class suburbia. Product integration is also easily tied to the series' other two families: that of Claire Dunphy's wealthy father Jay Pritchett and his second wife Gloria Delgado-Pritchett and stepson Manny, and that of Claire's brother Mitchell, a lawyer who lives with his male life partner Cam Tucker and their adopted Vietnamese daughter Lily. The Tucker-Pritchetts drive a Toyota Prius and are part of the consumer category Procter & Gamble calls "the sustainable mainstream." They shop at Whole Foods, although they sometimes mock the more militant "green" consumers they see there. They are also upscale mall shoppers, as is shown in several episodes, and their upscale, first floor duplex condo is decorated with some design touches reminiscent of upscale contemporary furniture retailers like West Elm. As owner of a *California Closets*-style company, Jay Pritchett is an over-60 luxury consumer who has various new model cars, which signal his status as a wealthy businessman. His wife Gloria, who emigrated from Colombia, represents the aspirational ethnic American and the luxury car brands she drives signal her achieved social mobility. The latter two variants of the suburban norm are less like variants on the suburban norms when considered in terms of each couple's breadwinner–homemaker family structure.

The Pritchetts embrace the trade-in logic encouraged by the auto industry, as is evidenced in several episodes, including "Punkin Chunkin" (3.9) when Jay comments on getting a new Audi. The adoption of the new model year concept was a game changer for the auto industry, which then influenced the appliance industry to circulate messaging that normalized replacing perfectly good products and often almost-new products with latest models. Phil Dunphy certainly adopts this philosophy for his tech device consumption.

As the next chapter demonstrates, an analysis of the entire output of ABC programming since the midcentury indicates that ABC has specialized in series like *Modern Family*, which have tween-inclusive elements. Coming on air in 2009 along with *Modern Family*, *The Middle* also had some memorable product integration episodes. The difference, however, is that unlike the Dunphys (or for that matter *Modern Family*'s "sustainable mainstream" gay family, its over-60 luxury consumer, or its aspirational ethnic Americans), the Heck family has barely enough money to buy one new appliance or tech device, let alone replace them when new models come out. While *Modern Family* gets higher ratings and much more critical attention, *The Middle* is more intriguing for its representation of a "barely-making-ends-meet," two-earner lower-middle-class (or perhaps working-class?) household. More to the point, the producers manage to turn the series into a brandcasting platform despite the family's lack of purchasing power and the fact that the Hecks are financially frozen in the flip-phone era.

Several episodes of *The Middle* illustrate the creative ways producers can make a series focused on a lower-middle-class family into an advertising platform, while still maintaining class-appropriate possessions and setting. Watching *The Middle* makes evident just how normal it is for television families to have gleaming stainless steel appliances and granite countertops in their kitchens. The Hecks have almost no countertops and the little they do have is covered with small appliances, food packages, and junk. The Hecks' kitchen "design" includes an old, outmoded avocado-colored refrigerator and an empty hole where the matching energy-guzzling 1970s dishwasher used to be. Embarrassment over the state of this kitchen makes Frankie doubtful about whether she and Mike can host a holiday open house for the neighbors.

Frankie: "Do we really want them seeing our dishwasher hole?"
Mike: "I think they'll be embarrassed for us long before they see the hole."

Mike, later jokes that they should "pick up a scratched and dented floor model. That way it will fit in with everything else."

The Hecks host the party even though they are clearly depressed by their outmoded kitchen even after they cover the hole with wrapping paper like a Christmas present to disguise it. At the party a tipsy Frankie makes fun of how cheap Mike is for not getting a new dishwasher. Her goading prompts some neighbors to shout at Mike across the room, "Oh Mike why don't you buy poor Frankie a dishwasher." It is a bit mean-spirited, as Frankie knows that they just can't afford to replace it. The comedy becomes cringe worthy when it is revealed that Mike has splurged for the dishwasher as a gift he planned as a Christmas morning surprise. When he can't take the mocking any more, Mike defiantly rolls out the dishwasher to prove he is not a bad guy. Everyone is stunned and a bit ashamed. The neighbors make their excuses and the party abruptly ends. All is forgiven by the final beat when the whole Heck family is gathered around the dishwasher, staring at its shiny newness in awe. The angle of the shot makes it look like the Hecks are gathered around a new baby's bassinet, staring in wonder at the new arrival. In her final voiceover Frankie marvels at the change this new appliance brought to their outlook: "Yes Christmas is a season of wonder."

As this example suggests, the humor in *The Middle* often revolves around the inability of the Heck family to afford the typical television-family basics, which include both appliances and new personal tech devices. To that end, it is not surprising that in "The Smile" (4.14) youngest son Brick lobbies for an iPad. His father just laughs at the ridiculousness of the request. His mother does too, and adds, "The only way you're getting an iPad is if you're in Steve Jobs' will!" After Brick wears her down, Frankie agrees that it does seem like a necessity for their studious youngest son. In the end, she manages to get Brick a refurbished iPad. After she gives it to him, she says to the audience: "This is *better* than good parenting!" because Brick is happy to get it, even if it's refurbished. Of course, the incident has probably inculcated in him a determination to make enough money in adulthood to buy all the new tech devices he wants. The episode ends with some actual product integration, which seems very character consistent: the Hecks have a celebratory dinner at the chain restaurant Red Lobster. The episode also includes the standing joke that Mike has to run the hair dryer to get the microwave to work in order to warm up his coffee (other episodes show that they duct tape the washer shut during the agitation cycle).

Oldest son Axl also has a clear understanding of the kinds of consumer powers he wants as an adult. His role models are the Donahues, the idealized middle-class family next door and the ones who get a shiny new Volkswagen Passat. In the episode "Hecking it Up" (3.13), Axl describes the Donahues as his surrogate family during a scene in which his real family is dashing around trying to clean up the Donahues' car, which they borrowed without asking. Axl is panicking: "I can't afford to lose the Donahues, they feed me real food. They taught me how to brush my teeth! If I lose that family, I've only got this family."

The Hecks cannot trade in their car or even buy a new one when the old one is worn out. Frankie drives a barely functional dilapidated old car. When Axl starts to drive, he buys a car that is in such bad shape, it is mistaken for an entrant in a demolition derby. Over the season many jokes focus on incidents related to the dilapidated state of the Hecks' cars. While the matter-of-factness of the buying power of the extended Pritchett family makes new cars logical for the characters, it would seem impossible to use any car placement within *The Middle*. The writers managed to pull it off in the "Hecking it Up" episode. The premise is that the Donahues get last-minute tickets to the Super Bowl and ask Frankie to go over to their house and move their new car into the garage. Instead Frankie puts it in her own garage and soon starts driving it around town. Unbeknownst to Frankie her son Axl does the same thing and every other member of the family puts the car to use in some way. Riding around in a roomy, new family sedan inspires Frankie with new-found confidence that is rewarded by a better volunteer position at the Super Bowl, which is being held that year in Indiana.

Frankie's good mood rubs off on the rest of the family and soon we see them using the car all the time. The family even bonds because of the car when they all participate in a sing-a-long to cheer up Sue, who thinks she has been dumped by her new boyfriend. The Hecks have become new people while driving in this new car, which aligns with car commercial messaging. Their consumer product-enabled happiness is cut short when Nancy Donahue calls to say they are on their way home and will be there in a half-hour. Nancy and Ron show up just after the Hecks have cleaned the mess they made of the car and placed it back in the

FIGURE 1.12 In *The Middle*, the Hecks are filled with happiness when they secretly drive their neighbours' new Volkswagen Passat. When they get caught, they are all dejected, especially eldest son Axl, who thinks of the solidly middle-class Donahues as his fantasy family.

Donahues' driveway. The Hecks stand near the car, guilty and nervous. Then Ron Donahue notices a scratch. At first, Frankie panics and blames her eldest son Axl, but she soon confesses that they've been secretly driving the car and begs for their forgiveness. Nancy Donahue responds, "Why would I ever hate you? I hate myself for not telling you to drive it in the first place! Seriously. What is the point of having a brand new car if you can't share it with your neighbors? I'm *thrilled* you drove it!" Ron adds, "Absolutely! You saved one of us from getting the first scratch and fighting with each other about it," and then he laughs. Their behavior is at odds with the "use new cars to one-up your neighbors" messaging often seen in suburban-address car commercials. The Hecks conclude that the Donahues are the nicest people on the planet, or just in a perpetual good mood from having the money to buy new things.

1.10   Re-contextualizing Sponsored Sitcoms of the 1950s

Thanks to TVLand and other decontextualized rerun outlets (including You-Tube) many viewers continue to believe that modern sitcoms like *The Middle* are a counterpoint to an anxiety-free "the way we were" 1950s.[34] According to Stephanie Coontz, the 1950s does not represent the last gasp of traditional family life, but rather the beginning of such a model centered on the idea of the "sexually charged, child-centered family," one "that would fulfill all its members' personal needs through an energized and expressive personal life."[35]

TV families have become emblematic of sequentially organized conceptions of the discrete times associated with different kinds of families—from the immigrant Hansens to the assimilating Goldbergs to the already-arrived ethnic strivers like the Williamses from *The Danny Thomas Show* to the generationally middle class Andersons, and diverse millennial-era families of sitcoms like *Modern Family*. Upon closer examination of TV schedules and rerun practices, these families are placed in this linear narrative so that they can be made to seem to represent stages in an evolutionary narrative. The next chapter's analysis of the actual dynamics of ABC's 1950s and 1960s schedules reveals that this interplay did not exist in actuality. Paying attention to the architecture of all the networks' schedules of the era would reveal that the Andersons, the Stones, and the Cleavers actually occupied slots on a television schedule with single-parent families, replacement parent families, and all-male families, and some of those families lived in cities and some in rural locales.[36]

The other kinds of programs on the 1950s schedule that dominated the top spots had less rerun potential, sometimes because of their poor archival format and often because of their era-specific content, dependent on knowledge of the then-current events and personalities. Rerun audiences have not been exposed to the early ethnic sitcoms or to the sponsored programming/variety shows that actually dominated the early TV schedule and its ratings charts. When watching suburban sitcoms in reruns or on DVD, viewers remain unaware of the complexities of the historical time period in which these shows originally aired or the time-based scheduling and programming practices that first introduced the nation to TV families and familial corporations as representative caretakers of "the common good."

It is only when looked at outside of the social and political conflicts of their own time that we can imagine that the suburb sitcoms offer a window onto history, rather than trace evidence of the shop windows of the era and the lifestyles and products displayed therein. It was not assumed that everyone could afford these products, at least not without the opportunity to buy them on time (credit) or in time (generational aspirations). In their original contexts these shows offered a mise-en-scène of desire—in the form of the single-family homes, cars, and household goods they put on display. As Halberstam explains of the constant roll out of new model years, "they made car owners restless by playing off their broader aspirations."[37] As is also the case on contemporary television, it is hardly surprising that the sitcom set design of the era bears little resemblance to the style of living that would be feasible for the characters' social and economic conditions. Their living spaces were on display to generate desire in their viewers. Clearly, television programming and advertising depicts lifestyles and consumer patterns as universal when they are representative only of a specific class and available only to those with consumer purchasing power. U.S. television works to legitimate the values of that class as those that would be most universally beneficial to all Americans at the same time that it implicitly excludes certain families from its representation of typicality. This exclusion was not only representational, but also industrial in that the scope of early television developed as the industry and its technologies did. Television started as an east coast phenomenon, then became bicoastal, then expanded more and more nationally. The content of television has developed in tandem with its geographical reach and the resulting understandings of the "mass" audience that it was reaching. Indeed, television has always had elements of narrowcasting in its broadcast address as it was always courting selected audiences.[38]

Since TVLand stopped airing its "Better Living Through Television" blocks, the typical way to watch classic TV is online, on DVD, or on YouTube. None of these formats offer a complete series and many companies just release random episodes. Most TV on DVD does not offer captured flow broadcasts (meaning with commercials/promos intact so that the contextualized meaning not offered by story segments would remain). Within the episode we just see the traces of the spaces in which the network and corporate promotion would have been scheduled. Packaged by nostalgia companies, such as the aptly named TimelessTV, such DVDs tell us little about the historical or industrial time that would have been the context for such programming. Given that such DVDs usually offer selections of episodes rather than full seasons, they can contribute to the continued misrepresentations of the era and its programming. Until the UCLA Film and Television Archive in partnership with Shout Factory released a compilation DVD spanning several seasons of *The Goldbergs* in 2010, for example, the episodes available on DVD were only those from the final season when Molly's gender and ethnic challenges to consensus culture are contained and the family is shipped off to the suburbs for a lesson in how to live like a *Father Knows Best* consumer-oriented typical American family. It is much more interesting to see the earliest episodes, or to find an episode with intact sponsor dramatizations. To look at these television episodes outside of their "captured flow broadcasts" is to study texts without the commercial system that moves them along. Taking the story segments out of their original timed-segmentation and commercial context and disrupting the commercial flow, changes their meaning. In the case of the suburban sitcom, looking at it in ahistorical TV Time makes what was actually a contestation of new concepts about family and nation appear to be a simple consensus.

As I established at the outset of this chapter, the early 1950s U.S. television industry was characterized by sponsor-driven schedules dominated by time franchises. Networks existed, but they really couldn't have channel brands as they had little control over what was scheduled and where it was scheduled. Sponsors often picked up their shows and moved them to new networks, which also disrupted any sense of series–channel entwinement, which is necessary for effective channel banding. *Leave It To Beaver*, for instance, began on CBS, but then moved to ABC as a result of the sponsor making a better deal with ABC. More typically, ABC lost series because it was a network with fewer affiliates and owned and operated stations than CBS and NBC. If a series moved to one of those networks, it would be seen in more markets and would be more likely to become highly rated (e.g., on CBS *The Danny Thomas Show* was a ratings hit).

As the many examples in this chapter indicate, the sponsorship model had an impact on the kinds of programs that aired on 1950s television. As a result, network schedules often had very little continuity because of the slots controlled by sponsors. By the end of the 1950s this system was coming to an end. Networks wanted to gain full control of their schedules by having every slot under network rather than sponsor control. When a national scandal erupted over sponsor rigging of quiz shows, network executives exploited it and used it as a way to dismantle the time franchise model for good and take full control of schedules for their own brand messaging needs. With the switch to a participating advertising model, companies bought timed increments within the flow of a network's programming. The "magazine" flow, in turn, came under control of the network. In this new model a loss of an advertiser would not threaten program viability. For their part, advertisers no longer had to rely on a single series to carry its brand messaging. With what we think of today as traditional commercial spots running between segments of many programs, advertisers were more likely to reach a broader population. In addition, it was also now cost effective to advertise small ticket items, a change that worked especially well for packaged goods companies that produced a family of brands (like Procter & Gamble or Quaker Oats). The next chapter addresses how networks gradually moved away from sponsorship and adopted the participating advertising model of "magazine-concept" commercial spots. Networks understood that participating advertising was a way to support their own messaging goals and take control of programming away from sponsors, thereby undercutting their power.

Notes

1 The broad comedy in *Welcome Back, Kotter* came from the interactions of "Mr. Ka-TER" with the ethnically diverse students in the history class he teaches at the same Brooklyn high school he attended in the 1960s.

2 Containment culture is Alan Nadel's term from the book of the same name. He claims that the drive to conform was related to the national foreign policy of containment. On the domestic front, a containment culture surfaced in which all differences were kept in check so that the United States could project a unified front in the global arena. Nadel categorizes 1950s America as a "containment culture," that is, one that strives to contain anxieties about the stability of categories of gender, class, race, and other areas of difference (xi, 3). The 1950s, he says, was a decade in which "'conformity' became a positive value in and of itself" (4).

3 Gillan 2010, 181–200.

4 Boddy (1993) provides an overview of the new consumer market for television advertising.

5 Consumer spending on automobiles, according to Marling (1994, 140–5), had grown from $22 billion in 1950 to $65 billion in 1956.

6 Bird (1999) offers a particularly good analysis of time franchises in *Better Living*.

7 All the quotations from Caldwell in this section are from *Televisuality*, 1995, 117. Such stamping of ownership is even more complicated today when a variety of networks, media conglomerates, production companies, and sponsors want to stamp their ownership on a TV program.

8 Meehan (2005) argues that what's on television does not, as is often assumed, reflect some general good or bad taste of the public: "Because advertisers pay for time slots in programs, they are the primary customers of networks and channels; that makes programming a vehicle for advertising . . . Increasingly, the Big Five have treated programs as commercials—writing brand names into dialogue, using products to decorate sets, having actors hold products as props, and using a show's sound track to plug their recording artists" (5).

9 For these quotations from Hine, see *Populuxe*, 1986, 9, 3, 27.

10 The series aired on ABC as *Make Room for Daddy* from 1953–6. After the lead actress quit in a contract dispute, ABC made Danny a widower and renamed the sitcom, *The Danny Thomas Show* for 1956–7. For 1957, Danny had a new wife and stepdaughter and the series moved to CBS, where it finished its run in 1964.

11 As Chapter 3 demonstrates, this same "best of both worlds" claim is at the heart of Disney Channel's star sitcoms such as *Hannah Montana*.

12 This combination is why some scholars use the term television personality, I keep the term star as it makes it easier to talk about star sitcoms, but I recognize the problems with the term.

13 Negra (2002, 112) offers a compelling analysis of "residual stardom" in the case of Hedy Lamarr.

14 Donna Reed was a movie star as well, appearing as gentleman's club worker and the love interest of Montgomery Clift's character in *From Here to Eternity* (1953), a film for

which she won the Best Supporting Actress Academy Award. See an excellent analysis of the series by Morreale (2012).

15 Perhaps Ozzie Nelson chose the legal profession for his fictional sons because it was his own "road not taken." He earned a law degree, but had become a professional musician with a solid career even before his graduation.

16 Although many scholars touch on the limitations of such representations, two targeted studies are Maurice Manring, *Slave in a Box: The Strange Career of Aunt Jemima* (Charlottesville, VA: University of Virginia, 1998) and Marilyn Kern-Foxworth, *Aunt Jemima, Uncle Ben, and Rastus: Blacks in Advertising, Yesterday, Today, and Tomorrow* (Westport, CT: Praeger, 1995).

17 Pendergrast 2000, 272.

18 Samuel 2001, 153.

19 Pendergrast 2000, 272.

20 *Father Knows Best* was a traveler, a show that moved between networks, something that was more common in its era. Its network history is as follows: CBS 1954–5; NBC 1955–8; CBS 1958–60. It was already in syndication in its own time with CBS airing primetime reruns in 1960–2, followed by primetime reruns on ABC for 1962–3.

21 The connection between *The Donna Reed Show*'s low ratings and the limited range of the ABC network is addressed in Chapter 2.

22 Lipsitz briefly discusses the rent strike episode and the move to the suburbs. See *Time Passages*, 1990, 39.

23 Chevrolet continued to sell many cars when its time franchise was hosted by the covertly Jewish Dinah Shore. See Bratten 2002, 88–104.

24 Brook argues that when *The Goldbergs* was recreated as *Molly* for the 1955–6 season on the Dumont Network, it was essentially a new show (50, 56). It was also no longer a live television show, but was instead filmed for syndication. See also Jones 1992, 90.

25 Brook (1999) and Marc (1989) claim Haverville is meant to contrast to the Goldbergs' former have-not neighborhood in the Bronx. Of course, technically the Goldbergs already left the have-nots behind when they moved away from the Lower East Side. Also having at its center characters who combine bourgeois behavior and racial/ethnic stereotypes, *Amos 'n' Andy* proved too problematic for television with a CBS run that lasted only from 1951–3. Henry Louis Gates' memoir piece about how appealing he found the show because, despite its stereotyping, it had an all-black cast, suggests some of the complexities of the program's address. For more on the controversy surrounding the program, see Doherty 2003 and Cripps 2003.

26 For Gillan and Ponte (2005), I conceived of the phrase "beneficial family" as a play on the type of family formation historically rewarded in corporate benefits programs because it is also the one that U.S. TV programming has represented as the most beneficial, not only for the individuals living within it, but also for a nation comprised of millions of such households. In our law review article on corporate benefits programs, Lucille Ponte and I examined how and why this idea of the TV family ideal had a real world impact on the conceptualization of family benefits packages.

27 Molly's Bronx neighbors still carried with them some of the Hester Street emphasis on the bonds of mutuality that provided a safety net in times of personal or economic crisis, as suggested in one of the first Haverville episodes. Molly's family phones her former Bronx neighbor to tell her how miserable Molly is in the suburbs. Although the woman says that she is preparing for her granddaughter's birthday, she still puts her friend before her nuclear family and gets on a train and comes to visit. Her behavior suggests that *The Goldbergs* might be more representative of the extended ethnic

community and the kinds of social and political organizations with which it was associated. Berg once commented on trying to avoid controversial issues on the show: "I don't bring up anything that will bother people. That's very important. Unions, politics, fundraising, Zionism, socialism, inter-group relations. After all, aren't all such things secondary to daily family living" (41). For involvement in such organizations, Philip Loeb, the original TV Jake, was put on the Red Channels list. General Foods, the sponsor of the CBS seasons was certainly not pleased with the connection and tried to get Berg to fire him in 1950. When she refused, it kept sponsoring the show for the year and let its sponsorship lapse in 1951. Then CBS dropped the show despite the fact that it had been a hit and Sanka sales had risen 57 percent after being promoted on the show. When NBC snapped up the show the next year, it forced Berg to fire Loeb when it discovered the connection, and after it could find no one to sponsor the show until she did. For a history of these controversies see Doherty 2003, 37–48.

28 Lipsitz 1990, 40.
29 See Caldwell 2008.
30 Gerard Jones notes these sponsor changes in *Honey I'm Home!*, 1992, 104–7.
31 Halberstam (1993) discusses which cars went with which class levels on page 120.
32 Lizabeth Cohen (2003) and many other historians have noted that this change is connected to the circulation of the idea that Americans should think of themselves as citizen consumers.
33 Cohen examines how the suburbs and the material goods associated with them were linked to patriotism and national identity (1993, 194–213).
34 Coontz addresses the detrimental effects of overly idealized families on actual Americans and their views of their own families (1992, 27–8). It was also an era in which about 25 percent of all families lived in poverty and had no possibility of attaining the consumer family ideal. To gauge the salary differential, consider that Tom Raft, the character in the film version of *The Man in the Gray Flannel Suit*, is approximately at the economic level of the Andersons. During that 1956 film he is making $7,000, but as he climbs the corporate ladder and moves into a new job, he asks for $10,000. This climb would move him from the upper-middle class to the lower end of the high-income class. Hine explains the variation in middle-class economic and social levels, noting that "[t]he absolute number of high-income people, which *Fortune* defined as those making more than $7,500 annually in 1953 dollars, more than doubled from 1929 . . . . The biggest increase came in the number of families in the $4,000–$7,000 salary range, which was understood to be solidly middle class. There were 5.5 million families in this category in 1929, 17.9 million in 1953. They accounted for thirty-five percent of the nation's population."
35 Coontz 1992, 28, 27.
36 The 1950s primetime schedule also had workplace shows and westerns and was dominated by anthology programs, variety shows, and the infamous quiz shows.
37 Halberstam 1993, 120.
38 Advertising certainly has been narrowcast, Sivulka (1998) claims, "Advertising excluded not only African Americans but residents of ethnic urban neighborhoods, the single, the widowed, and single parents" (263).

Bibliography

Aaker, David. "Beyond Functional Benefits." *Marketing News*, September 30, 2009: 23.
Aaker, David and Enrich Joachimsthaler. "The Brand Relationship Spectrum: The Key to the Brand Architecture Challenge." *California Management Review* 42, no. 4 (Summer 2000): 8–23.

"ABC-TV's 'Get 'em Young': Major Payoff in Kid Accent." *Variety*, March 23, 1955: 21, 38.

Alvey, Mark. "The Independents: Rethinking the Television Studio System." In *The Revolution Wasn't Televised: Sixties Television and Social Conflict*, eds. Lynn Spigel and Michael Curtin, 139–58. New York, NY: Routledge, 1997.

Anderson, Benedict. *Imagined Communities: Reflections on the Origin and Spread of Nationalism*. New York, NY: Verso, 1983.

Anderson, Christopher. "Creating the Twenty-first-Century Television Network: NBC in the Age of Media Conglomerates." In Hilmes 2007, 275–90.

———. *Hollywood TV: The Studio System in the Fifties*. Austin, TX: University of Texas Press, 1994.

Aucoin, Don. "Why the Dr. Is Out: Advertisers, Not Viewers, Dictate Which Shows Live and Which Die." *The Boston Globe*, May 29, 1998, C1.

Banet-Weiser, Sarah. *Authentic: The Politics of Ambivalence in a Brand Culture*. New York, NY: New York University Press, 2012.

———. *Kids Rule!: Nickelodeon and Consumer Citizenship*. Durham, NC: Duke University Press, 2007.

Barnouw, Erik. *The Sponsor: Notes on a Modern Potentate*. New York, NY: Oxford, 1979.

———. *Tube of Plenty: The Evolution of American Television*, 2nd edition. Oxford, UK: Oxford University Press, 1990.

Bauer, Douglas, ed. *Prime Times: Writers on Their Favorite TV Shows*. New York, NY: Crown, 2004.

Baughman, James L. *Same Time, Same Station: Creating American Television, 1948–1961*. Baltimore, MD: The John Hopkins University Press, 2007.

Becker, Ron. *Gay TV in Straight America*. New Brunswick, NJ: Rutgers University Press, 2006.

Bennet, James. *Television Personalities: Stardom and the Small Screen*. New York, NY: Routledge, 2011.

Berlant, Lauren. *The Queen of America Goes to Washington City: Essays on Sex and Citizenship*, Durham, NC: Duke University Press, 1997.

Best, Natalie, "Ozzie Nelson Takes His Family to TV!" *TV Trade News*, September 1952: 13. Available in The Hal Humphrey Collection at the University of Southern California Cinema-Television Library.

Bird, Elizabeth S. *The Audience in Everyday Life: Living in a Media World*. New York, NY: Routledge, 2003.

Bird, Jr., William L. "*Better Living:" Advertising, Media, and the New Vocabulary of Business Leadership*. Evanston, IL: Northwestern University Press, 1999.

Boddy, William. *Fifties Television: The Industry and its Critics*. Urbana and Chicago, IL: University of Illinois Press, 1993.

———. "New Media as Old Media: Television." In Harries 2002, 242–53.

———. *New Media and Popular Imagination: Launching Radio, Television, and Digital Media in the United States*. Oxford, UK: Oxford University Press, 2004.

Bodroghkozy, Aniko. *Groove Tube: Sixties Television and the Youth Rebellion*. Durham, NC: Duke University Press, 2001.

Bratten, Lola Clare. "Nothin' Could be Finah: *The Dinah Shore Chevy Show*." In Thumim 2002, 88–104.

Broadcasting & Cable. "A Strategy for Stemming the Slide." *Broadcasting & Cable*, May 20, 2002: 21.

Brook, Vincent "The Americanization of Molly: How Mid-Fifties TV Homogenized *The Goldbergs* (and Got 'Berg-larized' In the Process)." *Cinema Journal* 38, no. 4 (Summer 1999): 45–67.

Brooks, Tim and Earle Marsh. *The Complete Directory to Primetime Network and Cable TV Shows: 1946–Present*. 8th edition. New York, NY: Ballantine, 2003.

Brown, Les. *Television the Business behind the Box*. New York, NY: Harcourt Brace Jovanovitch, 1971.

Butler, Judith. *Gender Trouble*. New York, NY: Routledge, 1990.

Caldwell, John Thornton. "Convergence Television: Aggregating Form and Repurposing Content in the Culture of Conglomeration." In Spigel and Olsson 2004, 41–74.

——. "Critical Industrial Practice: Branding, Repurposing, and the Migratory Patterns of Industrial Texts." *Television & New Media* 7, no. 2 (May 2006): 99–134.

——. *Production Culture: Industrial Reflexivity and Critical Practice in Film and Television*. Durham, NC: Duke University Press, 2008.

——. *Televisuality: Style, Crisis, and Authority in American Television*. New Brunswick, NJ: Rutgers University Press, 1995.

——. "Welcome to the Viral Future of Cinema (Television)." *Cinema Journal* 45, no. 1 (Fall 2006): 90–7.

Carter, Paul A. *Another Part of the Fifties*. New York, NY: Columbia University Press. 1983.

Cashmore, Ellis. *. . . And There Was Television*. New York, NY and London, UK: Routledge, 1994.

Castleman, Harry and Walter J. Podrazik. *Harry and Wally's Favorite TV Shows*. New York, NY: Prentice Hall, 1989.

——. *The TV Schedule Book: Four Decades of Network Programming from Sign on to Sign off*. New York, NY: McGraw-Hill, 1984.

——. *Watching TV: Six Decades of American Television*. Syracuse, NY: Syracuse University Press, 2003.

Caves, Richard E. *Creative Industries: Contracts between Art and Commerce*. Cambridge, MA: Harvard University Press, 2000.

Chang, Lan Samantha. "Like Robinson Crusoe." In Bauer 2004, 121–30.

Cheever, Susan. "Father Knows Best." In Bauer, 2004, 45–51.

Cohen, Lizabeth. *A Consumer's Republic: The Politics of Mass Consumption in Postwar America*. New York, NY: Vintage/Random House, 2003.

Collins, Gail. *When Everything Changed: The Amazing Journey of American Women from 1960 to the Present*. New York, NY: Little, Brown and Company, 2009.

Coontz, Stephanie. *The Way We Never Were: American Families and the Nostalgia Trap*. New York, NY: Basic Books, 1992.

Cripps, Thomas. "*Amos 'n' Andy* and the Debate Over Racial Integration." In *Critiquing the Sitcom: A Reader*, ed. Joanne Morreale, 25–40. Syracuse, NY: Syracuse University Press, 2003.

Davis, Aeron. *Promotional Cultures: The Rise and Spread of Advertising, Public Relations, Marketing and Branding*. Cambridge, UK: Polity Press, 2013.

DeCordova, Richard. *Picture Personalities: the Emergence of the Star System in America*. Urbana, IL: University of Illinois Press, 1990.

Deery, June. *Consuming Reality: The Commercialization of Factual Entertainment*. New York, NY: Palgrave Macmillan, 2012.

——. "Reality TV as Advertainment." *Popular Communication* 2, no. 1 (2004): 1–19.

Denis, Christopher Paul and Michael Denis. *Favorite Families of TV*. New York, NY: Citadel Press, 1992.

Dennis, Saul. "Brands Begin by Believing." *Promo Magazine* (June 2004): 121.

Desjardin, Mary. "Lucy and Desi: Sexuality, Ethnicity, and TV's First Family." In *Television, History, and American Culture*, eds. Mary Beth Haralovich and Lauren Rabinowitz, 56–74. Durham, NC: Duke University Press, 1999.

Deuze, Mark. "Convergence Culture in the Creative Industries." *International Journal of Cultural Studies* 10, no. 2 (2007): 243–63

———. *Media Work*. Cambridge, UK: Polity, 2007.

Doherty, Thomas. *Cold War, Cool Medium: Television, McCarthyism, and American Culture*. New York, NY: Columbia University Press, 2003.

———. *Teenagers and Teenpics: The Juvenilization of American Movies in the 1950s*. Boston, MA: Unwin Hyman, 1988.

Donaton, Scott. *Madison and Vine: Why the Entertainment and Advertising Industries Must Converge to Survive*. New York, NY: McGraw-Hill, 2005.

Doty, Alexander. "The Cabinet of Lucy Ricardo: Lucille Ball's Star Image." *Cinema Journal 29*, no.4 (Summer 1990): 11.

Douglas, Susan J. *Where the Girls Are: Growing Up Female with the Mass Media*. New York, NY: Times, 1995.

Dyer, Richard. *Stars*. London, UK: BFI Publishing, 1986.

Eckert, Charles. "The Carole Lombard in Macy's Window." In *Fabrications: Costume and the Female Body*, eds. Jane Gaines and Charlotte Herzog, 100–21. New York, NY: Routledge, 1990.

Elliot, Stuart. "Madison Avenue Likes What it Sees in the Mirror." *New York Times* June 23, 2008. Available: www.nytimes.com/2008/06/23/business/media/23adcol.html.

———. "What Was Old is New as TV Revisits Branding." *New York Times*, June 13, 2007. Available: http://query.nytimes.com/gst/fullpage.html?res=9B01E1D6173FF930A25755C0A9619C8B63&sec=&spon=&pagewanted=all.

Ellis, John. "Interstitials: How the 'Bits in Between' Define the Programmes." In Grainge 2011, 59–69.

———. "Scheduling: the Last Creative Act in Television?" *Media, Culture and Society* 22, no. 1 (2000): 25–38.

———. "Stars as a Cinematic Phenomenon." In *Stardom and Celebrity: A Reader*, eds. Sean Redmond and Su Holmes, 90–7. London, UK: Sage, 1982.

Feuer, Jane. "The Concept of Live Television: Ontology as Ideology." In *Regarding Television: Critical Approaches—An Anthology*, ed. E. Ann Kaplan, 12–21. Los Angeles, CA: The American Film Institute, 1983

Feuer, Jane, Paul Kerr, and Tise Vahimagi. *MTM: "Quality Television."* London, UK: BFI Publishing, 1984.

Finkle, Jim. "New Shows, New Marketing." *Broadcasting & Cable*, February 21, 2005: 8.

Frank, Thomas. *The Conquest of Cool: Business Culture, Counterculture, and the Rise of Hip Consumerism*. Chicago, IL: University of Chicago Press, 1997.

Friedberg, Anne. "The Virtual Window." In Thornburn and Jenkins 2004, 337–53.

Gaines, Jane. "Costume and Narrative: How Dress Tells the Woman's Story." In *Fabrications: Costume and the Female Body*, eds. Jane Gaines and Charlotte Herzog, 180–211. New York, NY: Routledge, 1990.

Gertner, Jon. "Our Ratings, Ourselves." *New York Times Magazine*, April 10, 2005: 34.

Gillan, Jennifer. "From Ozzie Nelson to Ozzy Osbourne: the Genesis and Development of the Reality (Star) Sitcom." In *Understanding Reality Television*, eds. Su Holmes and Deborah Jermyn, 54–70. London, UK: Routledge, 2004.

———. *Television and New Media: Must-Click TV*. New York, NY: Routledge, 2010.

Gillan, Jennifer and Lucille Ponte. "*From Our Family to Yours*: Rethinking the 'Beneficial Family' and Marriage-centric Corporate Benefit Programs." *Columbia Journal of Gender & the Law* 14, no. 2 (Summer 2005): 1–85.

Gillan, Maria Mazziotti. "Daddy, We Called You" and "Learning Silence." In *Identity Lessons: Contemporary Writing about Learning to Be American*, eds. Maria Mazziotti Gillan and Jennifer Gillan. New York, NY: Penguin Books. 1999.

Gitlin, Todd . *Inside Prime Time*. New York, NY: Routledge, 1985.

Gledhill, Christine, ed. *Stardom: Industry of Desire*. London, UK: Routledge, 1991.

Gobé, Marc. *Brandjam: Humanizing Brands Through Emotional Design*. New York, NY: Allworth Press, 2007.

Gomery, Douglas. *A History of Broadcasting in the United States*. London, UK: Blackwell, 2008.

———. *The Hollywood Studio System: A History*. Berkeley, CA: University of California Press, 2005. Expanded and revised from New York, NY: St. Martin's, 1986.

———. "Talent Raids and Package Deals: NBC Loses Its Leadership in the 1950s." In Hilmes 2007, 153–68.

Grainge, Paul. *Brand Hollywood: Selling Entertainment in a Global Media Age*. New York, NY: Routledge, 2008.

———. ed. *Ephemeral Media: Transitory Screen Culture from Television to YouTube*. London, UK: BFI, 2011.

———. "TV Promotion and Broadcast Design: An Interview with Charlie Mawer, Red Bee Media." In Grainge 2011, 87–101.

Gray, Herman. *Cultural Moves: African Americans and the Politics of Representation*. Berkeley, CA: University of California Press, 2005.

Gray, Jonathan. *Show Sold Separately: Promos, Spoilers, and Other Media Paratexts*. New York, NY: New York University Press, 2010.

———. "Television Pre-views and the Meaning of Hype." *International Journal of Cultural Studies*, 11, no. 1 (2008): 33–49.

Gripsrud, Jostein. "Broadcast Television: The Chances of Its Survival in a Digital Age." In Spigel and Olsson 2004, 210–23.

Halberstam, David. *The Fifties*. New York, NY: Villard, 1993.

Hamamoto, Darrell Y. *Nervous Laughter: Television Situation Comedy and Liberal Democratic Ideology*. New York, NY: Praeger, 1991.

Haralovich, Mary Beth. "Sit-coms and Suburbs: Positioning the 1950's Homemaker." In Spigel and Mann 1992, 111–41.

Harries, Dan, ed. *The New Media Book*. London, UK: BFI Publishing, 2002.

Hartley, John. *The Uses of Television*. New York, NY: Routledge, 1999.

Hill, Annette. "Big Brother, the Real Audience." *Television & New Media* 3, no. 3 (August 2002): 323–40.

Hills, Matt. "*Dawson's Creek*: 'Quality Teen TV' and 'Mainstream Cult?'" In *Teen TV: Genre, Consumption and Identity*, eds. Glyn Davis and Kay Dickinson, 54–67. London, UK: BFI Publishing, 2004.

———. *Fan Cultures*. New York, NY: Routledge, 2002.

Hilmes, Michele. *Hollywood and Broadcasting: From Radio to Cable*. Urbana, IL: University of Illinois Press, 1990.

———, ed. *NBC: America's Network*. Berkeley, CA: University of California Press, 2007.

———. *Only Connect: A Cultural History of Broadcasting in the US*, 2nd edition. Belmont, CA: Wadsworth, 2008.

——. *Radio Voices: American Broadcasting, 1992–1952.* Minneapolis, MN: University of Minnesota Press, 1997.

Hilmes, Michele and Jason Jacobs, eds. *The Television History Book.* London, UK: BFI Publishing, 2004.

Hine, Thomas. *Populuxe.* New York, NY: Knopf, 1986.

Holt, Douglas B. *How Brands Become Icons: Principles of Cultural Branding.* Boston, MA: Harvard Business School Press, 2004.

Holt, Douglas B. and Douglas Cameron. *Cultural Strategy: Using Innovative Ideologies to Build Breakthrough Brands.* Oxford, UK: Oxford University Press, 2010.

Holt, Jennifer. "Vertical Vision: Deregulation, Industrial Economy and Prime-time Design." In Jancovich and Lyons 2003, 11–31.

Holt, Jennifer and Alisa Perren, eds. *Media Industries: History, Theory, and Method.* Malden, MA: Wiley-Blackwell, 2009.

Jancovich, Mark and James Lyons, eds. *Quality Popular Television.* London, UK: BFI Publishing, 2003.

Jenkins, Henry. *Convergence Culture: Where Old and New Media Collide.* New York, NY: New York University Press, 2006.

Jenkins, Henry and David Thornburn, eds. *Democracy and New Media.* Cambridge, MA: MIT Press, 2003.

Jenkins, Henry, Sam Ford, and Joshua Green. *Spreadable Media: Creating Value and Meaning in a Networked Culture.* New York, NY: New York University Press, 2013.

Johnson, Catherine. *Branding Television.* New York, NY: Routledge, 2012.

——. "Tele-branding in TVIII: the Network as Brand and the Programme as Brand." *New Review of Film and Television Studies* 5, no. 1 (2007): 5–24.

Johnson, Victoria E. *Heartland TV: Primetime Television and the Struggle for U.S. Identity.* New York, NY: New York University Press, 2008.

Jones, Gerard. *Honey, I'm Home! Sitcoms: Selling the American Dream.* New York, NY: Basic Books, 1992.

Kamp, David. "Rethinking the American Dream." *Vanity Fair* (April 2009): 118–23, 177–80.

Keats, John. *The Crack in the Picture Window.* Boston, MA: Houghton Mifflin, 1957.

Keply, Vance Jr., "From 'Frontal Lobes' to the 'Bob-and-Bob Show': NBC Management and Programming Strategies, 1949–65." In *Hollywood in the Age of Television*, ed. Tino Balio, 41–62. Boston, MA: Unwin Hyman, 1990.

Klein, Naomi. *No Logo.* New York, NY: Picador, 2002.

Klinger, Barbara. *Beyond the Multiplex: Cinema, New Technologies, and the Home.* Berkeley, CA: University of California Press, 2006.

——. "Digressions at the Cinema: Reception and Mass Culture." *Cinema Journal* 28 no. 4 (1989): 3–19.

Kompare, Derek. "I've Seen This One Before: The Construction of 'Classic TV' on Cable Television." In Thumim 2002, 19–34.

——. *Rerun Nation: How Repeats Invented American Television.* New York, NY: Routledge, 2005.

Kozinets, Robert V. "E-tribalized Marketing?: The Strategic Implications of Virtual Communities of Consumption." *European Management Journal* 17, no. 3 (June 1999): 252–64.

Kunz, William. *Culture Conglomerates: Consolidation in the Motion Picture and Television Industries.* Lanham, MD: Rowman and Littlefield, 1997.

Langer, John. "Television's 'Personality System.'" *Media Culture & Society* 4 (1981). Reprinted in Marshall, 2006, 181–95.

Landay, Lori. *I Love Lucy*. Detroit, MI: Wayne State University Press, 2010.

Leibman, Nina C. *Living Room Lectures: The Fifties Family in Film & Television*. Austin, TX: University of Texas Press, 1995.

Lipsitz, George. "The Meaning of Memory: Family, Class, and Ethnicity in Early Network Television Programs." In Spigel and Mann 1992, 71–108.

———. *Time Passages: Collective Memory and American Popular Culture*. Minneapolis, MN: University of Minnesota Press, 1990.

Lotz, Amanda. "How to Spend $9.3 Billion in Three Days: Examining the Upfront Buying Process in the Production of US Television Culture." *Media, Culture and Society* 29, no.4 (2007): 549–67.

———. *The Television Will Be Revolutionized*. New York, NY: New York University Press, 2007.

"Madison Ave.'s Program Taboos." *Variety*, October 26, 1960.

Mann, Denise. "The Spectacularization of Everyday Life: Recycling Hollywood Stars and Fans in Early Television Variety Shows." In Spigel Mann 1992, 41–69.

Marc, David. *Comic Visions: Television Comedy and American Culture*. Boston. MA: Unwin Hyman, 1989.

———. *Demographic Vistas: Television in American Culture*. Philadelphia, PA, University of Pennsylvania Press, 1984.

Marchand, Roland. *Advertising and the American Dream: Making Way for Modernity, 1920–1940*. Berkeley, CA: University of California Press, 1986

Marling, Karal Ann. *As Seen On TV: The Visual of Everyday Life in the 1950s*. Cambridge, MA: Harvard University Press, 1994.

Marshall, P. David. "Introduction." *Celebrity Culture Reader*, 1–20. New York, NY: Routledge, 2006.

Mashon, Mike. "NBC, J. Walter Thompson, and the Struggle for Control of Television Programming, 1946–58." In Hilmes 2007, 135–52.

Mayne, Judith. *Cinema and Spectatorship*. London, UK: Routledge, 1993.

McAllister, Matthew. *The Commercialization of American Culture: New Advertising, Control, and Democracy*. Thousand Oaks, CA: Sage, 1996.

———. "Television Advertising as Textual and Economic Systems." In *A Companion to Television*, ed. Janet Wasko, 217–37. Oxford, UK: Wiley-Blackwell Publishing, 2005.

McCarthy, Anna. *The Citizen Machine: Governing by Television in 1950s America*. New York, NY: New Press, 2010.

McCracken, Grant. *Culture and Consumption II: Markets, Meaning, and Brand Management*. Bloomington, IN: Indiana University Press, 2005.

McDonald, Paul. *The Star System: Hollywood's Production of Popular Identities*. London, UK: Wallflower, 2000.

McLean, Adrienne. *Being Rita Hayworth: Labor, Identity, and Hollywood Stardom*. New Brunswick, NJ: Rutgers University Press, 2004.

Meehan, Eileen. *Why Television is Not Our Fault: Television Programming, Viewers, and Who's Really in Control*. Lanham, MD: Rowman and Littlefield, 2005.

———. "Why We Don't Count: The Commodity Audience." In *Logics of Television: Essays in Cultural Criticism*, ed. Patricia Mellencamp, 117–37. Bloomington, IN: Indiana University Press, 1990.

Mellencamp, Patricia. "Situation Comedy, Feminism, and Freud: Discourses of Gracie and Lucy." In Morreale 2012, 41–55.

Metz, Walter. *Bewitched*. Detroit, MI: Wayne State University Press, 2007.

Miller, Douglas T. and Marion Nowak. *The Fifties: The Way We Really Were*. Garden City, NY: Doubleday, 1977.

Miller, Margo. "The Bob Cummings Show's 'Artist's At Work': Gender Transitive Programming and Counterpublicity." *Spectator* 28, no. 1 (Spring 2008): 10–28.

Mittell, Jason. "Generic Cycles: Innovation, Imitation, and Saturation." In Hilmes and Jacobs 2004, 44–9.

——. *Genre and Television: From Cop Shows to Cartoons in American Culture*. New York, NY: Routledge, 2004.

Morreale, Joanne. *The Donna Reed Show*. Detroit, MI: Wayne State University Press, 2012.

Mullen, Megan. "'Surfing through TVLand': Notes toward a Theory of 'Video Bites' and their Function on Cable TV." *Velvet Light Trap* 36 (1995): 60–8.

Murray, Simone. "Brand Loyalties: Rethinking Content within Global Corporate Media." *Media, Culture, Society* 27, no. 3 (2005): 415–35.

Murray, Susan. *Hitch Your Antenna to the Stars: Early Television and Broadcast Stardom*. New York, NY: Routledge, 2005.

Nadel, Alan. *Containment Culture: American Narratives, Postmodernism, and the Atomic Age*. Durham, NC: Duke University Press, 1995.

Napoli, Philip M. *Audience Economics: Media Institutions and the Audience Marketplace*. New York, NY: Columbia University Press, 2003.

Negra, Diane. "Re-Made for Television: Hedy Lamarr's Post-War Star Textuality." In Thumim 2002, 105–17.

Nelson, Ozzie. *Ozzie*. New York, NY: Prentice Hall, 1973.

Newcomb, Horace M. and Robert S. Alley. *The Producer's Medium*. New York, NY: Oxford University Press, 1983.

Oswald, Laura R. *Marketing Semiotics: Signs, Strategies, and Brand Value*. Oxford, UK: Oxford University Press, 2012.

Ouellette, Laurie and James Hay, *Better Living Through Reality TV: Television and Post-Welfare Citizenship*. Malden, MA: Blackwell, 2008.

"Performer or Pitchman?" *Variety*, November 11, 1953: 31.

Pendergrast, Mark. *For God Country and Coca-Cola*. New York, NY: Basic Books 2000.

Sampson, Anthony. *Company Man: The Rise and Fall of Corporate Life*. New York, NY: Random House/Times Business, 1995.

Samuel, Lawrence R. *Brought to You By: Postwar Television Advertising and The American Dream*. Austin, TX: University of Texas Press, 2001

Sanders, Coyne S. and Tom Gilbert. *Desilu: The Story of Lucille Ball and Desi Arnaz*. New York, NY: William and Morrow, 1993.

Sandler, Kevin. "*Modern Family*: Product Placement." In *How to Watch Television*. eds. Ethan Thompson and Jason Mittell. 253–61. New York, NY: New York University Press, 2013.

Schatz, Thomas. "Desilu, I Love Lucy, and the Rise of Network TV." In *Making Television: Authorship and the Production Process*, eds. Robert J. Thompson and Gary Burns, 117–35. New York, NY: Praeger, 1990.

——. "The New Hollywood. "In *Film Theory Goes to the Movies*, eds. Jim Collins, Hilary Radner and Ava Preacher Collins, 8–36. London, UK: Routledge, 1993.

Sella, Marshall. "The Remote Controllers." *New York Times Magazine*, October 20, 2002. 68+.

Shattuc, Jane M. "Television Production: Who Makes American TV?" In *A Companion to Television*, ed. Janet Wasko, 142–54. Oxford, UK: Blackwell, 2005.

Shrum, L.J. *The Psychology of Entertainment Media: Blurring the Lines Between Entertainment and Persuasion.* New York, NY: Routledge, 2012.

Sivulka, Juliann. *Soap, Sex, and Cigarettes: A Cultural History of American Advertising.* Belmont, CA: Wadsworth Publishing Company, 1998.

Soto, Gary. "Looking for Work." In *Growing Up Ethnic in America: Contemporary Fiction about Learning to Be American*, eds. Maria Mazziotti Gillan and Jennifer Gillan, 32–8, New York, NY: Penguin Books, 1999.

Spigel, Lynn. *Make Room for TV: Television and the Family Ideal in Postwar America.* Chicago, IL: University of Chicago Press, 1992.

——. *Welcome to the Dream House: Popular Media and Postwar Suburbs.* Durham, NC: Duke University Press, 2001.

Spigel, Lynn and Denise Mann, eds. *Private Screenings: Television and the Female Consumer.* Minneapolis, MN: University of Minnesota Press, 1992.

Spigel, Lynn and Jan Olsson, eds. *Television After TV: Essays on a Medium in Transition.* Durham, NC: Duke University Press, 2004.

Stacey, Jackie. *Star Gazing: Hollywood Cinema and Female Spectatorship.* London, UK: Routledge, 1994.

Streeter, Thomas. *Selling the Air: A Critique of the Policy of Commercial Broadcasting in the United States.* Chicago, IL: University of Chicago Press, 1996.

Stuever, Hank. "The Best and Worst of 2009: TV." *Washington Post*, December 20, 2009. Available: www.washingtonpost.com /wp-dyn/content/article/2009/12/18/AR2009121800193.html.

Tasker, Yvonne and Diane Negra. "In Focus: Postfeminism and Contemporary Media Studies." *Cinema Journal* 44 (2005):107–10.

Taylor, Ella. *Prime Time Families: Television Culture in Postwar America.* Berkeley, CA: University of California, 1989.

Taylor, Timothy D. *The Sounds of Capitalism: Advertising, Music, and the Conquest of Culture.* Chicago, IL: The University of Chicago Press, 2012.

Thornburn, David and Henry Jenkins, eds. *Rethinking Media Change: The Aesthetics of Transition*, Cambridge, MA: MIT Press, 2004.

Thumim, Janet, ed. *Small Screens, Big Ideas: Television in the 1950s.* London, UK: I.B. Tauris, 2002.

Turow, Joseph. *Breaking Up America: Advertisers and the New Media World.* Chicago, IL: University of Chicago Press, 1997.

——. *Niche Envy: Marketing Discrimination in the Digital Age.* Cambridge, MA: MIT Press, 2006.

Ulin, Jeffery C. *The Business of Media Distribution: Monetizing Film, TV, and Video Content in an Online World.* 2nd edition. New York, NY: Focal Press, 2014.

Uricchio, William. "Historicizing Media in Transition." In Thornburn and Jenkins 2004, 23–38.

——. "Old Media and New Media: Television." In Harries 2002, 219–30.

——. "Television's Next Generation: Technology/Interface Culture/Flow." In Spigel and Olsson 2004, 163–82.

Vogel, Harold. *Entertainment Industry Economics: A Guide for Financial Analysts.* 7th edition. New York, NY: Cambridge University Press, 2007.

Wasko, Janet. *How Hollywood Works.* Thousand Oaks, CA: Sage, 2003.

Weber, David. "Memory and Repression in Early Ethnic Television: The Example of Gertrude Berg and *The Goldbergs*." In *The Other Fifties: Interrogating Midcentury American Icons*, 144–67. Urbana, IL: University of Illinois Press, 1997.

Weisblat, Tinky, "What Ozzie Did for a Living." *Velvet Light Trap* 33 (Spring 1994).

Weisman, Jon. "'Modern Family' is a 'Cosby' Celebre." *Variety*, October 21, 2010.

Weiss, Jessica. *To Have and to Hold: Marriage, the Baby Boom & Social Change*. Chicago, IL: University of Chicago Press, 2000.

Wernick, Andrew. "Vehicles for Myth: the Shifting Image of the American Car." In *Cultural Politics in Contemporary America*, eds. Ian Angus and Sut Jhally, 198–216. New York, NY: Routledge, 1989.

Williams, Raymond. *Television, Technology and Cultural Forms*. London, UK: Fontana, 1974.

Witchel, Alex "'Mad Men' Has its Moment." *New York Times Magazine*. June 22, 2008. Available: www.nytimes.com/2008/06/22/magazine/22madmen-t.html?partner=permalink&exprod=permalink.

Wyatt, Justin. *High Concept: Movies and Marketing in Hollywood*. Austin, TX: University of Texas Press, 1994.

Zimmerman, Shirley. *Family Policies and Family Well-Being: The Role of Political Culture*. Newbury Park, CA: Sage, 1992.

2

NARROWCASTING SCHEDULES AND STARS

2.1   Narrowcast Broadcasting

Scheduling is an industry practice that is incorrectly perceived to have changed completely in the post-network era. While the U.S. schedule itself has certainly expanded exponentially, many core elements of scheduling logic have remained constant since the 1960s. More to the point, schedule-related elements that are typically characterized as a byproduct of the current multiplatform television industry have parallels in the United States' three-network schedule when CBS, NBC, and ABC competed with each other for the highest ratings. Those ratings allowed the winning network to sell to advertisers the idea that its programs would reach the most potential consumers. It has been taken for granted that networks did not get in the business of narrowcasting to niche audiences or building of distinct channel brands around those niches until the post-network era of the 1990s. At that time the power of the three-network system was displaced in the expanding U.S. channel spectrum.

Looking closely at some ABC schedules of the 1960s and 1970s, however, indicates that the network engaged in narrowcasting on some of its weeknight schedules and, in doing so, ventured into a nascent form of channel branding. Of course, channel branding is more evident today on basic cable channels. Premium channels are technically generalists, but Showtime leaned toward a more precise channel brand when it specialized in bleak comedies and was perceived to be narrowcasting through a cycle of half-hour series that featured women in the lead roles. While journalists critiqued the schedule for being redundant, Showtime did convey a clear brand identity in the marketplace when its schedule included female-headed "bleak comedies" such as *Weeds*, *Nurse Jackie*, *The Big C*, and *United States of Tara*.

Instead of looking at such series only as stand-alone creative works or as registers of cultural assumptions, we also can consider them as part of a series cycle emblematic of Showtime's brandcasting at the level of its schedule pairings. In "Scheduling: The Last Creative Act in Television?" John Ellis makes a compelling case for studying the overlooked industry practice of scheduling. If we consider the "architecture of the entire output" of a single channel, he argues, we can find a brand identity embedded not only within the choice of programs, but also in the way they are placed in a "recognized pattern" designed to attract specific audiences. Although Ellis is only talking about channels within the current brandcentric context, his assertion that even generalist channels have brands is applicable to ABC of the 1960s and 1970s as well as today. "The brand of all generalist channels," Ellis explains, "lies in the schedule and how that schedule is known by their client audiences."[1]

By way of exemplifying these points, I begin with an analysis of how in the late 2000s Showtime began to differentiate its channel brand through a narrowcast inflection to its cycle of "bleak comedies" and comedy/drama hybrids. The scheduling of *Weeds* is of particular note because it acted as a lead-in or lead-out for some of Showtime's signature series such as *Californication*, *The Big C*, and *Nurse Jackie* during the 2005–11 period when the premium cable channel's tagline was, *TV. At Its Best*. The disparaged position of mid-2000s Showtime in relation to HBO prior to this successful series cycle parallels the position of 1960s ABC in relation to CBS and NBC. The body of the chapter looks at key schedules through which ABC differentiated itself and the kinds of channel branding it utilized in the 1960s prior to achieving its first time at the top of the ratings in the mid-1970s. Building to that discussion the chapter offers an overview of scheduling logic and logistics on the U.S. broadcast networks.

2.2 Showtime's "Bleak Comedy" Schedule Pairs

In a dramatized promotion for Showtime's pairing of its hit series *Weeds* with newcomer *The Big C*, the lead female characters of each meet at a fence, and the visuals embody the fact that the two series are housed next to each other on the schedule. The distinctiveness of each series is signaled by the California hillside desert terrain on Nancy Botwin's side of the fence, and the rolling green grass of Midwestern suburbia on Cathy Jamison's side. When Nancy compliments Cathy on her grass, it is both a joke about the fact that Nancy deals "grass" and an implied commentary on their rebellion against the surface politeness and interactions associated with the suburbs. Both series imply that these women were raised to believe in the importance of acquiring their own personal patches of grass in suburban America. Then, through an unexpected life circumstance (Cathy's cancer diagnosis and the sudden death of Nancy's husband), each is forced to reevaluate her old life as an outsider might. Obviously, the "nice grass" compliment is indicative of the kind of over-the-fence conversation many suburbanites have with their neighbors. The humorous payoff for a viewer of *The Big C* is that Cathy has a battle with her neighbor Marlene over uncut grass. Cathy's outburst at Marlene over the grass is retaliation for complaints Marlene made to the city over Cathy's unfilled swimming pool hole in her lackluster yard.

season premiere | series premiere
weeds | the big C
monday august 16
starting 10 | 9c

FIGURE 2.1 A dramatized schedule promotion for Showtime's pairing of its hit series *Weeds* with newcomer *The Big C*. The promotion visualizes the call-to-action: fans of *Weeds* and Nancy Botwin (right) should embrace *The Big C* and Cathy Jamison (left).

Cathy and Marlene soon become unlikely friends and this promo suggests Cathy and Nancy would be friends as well if they occupied the same fictional universe. In the dramatization, Cathy and Nancy vent to each other about their crappy lives and about their needy (and often useless) family members. Then Cathy stops to marvel, "You really get me!" Nancy and Cathy hug and come together in a way suburban neighbors typically do not. Through its schedule pairing, Showtime was hoping that viewers would feel the same way and embrace Cathy as they had already embraced Nancy. In other words, the dramatized promotion visualized the desired call-to-action: viewers who already watched *Weeds* should tune-in to *The Big C*, after all, it was already Nancy-approved.

The dramatized promotion is a literal representation of the relationship of the two series on the schedule and the role that Nancy Botwin and *Weeds* play in attracting viewers who it can then deliver to new series. *Weeds* proved quite successful in that regard, even acting as a lead-in to *Nurse Jackie* in 2009, which then was successfully paired with Emmy-winning *United States of Tara* for 2010. (see Schedule 2.1).

The three series are also emblematic of both a general "bleak comedy" series cycle that includes shows like *Californication* and of a more narrowcast subgroup of female-helmed bleak comedies. Of the success of the latter series, *The Independent* claimed that Showtime began to win Emmys because it gave actresses the chance to take "on the sort of flawed, amoral roles traditionally embraced by men." Robert Greenblatt's assessment of Hank Moody from *Californication* does apply equally well to Nancy Botwin of *Weeds* and most lead characters in Showtime series in the period during which he was entertainment president. They were dark comedies in which "the main character has a few very serious flaws, yet is always striving to get it right."[2] Although Dexter Morgan, a police blood splatter specialist/serial killer, and the series named after him has received more

SCHEDULE 2.1 *Weeds* acts as lead-in for new series (N) on Showtime, launching *Nurse Jackie*, which later became a lead-in for other series.

	Showtime Schedule Pairings	
Years	Weeds (2007–12)	Nurse Jackie (2009–14)
2007	Californication (N)	—
2008	Secret Diary of a Call Girl (N)	—
2009	Nurse Jackie (N)	Weeds
2010	The Big C (N)	United States of Tara
2011	The Big C	United States of Tara
2012	Episodes	The Big C
2013	—	The Big C*
2014	—	Californication

*as a limited-run miniseries

press, Showtime's status as a premium cable channel airing Emmy-winning series was set in motion by the acquisition of *Weeds*, which then became the lead-in delivering audiences to a slate of other bleak comedies. In 2007, for instance, schedulers used "danger junkie" Nancy Botwin to introduce viewers to *Californication*'s Hank Moody, a sex addicted writer whom actor David Duchovny strove to make "relatable" despite the fact that Hank has "a kind of reprehensible quality."[3] Similarly, in the PBS documentary *America in Primetime*, Mary-Louise Parker described her character Nancy Botwin as "mildly intolerable," and, consequently, she was a delight to portray.

In 2006, Tim Goodman characterized *Weeds* as a series poised "to open the door for more great series, writers, and actors to flood into the Showtime family" and he correctly predicted that the series would help to propel Showtime into the "must-buy arena dominated by HBO." *Weeds* did so through its ability to be a promotional platform for new shows. In relation to scheduling, it is clear that Showtime understood how pairing an established and a new series on its schedule would be essential for its ability to launch new series.

Other journalists concurred that *Weeds* signaled a significant shift at Showtime. Scott Collins of *The Los Angeles Times* predicted in 2006 that the series "could prove a game changer for Showtime, which labored for years in the shadow of pay-cable rival HBO." The *Seattle Post-Intelligencer* was still calling Showtime itself second rate, a description also explicitly used or implied in most 2006 reviews. Yet, soon the tone changed after *Weeds* succeeded in being a lead-in for other series. Soon, *The Washington Post* was proclaiming, "All eyes are on Showtime."

Goodman was calling Showtime "Must-Pay-For-TV" in 2006. With the addition of some new series, it was "a new dawn for Showtime," according to *The Los Angeles Times*, which later declared the channel to have "the best shows on television." "Showtime's moment has arrived," said the *New York Post*, while *The New York Times* described its series as "impossible to resist." Saying the magic words for a subscription-funded channel, Goodman declared it was "Time To Get Showtime."

The scheduling of *Weeds* points to the hybrid function of television series, both as stand-alone entertainment brands and as promotional platforms. The strategic use of *Weeds* on the Showtime schedule in the mid-to-late 2000s highlights how a half-hour show has the most potential to serve as a lead-in, because it can drive tune-in and encourage viewers to stay around for the rest of the hour to sample other shows. Eventually, such a schedule cycle of similar series can cement an identity with viewers and advertisers. Brand identity is conveyed through a channel's choice of programs and in its "overall narrative patterns," as Philip Napoli puts it. Yet, he explains, it is also dependent on whether desired audiences recognize and value those patterns and connections.[4]

When it found success with its first critically acclaimed and buzzed about original series, Showtime was elated to achieve some program parity with its premium cable competitor. Once it had enough original series to contribute to a brand identity, the critical commentary about its fare being too formulaic began. Some assessments find Showtime wanting, both in terms of its narrowcast leanings toward female audiences and the popularity of its "'add Indie actress' and stir" black comedy formula for its original series. Rattled by some negative press, which faulted the channel for not having enough generalist reach (which translated to starring roles for men), Showtime added Don Cheadle in the bleak comedy *House of Lies*. It had already paired William H. Macy with Emmy Rossum for its dramedy *Shameless* and Mandy Patinkin with Claire Danes for *Homeland*. This trio of series was part of why in March 2012 *The Hollywood Reporter* was calling Showtime "cable's buzziest network" and describing its new schedule as a welcome change from the earlier series cycle of "half hours centered on damaged 40-something women." Writing for *The Atlantic*, Kevin Fallon said he did not mind the casting or tone of the half-hours, which were "at once warmly relatable and darkly humorous." He continued, "While it's easy to joke about Showtime's cookie-cutter mold, it's an undeniably successful formula for them. It's paid off." Even when the Gawker blog said Showtime specialized in "ladies in peril" or "ladies with problems" series, it did so with more affection than hostility.

The Hollywood Reporter commentary overlooks the role the half-hours had played in rebranding Showtime, which in the early 2000s was a premium cable channel that had been a non-contender in the original content arena. *Weeds* and *Nurse Jackie* generated buzz and, more significantly, could act as promotional platforms for new programs. Implying they work well as pairs, Fallon attributes Showtime's success at this time to the way the channel branded its series "around sexy, hot-button issues that draw in buzz and viewers—things like pill-popping nurses [*Nurse Jackie*], a suburban mom dealing pot [*Weeds*], multiple personalities [*United States of Tara*], refusing cancer treatments [*The Big C*]—and capitalize on that initial intrigue to create fully realized female characters."

Showtime first garnered substantial buzz in 2006 when *Dexter* was added to the schedule, giving Showtime a hip black comedy in *Weeds* paired with a "quality popular" drama that could challenge HBO by offering a fresh twist on the dysfunctional family business drama cycle embodied by *The Sopranos* and *Six Feet Under*. The latter series had just ended its run, leaving Michael C. Hall (David in *Six Feet Under*) free to sign on as the title character in *Dexter*. With the ending of *The Sopranos* in June 2007, HBO floundered to find its next hit. In that lull, Showtime began generating buzzworthy series. In 2007, Showtime used *Weeds* as a lead-in to its then new half-hour series *Californication*, which brought quality popular favorite David Duchovny from *The X-Files* back to TV and drew even more new subscribers to Showtime. Hank Moody's sexcapades would be countered with the British import *Secret Life of a Call Girl*, a series that would get a boost from *Weeds* as its lead-in during June 2008. *Six Feet Under* creator Alan Ball helped HBO strike back through the September 2008 premiere of *True Blood*. Ostensibly about vampires, the series was acclaimed for the gay rights parallels that could be found in its "newly out" vampires storylines. The series also made liberal use of a premium cable channel's ability to show nudity and graphic sex. Counterpunching, Showtime picked off *Sopranos* alum Edie Falco for its June 2009 series *Nurse Jackie*.

Falco joined a roster that included indie actress Toni Collette, who won the 2009 Lead Actress in a Comedy Emmy for her series *United States of Tara* (premiering in January 2009). Edie Falco followed with her 2010 Lead Actress in a Comedy Emmy for *Nurse Jackie*. The ultimate prestige prize came through terrorism drama *Homeland*, which took home Showtime's first Best Drama Emmy in 2012. Series star Claire Danes won the 2012 Emmy for Lead Actress in a Drama, and her costar Damien Lewis won the 2012 Best Lead Actor Emmy. Danes took home another Lead Actress Emmy for 2013 with *Nurse Jackie*'s Merritt Weaver winning Best Supporting Actress in a Comedy. The condensed format in which the final season of *The Big C* aired also enabled Linney to compete in a new category and win for 2013's Lead Actress in a Miniseries. All of these wins represent the fact that for a few years Showtime built its reputation for quality programming through series starring some of the most significant independent film actors. Their already established credentials helped drive up the Showtime subscriptions upon which its premium cable revenue model is based. By January 2014, Showtime had reached 23 million subscribers compared to HBO's 28 million. It will probably never catch HBO, but it is closing the gap, with new subscribers almost doubling the 12.2 million subscribers posted for 2003.

2.3   From Premium to Broadcast Channel Brands

To return to the dramatized promotion for Showtime that aired in 2010 when the channel was still building that base, Nancy and Cathy's "nice grass" exchange is intriguing given the implied reference to the suburban American Dream. Several Showtime series called attention to the typical desirable elements of that dream— upscale furnishings in a large single-family house, new appliances in a customized kitchen, and designer linens in a master bedroom suite with an oversized bed. Showtime series often feature consumer dissatisfaction story arcs that deconstruct that desire. On a subtle level, some of the series' characters affirm the desirability of the consumer-oriented suburban American Dream, even though they understand intellectually that it is an unattainable fantasy. In this way, Showtime series speak to those viewers cynical about, and yet still attracted to, the myth story of personal fulfillment via such consumer acquisitions. While all Showtime series call attention to the ultimately dissatisfying nature of a consumer-oriented identity, both Nancy Botwin and Cathy Jamison take out that dissatisfaction on their former objects of consumer affection. In *Weeds* Nancy burns down the whole dream house, starting in the designer kitchen and in *The Big C* Cathy uses her once-loved couch to start a bonfire in the gaping hole for her un-built swimming pool. These series counter the "suburban good life" mythology through depictions of characters who worry that it came at too steep a price.

As discussed in Chapter 1, the set design and dramatized advertisements linked to 1950s series put on display the origins of an American culture in which a typical aspiration would be to acquire a suburban, single-family home with a picket fence enclosing that "nice grass." Inside there would be a designer kitchen stocked with modern convenience products and outfitted with the latest appliances. The aspiration is affirmed in ABC's *Modern Family* in the matter-of-factness of the Dunphys toward their designer kitchen and new appliances and in the dejection of the characters in *The Middle* about their dilapidated kitchen and partially or totally broken appliances.

Only a premium cable series liberated from spot advertising could offer a true critique of these signifiers of the consumer versions of success and fulfillment. Broadcast television series have to affirm consumer culture on some basic level because they are financially supported by consumer–products companies that buy television advertising. They also have more slots to fill on their schedules and more need to attract attention to their series to get the ratings numbers that inspire advertisers to write big checks. Typically, the U.S. networks are thought of as generalists because of the need for programs that have mass appeal. When ABC of the 1960s was in third place behind CBS and NBC, it tried out some narrowcasting strategies and dramatized promotions to try to increase its market share. It finally succeeded, and in the mid-1970s ABC found itself in first place. As the following close look at its 1960s and early 1970s schedules reveals, ABC took some surprising turns toward narrowcasting to achieve that status. Before turning to that analysis, I offer a general overview of how scheduling works on a broadcast network, which has many more slots to fill than a premium cable channel like Showtime.

Showtime is also an interesting channel to consider in relation to the rest of this study as its position in the marketplace has some parallels to the position of midcentury ABC, especially in relation to the limits of its audience reach and a lingering public perception of its less prestigious status in relation to its primary competitor. It is important to understand that ABC of the 1950s was not a broadcaster in the same category as U.S. industry leader CBS. ABC had a limited number of stations and affiliates, which prevented the network from achieving true *broadc*ast reach. ABC continued to struggle because of its lack of affiliates until the early 1970s, when rule changes evened things out among the three networks. Between 1968–73, ABC gained 30 new affiliate stations. It also benefited from the FCC's Prime-Time Access Rule (PTAR) changes in that the network gave back the 7:30 p.m. block to the local stations and, in doing so, got rid of a block that had long run at a loss. While the PTAR was supposed to open up the 7–8 p.m. block for local and public affairs programming, it mostly became the home of cheap gameshows. The body of this chapter looks at how ABC took several decades to build to the kind of primetime programming that helped it craft a channel brand compelling enough to help it take first place in the ratings in the mid-1970s. By examining some specific scheduling grids, we can clearly see how ABC of the 1960s engaged in brandcasting through its scheduling of demographically inflected series cycles.

To contextualize these specific schedules, we need to establish the general assumptions about the scheduling strategies and channel branding in what is known as the classic network era. When commentators speak of the displacement of "classic network era" strategies employed by the Big Three U.S. networks, they are not thinking of 1950s or even 1960s schedules, as this chapter's explication of grids from those eras will detail. Instead, the "classic network" schedule refers to the standard primetime flow that had been the norm for many television seasons prior to the schedule disruptions of the early 2000s. The "classic" schedule is often recalled as some version of NBC's 1980s and 1990s *Must-See TV* primetime formula of "four sitcoms, plus one quality drama" slotted into the 8 p.m. through 10 p.m. blocks. This formula worked well until FOX's *American Idol* hijacked Nielsen's ratings, the sitcom as a genre was pronounced dead, and the audience for the 10 p.m. broadcast television version of the quality drama migrated en masse to cable for *The Sopranos* and other *It's Not TV* quality dramas.

Glimmers of hope for the viability of scripted original programs on broadcast networks returned when ABC's quality popular drama, *Lost*, ushered in a new network television era of the long-arc serial and ABC's *Modern Family* revived the socially liberal sitcom. CBS had never lost faith in the more traditional three-camera sitcom and was rewarded in the ratings for its steadfastness. CBS also won ratings when it gave its 10 p.m. drama slots to *CSI* and its other franchise procedurals. Despite critiques of the formulaic structure of its programming, CBS continued to lead in the ratings race and even managed to find some critical acclaim through quality procedurals like *The Good Wife*. NBC billed itself as the home of the smart sitcom, but its series faltered in the ratings and the network often found itself in last place. Since FOX became a contender in the network race after its initial launch in the late 1980s, there had been a four-way battle to be the ratings leader and NBC was often coming in last. The network still had its fans and its continuing viability had to do with the rise in channel brand identification. Even though they were all supposed to be broadcast networks with an array of programming calculated to appeal to a range of viewers, each broadcast network had become associated with a brand of sorts: Smart and Liberal NBC; Staid and Conventional CBS; Irreverent and Confrontational FOX; and Soapy and Aspirational ABC. While most of these are self-explanatory, ABC's shorthand identity has not been easy to pinpoint, and yet, its narrowcast inflection is actually the most consistent over the decades.

Today, ABC simply has a reputation of having a narrowcast leaning toward female viewers. Yet, it is not generally acknowledged that ABC has a long history of elements of narrowcasting, already targeting young women and airing tween-inclusive sitcoms in earlier decades. Closer study of its output over time reveals that ABC's programming is often aspirational in tone. Series focus on fantasies, whether they are about relationships with friends, family, or significant others, or about achieving the American Dream of suburban and professional success. ABC series often embody these aspirations in their representations of new kinds of families, new kinds of teenagers, new kinds of best friends, new kinds of odd couple roommates or romances, and, most noticeably, "new girls" of various kinds. Within these otherwise upbeat series, there were also some undercurrents of anxieties about the feasibility or desirability of the fantasies on display.

The association of today's ABC with aspirational programming is linked to its position as a broadcast network within the Disney–ABC Television Group. This portfolio includes truly narrowcast channels such as ABC Family (perceived to attract teens and twenty-something females with its "friends as family" ensembles promoted with the new tagline, *a new kind of family*), and Disney Channel (for tweens, especially females, but also inclusive of co-viewing caregivers and "kids of all ages"). Yet, long before the Disney acquisition of ABC in 1995, ABC's historical association with Disney, tweens, and young females helped ABC survive to become the third network in the 1950s and move into the 1960s with a viable market share, even if well behind market leader CBS.

2.4   ABC as Middlecaster

The commonly accepted shorthand descriptor is that ABC programs address "young families with kids," but a closer look at ABC's schedules over the decades makes evident that its address was a bit more nuanced. Similarly, ABC's 1960s and 1970s series did more than appeal to the *lowest common denominator* in the general adult audience (as has been said of CBS's rural sitcoms of the era). More precisely, ABC is a network airing generalist series with narrowcast elements designed to target the *youngest common demographic* in the assumed audience for a given genre category—whether that is tweens, teens, young females, or young parents. Over its history, ABC has aired many suburban sitcoms about families, for instance. While the sitcoms were assumed to appeal to advertisers interested in marketing brands to suburbanites, such series also accommodated the fantasies of the newest American dreamers: those who did not live in American suburbs, but aspired to live there. This included tweens born into lower-income and/or immigrant families, but encouraged to strive for "typical American" futures as shaped by television representations of Anglo American, middle-class suburbia. ABC trafficked in fantasies, and so it is not surprising that the broadcast appeal of its series might attract those for whom the characters and lifestyles on display represented aspirations rather than any achieved state. As John Hartley says, we should never underestimate the appeal of "suburbanality."[5]

Along these lines, series featuring young women and teens had appeal beyond those demographics, especially among tweens "aging up" or adults "aging down" in their character identification. This diversity of appeals became part of ABC's channel brand. Considering programming like *Bewitched*, which is calculated to appeal to a range of demographics from young in actual age to young in attitude, it is clear that by 1960 ABC's broadcast target market was inflected with a core address to "think youngs," as I detailed in the previous chapter. This segment of the population is grouped into a cohort through their attraction to appealing lifestyles (rock 'n' roll, beach culture, and the mod or "swinging" single life) and often to youthful aspirations about fantasy professions, flirtatious or romantic relationships, or even friction-free family dynamics. After all, ABC's "family" sitcoms most often featured a new kind of parents: the peer-ents who were less likely to critique their teenagers than to live vicariously through them or try to consume elements of their lifestyles.

ABC moved toward a definite "think young" channel brand both through the sitcoms on its schedule and promotions utilizing teen actors like Sally Field and Patty Duke or its twenty-something females like Marlo Thomas and Elizabeth Montgomery. Speaking in direct address to viewers, these actors (from a hybrid position as themselves/their characters) implicitly told tweens, teens, and young women that ABC was a network that accommodated their points of view.

As background for the analysis of specific schedules that support these claims about ABC, we need to establish some specifics about the importance of scheduling as an industry practice. A schedule is the "defining artifice that gives meaning" to program blocks. Through its schedule a network creates a narrative about itself and about the audience it intends to sell to advertisers, which is why Ellis compares scheduling "to narrative construction."[6] Most literally, a schedule is a mechanism for dividing time slots and creating expectations about what kinds of programming one might find in them. As I implied earlier, American television viewers were trained in the era of NBC's *Must-See TV* schedules to expect a typical primetime flow to move from four sitcoms into a quality drama, and see the higher-rated sitcoms scheduled as lead-ins at 8 p.m. and 9 p.m. in the hope that they would act as tentpoles to prop up the newer or weaker sitcoms in between. Successful scheduling does more than calculate how to attract and maintain audiences for an entire evening's programming. Scheduling reveals network assumptions about the viewing habits of its perceived audiences. Embedded within a schedule is a channel's desired brand identity and the cultural expressions through which it intends to convey the brand and attract national audiences.

A closer look at assumptions about the strategies and branding of generalist channels today and in the classic network era helps to clarify this point. U.S. television schedules are conceptualized as grids and standardized in terms of length (30- and 60-minute blocks) and time of day (morning, daytime, early evening, prime-time, late-night). The daypart divisions are often linked to assumptions about desirable programming for the gender and age breakdowns associated with them and the presumed daily routines of target audiences (e.g., young families). As Ellis explains, before there is a schedule there are assumptions about desirable target audiences and when they might be available to watch programs. Walt Disney Studios understood the potential interplay between demographics and dayparts when it offered ABC *The Mickey Mouse Club* in 1955 to slot into the dead zone of the late afternoon/early evening. The studio and the network already had success with the initial season of *Disneyland*, the studio's anthology series that aired from 7:30 to 8:30 p.m. to accommodate its hybrid generalist/tween target audience. While I will return to those series in Chapter 4, I want to note for now that having Disney programs on ABC's mid-1950s schedule kickstarted ABC's narrowcasting to the tweens, while still allowing for a more broadcast address to a generalist audience.

ABC also benefited from having two star sitcoms, *Ozzie & Harriet* and *Make Room for Daddy/The Danny Thomas Show*, which had wisecracking tween males as a signature element of their comedy styles. *The Danny Thomas Show* jumped to CBS, a move that was common at the time because sponsors were always looking for the best time slots and the best terms. *Danny Thomas* inherited *I Love Lucy*'s premium time slot (Mondays at 9 p.m.). In its new CBS slot the sitcom shot to number two in the ratings. *The Danny Thomas Show* was now seen by more people than ever before, in part because it secured a coveted schedule slot on a night when people had already been "appointment viewing" *I Love Lucy*, the number one series in the ratings for 1956–7. It was also the case that any CBS show was literally seen in more homes than any ABC show because CBS had many more owned and operated stations and affiliate stations in markets across the country. Later, ABC's *My Three Sons* (ABC 1960–5) made a similar move to CBS where it stayed on air from 1965–72. Sometimes the leap in networks went in the other direction, as in the case of *Leave It to Beaver*. After its initial 1957–8 season the kid-focused sitcom moved to ABC for 1958, apparently because the sponsor deal was better.

Leave It to Beaver was a schedule addition that would pay off in its final two seasons when Tony Dow as Wally, older brother to Theodore "Beaver" Cleaver (Jerry Mathers), achieved teen heartthrob status. For its final season in 1962–3, *Leave It to Beaver* aired alongside other teen-inclusive series, including *The Donna Reed Show*, *My Three Sons*, and even *The Adventures of Ozzie & Harriet*. By that point, teen idol Ricky Nelson was a 22 year-old who wanted to be called Rick, although his active rock 'n' roll career was still keeping him on magazine covers.

2.5   *Ozzie & Harriet* and the Peer-ent

Tracking the changing role of both Ricky Nelson and the Nelson family sitcom, *The Adventures of Ozzie & Harriet*, on 14 years worth of ABC schedules can help us to understand how a teen narrowcast streak developed at ABC. We can also use the industry practice of scheduling to chart some of the more general changes happening in the U.S. television industry during the 1950s and 1960s. The schedule pairings indicate which thematics ABC programmers thought were marketable during different seasons, and they reveal the emergence of different series cycles.

In the first iteration of the series ranging from 1953 to 1956, Ozzie is a bumbler who humorously avoids responsibility for his actions. In this era Harriet retained some of her fast-talking female persona from the 1940s radio version of the "Ozzie & Harriet" act. She banters with Ozzie and offers wry comments on his behavior. Far from the June Cleaver model of fussy mothering and anxious

SCHEDULE 2.2 An overview of the different kinds of programming airing alongside *The Adventures of Ozzie & Harriet* during its 1952–66 run.

ABC	Day of Week	7:30	8:00	8:30	9:00	9:30
1952–3	Friday	The Stu Erwin Show	**Ozzie & Harriet**	All-Star News		Tales of Tomorrow
1953–4	Friday	The Stu Erwin Show	**Ozzie & Harriet**	Pepsi-Cola Playhouse	The Pride of the Family	The Comeback Story
1954–5	Friday	Adventures of Rin Tin Tin	**Ozzie & Harriet**	Ray Bolger Show	Dollar a Second	The Vise
1955–6	Friday	Adventures of Rin Tin Tin	**Ozzie & Harriet**	Crossroads	Dollar a Second	The Vise
1956–7	Wednesday	Disneyland	Disneyland	Navy Log	**Ozzie & Harriet**	Ford Theatre
1957–8	Wednesday	7:00 Local / 7:15 John Daly and the News	Disneyland	Disneyland	Tombstone Territory	**Ozzie & Harriet**
1958–9	Wednesday	Lawrence Welk's Plymouth Show		**Ozzie & Harriet**	The Donna Reed Show	Patti Page Oldsmobile Show
1959–60	Wednesday	The Court of Last Resort	Charley Weaver's Hobby Lobby	**Ozzie & Harriet**	Hawaiian Eye	
1960–1	Wednesday	Hong Kong		**Ozzie & Harriet**	Hawaiian Eye	
1961–2	Thursday	**Ozzie & Harriet**	The Donna Reed Show	The Real McCoys	My Three Sons	Margie
1962–3[7]	Thursday	Local	**Ozzie & Harriet**	The Donna Reed Show	Leave It to Beaver	My Three Sons
1963–4	Wednesday	**Ozzie & Harriet**	The Patty Duke Show	The Price Is Right	Ben Casey	
1964–5	Wednesday	**Ozzie & Harriet**	The Patty Duke Show	Shindig!	Mickey	
1965–6	Wednesday	**Ozzie & Harriet**	The Patty Duke Show	Gidget	The Big Valley	Burke's Law

worrying about male behavior she could not quite understand, Harriet was also a relaxed ruler of the roost. At the outset, the Nelsons were paired with other star-helmed sitcoms. First, there was *The Stu Erwin Show*, a "trouble with father" sitcom starring a real life couple, but transforming Stu Erwin into a simpleton school principal and giving the show couple some fictional children. *Stu Erwin* was replaced by *The Adventures of Rin Tin Tin*, with the titular dog ostensibly counting as another "star" who made the transition to television. In this adventure series the dog and his tween owner rode with the U.S. Cavalry on the western frontier. For 1954, the Nelsons became the lead-in for *The Ray Bolger Show*, centering on the Broadway star best known as the tin man from *The Wizard of Oz*. The real life song and dance man played one on TV. His sitcom tried to capitalize on Bolger's recent success in *Where's Charley?* (a film made from his hit Broadway musical). The comedic situations arose because Bolger's character was always running late. In playing a flawed character, Bolger's performance aligned well Ozzie Nelson's on-screen persona of this era, which had little in common with the popular memory of *Ozzie & Harriet* as a sitcom like *Father Knows Best*, depicting parents as authority figures who offer "clear-cut rules for moral guidance."[8] Instead, Ozzie often set a bad example by trying to avoid blame for things that happened when he cut corners or bent the truth.

When Bolger did not return for the 1955 season, *Ozzie & Harriet* was paired with adventure series and anthology programs, the most significant being *Disneyland* in 1956 and 1957, because the program's high ratings made it more likely for viewers to stay tuned for *Ozzie & Harriet*. Chapter 4 offers a fuller discussion of the Disney anthology program as a literal brandcasting series, which promoted all things emanating from Walt Disney Studios and its subsidiaries. For the purposes of the discussion in this chapter, we can simply place it within the general category of the anthology series, one that also included *The Pepsi-Cola Playhouse*. Such a series aired a different drama each week, but always had the same kind of sponsor plugs. The anthology drama time franchise format emanated from the assumption that viewers would feel grateful to the sponsor for giving airtime to their favorite performers. This gratitude effect would, in turn, prompt the purchase of the sponsors' brands. Other companies took a different approach to the time franchise and operated a variety show hosted by a star, so there would be some level of continuity even as the guest acts changed each week. *Lawrence Welk's Plymouth Show* and *The Patti Page Oldsmobile Show*, musical/variety formats, shared the 1958–9 Wednesday night schedule with the Nelsons. Such time franchises had fixed time slots on the schedule, which often limited a network's ability to convey continuity in its offerings. In contrast, ABC had control of where it would move *Ozzie & Harriet* each season. The network worked to find somewhere to put the series because Ozzie had negotiated an unprecedented non-cancelable ten-year contract with ABC in 1949 when Ricky and David joined their parents' long-running radio show.

2.6 The Rock 'n' Roll Era Arrives on ABC

Time franchises were problematic for networks as the sponsors only cared about their own blocks and not the flow of programming across the schedule. In the 1960s, networks would take control away from the sponsors and have more power in crafting network schedules that worked to brand the network in specific ways. This new dynamic is especially evident on the schedule for Wednesdays in 1962–3, when ABC schedulers grouped all the teenage-appeal sitcoms in one spot. One of these was *The Donna Reed Show* with which *Ozzie & Harriet* was paired initially during 1958–9 because *Ozzie & Harriet* was seen as an effective lead-in for the newcomer sitcom created for Hollywood star Donna Reed by her producer husband Tony Owen. Reed transformed herself into Donna Stone, the patient wife of a pediatrician and the "mother who knew best." Young actors culled from *The Mickey Mouse Club*'s stable of stars played the Stone children. Former Mouseketeer Paul Peterson was Jeff, the "irrepressible" tween. Shelley Fabares played his often exasperated, teenage sister Mary. Fabares was already known from *The Mickey Mouse Club* serial *Annette* and was more famous to teens as a friend of its star Annette Funicello. Fabares, who would go on in the later 1960s to play female leads opposite Elvis, was linked through this schedule to Ricky Nelson, who was giving Elvis a run for his money in 1958 on the newly created Billboard Top 100 charts.

By the time the Stones and the Nelsons had neighboring slots on the 1958–9 ABC schedule, Ricky had completed his transformation from an "irrepressible" tween to irresistible teen, trading less on the comic timing of his zingers than on the musical timing in his performances embedded into sitcom episodes. Recall that Ricky was only 12 years old when *Ozzie & Harriet* started in 1952 (brother David was already 16), and was 16 when his first performance was included on *Ozzie & Harriet*. Already known as a producer skilled at product integration, Ozzie Nelson pioneered the embedded music video. He first utilized the strategy in "Ricky, the Drummer" (April 10, 1957), when Ricky made his singing debut four months before ABC took *American Bandstand* to a national audience. With the subsequent success of Ricky's cover of "I'm Walkin'" Ozzie Nelson recognized that the sitcom's call-to-action could prompt viewers to buy Ricky's music at local record stores as well as to encourage them to visit local retailers for sponsor products. Nelson was the first of many producers to understand that television could function as a highly effective platform for promoting potential Billboard Top 100 singles, particularly to those 9- to 14-year-olds marketers now call tweens. In a cultural sense, the embedded music video structure of *Ozzie & Harriet* episodes, especially those in which Ricky performs for his parents and their friends, helped him have more general audience appeal or at least ease anxieties about the new generation.

While retaining elements of his original sitcom persona, Ozzie revised his own character to align with the new life stages of the boys. Now, he was less the bumbler-in-chief and more the middle class, suburban "peer-ent": a parent who participates alongside his sons in their leisure activities and advocates for rather than chafes against their points of view. Ozzie is depicted as supportive of his sons' leisure-oriented aspirations, rejecting the generational discord narrative ("the problem with kids today is . . ."). Recalling in his autobiography his desire to play the role of peer recommender, Nelson said he intended to address fellow members of his Big Band-era generation and use the depiction of Ricky to help de-stigmatize rock 'n' roll music and the teen rock musician or listener. The series also enabled Ricky to speak directly to his generational peers and launched him as a teen idol with Billboard-charting singles and several albums.

The official transition of *Ozzie & Harriet* into peer-ent sitcom began in the 1957–8 season after Ricky's first performance. Yet, Ozzie and Harriet's willingness to appreciate Ricky's taste in rock 'n' roll music could already be seen in "Music Appreciation," a 1955 episode in which older brother David is the one who can't tolerate Ricky's rock 'n' roll records. In 1956's "Kappa Sigma Party" and 1957's "The Man Without a Family," Ozzie is still the more stereotypical oblivious peer-ent, the precursor of the modern type who wants to participate in new generation trends and be accepted as "one of the gang."

The post-1957 episodes with integrated performances by Ricky stand out for conveying the series' signature peer-enting characterization. In them Ozzie and Harriet have close ups to display their enthusiastic expressions and their tendency to start bopping to the beat and/or clapping at the end of a song. These types of episodes include insert shots of crowds of adoring female listeners or long shots from the audience's position looking at Ricky perform on stage for some supposedly in-series group of young people. Most of these performances feel more like small venue concerts in which there is an intimacy between the audience and performer. Even when Ricky's band is playing for a party or another event within the story world, the performance still feels like a concert video with actual Ricky Nelson fans in the audience. The function of these inserted music videos is to capture and construct Ricky Nelson's extratextual stardom and bolster his brand as a singer. These music videos played as content–promotion hybrids that ran as a content bumper to the credits.

One of the oddest of these hybrids is built in to end of the May 1961 episode, "The Built-in TV Set." The main episode is about Ozzie's attempt to get a television installed into the bedroom wall and his willingness to manipulate some kids and his neighbor to do so (his "frenemy" neighbor manipulates Ozzie right back). Before the episode officially ends, we get a sense of Ozzie as peer-ent when Rick, David, and Ozzie lounge in his bed. With them all in the same pose, the shot composition conveys that they have the same leisure-time tastes. The episode's actual last segment, which comes after a brief snippet of the credits, looks like part of the episode because we are back in the Nelsons' bedroom. Although they share the same double bed on screen (a rarity at the time), the Nelsons are far from sexy in their pajamas. They are propped up against the

FIGURE 2.2   In an episode of *Ozzie & Harriet*, Ricky Nelson's performance captivates female fans (upper). In the "Make a Wave" music video airing on Disney Channel in 2010, Demi Lovato occupies both positions: the pop idol and the admiring fan of Joe Jonas, her male pop idol counterpart (lower).

headboard enjoying their newly installed television set. The "show" they watch is a small venue performance of Rick and his band. The scene represents the series' usual slippage between series persona and star, as there is no narrative logic offered for the character to appear on television. The shots capture Ozzie and

Harriet (as a hybrid of the characters and the star couple) beaming at the television and bopping to the music, although in a more histrionic way than usual. The surreal element to the scene feels like meta commentary on the significance of television as a platform for brandcasting to a broad range of viewers beyond those who would go to a live musical performance. Affirming the metatextual function of the segment, the final beat calls attention to Ozzie and the cheeky look on his face, as he breaks the fourth wall and points to the viewer and then to the television. It is as if he is saying with a wink, "what's the use of having a television show if you can't use it to promote the hell out of your son's career?! Nobody else is going to do it for him."

In this music video, Ricky the teen idol with his name emblazoned across his guitar is on full display. First, he sings "Hello Mary Lou," his hit about true love, and then "Travelin' Man," his hit about having a girl in every port. The ambivalence of him as romantic teen idol and rock 'n' roll star is embodied in those choices. Of course, the lyrics are sung in the characteristic romantic mode of this early rock 'n' roll style. The latter is the kind of song to which people sing along without paying much attention to sexual implications beneath the romantic tone of the lyrics. In the case of this music video the meaning of the lyrics are domesticated by the way that shots of Ozzie and Harriet as middle-aged parents are intercut before and after each song. The sequence becomes a literal manifestation of the way Ricky makes rock 'n' roll safe for suburban America by domesticating it, diffusing some of its more "raucous elements," and making it ready for prime time.[9]

Ricky quickly grew much bigger than his primetime persona, which made many of the episodes between 1958–62 seem surreal because his extratextual stardom seemed to erupt within very ordinary scenes or even in the dramatized advertisements. A case in point is the Kodak dramatization in which Ricky demonstrates the new functions of a camera for a pretty girl (see Figure 1.10 from Chapter 1). When the actress looks at Ricky, as she is required to do by the scenario, she seems a bit star struck, as if marveling at the fact that she is standing next to "*the* Ricky Nelson." After all, Ricky's "Poor Little Fool" was the number one single for August 4, 1958 on the newly created Billboard Hot 100. Ricky had 12 hits on the charts to Elvis' 11 in 1958 and 1959, and between 1957–62, he had 30 hits in the Top 40. Ricky was making the cover of magazines and headlines in newspapers, even being billed at 18 years old as one of Hollywood's ten most eligible bachelors and young movie stars to watch.[10] He had garnered some box office buzz that year from his role *Rio Bravo* (1959) with John Wayne, Dean Martin, and Angie Dickinson.

Within this context, it made sense that for 1959–61 ABC shifted its schedule around to pair *Ozzie & Harriet* with *Hawaiian Eye*, one of several Warner Brothers detective series featuring good-looking male leads who also released singles or albums. A standout was Edd Byrnes, who starred as a sexy amateur detective and rock 'n' roll hipster in *77 Sunset Strip*, and also made the Hollywood top 10 in 1959. Lindsay Giggey has argued that *77 Sunset*'s sister series *Hawaiian Eye* was also a crosspromotion platform for the music career of Connie Stevens,

FIGURE 2.3 The shots capture Ozzie and Harriet (as a hybrid of the characters and the star couple) beaming at Ricky Nelson's on-air performance. The sequence from "The Built-in TV Set" offers meta-commentary on the significance of television as a brandcasting platform.

FIGURE 2.4 Ricky Nelson performs on *Ozzie & Harriet* in a new televisual form: the embedded music video. Despite his insistence on being called Rick, he had a hard time breaking away from his "Ricky Nelson: pop idol" image.

SCHEDULE 2.3 Linking *My Three Sons* and *The Donna Reed Show* on the ABC schedule. 1962–3 launched a full teen lineup; 1963–4 offered a second night for teen pairs.

ABC	Day of Week	7:30	8:00	8:30	9:00	9:30
1960–1	Thursday	Guestward, Ho!	The Donna Reed Show	The Real McCoys	**My Three Sons** #13	Untouchables
1961–2	Thursday	Ozzie & Harriet	The Donna Reed Show	The Real McCoys	**My Three Sons** #11	Margie
1962–3	Thursday	Local	Ozzie & Harriet	The Donna Reed Show	Leave It to Beaver	**My Three Sons**
1963–4	Thursday	Flintstones	The Donna Reed Show	**My Three Sons**	The Jimmy Dean Show	
1964–5	Thursday	Flintstones	The Donna Reed Show	**My Three Sons** #11	Bewitched	Peyton Place
CBS			From fall 1965–72, *My Three Sons* aired on CBS			
1965–6	Thursday	The Munsters	Gilligan's Island	**My Three Sons**	The CBS Thursday Night Movie	

who, in turn, did a song with Edd Byrnes that reached #4 on the Billboard 100. As Cricket Blake, nightclub singer and sometime sleuth, Stevens was gaining a following. She is also emblematic of a character type in which ABC would continue to show interest.[11] Susan Douglas describes her as a sidekick girl, and sees the character type as a first step toward building a sitcom around a spunky single girl, as ABC would do later in the decade. In any case, ABC's narrowcast leanings were already becoming more evident in these late-1950s programs.

As already noted, the Warner Brothers' action/adventure series were generating some teen idols of their own. At the time, the turn to teens was happening in part because of the kinds of programs Warner Brothers, Disney, and independent producers were supplying in fulfillment of their contracts with ABC. By 1960, teenagers and young adults soon became central marketing hooks on ABC. Its 1962–3 Thursday night schedule, for example, brought together *Ozzie & Harriet*, *The Donna Reed Show* (ABC 1958–66), *Leave It to Beaver* (CBS 1957–8; ABC 1958–63), and *My Three Sons* (ABC 1960–5; CBS 1965–72).

2.7 *My Three Sons* and the Generational Accord Sitcom Cycle

My Three Sons is the most intriguing because it has a Disney Studios connection and is the one series of the 1962–3 teen block with the same kind of longevity as *Ozzie & Harriet*. Yet *My Three Sons* had much more success in the ratings, placing in the top 30 for most of its 12-year run. I focus only on the role it played on the schedule when it was an ABC series, between 1960–5. Parallels between *My Three Sons* and *Ozzie & Harriet* are more noticeable when they both aired on Thursdays from 1961–3. Of particular interest to the discussion in this chapter is the way in which the two series represent interactions between sitcom parents and their rock 'n' roll-generation children in the period before youth culture becomes a truly transgressive movement.

Both *Ozzie & Harriet* and *My Three Sons* are series in which a television father, a musician himself during the Big Band era, advocates for the rock 'n' roll generation via his support of the aspirations of his teenage son. Like Ozzie Nelson, widower Steve Douglas (Fred MacMurray) often endorses the musical aspirations of his son Robbie (Don Grady). A few episodes about Robbie also have performance segments in which Grady sings and plays guitar, often accompanied by MacMurray on saxophone and background vocals. The series contrasts to later ones such as *The Monkees* (NBC 1966–8), which become sites for "displaying the generational rift between the tastes of the young and the older generation."[12] Explicitly rejecting "the problem with kids today" generational discord theme, Steve's advice to his father-in-law "Bub" doubles as advice to the adult audience to learn to appreciate or at least understand the tastes of rock 'n' roll-era teenagers. It helps that Steve is a former musician, and Bub a former vaudeville performer.

Ozzie and Harriet are unified in their support of Ricky's music, but in *My Three Sons*, Steve is Robbie's chief advocate and often has to convince Bub that rock 'n' roll is not just noise. A few episodes such as 1963's "When I Was Your Age" (3.34) center on proving that one of Bub's assumptions about the generation is false or misleading. Steve is always willing to represent himself and Bub as flawed and even comments explicitly on the error of assuming their generations were better than the current one. The dynamic is evident in December 1961's "Robbie's Band" (2.12). The situation is set in motion after Bub complains to Steve about the volume of the music coming from the kitchen where Robbie's band is practicing. Steve takes on the role of mediator. He tells Bub and eldest son Mike that being in a band "is a good outlet for boy Robbie's age." Steve goes into the kitchen and encourages the teens even though they aren't sounding great and he subtly tries to convince them to practice elsewhere. When that fails, he gives them some tips for improvement. Once they find out he was a saxophone player in a band in his schooldays, Robbie's friends want Steve to be their "mentor." This makes Robbie smile and father and son are positioned in a friendly peer-to-peer stance in some medium shots (see Figure 1.7 from Chapter 1). The rest of the band urges Steve to sit in with them, but he declines: "I don't think a parent should butt in on a kid's activities." He quips, "I figured that out when I was a kid." With a chuckle and a quick exit he indicates that he has no intention of being that sad kind of peer-ent who tries to become a teen again. Later in the episode, one of the band members gets sick and the rest beg Steve to join them. For a gig at Mike's fraternity party, Robbie's band even decides to dress in Jazz Age costumes like the one Steve wore when he was in a band. The performance segments show that Steve enjoys his time in the band because they really want him there (see Figure 2.9 later in this chapter). The performance also highlights the musical talent of Don Grady, who would go on to have a professional career. His actual band The Greefs would also be Robbie's band on the series in later seasons, such as in the December 1966 episode, "Falling Star" (7.12). A few years later Chip would become the teen and, like his brother Robbie before him, play in a rock 'n' roll band, and the series would again raise the "is rock and roll just noise?" debate.

My Three Sons had many levels of multi-generational credibility built into its casting. First, it reunited Fred MacMurray and Tim Considine (eldest son Mike) one year after they starred in Disney's surprise hit of 1959, *The Shaggy Dog*. Considine had also played one of the main leads in both *The Hardy Boys* and *Spin & Marty*, the two most popular serials that aired in installment format during *The Mickey Mouse Club*. Don Grady was formerly Don Agrati, tween Mouseketeer, and as Robbie he would start to age into a teen heartthrob role a few years prior to Considine aging out of the series in 1965. The third son was cute kid Chip (Stanley Livingston) who would eventually age into the teen role once the series moved to CBS (1965–72). There are obvious demographic appeals of a series with a recent teen idol, a soon-to-be teen idol, and a cute kid who could grow into the teen role, but the adults had some cross-demographic appeal as well. The *My Three Sons* for Hunt's or Chevrolet end credits had a doorway shot of this range of males (see Figure 1.9 in Chapter 1). The series also got a boost from getting William Frawley (Fred Mertz from *I Love Lucy*) for the role of the boys' maternal grandfather Bub. He was their primary caregiver because their widowed dad traveled as an aerospace engineer working on government contracts, including a mysterious "moon project."

My Three Sons is obviously notable for its representation of *a new kind of family*—one with two males in the parental roles. It is also significant for its positioning of Steve as a new kind of parent. Yet, as established above, the originator of this new type is actually Ozzie Nelson, as we saw in the discussion of "The Built-In TV Set." The episode aired in the same 1961 primetime block as *My Three Sons*, creating continuity between the depiction of these two fathers who learn to appreciate or at least understand the tastes and behaviors of their rock 'n' roll-generation sons. ABC was coming to value the peer-ent character type and see the demographic reach enabled by an on-screen paring of a representative of one generation with one from another. These shows are the light television precursors to the more weighty generational relevance sitcoms in which CBS would specialize, starting with *All in the Family* in 1971. *Ozzie & Harriet* paved the way for ABC's longer term investment in a generational accord series cycle that has yet to be recognized, even though it provides an interesting parallel to the generational discord programming of the 1960s and early 1970s.

The constant on *My Three Sons* was that it remained, first and foremost, a star vehicle for Fred MacMurray. While he had a substantial film career in the 1930s

FIGURE 2.5 *My Three Sons*' Bub is the all-male family's caregiver serving at the breakfast table. It is equipped with a turntable to showcase Hunt's condiments (upper). Actor William Frawley (Bub) was already famous as Fred Mertz from *I Love Lucy* (lower).

and 1940s, he had begun what would be another successful film cycle for him with *The Shaggy Dog* and would appear in many more Disney family comedies over the subsequent decade. A simultaneous film and television career was possible for the actor because of the deal the producers brokered to lure MacMurray to work on the sitcom. Known as the MacMurray method, producers shot all of his scenes at once and hundreds of reaction shots. Then the rest of the cast had to work around these limitations and deal with the continuity issues while MacMurray was off shooting feature films.

Because of this method there were many scenes in which MacMurray didn't appear or only appeared in reaction shots (all filmed in one day). One effect of MacMurray's shooting schedule is that it made Steve feel literally separate from his family, paralleling the plot device that Bub is the caretaker because his widowed son-in-law is a traveling consultant. Steve is often not at home or leaving for a trip and the boys are parented mostly by Bub. As Steve is away a lot, it is arguably easier for him to take on the role of peer-ent, especially because he is not in the home everyday to become frustrated with the boys.

In the ABC seasons, eldest son Mike sometimes tried to play the role of stand-in parent, but Steve's peer-ent character always set him straight when he came home. Contrary to assumptions about this kind of midcentury family sitcom, it does not rely on "a developmental psychology of growing up."[13] Steve, Ozzie, and later Russ Lawrence (*Gidget*) reject the developmental psychology approach that would be the foundation of the later idealized re-imaginings of the midcentury father type on series like *Happy Days* and *The Cosby Show*. Instead, the writers allow the eldest sibling to represent that point of view and then dismiss it and him or her as an authority figure. Displacing more critical parenting onto the eldest sibling enables the fathers in *My Three Sons*, *Ozzie & Harriet*, and *Gidget*, to be peer-ents, reinforcing the generational accord thematics.

One hallmark of their peer-enting is that the fathers try to let their kids work out their dilemmas for themselves. When authoritative solutions are offered, they come from these parent-like older siblings whose points of view are rejected. While this begins with David Nelson, it is more overt in the case of Mike Douglas from *My Three Sons* and Anne (Lawrence) Cooper and her husband John in *Gidget*. Additionally, Mike and John often frame their advice as based on knowledge gleaned from their university psychology courses, but both the fathers and the teen siblings reject it.

2.8 Wally, Ward, and Eddie Haskell on *Leave It to Beaver*

This dynamic is less at play in *Leave It to Beaver* because the older sibling Wally Cleaver is just a teen when the series starts. Wally does analyze Beaver's behavior and discuss it with his parents, but he also is often in cahoots with Beaver in some scheme that would not be parent-approved. Still, even *Leave It to Beaver* began to have more generational accord moments between Ward and Wally in its final season in 1962–3, when it moved to 9 p.m. as the lead-in to *My Three Sons*. This change is significant given that the early years of the series had at least one moment in every episode in which Ward conveyed a moral lesson in what we think of today as a classic midcentury father manner. Nevertheless, *Leave It to Beaver* remained distinct from *Father Knows Best*, although commentators often treat them as if they are the same father-as-patriarch sitcom format.[14] *Leave It to Beaver* was more kid-focused and it took the time to detail the logic motivating Beaver's actions and then later Wally's. A good amount of screen time was given over to Beaver's conversations with Wally in their shared bedroom. Scenes in the boys' bathroom had the same effect, but doubled as sites of product integration for Listerine toothpaste. The boys most often concluded that parents didn't make much sense.

This belief might explain Wally's friendship with Eddie Haskell. Eddie was usually shown telling Ward and June things he assumed parents wanted to hear, although his phony delivery was not very effective in fooling them. By the time of the final season, Wally's conversations with Eddie got more airtime and we learned more about his theory that adults were hypocritical. There were many scenes in which Eddie acted overly deferential to adults and then "talked trash" behind their backs. In subtle ways, Eddie's father was represented as the source of the trouble because the dialogue implied that George Haskell gave terrible advice to Eddie. This dynamic was evident in Eddie's many lines that started with, "Well, my father says . . ." and ended with some questionable viewpoint.

Eddie is one of the most remembered sitcom characters of the era as he brought some spunk to episodes and seemed very realistic for the way he harassed Beaver, instigated bad behavior, and then denied responsibility or a helping hand when the schemes he concocted went awry. When Beaver asks Wally why Eddie is "such a creepy guy," Wally retorts, "Because he works at it!" While Eddie Haskell's rebelliousness might have been validated at the level of subtext, the series often overtly affirmed Beaver's logic and always gave him a chance to express his worldview and have others take it seriously. In its early years, *Leave It to Beaver* was a sitcom about parents who don't get kids' motivations, kids who don't get the logic of their parents' rules, and the humorous scenarios that result. As Beaver aged from cute kid to awkward tween, his logic was not always as cute or appealing, and stories sometimes shifted to older brother Wally. While it always maintained an authoritative parents dynamic overall, there were moments in the final seasons when Ward treated Wally as more of a peer, perhaps because he was about to turn 18 and start college. Such episodes were also a chance to showcase the very marketable Tony Dow, then a teen heartthrob.

The changes are registered visually in the shots of the June 1962's "Untogetherness" (5.39). In this episode, as in many, Eddie Haskell acts as a foil to Wally. Eddie is always trying to make a fast buck, borrowing from friends, and "forgetting" to pay them back. The realism of the teen character may have been a particular attraction of the series in these years. His negative parent–child relationship and the sneaky behavior it produces are set up as a contrast for the aspirational depiction of mutual respect between Wally and Ward, at least at this point in the series when Wally is finishing high school.

In the episode's parallel car shots, we are encouraged to compare Wally and Eddie (but also to look at the new model from Plymouth, the episode's sponsor). In Eddie's shot sequence, he is visually aligned more with Beaver, the tween, than with the adults. Ward even backs the car away from Wally rather than simply turning around so that he does not have to talk to Eddie directly. We know from earlier in the episode and from many episodes that Ward just does not like Eddie and usually can't get away from him fast enough. Eddie knows it, too. Commenting on how Ward looks at him when he opens the front door, Eddie tells Wally, "Sometimes I think he'd be happier to see Khrushchev standing there."

When they saw Eddie walking down the street, the Cleavers had been heading off to their family vacation without Wally. June wanted to stop to talk with Eddie because Wally would be staying with the Haskells instead of going on the vacation, ostensibly to work at a summer job, but really to spend more time pursuing a girl he hoped to date. The Cleavers learn from Eddie that the girl told Wally a few days before that she would be away with her family the whole time. Wally tried to "take it like a man" and keep the information to himself. While he does not want to look foolish or immature, Wally was lingering by the family car when they were heading off because he clearly would rather be on a vacation than stay with the horrible Haskell family. During that original conversation, Wally is on Ward's side of the Plymouth Fury and they appear more like equals who share a genial relationship. Ward admires his son's acceptance of the "I made my bed, and now I have to lie in it" resignation, but he still heads home to pick him up. In this episode and in several others focused on Wally, Ward shows pride in his son's behavior. It helps that Wally is a good, middle-class achiever who embraces the Protestant work ethic. He is always working for what he wants and showing initiative by finding a variety of jobs to pay for the things that his friendship with Eddie the moocher and his active dating life require.

Establishing how this kind of sitcom with elements of narrowcasting to teens also had to have generalist appeal, the episode is also about parents trying to think of their son as an adult, while still seeing him as a child. Wally, who is relieved when they come back for him, is struggling with the transition as well. Ozzie Nelson delivered a similar message to his eldest son David in "The Kappa Sigma Party." As already noted, the 1956 episode undercuts one of the most persistent misperceptions about *Ozzie & Harriet*: that it depicts parents as authority figures who offer "clear-cut rules for moral guidance." If in its first phase, the sitcom focused on Ozzie as a flawed, bumbling father, in its second phase *Ozzie & Harriet* focused on more equal than authoritarian relations between parents and teenagers. This thematic aligned it with the series airing alongside it on the ABC schedule.

The generalist appeal of this kind of parent and older teen dynamic is parallel to some 1962 and 1963 episodes of *The Donna Reed Show*. Following Ozzie

FIGURE 2.6 Later seasons of *Leave It to Beaver* showcase Ward Cleaver's Plymouth. Ward develops a "peer-ent" relationship with teenaged son Wally (upper) and an increased distrust of Wally's "frenemy" Eddie Haskell (middle). In the final seasons both Wally and Beaver (right) are shown in the final shot of the credits sequence (lower).

Nelson's example of utilizing a sitcom as a launch pad, *The Donna Reed Show* was a brandcasting platform that launched singles for Paul Peterson (Jeff Stone) and Shelley Fabares (Mary Stone). As the older actor, Fabares got two integrated music videos on the series and she would go on to star in a series of beach-themed musicals.

2.9 From Bobby Soxer to Beach Bunny on *Donna Reed*

When it was paired with the other teen series *The Donna Reed Show* also put more focus on the point of view of Mary. Of particular interest is the 1963 episode "Where the Stones Are," as it not only offers an understanding of the teen female point of view, but also previewed Fabares' new star image linked to beach films. In the episode Mary's costuming functions as excess, which signals the transition of Shelley Fabares from the Stones' daughter to Elvis' leading lady. As Jane Gaines explains, costumes sometimes have "a visual excessiveness that transgresses the basic requirements of cinematic storytelling" and when they do they can distract from the narrative. Before turning to an episode in which Mary's costume completely stops the narrative, I should note that Mary had already begun a transition through consuming into more of a rock 'n' roll era teenager. In a few episodes Mary even analyzes her mother's limited lifestyle and asserts that she has no intention of immediately following in her footsteps. In other episodes Mary acknowledges that she admires her mother for being in an affectionate marriage characterized by the mutual respect her parents have for each other. Still, she seems to want that kind of relationship because the series represents it as so atypical of the time.

Mary's storyline is never resolved as she just heads off to college (after which Fabares returned only for guest spots).[15] Younger brother Jeff was waiting in the wings to take over the teen storyline and the series added a younger sibling through an adoption scenario to restore the sitcom's teen plus kid balance.[16] To return to Mary, a striking contrast occurs between Mary of the 1962–3 season and Mary of the early seasons when she was represented as a junior version of Donna. Understanding that Fabares was a marketable brand in her own right in relation to her extratextual stardom as a singer and a member of Annette Funicello's social circle, producers put Mary's viewpoint on display more as well, with more episodes focused on her in her final seasons. The problem was that Fabares' extratextual stardom bubbled up and created excess in the story world of the Stones. This excess becomes most evident in the episode, "Where the Stones Are," airing March 7, 1963. The title references a beach party film, and as a sign of the actor's extratextual teen idol status, Mary Stone is suddenly (and unaccountably) friends with Miss Teen USA, Darla Banks. The premise of the episode is that Donna and Alex reluctantly agree to let Mary go with her girlfriends to a waterside resort. Then they arrange it so they can borrow a boat and "happen" to vacation there too.

FIGURE 2.7 Shelley Fabares begins as Mary Stone, good 1950s mini-mommy in *The Donna Reed Show*, but evolves into the rock-'n'-roll-era teen looking beyond the staid suburbs.

FIGURE 2.8 Mary Stone's resort wear registers the beginning of Shelley Fabares' move from sitcom daughter to Elvis' leading lady in a beach party film cycle.

Shelley Fabares' brand repositioning is evident in Mary Stone's resort outfit in a boat scene in the episode. Gaines would point to the excess created by Mary's outfit, as it was signaling much more than the maturity of Fabares. Her costume changes track her movement away from her original branding as the representative middle-class daughter. Mary had been a supporting player in storylines about Donna's ability to adjudicate disputes, problem-solve in her household, and adjust to the changes in her growing children. Mary's dramatic costume change in "Where the Stones Are" disrupts that characterization in a way that goes beyond the theme of the Stones having to adjust to Mary's impending adulthood and her new generation viewpoints. While they are concerned enough to follow Mary to the resort, the Stones don't seem at all worried about their daughter's outfit, which seems unlikely given what she is wearing. The outfit registers that Fabares needed to leave the show because her star image would soon be linked to sexier roles. For this on-location episode, Donna trades in her usual pretty, perky wife look for more frumpy attire, perhaps to offset Fabares' sexiness or to distance Donna Reed from implied approval of it. The shadows in the shot sequence also reinforce this dynamic. While Mary's outfit makes her female body dangerous, to borrow Gaines' phrasing, Donna's loose-fitting clothes keep her safely under wraps, at least for this episode. She would return to her dresses with the cinched waists and tight bodices for the next episodes.

In terms of star brand, explicit sexiness would be necessary for Fabares to succeed in beach musicals in which she would play a love interest for the era's male teen idols. In 1964, the idol was Fabian and the film was *Ride the Wild Surf*, set in Hawaii, but the next three were Elvis films. This movement toward beach musicals was set in motion when her single "Johnny Angel" made it to #1 in April 1962. By 1965, she was costarring in *Girl Happy*, her first of three Elvis films. Her association with Elvis and beach culture continued in *Spinout* (1966) and *Clambake* (1967).

2.10   Rock 'n' Roll (& Lose Control) on *Patty Duke* and *Gidget*

With Shelley Fabares and Tony Dow gone from the roster of ABC teens, schedulers moved *Ozzie & Harriet* to Wednesdays in 1963–4 to act as the lead-in to the rock 'n' roll teen sitcom, *The Patty Duke Show* (ABC 1963–6). The teen-centric series premiered at 18 on Nielsen's ratings and likely contributed to *Ozzie & Harriet* coming in 29th for its first top-30 showing. The pair got a third series for 1964–5 when *The Patty Duke Show* played lead-in for ABC's *Shindig!*, the new teen music party variety series. Although only 17 when her sitcom began, Patty Duke had just won the 1962 Best Supporting Actress Oscar for her portrayal of Helen Keller in *The Miracle Worker*. For *The Patty Duke Show*, the first star sitcom built around a teen actor, Duke played dual roles as Patty Lane, the rock 'n' roll teen, and Cathy Lane, her Scottish cousin with old world/old school tastes.

The constant parental endorsements of Ricky by the Nelsons contrast with the behavior of the Lanes toward Patty Duke. While Mr. and Mrs. Lane do not necessarily embrace rock 'n' roll, neither do they dismiss it completely. In "Partying is Such Sweet Sorrow" (3.3), they even look on approvingly at Patty as she sings in the living room with a band she hired for a party. They are the Shindogs, the house band on *Shindig!*—*a bright new showcase for the big beat dance music*. The in-episode performance in this 1965 sitcom episode doubles as promotion not only for ABC's *Shindig!*, but also for Patty Duke's appearance in the feature film *Billie* and for her single, "Funny Little Butterflies." In the same episode, Patty sings a more lively song at the party itself, giving her a second moment of brandcasting. She sings a rendition of "I Am Henery the XIII, I Am," a number one hit that year for British invasion band, Herman's Hermits. As the song choices, episode title, and series name confirm, this Brooklyn Heights-set sitcom is told from the point of view of the rock 'n' roll teenager, which helps explain why Patty's logic wins over her father's in the final beat of the episode. Patty's logic is similarly privileged over that of her "identical cousin" Cathy, who is a prim Scottish girl with classical music and lifestyle tastes (as noted earlier, she is played by Patty Duke via some "cutting edge" camera tricks).

The Patty Duke Show marks ABC's movement toward teen-centric series and the emergence of the tween female pitchperson. In one embedded dramatized advertisement, for example, Patty promotes Breck hair care to Cathy, while they hang out "together" at home. This narrowcasting potential had market appeal, and ABC tried out a few more series led by or costarring spunky females. It had success with its magical sitcom *Bewitched*, but other series about young, newly married couples floundered, perhaps because they lacked tween crossover appeal. ABC tried out some notable one-season series such as *Honey West* (with Anne Francis as a sexy female detective) and *Gidget* (with Sally Field as a spunky surfer girl), before launching Marlo Thomas in *That Girl*, its first true single-girl sitcom.

Before turning to that series and its schedule pairings with Elizabeth Montgomery's *Bewitched*, among other female-centered sitcoms including one starring Sally Field, we need to consider Field's 1965 series *Gidget* because it was ABC's failed attempt to develop series whose primary focus was on California teen culture.

After Shelley Fabares left the network, the beach party briefly came to ABC both through *Gidget* in 1965–6 and 1967's *Malibu U*, the filmed on-location, musical variety, "summer beach-in" series. *Malibu U* is remarkable because it was hosted by Rick Nelson and featured performances by The Doors, Buffalo Springfield, and The Turtles, as well as many of the era's pop idols. *Gidget* is the more interesting series, but the short run of both series suggests how hard it is for a broadcast network to sustain any true narrowcasting. *Gidget* has features that are quite similar to today's successful tween sitcoms on basic cable narrowcasters:

- a young person offering advice to her peers [via direct address in this case];
- a central best friend relationship [a single dad/peer-ent];

FIGURE 2.9 Steve Douglas, peer-ent, plays with Robbie's band in *My Three Sons* (upper). Patty Duke sings with the Shindogs on her self-titled sitcom (lower). *The Patty Duke Show* was the 1964 schedule lead-in to *Shindig!* (a music showcase series).

- a trendy youth culture focus [Southern California surf culture];
- the validation of a young female point of view and of her position as a potential stylist for viewers; and
- narrowcast advertising [in *Gidget*'s case, for hair care products].

Gidget was ahead of its time, offering viewers a more modern character in comparison to characters in the other ABC series. Several newspapers heralded the arrival of this appealing and winsome character. As Field put it in an interview with Vince Leonard of *The Pittsburgh Press* at the time, "There has never been a show about teens . . . the pains they go through. This is real to life." Sylvie Reice addressed the difficulties of speculating on teen tastes: "You can't pin teens down. Make the generalization that they're all reading escape literature now (the Tolkien books) and you find just as many are reading James Baldwin. Decide that teens want westerns and/or violence on TV (Don't they just adore those *Men from U.N.C.L.E.*) and you get letters and letters asking you to write about typical American teen: Sally Field."

Field plays Frances "Gidget" Lawrence as a spunky, self-assured teen who has an enviable peer-to-peer relationship with her dad. Don Porter described his portrayal of Professor Russell Lawrence as a father who often "loses with dignity" because he sees the validity of his daughter's point of view and does not feel the need to assert blanket authority over her. It helps that he's a widower because there is no mother modeling female norms. As a budding surfer, Gidget spends most of her time at the beach and is accepted by the gang of mostly male surfers. To keep dating storylines at a safe distance, Gidget has a long distance boyfriend (Jeff, a surfer now attending Princeton).

With Jeff away, the series does not even have to deal with kissing very often, but there are episodes that hint at the more sexually free beach culture, and Gidget's attraction to that world. In "The Great Kahuna" (1.3), for instance, Gidget's father Russ shows up at the beach to get a look at the object of Gidget's sudden affection, the Big Kahuna, an older surfer whose been traveling the world. Gidget's usual crowd of young, male surfers has never met her dad, but welcomes him like the good "clean teens" they are at heart. The costuming acknowledges Gidget's "new girl" status, conveying through her sportier bikini that she directs her energies toward leisure activities more typically associated with boys. Other elements in this episode and previous ones confirm that Gidget has little interest in preparations to be good wife like her married sister. Gidget rejects her sister Anne's attempts to parent her, and Russ shows more respect for his younger daughter and her interests. The episode ends with Gidget getting over her attraction to Kahuna and reminding herself that she is lucky to have Jeff. Yet, it does not foreclose the possibility or the appeal of alternative lifestyles by ending on an ambivalent note after Gidget reads a letter from Jeff saying he is planning to take time off after graduating and just "bum around."

Bumming around is already the daily routine at the beach, where many scenes are often set. Episodes typically revolve around the screwball antics of Gidget and her often reluctant best friend Larue, as is evident in "My Ever Faithful Friend" (1.11). The episode is also rich in what Gaines calls "storytelling costuming." The beach attire of each female points to how she "wears" gender a different way. A sporty bikini becomes the shorthand that tells us Gidget is the representative of the middle ground between two extreme female types. On her left is Larue, as the overly conservative and covered up female completely uninterested in dating. On her right is a popular girl dressed in a "lipstick kisses" patterned bikini, which Gidget disdainfully describes as "mostly skin." The dialogue confirms that the popular girl directs her energies to attracting male suitors (and competing with other women). Putting Gidget in the middle of these poles calls into question the contradictory values society places on both female chastity and sexiness.

The scene also establishes that Gidget is interested in dating, but that she prioritizes friendship over all else. She stands up to the popular girl who calls Larue an ox and pokes fun at her. Yet, Gidget is not above trying to transform her childhood friend into a slightly more normative female so she can blend in a bit better. Larue's cover-up makes her look old-fashioned, whereas Gidget's sunglasses suggest her modern outlook. They also signify that she doesn't see as clearly as Larue, who is happy with being herself and not interested in "fashioning" a consumer-inflected identity. In the shot of the trio on the beach blanket, Larue's body is the most literally grounded, whereas the popular girl has merely alighted momentarily like "one of those 'wiggy' birds" Gidget describes as flitting around from blanket to blanket. Gidget does not totally reject the logic of drawing attention to your physical appearance and spends the rest of the episode working on a misguided makeover of Larue. As it is a middle-ground series, *Gidget* still implies that Larue should desire to be a bit more normative. After all, advertisers need teens to buy their latest offerings in nail polish, hair care, and beachwear.

Despite only lasting one year, *Gidget* is an important series because it moved the era's new girl type from spunky sidekick in the Warner Brothers detective fare circa 1959–63 to the center of the action. ABC did not have faith in the series and cancelled it prematurely. It is interesting to note that the ratings saw an uptick in viewers for *Gidget* during summer reruns. Too bad the series was already cancelled, prompting an outpouring of fan complaint and some newspaper commentary. *The Morning Record and The Meriden* (Connecticut) reported in September 1967 that ABC had made a major scheduling error when it cancelled *Gidget*. It explained that by the summer rerun season, the sitcom had "edged its way into the top ten and ABC brass not only had to face up to the hasty decision, but even work its way through thousands of angry letters from disappointed fans."

Much to Sally Field's annoyance, ABC next cast her in *The Flying Nun* (1967–70). Costumed in a full habit as Sister Bertrille, the girl formerly known as Gidget was shifted to the Larue end of the spectrum. The series took the idea of a "new girl" type pitted against the establishment and buried it safely in subtext. She played a spunky, young nun character whose headgear and small size combined to enable her to fly. Using such a character to stand in for the "new girl" of the era may

FIGURE 2.10 Costuming and shot composition position Gidget as the "new girl" of 1965 and the middle ground between female types (upper). While *Gidget*'s main focus is on best friends (middle), it also features a peer-ent. This is evident when Gidget's usual crowd of young, male surfers welcomes her dad to the beach (lower).

seem off to us today, but spunky nuns were already the subject of a popular 1966 Hayley Mills film, *The Trouble With Angels*, and its November 1968 sequel. The sitcom became part of what Reice and other entertainment columnists called a "massive realignment of its Thursday night schedule," with *The Flying Nun* paired with the "witch marries a mortal" series, *Bewitched*. Both shows displaced female power onto magical or unlikely circumstances. The new Thursday schedule placed the pair alongside *That Girl*, a more grounded, although screwball style sitcom, which had a "Gidget moves to Manhattan" vibe.

2.11   *That* Kind of Girl on *That Girl* and *Bewitched*

Through *That Girl* (1966–71) ABC aged up its teen type. Changing from a teen to a 20-something character, one who moves alone to Manhattan to pursue an acting career, enables the sitcom to appeal to a range of demographics but still remains tween-inclusive. As a cheeky TVLand promo made clear, *That Girl* was not about "that kind of girl," but about wacky antics. In early episodes Ann's father was always appearing at the apartment to check and make sure Ann was not having a sexual relationship with her boyfriend Donald. Despite his disapproval, Lew Marie accepts Ann's move because of how much he values his relationship with his daughter. Ann does have a conversation with Donald when she reminds him of how often she has said "no," but there are many moments when the series seems to be winking at the idea that the two would be in such a chaste relationship for so long.

That Girl would move the spunky girl to center stage and keep her there for five seasons. It helped the series' broadcast appeal that Ann Marie is played by Marlo Thomas, daughter of Danny Thomas. The characterization of Ann's father Lew Marie as a good-hearted man who covers his emotional sensitivity with a veneer of bluster aligns with the character Danny Thomas played on his own sitcom. The extratextual knowledge of the connection generated buzz for *That Girl* and that family connection enabled Marlo Thomas to get a pitch meeting at ABC and secure the in-demand writing team of Sam Danoff and Bill Persky, who had worked together on *The Dick Van Dyke Show*.

One of the iconic images from *That Girl* is the credits' shot sequence of Ann looking in the display window of luxury retailer Bergdorf Goodman and doing a double take when she realizes the mannequin IS her, or a fantasy version of her. Ann's alternate self wears a tiara with a veil. She is dressed in a dark, luxurious medieval gown and is posed in front of a unicorn tapestry. The living mannequin winks at Ann, who smiles broadly in response. Ann seems pleased by the fantasy: perhaps a future in which she is a successful actress and "fashionista" who rules Manhattan, or perhaps just a future of luxury shopping enabled by Ann's ability to support herself with a well-paying career, hopefully as an actress. Or maybe it is that the mannequin is stuck in her position, wearing what could be a wedding veil and medieval wedding dress. In contrast, Ann is shown on the move in various parts of New York. She is independent, mobile and, as the narrator in promotions characterizes her, "fully alive." It's unclear if Ann's attraction is solely to the regal gown or if it is to the contrasting regal independence of her own life, and her fantasy of a future of financial independence that would keep her closets full of British-mod mini-dresses and pencil pants. In any case, the shot sequence is definitely a rejection of the idea of a woman as window dressing, mixed ambivalently with an embrace of the centrality of fashion to female self-expression. Ann wants control of her own decision making, but more so of her own consumer spending. This makes Ann similar not only to today's postfeminists, but to her predecessor Gidget in that she is depicted as empowered but often seeking self-expression through fashion choices. *That Girl*'s last season had Ann finally get engaged to Donald. Continuing the ambivalence of the series' representation of gender, the final episode is not a wedding, but Ann taking Donald along to a consciousness-raising women's lib meeting.

While the sexual revolution issues are still an undercurrent in *That Girl*, it is easier to have a 30-year-old actress in the "new girl" role, as producers could control the changes in the way she looked. With teen actors, there is the unknown factor of how they will grow out of their original characterization and look. The ambivalent depictions of Ann register the gendered tensions that Susan Douglas argues are at the heart of many 1960s sitcoms. She characterizes *Bewitched* as another series that negotiates "the impending release" of feminine power and sexuality. Gender issues abound in *Bewitched* because its premise is that a pretty, young witch marries a mortal and tries (and often fails) to conform to mortal gender norms to please him.

Bewitched was more sexual than earlier suburban sitcoms. Samantha is sometimes costumed in sexy nightgowns and the couple is often shown in their bedroom and even sometimes in their double bed. The January 1967 episode "Sam in the Moon" (3.17) exemplifies this dynamic. Darrin fears that Sam and her mother have taken a literal trip to the moon. The last scene is framed so that we see Samantha, dressed in a sexy negligee, sitting on the bedroom windowsill, and basking dreamily in moonlight. A subtextual conversation follows:

> Darrin: "Well . . . have you . . ."
> Sam: "Have I what?"
> Darrin: "Been to the moon . . . ever?"
> Sam: (In the final line of the episode): "There are some things a wife shouldn't tell a husband. And whether she's been to the moon is one of them."

Only the audience can see the subsequent look on her face, which seems to suggest that a girl who kisses like Sam does in the pilot episode has probably "been to the moon" before! Darrin is probably thinking that too as the script direction is that "Darrin looks vaguely dissatisfied." Of course, the series contained Sam's sexuality in marriage, and she had already had her first child in season two.

While a good deal of the commentary on *Bewitched* explores its fascinating gender politics, the sitcom is also interesting for the way it deals with ethnicity through its witch–mortal "mixed marriage" premise. *Bewitched* represents a displacement of ethnic issues onto a fantasy scenario of middle-class, Anglo American Darrin marrying Samantha, a witch from an elite line of witches and warlocks. On a subtextual level, Samantha might represent the ethnic American in a mixed marriage with a WASP, whereas Darrin would be the upwardly mobile, middle-class, ordinary American who has married a woman from an eccentric, wealthy family. Her family is certainly disapproving of how Samantha has stepped down in the world. Her relatives even use the term "mixed marriage" and her mother Endora, her cousin Serena, and a variety of aunts and uncles spend a good deal of time "popping in" on Samantha. This behavior points to the expectations of an extended family in relation to the closeness to non-nuclear family relatives, as opposed to the "typical American" model of the contained and isolated nuclear family, which maintains its distance from extended family members except during the holidays.[17]

This thematic concern could be argued to reflect the fact that the 1960s was an era of assimilation in which the children born to immigrant parents or the children from poor or working class backgrounds were graduating college and often marrying people from different ethnic and/or class backgrounds. In any case, the magic sitcoms (and many of the rural sitcoms) are series about atypical Americans, whether because of class, ethnicity, or some other difference.[18]

These series had particular appeal for younger viewers because of their screwball antics, which is suggested in a 1967 ABC promo in which Elizabeth Montgomery (Samantha) reminds viewers that *Bewitched* will be on "a half an hour earlier so the whole family can watch." This schedule shift suggests that programmers were aware of the tween-inclusive aspects of the magical sitcom. This shift started in earnest in season three when more episodes focused on Samantha's wacky extended family, most often dotty, old Aunt Clara and prank-happy Uncle Arthur. While the popularity of the wacky antics sitcoms of the 1960s tend to be attributed to their appeal to *lowest common denominator* in the population, their ratings might be explained by their accommodation of tweens, *the youngest common demographic* in many television households. Lan Samantha Chang's memoir piece on *Gilligan's Island* indicates as well that screwball sitcoms about characters who don't fit in or characters who are reprimanded for their social guffaws also may have had appeal for immigrants and their "born here" children. In any case, Montgomery's "the whole family can watch" pitch indicates that programmers realized that these screwball sitcoms had appeal beyond the adults attracted to the lead actresses or to the subtextual gender rebellions. The same kind of multiple potential appeals helps explain the popularity of *That Girl* as well, so it is not surprising that the sitcom shared the Thursday night schedule with *Bewitched*.

FIGURE 2.11 Samantha from *Bewitched* is caught between her atypical mother (upper) and her typical American husband in a sitcom whose magical premise displaces "mixed-marriage" conflicts of ethnicity and social class. In *Make Room for Daddy*, Danny returns home from a nightclub tour to class and ethnic conflicts with a governess and his class-climbing wife (lower). Danny proudly acknowledges his background, but his wife is ashamed of her class origins and her show business mother (in the foreground).

2.12   ABC's *Thursday's Girls* Schedule Promotions

The most intriguing season was 1966–7 because ABC began running promotions indicating that programmers were narrowcasting to audiences interested in watching young women in leading roles. In one dramatized promotion alerting viewers to some midseason schedule shifting on Thursday nights in 1967, two young women join Elizabeth Montgomery on the couch in Samantha Stephens' living room and directly address the audience. Elizabeth/Samantha is the most known to the audience, programmers assume, given that *Bewitched* was then placing seventh in the ratings and had been on air since 1964–5. The seating arrangement becomes a physical embodiment of the 1966–7 schedule shifting, of the promotional tagline, and of ABC's narrowcast address on Thursdays. When Elizabeth/Samantha says that Thursday's are getting a "new look" and then gestures to the other women, the longer shots reveal that Ann/Marlo and Judy/Julie are dressed in mod outfits of the time. The costuming might appeal to viewers interested in the latest London fashion arriving with the British Invasion, especially given Ann's penchant for Mary Quant style mini-dresses. The "new look" references the more general appeal of casting the three pretty young women (ages 28 to 34).

Judy/Julie is located between Elizabeth/Sam and Marlo/Ann, as it is the role of their series to act as "tentpoles" on the schedule, delivering an audience to her sitcom *Love on a Rooftop*.[20] The schedule dramatization is intriguing as an indirect and visual way of encouraging desired viewing behavior. The three women pitch the schedule to viewers from some in-between position as both their characters (Marlo Thomas has Ann's signature sunglasses on her head) and themselves (the announcer addresses them by their real names). Thomas' delivery of her lines and her confused way of explaining the schedule shuffling is similar to the screwball character she plays on *That Girl*. When it is her turn to talk she looks into the camera and says, "Yes, I'm that girl," and then launches into a very daffy explanation of the schedule shift. She cuts herself off and simplifies: "Look, if you just tune in at 8:30 and stay until 10, you won't miss a thing." Sam/Liz reiterates her earlier point: "There'll be a whole new look on Thursday Nights." Then she repeats the details of the schedule shift: "*Bewitched* a half an hour earlier, followed by *Love on a Rooftop*, and then *That Girl*" (as she points at Marlo/Ann). After a pause, she says, "Please join us, in color, on ABC." The final shot of the dramatization is followed by a shot of the actual schedule on a text-based billboard.

It's notable that *Bewitched* is also a generational discord series, and the paring with *Love on a Rooftop* and *That Girl* makes the generational theme more noticeable. Although it is not addressed in the promotion, they are a trio of series in which young women are badgered about their life choices by loving, but disapproving, parents. Yet, the women continue to do things their own ways even though they know their parents disapprove. In *Love on a Rooftop*, for instance, Judy Carne plays Julie, an art student and daughter of wealthy parents who disapprove of her impulsive marriage to David Willis, an apprentice architect surviving

SCHEDULE 2.4 The schedule parings for ABC's *Bewitched*, most notably the 1966–9 lineups promoted as "Thursday's Girls, in color, on ABC."

ABC	Day of Week	7:30	8:00	8:30	9:00	9:30
1964–5	Thursday	Flintstones	Donna Reed Show	My Three Sons #13 (25.5 rating)	Bewitched #2 (31.0 rating)	Peyton Place #9 (26.4 rating)
1965–6	Thursday	Batman #5 (27.0 rating)	Donna Reed Show	O.K. Crackerby! Double Life of Henry Phyfe	Bewitched #7 (25.9 rating)	Peyton Place
1966–7[19]	Thursday	Batman	F Troop	The Dating Game/ **Bewitched #7**	Bewitched #7 (23.4 rating)/ **That Girl**	**That Girl**
1967–8	Thursday	Batman	**Flying Nun**	**Bewitched #11** (23.5 rating)	**Love on a Rooftop** / **That Girl**	Peyton Place
1968–9	Thursday	Ugliest Girl in Town	Flying Nun	Bewitched #11 (23.3 rating)	That Girl	Journey to the Unknown
1969–70	Thursday	Ghost & Mrs. Muir	That Girl	Bewitched #24 (20.6 rating)	This is Tom Jones	
1970–1	Thursday	Matt Lincoln Alias Smith and Jones		Bewitched	Barefoot in the Park Make Room for Granddaddy	Odd Couple Dan August
1971–2	Wednesday	Local	Bewitched	Courtship of Eddie's Father	Smith Family	Shirley's World

FIGURE 2.12 Marlo Thomas in her direct-to-viewer schedule pitch for *That Girl*. The ABC's *Thursday's Girls* schedule line-up promotion below signaled a move away from the prior season's sexy girl sitcoms to screwball sitcoms with tween appeal, including *The Flying Nun*.

on a $85.37 per week salary. Judy and David are happy living in a tiny San Francisco apartment, especially because it has access to the roof and a really good view (of the San Francisco home base of the 1967 counterculture). As already noted, Ann is living alone in a New York City apartment, much to her father's chagrin. One pre-premiere ABC promotion for *That Girl* attempted to contain the association of Ann with a "sexual liberation in the city" subtext using a narrator who assured viewers that Ann was "young and alive AND very much in love" with her serious boyfriend Donald. Although the other two are married characters, Ann, Julie, and Samantha all have parents who treat them like girls and vocally disapprove of their lifestyles. In doing so, they put their daughters in the position of articulating their reasons for making specific new generation choices. Episodes allow the women to voice their belief systems and, in the end, the young women prevail and the parents back down (until the next episode, of course). While the situations are banal and the characters engage only in minor acts of rebellion, they represent early prototypes of new kinds of female characters. This first step, we might argue, was to offer good girl characters with rebellious streaks.

Later seasons of *Bewitched* took this a step further and integrated a fully rebellious female alter ego for Sam in the person on her "identical cousin," Serena (also played by Elizabeth Montgomery). The simplistic visual register of the series depicts Serena as the smoldering version of Samantha through Serena's dark hair and mod style. Added to the characterization is her bombshell beauty mark (sometimes a peace sign), oversized eyelashes, and contemporary fashions that range from sexpot to hippie to the Twiggy-style mod look. This characterization is especially obvious in an episode, "Serena Stops the Show" (6.22), when Serena becomes a fan of the then well-known pop act and songwriting duo of Boyce & Hart (Tommy and Bobby). Adding a narrowcast inflection to a broadcast series was more effective than offering a narrowcast series such as *Getting Together*. This 1971 ABC sitcom was supposedly modeled on the songwriting career of Boyce & Hart and their experiences writing hits like "(I'm Not Your) Steppin' Stone" and "Last Train to Clarksville," among many other songs for *The Monkees* on NBC 1966–8.

In "Serena Stops the Show" Sammy, as Serena calls her, does bop along to the Boyce & Hart song, but she still remains more suburban than mod, a fact registered by the shots that capture the difference in the characters' costuming. Samantha of season one is a demure blond (and Clairol spokesperson), with a modern edge and a flip hairstyle (see Figure 2.11). Sam of later seasons was increasingly spunky, a woman advertisements of the time might have called "vital" and "modern." Her outfits changed from shift dresses and ladylike outfits to modern relaxed suburban attire to youth culture inspired mini-dresses. As Sam's look evolved over the course of *Bewitched* (1964–72) it reflected cultural changes and the evolving depiction of young women on ABC (and other networks). By later seasons, Sam has long straight hair and dresses more frequently in mini-skirts, looking more like a teen than a housewife.

FIGURE 2.13 Costuming and musical taste signal the difference between blond, suburban Sam and her dark-haired and dangerous alter ego and "identical cousin" Serena (both played by Elizabeth Montgomery in *Patty Duke* style).

Similarly, Ann Marie of *That Girl* starts out as modern girl with a jaunty hairdo, but by the 1970–1 episodes has longer, sleeker, straighter Cher-style hair.[21] In 1967–8 Marlo/Ann and Liz/Sam got a decidedly unfashionable companion in Sally Field as Sister Bertrille when Thursday's Girls were now *The Flying Nun*, *Bewitched*, and *That Girl* and a simple title card insert replaced the on-the-couch promotion (see Figure 2.12).

The replacement of *Gidget* with *The Flying Nun* might have been only partially about general fears about the possible risqué content of a teen beach show as Gidget grew up, and more about that content in relation to the series' attraction for viewers who were younger than the characters. While any actual teen might find the dilemmas of a television teen at odds with real experience, a tween or even a kid might be attracted to the representative fun and independent teen lifestyle that they imagine they will experience in the future. Whether correct or not, programmers seemed to assume that tweens would be more interested in seeing a Gidget-type do spunky things in screwball situations than in being involved physically with boyfriends. As targeting tweens and teens in overt ways was clearly a tricky business, it is not surprising that the teen-exclusive shows did not last.

2.13 Family Fridays and Tween Tuesdays

While Thursdays were being reserved for tween-and-teen-appeal "new girls," Fridays were for actual tweens. The larger families on *The Brady Bunch* (1969–74) and *The Partridge Family* (1970–4) were precursors to the ensemble casts strategies of the present. With more kids came more potential sites of identification. The Bradys were a blended family of eight, with two kids, two tweens, two teens, two trying-to-be-hip peer-ents, a shaggy dog, and a veteran comedian playing the housekeeper and providing comic relief. Starting in 1970, the Bradys were paired with another new kind of family, the Partridges. The family of six performed together in a rock 'n' roll band and toured the country in a school bus painted with Mondrian-inspired color blocks. *The Partridge Family* created comedy out of the everyday lives of a family headed by Shirley Partridge (Shirley Jones). The widowed mom was a new peer-ent type, as she went beyond approving of the kids' rock 'n' roll band to playing in a professional band. Lead guitarist and eldest son Keith (played by David Cassidy, the actual stepson of Shirley Jones) was even positioned as a potential stand-in, authoritarian parent in a few episodes. As we saw with Steve Douglas, the episodes resolve with Shirley asserting the peer-ent point of view, leaving Keith to return to hip, older brother status.

Beyond its teen idol, *The Partridge Family* included a pretty female teen, two almost-tween kids, and the obligatory "irrepressible" tween male. It was a parallel series to *Ozzie & Harriet* for its irrepressible tween, real life parent playing a peer-ent to a soon-to-be-teen-idol (David Cassidy), and its embedded musical performances, airing like stand-alone music videos and promoting actual singles

SCHEDULE 2.5 Tween Fridays on ABC reflected a narrowcasting streak already in place in 1970.

ABC	Day of Week	7:30	8:00	8:30	9:00	9:30
1969–70	Friday	Let's Make a Deal	Brady Bunch	Ghost & Mrs. Muir	Here Come the Brides	
1970–1	Friday	Brady Bunch	Nanny and the Professor	The Partridge Family #25 (19.8 rating)	That Girl	Love, American Style Odd Couple
1971–2	Friday	Local	Brady Bunch	The Partridge Family #16 (22.6 rating)	Room 222 #28 (19.8 rating)	Odd Couple
1972–3	Friday	Local	Brady Bunch	The Partridge Family #19 (20.6 rating)	Room 222	Odd Couple
1973–4	Friday	Local	Brady Bunch	Odd Couple Six Million Dollar Man #11 (22.7 rating)	Room 222	Adam's Rib Odd Couple

and albums. The comedy of the episodes sometimes revolved around teen situations faced by Laurie/Susan Dey as representative of the teen female point of view or by Keith/David Cassidy, as the long-haired heartthrob-in-residence. The two kids, Chris and Tracy were barely even supporting players. Over time, the majority of episodes showcased the tween-aged Danny (Danny Bonaduce) and concocted situations in which his antics exasperated the band's neurotic and long-suffering agent, Rueben Kincaid.

In terms of demographic range, *The Brady Bunch* offered comparatively more episodes about its kids, Bobby and Cindy, although episodes about Marcia and Greg dominate. Yet, like the emphasis on tweenage Danny, some of the most infamous *Brady Bunch* episodes focus on the tweens: irrepressible Peter and inconsolable Jan. She was often struggling with being in the shadow of her beautiful teen sister Marcia (played by Maureen McCormick who often graced the covers of teen magazines). Dad Mike Brady was sometimes a peer-ent type. His "think young" worldview was embodied in his Plymouth Barracuda Convertible. By this point, convertibles no longer only belonged to bachelor uncles or young people (e.g., the Pontiac GTOs of the Douglas boys in *My Three Sons*). They were now parked in the driveways of "think young" American dads. When Greg Brady aged into the older teen role, he and Mike became more equal in their interactions and were linked by the fact that they both were shown driving the convertible. Unlike a more typical peer-ent, Mike definitely positioned himself as the family's lesson-giving moral authority, just one dressed in more youthful

clothing. Carol also had a closet of youthful clothes and increasingly contemporary hairdos, although she was really more of a June Cleaver, in that Mike often
explained the kids' behavior to her. The fact that they were parents in a family
blended together after the death of their first spouses was only a culturally relevant issue for a few episodes before the family history and continuing problems
it might cause was conveniently forgotten.

As for the rest of the sitcoms on the schedule, short-run series *Nanny and the
Professor* and the final season of *Ghost and Mrs. Muir* (which had aired two seasons on NBC) also featured tween characters. The seeming anomaly is *The Odd
Couple* about two divorced men who become roommates. One might position
it as an attempt to offer more socially relevant programming on a hot button
social issue, and place it alongside *Room 222*, an Emmy-winning sitcom about
an idealistic bunch of city school teachers with the main focus on an idealistic
African American history teacher. Of course, a school-set series with a popular
young actress (Karen Valentine) playing a student teacher and a sitcom about
mismatched "roommates as family" have some older tween and teen appeal.
In the later 1970s, ABC would get some good ratings for its roommates as
family series, and CBS continues to have ratings success with its sitcoms about
roommates.

2.14   ABC's Mid-1970s Ratings Dominance

Beyond the logic of courting the youngest common demographic, such sitcoms
point to an emerging inflection to ABC as a channel—ensemble casts featuring
peer-ent types in series that were aspirational in tone and in which the ensemble
ranged in age from kids to tweens to teens. *Eight is Enough* (March 1977–August
1981) is an obvious standout in this regard. The dramedy is significant first for its
eight Bradford children, many of them over 18 and depicted as sexually active.
Episode segments are often focused on the four oldest girls (18, 19, 20, and 21),
but plenty of screen time was accorded to the boys, especially Nicholas, age 8,
and just-a-teen Tommy, who eventually drives a VW bus just like older brother
David. Only 22 at the start of the series, David eventually settles down, but he is
a rebel at the outset who forgoes college to work with his hands and live in his
own bachelor pad. At first his father Tom Bradford is exasperated by his son, and
often with the decisions of his other kids, especially when the girls sneak off to
use David's apartment. Tom eventually evolves into a peer-ent dad type, especially after he becomes a widower (due to the death of the lead actress). Then he
dates and marries a young teacher named Abby, who had been tutoring Tommy
when he was out of school with a broken leg. Given Abby's age and all the young
women in the house, *Eight is Enough* became more like a fantasy of a new kind
of family of peers. In relation to this chapter's focus on schedule branding, the
show is significant for the way it represents ABC's tween-inclusive programming
slate during the mid-1970s. *Eight Is Enough* would become part of the tween-and

SCHEDULE 2.6 Tween Tuesdays enabled ABC to reach its first #1 network finish in the three-way ratings race.

ABC	Day of Week	8:00	8:30	9:00	9:30
1976–7	Tuesday	Happy Days #1 (31.5 rating)	Laverne & Shirley #2 (30.9 rating)	Rich Man, Poor Man Book II #21 (21.6 rating)	
1977–8	Tuesday	Happy Days #2 (31.4 rating)	Laverne & Shirley #1 (31.6 rating)	Three's Company #3 (28.3 rating)	Soap #13 (22.0 rating)
1978–9	Tuesday	Happy Days #3 (28.6 rating)	Laverne & Shirley #1 (30.5 rating)	Three's Company #2 (30.3 rating)	Taxi #9 (24.9 rating)

teen-inclusive scheduling that helped give ABC its unprecedented first-place finish in the ratings ahead of its two competitors, CBS and NBC.

Playing a major role in propelling ABC forward to its first-place win for 1976–7, producer Gary Marshall provided the core programs for what I call the network's "Tween Tuesdays" line-up, with its central pairing of the 1950s-set sitcom *Happy Days* and its spinoff *Laverne and Shirley*.[22]

While they might seem simply like nostalgic takes on an as-it-never-was America, the sitcoms placed more emphasis on a 1970s rendition of the peer-ent: friends functioning as parents for friends. While this peer-ent dynamic could veer toward the serious depending on the situation and the advice, especially in the lower class sitcom world of *Laverne & Shirley*, episodes were dominated by more slapstick moments. Although designed to appeal to viewers of all ages, these sitcoms stand out for their tween-inclusive address, given their relatively young protagonists, juvenile humor, and, as Elana Levine has shown, middle school-level sexual titillation and innuendo.[23]

To trumpet its ratings win, the network aired the *ABC Silver Anniversary Special* in February 1978. This four-hour variety special/promotional hybrid program celebrated the broad success across the ABC schedule (it had seven of the top ten series in 1976–7), and recalled ABC's programming history more generally. On hand were some actors from *My Three Sons*, *Make Room for Daddy*, and *The Adventures of Ozzie & Harriet*—all long-running sitcoms that had young actors and tween-appeal situations. Representing some of the famous youth-appeal series cycles in ABC's history, the stars of the "kiddie" westerns of the 1950s and the sexy detectives of the past and present, including *Charlie's Angels*, made dramatic entrances. In reviewing this kind of history and showcasing recent ratings wins, ABC also had to acknowledge that less-than-prestigious thematic and demographic appeals had propelled it to the top for the first time. After all, ABC became successful by having broadcast series with narrowcast elements

appealing to tweens, thereby ending the era in which U.S. television was dominated by socially relevant and critically acclaimed sitcoms, including CBS's *All in
the Family* (1971–9), *Maude*, (1972–8), and *Mary Tyler Moore* (1970–7).

The network's ambivalence about the shows airing on its schedules over the
years and its most recent route to the number one placing in Nielsen's ratings was
palpable from the start of the evening. The special began with an introduction
by Penny Marshall and Cindy Williams, costars in broadcast television's number
one series *Laverne & Shirley* (1976–83). The special also called attention to the
unlikely superstar status of Kristy McNichol, the 15-year-old who won the 1977
Emmy for Best Supporting Actress for her portrayal of the pubescent tomboy
character Buddy in the 10 p.m. drama *Family* (1976–80).[24] Gary Frank, the actor
who played Buddy's college-age brother and best pal, won the 1977 Best Supporting Actor Emmy. If the special had aired after the September 1978 Emmys,
ABC promoters could have built up the Best Actress in a Drama win of Sada
Thompson (for her role as Kate Lawrence, their mother), thereby calling attention to the socially relevant aspects of the series. Although McNichol would win
the Emmy again in 1979, her diminutive presence on the stage aligned her less
with quality acting than with ABC's tween-inclusive and teen-inclusive brand of
programming.

FIGURE 2.14 Shirley shares her "obstinate optimist" advice with her best friend
Laverne, who is in need of a peer-ent pep talk. *Laverne & Shirley* was 1977's #1 show
and helped mid-1970s ABC reach its first #1 network ranking.

SCHEDULE 2.7 ABC's sitcom successes on [?]-ween Tuesdays during the run of *Happy Days*.

ABC	Day of Week	8:00	8:30	9:00	9:30	10:00
1975–6	Tuesday	Happy Days #11 (23.9 rating)	Welcome Back, Kotter #18 (22.1 rating) / Laverne & Shirley #3 (27.5 rating)	The Rookies		*Marcus Welby, M.D.*
1976–7²⁵	Tuesday	**Happy Days #1** (31.5 rating)	**Laverne & Shirley #2** (30.9 rating)	Rich Man, Poor Man Book II #21 (21.6 rating)		**Family**
midseason				**Eight is Enough #23** (21.1 rating)		
1977–8	Tuesday	**Happy Days #2** (31.4 rating)	**Laverne & Shirley #1** (31.6 rating)	**Three's Company #3** (28.3 rating)	**Soap #13** (22.0 rating)	**Family #26** (19.9 rating)
1978–9	Tuesday	Happy Days #3 (28.6 rating)	Laverne & Shirley #1 (30.5 rating)	Three's Company #2 (30.3 rating)	Taxi #9 (24.9 rating)	Starsky & Hutch
1979–80	Tuesday	Happy Days #17 (21.7 rating)	Angie	Three's Company #2 (26.3 rating)	Taxi #13 (22.4 rating)	Hart to Hart
1980–1	Tuesday	Happy Days #15 (20.8 rating)	Laverne & Shirley #20 (20.6 rating)	Three's Company #8 (22.4 rating)	Too Close for Comfort #15 (20.8 rating)	Hart to Hart #23 (19.9 rating)
1981–2	Tuesday	Happy Days #18 (20.6 rating)	Laverne & Shirley #20 (19.9 rating)	Three's Company #4 (23.3 rating)	Too Close for Comfort #6 (22.6 rating)	Hart to Hart #15 (21.1 rating)
midseason			Joanie Loves Chachi			
1982–3	Tuesday	Happy Days #23 (17.4 rating)	Laverne & Shirley #25 (17.8 rating)	Three's Company #6 (21.2 rating)	9 to 5 #15 (19.3 rating)	Hart to Hart #17 (18.9 rating)

The tone of McNichol's segment indicated that ABC executives were well aware that the network did not finally make it to first place because of quality acting across its series slate. The ratings boost came from the fact that many of its series were teen- and often tween-inclusive, even when they were about adult characters.

As noted above, the sitcoms tended to rely on the screwball antics of characters like Laverne and Shirley (and their neighbors Lenny and Squiggy). ABC viewers could soon also enjoy the disruptive antics of Robin Williams on *Mork & Mindy*, Danny DeVito on *Taxi*, and ensembles of comedians on *Soap*, *Barney Miller*, *Three's Company*, *What's Happening*, *Welcome Back, Kotter*, and *Happy Days*. Many of these series represented ABC's special brand of middle-school humor, and its ability to attract a broad range of viewers of all ages who enjoyed such light comedy.

ABC's programming for 1977–8 was shaped into the ultimate tween-inclusive and female-inclusive schedule. Tween-inclusive series kicked off the week, with Sunday Nights pairing *The Hardy Boys/Nancy Drew Mysteries* and *The Six Million Dollar Man*. As already noted, Tuesdays were for tween-coms, but Thursday comedies were tween-inclusive as well with *Welcome Back, Kotter*, *Barney Miller*, and *What's Happening*, among their offerings. Then Fridays kicked off with *Donny and Marie*, the Mormon singing duo from the famous Osmond family. She was "a little bit country" and he was "a little bit rock 'n' roll" and together their brand of clean pop and silly skits was perfect for white-bread tween sensibilities. Saturdays offered middle school-level titillation on *The Love Boat/Fantasy Island* combination, whereas the pairing of *Charlie's Angels* with *Eight is Enough* was a Wednesday night duo with a combined eight young women calculated as a female-centered, male-inclusive block.[26]

In relation to brandcasting at the level of the network schedule and early forms of channel branding that can be garnered from a network's programming slate, the special is most interesting for what it highlights about the history of narrowcasting at the heart of ABC's supposedly broadcast schedule. The broadcast narrowcast streak continues on ABC today, but much of the true tween narrowcasting has shifted to the cable channels, ABC Family and Disney Channel.

2.15 From *TGIF* to Disney Channel's Friendship Economy

Recalling this 1970s success with tween-inclusive fare and narrowcasting, ABC schedulers in the late 1980s crafted a *TGIF* programming block, explicitly inviting tween and family viewers to think of Friday nights on ABC as a lineup just for them. *Thank God It's Friday/Thank God It's Funny* promoted a tween-address line up which included *Full House*, *Perfect Strangers*, and its spinoff, *Family Matters*. Later schedules added *Boy Meets World*, *Step By Step*, *Hangin' With Mr. Cooper*, and *Sabrina, the Teenage Witch*. The night began with hosted lead-ins by series stars, initially the actors from *Perfect Strangers*, but later the lead adult actors from *Full House*. For 1991–2, this trio of "dads" moved back to its original Tuesday night slot to join *Roseanne* and *Coach* (with Shelley Fabares!). In this era ABC also aired many tween-inclusive sitcoms, including *The Wonder Years* (Fred Savage and Danica McKellar), *Doogie Howser, M.D.* (with Neil Patrick Harris as a teen genius doctor), *Who's the Boss* (Tony Danza and Alyssa Milano), *Home Improvement* (Tim Allen and Jonathan Taylor Thomas), and *Growing Pains* (Kirk Cameron and Leonardo DiCaprio). Today, Disney Channel and Disney-owned ABC Family air the series that most resemble or explicitly copycat elements of ABC sitcoms. Most notable is Disney Channel's highly anticipated 2014 newcomer, *Girl Meets World*. This sequel has the former tween stars of *Boy Meets World* playing the parents of the tweens Disney hopes to launch to multiplatform stardom through the sitcom. ABC Family already had success with *Melissa & Joey*, starring Melissa Joan Hart from *Sabrina, the Teenage Witch* and Joey Lawrence from *Blossom* in a *Who's The Boss?* scenario.

Disney Channel's *Shake It Up, The Wizards of Waverly Place, Liv & Maddie*, and *Good Luck, Charlie* have explicit parallels to *Laverne & Shirley, Bewitched, Sabrina, the Teenage Witch, The Patty Duke Show, Sister, Sister*, and *Growing Pains*.

While it is no surprise that the trio of besties dynamic of *The Wonder Years* has been replicated the most times on Disney Channel (e.g., *Lizzie McGuire, That's So Raven*, and *Hannah Montana*), the next chapter addresses how Disney's cable brandcaster bested the perennial market leader, Nickelodeon, by offering a compelling myth story about stars-in-the-making, which resonated with millennial tweens. Series such as *A.N.T. Farm*, had a trio of besties negotiating school day challenges, but updated it not only through an African American lead female, but also with the frame that the story was really a before-they-were stars backstory about Chyna Parks, future pop idol. At the same time, Disney groomed the series star, China Anne McClain for recording industry stardom and featured her in music videos for a series of singles, and put her in its friendship-themed corporate social responsibility shorts, *Disney's Friends for Change*. Chapter 3 details how friendship is at heart of the economics of Disney Channel, and central to its compelling address to a global cohort of millennial tweens.

Notes

1 Ellis 2000, quotations are from p. 36.
2 Greenblatt is quoted in Catlin (2007).
3 Catlin 2007.
4 Napoli 2003, 36.
5 Hartley 1999, 199.
6 Ellis 2000, 25.
7 For Thursday nights in 1962–3 ABC created a teen-inclusive schedule with four sitcoms featuring teen stars of the era.
8 Taylor 1989, 161.
9 Bashe 1992.
10 Seymour Korman, "Hollywood's 10 Bright Young Men." *Toledo Blade* [Ohio]. August 30, 1959. 1–2. Korman notes that Elvis had already amassed 20 gold records and

been in four films. Edd Byrnes of ABC's 77 *Sunset Strip* also made the list. On April 20, 1963 Rick Nelson (he had changed his name on his 21st birthday in May 1961) married Kris Harmon and they had their first child in October. As with David's wife June, Kris was eventually incorporated into the television show. Later, Rick described it as a shotgun wedding, and the speed with which all this happened definitely destabilized his brand identity. More generally, he was aging and his kind of sound was losing popularity as the British Invasion was providing new rock 'n' roll idols.

11 As Lindsay Giggey (2008–9) details, Connie Stevens would parlay the Cricket Blake role into costarring roles in feature films, including *Susan Slade* (1961) with fellow Warner Brother TV detective Troy Donahue.

12 Bodroghkozy 2001, 67.

13 Taylor 1989, 161.

14 *Father Knows Best* was an NBC series when it ended its original run in 1960, but was playing on ABC in reruns in 1962–3.

15 As *Donna Reed* was never truly a teen-focused series, for the two post-Mary seasons producers tried a "double couple" strategy, bringing in a younger couple. "Friends and Neighbors" from April 4, 1963 sets up the scenario that Alex's friend and fellow pediatrician, Dr. Dave Kelsey, is a mid-30s bachelor-for-life. Then he gets married to Midge, who is only a few years his junior, but acts more like a teenager. At first she makes him live with her parents, but with some coaching from the Stones, Dave manages to convince his wife to move into the house next door to the Stones. As a more recently married, thirty-something, childless couple, the Kelseys brought a youthful sensibility to the show and higher ratings. Dave Kelsey had particular appeal as he was played by Bob Crane, who would use his two-year stint on the series as a launch pad to star in his own sitcom, *Hogan's Heroes* (CBS 1965–71).

16 The Stones' adopted daughter Trisha was played by Patty Peterson, the real life little sister of Paul Peterson (Jeff Stone). Similarly, when *My Three Sons* lost eldest son Mike (Tim Considine both aged out of the series and had a contract dispute), producers used a similar adoption scenario to bring in a third son. Barry Livingston played Ernie and he was the real life younger brother of Stanley Livingston (Chip).

17 The mixing of different classes through marriage seems to also be at the heart of many of the rural sitcoms, such as ABC's *The Real McCoys*, which includes an episode where the series' granddaughter gets engaged to a wealthy neighbor, much to the disapproval of his parents. By the end of the episode, Grandpa (Walter Brennan) teaches them that they should reject their snobbishness and be happy their son is happy.

18 Whereas Ann Marie of *That Girl* is of ambiguous ethnicity, Marlo Thomas was widely known to be the Lebanese American daughter of Danny Thomas, even though she had surgery to make sure her nose bore little resemblance to his famous nose (the target of much of his self-deprecating humor). *The Danny Thomas Show* left the air in 1964 right before the debut of *Bewitched*. It directly addressed the mixed-marriage subject through Danny Williams' second marriage to Irish American Kathy. It sometimes explored the complications that the ethnic mix and their clashing relatives caused in their relationship. While Danny and Kathy's Irish father traded charged ethnic insults, *Bewitched*'s premise allowed for Sam's mother Endora to insult Darrin without insulting any audience segments.

19 ABC marketed its winter 1966–7 Thursday night line-up with the tagline *Thursday's Girls* to signal that its night of female-helmed sitcoms featured young, attractive, and modern "new girls": Elizabeth Montgomery, Judy Carne, and Marlo Thomas.

20 *Love on a Rooftop* did not succeed, although the concept was appealing enough that it was borrowed for *Dharma and Greg*, a series from 1997–2002 that was a minor success for ABC in trying to pick off viewers from NBC's then dominant "Must See TV"

block. *Love on a Rooftop* proved a good stepping-stone for the actors. Casting directors had good instincts in choosing Judy Carne as she went on to a decade-defining role as the "sock it to me" girl and go-go dancer on *Rowan and Martin's Laugh-In*, debuting as a special in September 1967 and then as a series in January 1968. *Love on a Rooftop* graduated Pete Duel to a starring role from his previous supporting role in *Gidget*. His bigger success would come later in *Alias Smith and Jones*. Although the series was a hit soon after it began in January 1971, it did not last long on the schedule because of the suicide of 31-year-old Duel on New Year's Eve 1971.

21 I look only at ABC's sitcom "girls" in this chapter, but there are some Serena types in *Batman*, *The Avengers* (the British import), and detective series like *Honey West* with Anne Francis as Aaron Spelling's "a private eyeful." Honey West has a male sidekick named Sam Bolt, a pet ocelot, her own detective agency, and a Shelby Cobra in the driveway. Created by Aaron Spelling, she is a precursor to his trio of mid-1970s female detectives in *Charlie's Angels*. Such series were, in turn, the precursors of Spelling's more recently produced female-helmed series, including WB's *Charmed* with Alyssa Milano of ABC's *Who's The Boss*.

22 *Happy Days* aired from 1974–84 and *Laverne & Shirley* from 1976–83.

23 Elana Levine (2007) offers astute analysis of these sitcoms. Her interest, however, is in examining how they mediate issues linked to the sexual revolution and how they register cultural shifts in attitudes about sex.

24 The 1977 supporting male actor Emmy went to Gary Frank, the actor who played Buddy's college-age brother and her best pal. He was 27 and was not emphasized in the special.

25 ABC achieved its first number one placement in the three-way ratings race through tween-inclusive programs such as *Happy Days* and *Laverne & Shirley*.

26 Once ABC did achieve number one status, NBC used a negative PR campaign that proved quite successful in disparaging ABC's programming. In her book, *Wallowing in Sex*, Levine (2007) covers the PR campaign through which NBC successfully branded ABC as a purveyor of "jiggle TV" and "kiddie porn."

Bibliography

"ABC-TV's 'Get 'em Young': Major Payoff in Kid Accent." *Variety*, March 23, 1955: 21, 38.

Abercrombie, Nicholas and Brian Longhurst. *Audiences: A Sociological Theory of Performance and Imagination*. London, UK. Sage, 1998.

Adalian, Josef. "Showtime Swears by Promo." *Variety*, August 20–6, 2007: 3.

America in Primetime. "The Independent Woman." PBS. October 30, 2011. Available: www.pbs.org/america-in-primetime/episodes/independent-woman/.

Alvey, Mark. "The Independents: Rethinking the Television Studio System." In *The Revolution Wasn't Televised: Sixties Television and Social Conflict*, eds. Lynn Spigel and Michael Curtin, 139–58. New York, NY: Routledge, 1997.

Anderson, Christopher. "Creating the Twenty-first-Century Television Network: NBC in the Age of Media Conglomerates." In Hilmes 2007, 275–90.

——. *Hollywood TV: The Studio System in the Fifties*. Austin, TX: University of Texas Press, 1994.

Anderson, Chris. "The Long Tail." *Wired* 12, no. 10, October 2004. Available: www.wired.com/wired/archive/12.10/tail_pr.html.

Ang, Ien. *Desperately Seeking the Audience*. New York, NY; Routledge, 1991.

Atkinson, Claire, "Netflix ends Q4 With an Astounding 31.7M subscribers." *The New York Post*. January 24, 2014. Available: http://nypost.com/2014/01/22/netflix-soars-on-sky-high-subscriber-numbers/.

Aucoin, Don. "Why the Dr. Is Out: Advertisers, Not Viewers, Dictate Which Shows Live and Which Die." *The Boston Globe*, May 29, 1998. C1.

Auletta, Ken. *Three Blind Mice: How the TV Networks Lost Their Way*. New York, NY: Random House, 1992.

Banet-Weiser, Sarah. *Kids Rule!: Nickelodeon and Consumer Citizenship*. Durham, NC: Duke University Press, 2007.

Barnouw, Erik. *The Sponsor: Notes on a Modern Potentate*. New York, NY: Oxford University Press, 1979.

Bashe, Philip. *Teenage Idol, Travelin' Man: The Complete Biography of Rick Nelson*. New York, NY: Hyperion Books, 1992.

Baughman, James L. *Same Time, Same Station: Creating American Television, 1948–1961*. Baltimore, MD: The John Hopkins University Press, 2007.

Becker, Ron. "Gay-Themed Television and the Slumpy Class." *Television & New Media* 7, no.2 (2006): 184–215.

Bierbaum, Tom. "The WB's Getting the Girls." *Variety*, November 2–8, 1998: 30.

Boddy, William. *Fifties Television: The Industry and its Critics*. Urbana and Chicago, IL: University of Illinois Press, 1993.

Bodroghkozy, Aniko. *Groove Tube: Sixties Television and the Youth Rebellion*. Durham, NC: Duke University Press, 2001.

Bradshaw, Lara. "Showtime's 'Female Problem': Cancer, Quality and Motherhood." *Journal of Consumer Culture* 13, no. 2 (2013): 160–77.

Broadcasting & Cable. "A Strategy for Stemming the Slide." *Broadcasting & Cable*, May 20, 2002: 21.

Brook, Vincent. "Convergent Ethnicity and the Neo-platoon Show." *Television & New Media 10*, no. 4 (July 2009): 331–53.

Brooke, Jill. "Counterpunch: WB Network's Programming Success." *Adweek*, March 30, 1998, 22–5.

Brooks, Tim and Earle Marsh. *The Complete Directory to Primetime Network and Cable TV Shows: 1946–Present*. 8th edition. New York, NY: Ballantine, 2003.

Brown, Les. *Television the Business behind the Box*. New York, NY: Harcourt Brace Jovanovitch, 1971.

Brunsdon, Charlotte. "What Is the 'Television' of Television Studies?" In Newcomb 2006, 609–28.

Butler, Judith. *Bodies that Matter: On the Discursive Limits of Sex*. New York, NY: Routledge, 1993.

Caldwell, John Thornton. "Convergence Television: Aggregating Form and Repurposing Content in the Culture of Conglomeration." In Spigel and Olsson 2004, 41–74.

——. "Critical Industrial Practice: Branding, Repurposing, and the Migratory Patterns of Industrial Texts." *Television & New Media* 7, no. 2 (May 2006): 99–134.

——. *Production Culture: Industrial Reflexivity and Critical Practice in Film and Television*. Durham, NC: Duke University Press, 2008.

——. *Televisuality: Style, Crisis, and Authority in American Television*. New Brunswick, NJ: Rutgers University Press, 1995.

——. "Welcome to the Viral Future of Cinema (Television)." *Cinema Journal* 45, no. 1 (Fall 2006): 90–7.

Campbell, Richard and Caitlin Campbell. "Demons, Aliens, Teens and Television." *Television Quarterly* 34, no.1 (Winter 2001): 56–64.

Carter, Bill. "Cable Juggernaut Continues With Emmy Award Nominations." *The New York Times*, July 18, 2008. E3.

——. *Desperate Networks*. New York, NY: Doubleday, 2006.

——. "TV Networks' Schedule Competition Is Starting to Resemble a Quilting Bee." *The New York Times*, January 19, 2008. C1, 20.

——. "With Focus on Youth, 2 Small TV Networks Unite." *The New York Times*, January 25, 2006. C4.

Castleman, Harry and Walter J. Podrazik. *Harry and Wally's Favorite TV Shows*. New York, NY: Prentice Hall, 1989.

——. *The TV Schedule Book*. New York, NY: McGraw-Hill, 1984.

Catlin, Roger. "Duchovny Back as a Sex-phile." *Hartford Courant*, August 13, 2007. Available: http://articles.courant.com/2007–08–13/features/0708130472_1_tom-kapi nos-adult-comedy-midlife-crisis.

Chang, Lan Samantha. "Like Robinson Crusoe." In *Prime Times: Writers on Their Favorite TV Shows*, ed. Douglas Bauer, 121–30. New York, NY: Crown, 2004.

Cheever, Susan. "Father Knows Best." In Bauer 2004, 45–51.

Cohen, Lizabeth. *A Consumer's Republic: The Politics of Mass Consumption in Postwar America*. New York, NY: Vintage/Random House, 2003.

Collins, Gail. *When Everything Changed: The Amazing Journey of American Women from 1960 to the Present*. New York, NY: Little, Brown and Company, 2009.

Collins, Scott. "Audience for 'Weeds' Grows." *Los Angeles Times*, "Quick Takes" section, August 16, 2006. Available: http://articles.latimes.com/2006/aug/16/entertainment/ et-quick16.4.

Consoli, John. "CW's Content Wraps May Keep DVR Viewer Interest." *Mediaweek*, January 29, 2007. 4+.

——. "CW Creates Content Wraps with Commercial Pods." *Mediaweek*, May 22, 2006. 4.

Coontz, Stephanie. *The Way We Never Were: American Families and the Nostalgia Trap*. New York, NY: Basic Books, 1992.

Crupi, Anthony and John Consoli, "Nets Testing VOD Waters." *Mediaweek*, November 14, 2005. 5.

Davis, Aeron. *Promotional Cultures: The Rise and Spread of Advertising, Public Relations, Marketing and Branding*. Cambridge, UK: Polity Press, 2013.

Davis, Glyn and Kay Dickinson, eds. *Teen TV: Genre, Consumptions and Identity*. London, UK: BFI Publishing, 2004.

Denis, Christopher Paul and Michael Denis. *Favorite Families of TV*. New York, NY: Citadel Press, 1992.

Dennis, Saul. "Brands Begin by Believing." *Promo Magazine*, June 2004: 121.

Doherty, Thomas. *Teenagers and Teenpics*, Philadelphia, PA: Temple University Press, 2002.

Donaton, Scott. *Madison and Vine: Why the Entertainment and Advertising Industries Must Converge to Survive*. New York, NY: McGraw-Hill, 2005.

Douglas, Susan J. *Where the Girls Are: Growing Up Female with the Mass Media*. New York, NY: Times, 1995.

Dow, Bonnie. *Prime-Time Feminism: Television, Media Culture, and the Women's Movement Since 1970*. Philadelphia, PA: University of Pennsylvania Press, 1996.

Dyer, Richard. *Stars*. London, UK: BFI Publishing, 1986.

Eckert, Charles. "The Carole Lombard in Macy's Window." In *Fabrications: Costume and the Female Body*, eds. Jane Gaines and Charlotte Herzog, 100–21. New York, NY: Routledge, 1990.

Ellis, John. "Interstitials: How the 'Bits in Between' Define the Programmes." In Grainge 2011, 59–69.

——. "Scheduling: the Last Creative Act in Television?" *Media, Culture and Society* 22, no. 1 (2000): 25–38.

Fabrikant, Geraldine. "Showtime's Perennial Struggle to Capture That HBO Aura." *The New York Times*, September 12, 2005. C1, 10.

Fallon, Kevin. "Showtime: Television for Women, for Everyone?" *The Atlantic*, August 16, 2010. Available: www.theatlantic.com/entertainment/archive/2010/08/showtime-television-for-women-for-everyone/61535/.

Feuer, Jane. "The Concept of Live Television: Ontology as Ideology." In *Regarding Television: Critical Approaches—An Anthology*, ed. E. Ann Kaplan, 12–21. Los Angeles, CA: The American Film Institute, 1983.

Feuer, Jane, Paul Kerr, and Tise Vahimagi. *MTM: "Quality Television."* London, UK: BFI Publishing, 1984.

Frank, Thomas. *The Conquest of Cool: Business Culture, Counterculture, and the Rise of Hip Consumerism.* Chicago, IL: University of Chicago Press, 1997.

Friedberg, Anne. "The Virtual Window." In *Rethinking Media Change: The Aesthetics of Transition*, eds. David Thornburn and Henry Jenkins, 337–53. Cambridge, MA: MIT Press, 2004.

Gaines, Jane. "Costume and Narrative: How Dress Tells the Woman's Story." In *Fabrications: Costume and the Female Body*, eds. Jane Gaines and Charlotte Herzog, 180–211. New York, NY: Routledge, 1990.

Gertner, Jon. "Our Ratings, Ourselves." *New York Times Magazine*. April 10, 2005. 34.

"Gidget Returns as the Flying Nun." *The Morning Record and The Meriden* (Connecticut). September 9, 1967. 1A.

Giggey, Lindsay. "Surf, Song, and Cricket Blake: Capturing the Emerging Teen Girl Market with Hawaiian Eye." UCLA Film and Television Archive Research and Study Center Award Paper, 2008–9.

Gillan, Jennifer. "From Ozzie Nelson to Ozzy Osbourne: the Genesis and Development of the Reality (Star) Sitcom." In *Understanding Reality Television*, eds. Su Holmes and Deborah Jermyn, 54–70. London, UK: Routledge, 2004.

———. *Television and New Media: Must-Click TV.* New York, NY: Routledge, 2010.

Gillan, Maria Mazziotti. "Daddy" and "Learning Silence." In *Identity Lessons: Contemporary Writing about Learning to Be American.* New York, NY: Penguin Books. 1999.

Gitlin, Todd. *Inside Prime Time.* New York, NY: Routledge, 1985.

Goodman, Tim. "Greatness of 'Weeds' Could Make Showtime Must-Pay-For Television." *San Francisco Gate.* August 11, 2006. Available: www.sfgate.com/entertainment/article/Greatness-of-Weeds-could-make-Showtime-2514299.php.

Gomery, Douglas. *A History of Broadcasting in the United States.* London, UK: Blackwell, 2008.

———. "Talent Raids and Package Deals: NBC Loses Its Leadership in the 1950s." In Hilmes 2007, 153–68.

Grainge, Paul. *Brand Hollywood: Selling Entertainment in a Global Media Age.* New York, NY: Routledge, 2008.

———, ed. *Ephemeral Media: Transitory Screen Culture from Television to YouTube.* London, UK: BFI Publishing, 2011.

———. "TV Promotion and Broadcast Design: An Interview with Charlie Mawer, Red Bee Media." In Grainge 2011, 87–101.

Gray, Herman. *Cultural Moves: African Americans and the Politics of Representation.* Berkeley, CA: University of California Press, 2005.

Gray, Jonathan. *Show Sold Separately: Promos, Spoilers, and Other Media Paratexts.* New York, NY: New York University Press, 2010.

———. "Television Pre-views and the Meaning of Hype." *International Journal of Cultural Studies* 11, no. 1 (2008): 33–49.

Gripsrud, Jostein. "Broadcast Television: The Chances of Its Survival in a Digital Age." In Spigel and Olsson 2004, 210–23.

Gwenllian-Jones, Sara and Roberta E. Pearson, eds. *Cult Television*. Minneapolis, MN: Minnesota University Press, 2004.

Halberstam, David. *The Fifties*. New York, NY: Villard, 1993.

"Halcyon Days for ABC—and All TV." *Business Week*, August 18, 1973.

Hamamoto, Darrell Y. *Nervous Laughter: Television Situation Comedy and Liberal Democratic Ideology*. New York, NY: Praeger, 1991.

Haralovich, Mary Beth. "Sit-coms and Suburbs: Positioning the 1950's Homemaker." In Spigel and Mann 1992, 111–41.

Hartley, John. *The Uses of Television*. New York, NY: Routledge, 1999.

Hills, Matt. "*Dawson's Creek*: 'Quality Teen TV' and 'Mainstream Cult?'" In Davis and Dickinson 2004. 54–67.

Hilmes, Michele. *Hollywood and Broadcasting: From Radio to Cable*. Urbana, IL: University of Illinois Press, 1990.

——, ed. *NBC: America's Network*. Berkeley, CA: University of California Press, 2007.

——. *Only Connect: A Cultural History of Broadcasting in the US*. 2nd edition. Belmont, CA: Wadsworth, 2008.

Hilmes, Michele and Jason Jacobs, eds. *The Television History Book*. London, UK: BFI Publishing, 2004.

Holt, Douglas B. *How Brands Become Icons: Principles of Cultural Branding*. Boston, MA: Harvard Business School Press, 2004.

Holt, Douglas B. and Douglas Cameron. *Cultural Strategy: Using Innovative Ideologies to Build Breakthrough Brands*. Oxford, UK: Oxford University Press, 2010.

Holt, Jennifer. "Vertical Vision: Deregulation, Industrial Economy and Prime-time Design." In Jancovich and Lyons 2003, 11–31.

"It's Showtime for Compelling Female Roles." *The Independent* (UK), April 20, 2010. Available: www.independent.co.uk/arts-entertainment/tv/features/its-showtime-for-compelling-female-roles-1948695.html.

Jancovich, Mark and Nathan Hunt. "The Mainstream, Distinction, and Cult TV." In Gwenllian-Jones and Pearson 2004, 27–44.

Jancovich, Mark and James Lyons, eds. *Quality Popular Television*. London, UK: BFI Publishing, 2003.

Jaramillo, Deborah L. "The Family Racket: AOL-Time Warner, HBO, *The Sopranos*, and the Construction of a Quality Brand." *Journal of Communication Inquiry* 26, no. 1 (2002): 59–75.

Jenkins, Henry. *Convergence Culture: Where Old and New Media Collide*. New York, NY: New York University Press, 2006.

Johnson, Catherine. *Branding Television*. New York, NY: Routledge, 2012.

——. "Tele-branding in TVIII: the Network as Brand and the Programme as Brand." *New Review of Film and Television Studies* 5, no. 1 (2007): 5–24.

Johnson, Derek. "Inviting Audiences In: The Spatial Reorganization of Production and Consumption in 'TV III.'" *New Review of Film and Television Studies* 5, no.1 (April 2007): 61–80.

Johnson, Victoria E. *Heartland TV: Primetime Television and the Struggle for U.S. Identity*. New York, NY: New York University Press, 2008.

Jones, Gerard. *Honey, I'm Home! Sitcoms: Selling the American Dream*. New York, NY: Grove Weidenfeld, 1992.

Keply, Jr., Vance, "From 'Frontal Lobes' to the 'Bob-and-Bob Show': NBC Management and Programming Strategies, 1949–65." In *Hollywood in the Age of Television*, ed. Tino Balio, 41–62. Boston, MA: Unwin Hyman, 1990.

Kompare, Derek. *Rerun Nation: How Repeats Invented American Television*. New York, NY: Routledge, 2005.

Korman, Seymour. "Hollywood's 10 Bright Young Men." *Toledo Blade* [Ohio]. August 30, 1959. 1–2. Available: http://news.google.com/newspapers?nid=1350&dat=19590830 &id=mwUkAAAAIBAJ&sjid=7wAEAAAAIBAJ&pg=5775,695420.

Lawson, Richard. "Showtime Does Lady Pain Just Right." *Gawker*, November 16, 2010. Available: http://gawker.com/5691421/showtime-does-lady-pain-just-right.

Leibman, Nina C. *Living Room Lectures: The Fifties Family in Film & Television*. Austin, TX: University of Texas Press, 1995.

Leonard, Vince. "The Young Set's Gal Sally" *The Pittsburg Press*, October 9, 1965. 1.

Leverette, Marc, Brian L. Ott, and Cara Louise Buckley, eds. *It's Not TV: Watching HBO in the Post-television Era*. New York, NY: Routledge, 2008.

Levine, Elana. *Wallowing in Sex: The New Sexual Culture of 1970s American Television*. Durham, NC: Duke University Press, 2007.

Littleton, Cynthia. "Dexter Injected Fresh Blood, Brand at Showtime." *Variety*, September 20, 2013: 24.

Lotz, Amanda. "How to Spend $9.3 Billion in Three Days: Examining the Upfront Buying Process in the Production of US Television Culture." *Media, Culture and Society* 29, no.4 (2007): 549–67.

——. "Must-See TV: NBC's Dominant Decades." In Hilmes 2007, 261–74.

——. *Redesigning Women: Television after the Network Era*. Urbana, IL: University of Illinois Press, 2006.

——. *The Television Will Be Revolutionized*. New York, NY: New York University Press, 2007.

Lowry, Brian. "Review: 'Nurse Jackie/United States of Tara.'" *Variety*, March 16, 2010.

Luckett, Moya. "Girl Watchers: Patty Duke and Teen TV." In *The Revolution Wasn't Televised: Sixties Television and Social Conflict*, eds. Lynn Spigel and Michael Curtin, 95–116. New York, NY: Routledge, 1997.

"Madison Ave.'s Program Taboos." *Variety*, October 26, 1960.

Mann, Denise. "The Spectacularization of Everyday Life: Recycling Hollywood Stars and Fans in Early Television Variety Shows." In Spigel and Mann 1992, 41–69.

Marc, David. *Comic Visions: Television Comedy and American Culture*. Boston, MA: Unwin Hyman, 1989.

——. *Demographic Vistas: Television in American Culture*. Philadelphia, PA: University of Pennsylvania Press, 1984.

Marling, Karal Ann. *As Seen On TV: The Visual of Everyday Life in the 1950s*. Cambridge, MA: Harvard University Press, 1994.

Mashon, Mike. "NBC, J. Walter Thompson, and the Struggle for Control of Television Programming, 1946–58." In Hilmes 2007, 135–52.

McCracken, Grant. *Culture and Consumption II: Markets, Meaning, and Brand Management*. Bloomington, IN: Indiana University Press, 2005.

McFarland, Melanie. "Second-rate Showtime Needs to Cultivate 'Weeds.'" *Seattle Post-Intelligencer*, August 11, 2006. Available: http://www.seattlepi.com/ae/tv/article/On-TV-Second-rate-Showtime-needs-to-cultivate-1211486.php.

Meehan, Eileen. *Why Television is Not Our Fault: Television Programming, Viewers, and Who's Really in Control*. Lanham, MD: Rowman and Littlefield, 2005.

——. "Why We Don't Count: The Commodity Audience." In *Logics of Television: Essays in Cultural Criticism*, ed. Patricia Mellencamp, 117–37. Bloomington, IN: Indiana University Press, 1990.

Metz, Walter. *Bewitched*. Detroit, MI: Wayne State University Press, 2007.

Mittell, Jason. "The Cultural Power of an Anti-Television Metaphor: Questioning the 'Plug-in Drug' and a TV-Free America." *Television and New Media* 1, no. 2 (2000): 215–38.

———. "Generic Cycles: Innovation, Imitation, and Saturation." In Hilmes and Jacobs 2004, 44–9.

———. *Genre and Television: From Cop Shows to Cartoons in American Culture*. New York, NY: Routledge, 2004.

Morreale, Joanne. *The Donna Reed Show*. Detroit, MI: Wayne State University Press, 2012.

Murray, Simone. "Brand Loyalties: Rethinking Content within Global Corporate Media." *Media, Culture, Society* 27, no. 3 (2005): 415–35.

Murray, Susan. *Hitch Your Antenna to the Stars: Early Television and Broadcast Stardom*. New York, NY: Routledge, 2005.

Napoli, Philip M. *Audience Economics: Media Institutions and the Audience Marketplace*. New York, NY: Columbia University Press, 2003.

Negra, Diane. "Re-Made for Television: Hedy Lamarr's Post-War Star Textuality." In *Small Screens, Big Ideas: Television in the 1950s*, ed. Janet Thumim, 105–17. London, UK: I.B. Tauris, 2002.

Nelson, Ozzie. *Ozzie*. New York, NY: Prentice Hall, 1973.

Newcomb, Horace M. "This Is Not Al Dente: *The Sopranos* and the New Meaning of Television" In *Television: The Critical View*. 7th edition. ed. Horace Newcomb, 561–78. New York, NY: Oxford University Press, 2006.

Newcomb, Horace M. and Robert S. Alley. *The Producer's Medium*. New York, NY: Oxford, 1983.

Osgerby, Bill. "'So Who's Got Time for Adults!': Femininity, Consumption and the Development of Teen TV- from *Gidget* to *Buffy*." In *Teen TV: Genre, Consumption and Identity*, eds. Glyn Davis and Kay Dickinson, 71–98. London, UK: BFI Publishing, 2004.

Oswald, Laura R. *Marketing Semiotics: Signs, Strategies, and Brand Value*. Oxford, UK: Oxford University Press, 2012.

"Performer or Pitchman?" *Variety*, November 11, 1953: 31.

Pomerantz, Dorothy and Lauren Streib. "Show and Sell." *Forbes*, August 11, 2008. 78–9.

Pope, Kyle. "For Showtime, Suburban Angst Is Fast Becoming A Ratings Delight." *New York Times*, Late Edition. August 6, 2006. 2, 26.

Reeves, Jimmie L., Mark C. Rodgers, and Michael Epstein. "Rewriting Popularity: The Cult Files." In *"Deny All Knowledge": Reading The X-Files*, eds. David Lavery, Angela Hague, and Marla Cartwright, 22–35. Syracuse, NY: Syracuse University Press, 1996.

Reice, Sylvie. "Sally Field: A Real Life Gidget." *The St. Petersburg Evening Independent*, April 13, 1966. 2.

Rogers, Mark C., Michael Epstein, and Jimmie L. Reeves. "*The Sopranos* as HBO Brand Equity: The Art of Commerce in the Age of Digital Reproduction." In *This Thing of Ours: Investigating The Sopranos*, ed. David Lavery, 42–57. New York, NY: Columbia University Press, 2002.

Rose, Lacey. "The Re-Rebirth of Showtime." *The Hollywood Reporter*, March 28, 2012.

Ross, Sharon Marie. *Beyond the Box: Television and the Internet*. Malden, MA: Blackwell, 2008.

Ross, Sharon Marie and Louisa Ellen Stein, eds. *Teen Television: Essays on Programming and Fandom*. Jefferson, NC and London, UK: McFarland, 2008.

Roush, Matt. "Matt's 2007 Top 10." *TV Guide*. December 12, 2007.

Sandler, Kevin. "Life Without *Friends*: NBC's Programming Strategies in an Age of Media Clutter." In Hilmes 2007, 291–307.

Samuel, Lawrence R. *Brought to You By: Postwar Television Advertising and The American Dream*. Austin, TX: University of Texas Press, 2001.

San Martin, Nancy. "'Must See TV': Programming Identity on NBC Thursdays." In Jancovich and Lyons 2003, 32–47.

Santo, Avi. "Para-television and Discourses of Distinction: The Culture of Production at HBO." In Leverette, Ott, and Buckley 2008, 19–45.

Schatz, Thomas. "Desilu, I Love Lucy, and the Rise of Network TV." In *Making Television: Authorship and the Production Process*, eds. Robert J. Thompson and Gary Burns, 117–35. New York, NY: Praeger, 1990.

—— "The New Hollywood." In *Film Theory Goes to the Movies*, eds. Jim Collins, Hilary Radner and Ava Preacher Collins, 8–36. London, UK: Routledge, 1993.

Sconce, Jeffrey. "What If? Charting Television's New Textual Boundaries." In Spigel and Olsson 2004, 93–112.

Shattuc, Jane M. "Television Production: Who Makes American TV?" In *A Companion to Television*, ed. Janet Wasko, 142–54. Oxford, UK: Blackwell, 2005.

Shrum, L.J. *The Psychology of Entertainment Media: Blurring the Lines Between Entertainment and Persuasion*. New York, NY: Routledge, 2012.

Soto, Gary. "Looking for Work." *Growing Up Ethnic in America: Contemporary Fiction about Learning to Be American*. New York, NY: Penguin Books. 1999.

Spigel, Lynn. *Make Room for TV: Television and the Family Ideal in Postwar America*. Chicago, IL: University of Chicago Press, 1992.

Spigel, Lynn and Denise Mann, eds. *Private Screenings: Television and the Female Consumer*. Minneapolis, MN: University of Minnesota Press, 1992.

Spigel, Lynn and Jan Olsson, eds., *Television After TV: Essays on a Medium in Transition*. Durham, NC: Duke University Press, 2004.

—— *Welcome to the Dream House: Popular Media Postwar Suburbs*. Durham, NC: Duke University Press, 2001.

Tasker, Yvonne and Diane Negra. "In Focus: Postfeminism and Contemporary Media Studies." *Cinema Journal* 44, no. 2 (2005):107–10.

Taylor, Ella. *Prime Time Families: Television Culture in Postwar America*. Berkeley, CA: University of California Press, 1989.

Turow, Joseph. *Breaking Up America: Advertisers and the New Media World*. Chicago, IL: University of Chicago Press, 1997.

——. *Niche Envy: Marketing Discrimination in the Digital Age*. Cambridge, MA: MIT Press, 2006.

Ulin, Jeffery C. *The Business of Media Distribution: Monetizing Film, TV, and Video Content in an Online World*. 2nd edition. New York, NY: Focal Press, 2014.

Uricchio, William. "Historicizing Media in Transition." In *Rethinking Media Change: The Aesthetics of Transition*, eds. David Thornburn and Henry Jenkins, 23–38. Cambridge, MA: MIT Press, 2004.

——. "Old Media and New Media: Television." In *The New Media Book*, ed. Dan Harries, 219–30. London, UK: BFI Publishing, 2002.

Vogel, Harold. *Entertainment Industry Economics: A Guide for Financial Analysts*. 7th edition. New York, NY: Cambridge University Press, 2007. Cambridge, MA: MIT Press, 2004.

Wasko, Janet. *How Hollywood Works*. Thousand Oaks, CA: Sage, 2003.

——. *Understanding Disney: The Manufacture of Fantasy*. Malden, MA: Polity Press, 2001.

Wee, Valerie. "Selling Teen Culture: How American Multimedia Conglomeration Shaped Teen Television in the 1990s." In Davis and Dickinson 2004, 87–98.

——. "Teen Television and the WB Network." In Ross and Stein 2008, 43–60.

Weiss, Jessica. *To Have and to Hold: Marriage, the Baby Boom & Social Change*. Chicago, IL: The University of Chicago Press, 2000.

Williams, Raymond. *Television, Technology and Cultural Forms*. London, UK: Fontana, 1974.

Wyatt, Justin. *High Concept: Movies and Marketing in Hollywood*. Austin, TX: University of Texas Press, 1994.

Zeitchik, Steven, "Fleshing Out The Sked." *Variety*, July 9, 2007, 4.

3

CABLE BRANDCASTING AND DISNEY CHANNEL'S COMPANY VOICE

3.1   Disney Channel as Brandcaster

The story of a brand is "a vital combination of documentary and inspiring narrative," or so says Saul Dennis, self-professed "Strategic Storyteller" and Creative Director at Sullivan New York. Walt Disney brand managers applied this same logic to their mid-2000s rebrand of Disney Channel. As the only literal brandcaster on the U.S. channel spectrum, Disney Channel merits in-depth analysis of how it realized the full potential of television as a brand circulation platform. Yet, academic commentary on Disney mostly overlooks the channel. The few studies of Disney Channel content tend to concentrate on its most famous franchises, *Lizzie McGuire*, *Hannah Montana*, or *High School Musical*. Such franchising is certainly central to Disney Channel's business strategy, and the isolated studies of single franchises or series are illuminating, especially in relation to gender and racial issues. For the purposes of my study, looking at sitcoms and DCOMs (Disney Channel Original Movies) detached from the larger channel flow experienced by on-air viewers reveals little about the effectiveness of Walt Disney's use of the channel as a brandcasting platform. To repeat John Ellis' useful advice, we need to look at "the architecture of the entire output" to understand a channel brand. In Disney Channel's case, the key is the role played by the omnipresent short-form content, as its brandcasting function works in conjunction with the channel's signature sitcoms and movies. How do these shorts create meaning for the series and movies? How do they provide links between series and point to the nuances of the channel brand? What role do the shorts play in circulating Walt Disney's company voice messaging, and in promoting specific brands or divisions of the parent company?

Everything on Disney Channel—its sitcoms, DCOMs, music videos, and short-form content—can technically be described as a content–promotion hybrid, as it is all entertainment content that promotes other Disney content. Close attention to this content about content reveals the specific brand messaging that has enabled Disney Channel to become such a cultural and industry force. Indeed, watching any hour block of Disney Channel programming, as I first did in 2009 before attending a faculty seminar at Disney Studios, is eye-opening, precisely because of the number and variety of its shorts. The channel is unique because no other channel invests as much in its content about content and in making sure that every element doubles as implicit channel branding. Studying Disney Channel over the course of several years now, I have concluded that these shorts have much to tell us about the channel's target demographic and about American culture more generally. Many commentators who have mythologized Disney Channel as a corporate monolith or a tween machine have failed to understand that the source of its power comes from its ability to counter ideological flashpoints with compelling embodiments of the brand's personality.

Disney Channel has succeeded because it taps into cultural desires and anxieties. In *How Brands Become Icons*, Douglas Holt argues that consumers are looking for brands that offer them ways to think through desired identities and, consequently, are receptive to innovative expressions of those identities. In *Cultural Strategy*, Holt and coauthor Douglas Cameron detail case studies of brands that figure out how to be "dynamic in terms of the cultural expressions that consumers value" and as a result craft "innovative cultural expressions that resonate perfectly with the ideological needs of their target." These brands offer "a potent new cultural viewpoint," by pursuing "radical innovations in culture, not product" and seizing "opportunities for innovation created by historical changes in society." Throughout their book, Holt and Cameron offer convincing assessments of how smart brand managers engage "ideological flashpoints" and then "assert the company's ideological counterpoints."[1]

My underlying argument is that Disney Channel achieves successful brand differentiation not only through interrelated cycles of original sitcoms and movies, but also through a slate of short-form content, which offers reassuring counter-narratives about current ideological flashpoints. The following table suggests some of these correspondences:

Ideological Flashpoints	Reassuring Counter-narratives
Economic recession, downsizing, and outsourcing	*Make Your Mark*
Environmental sustainability	*Friends for Change*
"The obesity epidemic"	*Pass the Plate*
	Try It!
Corrosiveness of celebrity and of a celebrity-obsessed culture	*TTI: The Time I . . .*
	Who I Am . . .

FIGURE 3.1 Phineas activates the "It's On!" Disney Channel brand campaign and amusement pier music video, ostensibly through a program created by his stepbrother Ferb and circulated online and in the air by their pet, Perry the Platypus.

I detail in this chapter how Disney Channel constructs two key types to embody its ideological counter-narratives: the brandcaster and the friend for change. Holt and Cameron would call these types cultural expressions, as they are embodiments of myths that consumers value. Both types are also obstinate optimists, those who accept challenges and display optimistic determination despite setbacks. They are convinced they can make an impact in their local communities or in a creative industry. Disney Channel programming often features obstinate optimistic character types such as Phineas and Ferb, the tween inventors/stepbrothers from Disney Channel's hit animated series named after them. Obstinate optimists challenge naysayers—those who view them as too young, too small, or too unseasoned to succeed. It's common knowledge that Disney Channel made its mark by explicitly targeting tweens (ages 9–12) in what was formerly known as the general kids market. Yet I am saying that its innovation is in implicit communication to these demographics, especially through the short-form content produced by a group of small "production company/multiplatform marketing" agencies with expertise in melding entertainment strategies and promotional messaging. I argue that Disney Channel is unique because its organization as a brandcaster enables it to be a leader in the creation of such interstitial content.

I explore Disney Channel and its innovative communication strategies in three parts. I begin with an analysis of the brandcaster. This populist type is on display in Disney Channel's short-form series and in its original sitcoms and movies. In part two I examine the friendship elements of Disney Channel's brandcaster sitcoms and DCOMs. Through a discussion of Disney Channel stardom and its stars-in-the-making programming, I transition to the third section's analysis of the other populist type, the friend for change. The type appears in a channel brand/cause marketing campaign hybrid, featuring the whole stable of Disney Channel stars circa 2009–10. In this section I consider how Disney Channel's focus on the "friend-com" enabled the focus on the friend for change, which was the populist type through which Disney Channel initially differentiated itself. In doing so, it surpassed Nickelodeon, the U.S. market leader in programming for kids and tweens.

3.2   Disney Channel: A Premium/Basic Cable Hybrid

Disney Channel is the most intensively promotional environment on the U.S. channel spectrum. It can devote so much of its space to short-form content and position that content to articulate a distinct channel brand because it is owned and primarily funded by The Walt Disney Company, the world's largest and most tightly organized transnational media conglomerate. Although originally commercial free, today's Disney Channel enters into cobranding partnerships with corporate sponsors who run some spots on the channel. These sponsors tailor their institutional messaging to suit Walt Disney branding. Given that these custom spots play more like the dramatized advertisements discussed in Chapter 1,

Disney Channel feels more commercial-free than other channels that share its basic cable tier in the U.S.

This hybrid structure of Disney Channel reflects its origins as a premium channel. Anne Sweeney, Co-Chair of Disney Media Networks, President of the Disney/ABC Television Group (2004–14), and former President of Disney Channel (1996–2004), oversaw the late-1990s transition of Disney Channel from premium to basic cable tier. This move expanded the channel's brand awareness among a broader range of American households. Sweeney helped to reorient Disney Channel toward a target demographic of tweens (and secondary demos of those who fall in between kid and tween, or tween and teen). Given Disney's brand promise about the quality of its offerings and its concern for kids and their families, the move could not be accompanied by the adoption of the same commercial structure as Nickelodeon, Disney Channel's direct competitor. Even in its 1990s heyday, Nickelodeon's acclaimed pro-social, live-action programming was at odds with the brash advertising for toys, as-seen-on-TV gimmick items, cereal, and snack foods. Disney Channel's flow between story segments is unique because it includes pro-social short-form content and corporate social responsibility messaging. Disney Channel has a distinct advantage over Nickelodeon because it can afford not to sell all the space between its sitcoms and movies for spot advertising. This distinctiveness remains despite its recent acceptance of sponsorships, because the deals are structured so that all sponsor messaging must reinforce Disney's desired self-representation. The custom sponsor spots are mixed in sparingly with short-form content about content, which helps Disney Channel to maintain the impression of uninterrupted premium channel flow even after its move to the basic cable tier in the U.S.

In the contemporary era of timeshifting, it may seem odd to study the "flow" of programming blocks, which on Disney Channel include original series, movies, music videos, and a variety of interstitial content (both more traditional channel identification elements and its content about content). Disney Channel offers a unique environment in which to study branded flow given the customization of its content, including the corporation's "proud sponsors of Disney Chan nel" spots. More to the point, all the content has promotional elements and all the promotion has content elements so that everything plays like a content–promotion hybrid.

Some of the short-form elements in the flow clearly act as promotion, such as the "trailer" for the Blu-ray/DVD release of *Teen Beach Movie* (*TBM*) or a music video starring the film's core cast or its main male star. The songs would also be in the rotation on Radio Disney, so the flow promotes that as well. Ross Lynch, the costar of *TBM*, also appears in music videos related to his sitcom persona Austin Moon (*Austin & Ally*) and videos for his own band R5. Lynch's band includes three siblings and the whole family was featured in the *Disney 365* promotional shorts for Disney vacations and parks, and R5 was an invited act for the televised 2014 Radio Disney Music Awards. Lynch appears as well on *Disney 365* with his *TBM* costar Maia Mitchell. As she is the newcomer, Lynch directly addresses the fans surrounding them in Disneyland and recommends her work to them. The presence of all these content–promotion hybrids indicates that flow still matters on Disney Channel, even as it is in decline across the rest of the broadcast and basic cable spectrum because of the prevalence of placeshifted, off-television viewing or fast-forwarding through programming flow on recorded broadcasts.

Whether or not their audience assumptions reflect actual behavior, Disney Channel schedulers and promoters have clearly invested in the flow. The choices they make indicate their expectations of typical audience behaviors to align more

FIGURE 3.2 Ross Lynch on *Disney 365*, a short that promotes "all things Disney," from sitcoms and movies to Disney's theme park rides and cruise ship attractions, such as Marvel's Avengers Academy.

closely to classic network-era audiences. In fact, Disney Channel operates as if most of its tween and kid viewers still watch original episodes (and reruns) on television. The relative lack of releases of whole seasons of the sitcoms on Blu-ray/DVD signals that schedulers have confidence that viewers watch episodes on television during their run and re-watch at some point during the 24-hour channel's generous schedule of reruns. This assumption is based in part on the fact that tweens and older kids have fewer choices on the U.S. channel spectrum and are therefore more likely to be watching blocks of television programming. In contrast to adult-address television, there is not an expectation of either binge viewing or delayed viewing (such as watching a series years after the original air-date). The more typical Disney Channel DVD releases contain four or five sitcom episodes connected to a loose theme. For example, the *Hannah Montana* thematic compilation DVDs include *Livin' the Rock Star Life* and *Keeping It Real*.

Disney Channel's rerun schedule also can be organized thematically to make it feel more like new content. With a large pool of reruns from which to choose, schedulers often create brand-centric thematic blocks of reruns. They also have the ability to mix in sitcom episodes and DCOMs with Disney Studios fare (whether A-level animation and popular live-action films or B-level film sequels or straight-to-DVD/Blu-ray films). Thematic organization is also evident in the channel's special event programming. A weekend might be programmed to include selected thematic episodes of signature sitcoms leading up to a dance-a-long encore of a DCOM like *High School Musical* or *Camp Rock*. To indicate how thematic organization can play out more loosely in the flow, dancing in front of the television is also encouraged by the schedulers of *Shake it Up* (a faux teen dance show sitcom) and its surrounding flow. It might include a short about learning to dance like *Beauty and the Beast*'s Belle as demonstrated by *Shake it Up* costars Zendaya Coleman and Bella Thorne. Zendaya appeared in other dance-related shorts, including a behind-the-scenes short about her experience appearing on *Dancing With the Stars* (2013's season 16), or a short in which she offered tips on dancing as exercise as part of the pro-social series, *Try It!*. As Zendaya advises her Disney Channel friends, "Part of staying healthy means staying active. Dance is one way that works for me and you can try it too."

Zendaya and Bella also appear in music videos for their dance song duets ("Watch Me," "This is My Dance Floor," and "Contagious Love") and for their singles (e.g., Zendaya's "Replay"). Zendaya appeared solo as the lead in the 2014 DCOM *Zapped*, but she and Bella Thorne costarred in the 2012 DCOM *Frene-mies*, in which their characters create *Geekly Chic*, a webzine about fashion which attracts the interest of a Manhattan publishing company. The duo also appear as some hybrid of themselves and their characters in international spots about them as representatives of the Disney Channel thematic and economic focus on BFFs. (see Figure 4.11 from Chapter 4). All of these elements rotate through the flow playing between episode segments and all are content–promotion hybrids, which have the ability to hold audience attention in a distinct way.

Disney Channel also has the advantage in its flow because of a wealth of available premium content controlled or produced by The Walt Disney Company. It has access to A-Level animation, from recent hits such as *Tangled* to Disney Studios classics. It helps that Disney now counts among its subsidiaries some of the companies producing the most popular franchises—Marvel films/*Avengers*, Jim Henson/*The Muppets*, Pixar/*Toy Story*, and LucasFilm/*Star Wars*. Yet, just listing all its subsidiaries and other holdings or making economically determinist arguments about Walt Disney as a media conglomerate does little to explain the appeal of Disney Channel. We need to look beyond easy generalizations. Too often, Disney Channel is just treated as the "bad object" in television studies or as part of mundane television output not interesting enough for academic study. To understand how it has captured such a large segment of its target market, Disney Channel needs to be examined in more depth and beyond the cultural impact of the infamous franchises.

3.3   Brandcasting Through Myth Stories

Disney Channel would not have become an "iconic global brand" with 100 channels/channel feeds in 169 countries/territories were it not for its embodiment of an iteration of the Disney brand that feels especially relevant to viewers. I trace Disney Channel's cultural and industry impact to its association with an incredibly "compelling myth story" or two. Disney Channel sitcoms, DCOMs, and short-form content draw on myth stories that speak to a generation anxious about sustainability—of the earth's resources and of their personal and generational aspirations. Disney's myths, as I explain later, are about an ecologically minded friend for change and an entrepreneurial brandcaster. The creation of these types responds to anxieties related to news reports about global warming and abysmal job prospects, and the more general predictions that current tweens, teens, and twentysomethings will be worse off in economical and environmental terms than their parents. A representative article from *The New York Times* in June 2012 began, "For this generation of young people the future looks bleak."[2]

To offset job and generational predictions, Disney Channel offers the *broadcast yourself* myth story about the feasibility of transforming teenage passions into adult professions. To embody this myth story, Disney Channel offers stars-in-the-making sitcoms built around a new populist type that I call the brandcaster. Emerging in a post-YouTube America, brandcasters are entrepreneurial individuals who take seriously the site's *broadcast yourself* imperative. They make the most of their access to YouTube video sharing as well as social media networks, platforms, and utilities and then create, circulate, sustain, and eventually monetize a marketable brand. Or so the brandcasting paradigm promises.

In U.S. culture at large the enterprising and self-actualizing worker paradigm emerged at a time when young men and women graduating from college were less likely to find a secure position as "company men and women" with long-term corporate affiliations. Richard Sennett examines why this career goal was embraced by many midcentury college graduates, especially those who saw the degree as a means of upward mobility into the middle or upper-middle class. Sennett says that the rejection of this kind of corporate life narrative by many young people in the 1960s has had a long-term impact. Today's corporation no longer has at its center the inclusive pyramid, with lots of workers at the bottom. Instead, there are fewer jobs at the bottom, fewer layers of management, and less likelihood of climbing the corporate ladder. Sennett argues that these working conditions produce anxiety because they are ill defined. Nick Shore claims, however, that millennials have a very different view of career aspirations and expectations for long-term employment. Sennett concurs, but worries about the impact of the contract worker culture that has been created. As he puts it, "Only a certain kind of human being can prosper in unstable, fragmentary social conditions."[3] Several recent scholars, many of whom are included in Roopali Mukherjee and Sarah Banet-Weiser's 2012 *Commodity Activism* anthology, would argue that the contradiction between the new ideology of neo-liberal entrepreneurialism and the actual state of jobs and behavior of corporations produced an enormous "demand for new myths" to manage these contradictions and, as Holt puts it, "shore up the nation's cultural contradictions."[4]

The brandcaster is what Holt would call a "populist type" that emerges in response to anxieties, specifically about the feasibility of upward mobility. The brandcaster as mythic type has proliferated on Disney Channel (and later on Nickelodeon) in response to the gap between the promise and the actuality of the old American work ethic paradigm in which steady hard work within a bureaucracy and loyal service to it would lead to the steady accrual of rewards.

Before turning to a closer analysis of Disney Channel's stars-in-the-making series cycle created to showcase its brandcaster character type and to transform the actors playing the roles into multiplatform stars, we need to consider other content on the channel, which reinforces the sitcom messaging. I contend that the distinctiveness of Disney Channel resides less in these sitcoms than in the short-form content airing on the channel and circulating the brandcaster ideology. These shorts enabled Disney Channel to remain distinctive even after its sitcoms were quickly copycatted by Nickelodeon once it started losing in the ratings game.

To create this content, Disney quietly hired outside contractors, including 7ate9 Entertainment, B2+, and Riverstreet Productions, a group of "production company/multiplatform marketing" agencies with expertise in melding entertainment strategies and promotional messaging. Paul Grainge and Catherine Johnson have written about how this emerging sector is fast becoming a key facet of the largely unstudied promotional screen industries.[5] As Johnson explains:

> In seeking to capture and manage attention within a competitive media landscape, promotion has become a major component of broadcast output,

from the exponential increase in promos, logos, idents and trailers, to new forms of branded and interactive content. In this broadcast ecology an industry sector has emerged specializing in promotional communication and digital screen design.[6]

The success of firms within this sector and the demand for the kind of content about content which they produce was made possible by a new era of negotiation among creative industries.

Through their case study of Red Bee Media, a West London media management company, Grainge and Johnson began the important work of bringing to light the specialized production houses that support the promotional screen industries. The work of these firms reflects the new de-centered production, distribution, and marketing models of today's creative industries. Paralleling the sector Grainge and Johnson studied in the U.K., a crop of Hollywood production houses have emerged. The work they produce is intended to engage viewers whose entertainment practices include watching YouTube video snippets; sharing videos and links through social media; and using entertainment preferences as a means of signaling desired self-representation to others in their social networks.

The Hollywood production sector is part of the emergence of the "diverse range of cultural intermediaries," that Chris Bilton describes as "competing to add value to cultural content through new forms of delivery and distribution." I argue that the hybrid nature of the content-about-content shorts on Disney Channel reflects Bilton's conception of an industry that is characterized by "a collapsing distinction between content and context." As Bilton proclaims, in today's creative industries "context is king." The emphasis is now on selling the experiences around content and shaping the meaning of a work through its framing. For Bilton, the shift "from the *what* of content to the *how* of delivery, branding, and customer relationships" is a turn toward brand management.[7] Designed for "distribution platform" flexibility and spreadability, Disney Channel's short-form content functions as paratextual framing and registers a change in reception practices. Commenting on that change, Lauren DeVillier, VP of Digital Media at Disney Channels Worldwide, says that her division is well aware that "Commenting, liking, and sharing are [now] forms of self expression"[8] and that Disney's audience "loves short form video."[9]

I aim to position the content-about-content shorts produced by B2+, 7ate9 Entertainment, and Riverstreet Productions as paratexts, as what Jonathan Gray calls "interpretive frames" through which producers encourage viewers to adopt specific understandings of a entertainment brand. While Gray looks at paratexts attached to particular texts, I broaden the scope to look how Disney Channel's content about content has an implicit function as channel branding and only sometimes has an explicit paratextual relation to a particular forthcoming work. I categorize the content as what I call Social Shorts, as they are high-concept versions of "social media profile" videography. They might be more typically termed as docu-tainment, keeping in mind Dennis' philosophy with which this chapter began: "The story of a brand is a vital combination of documentary and inspiring narrative."[10] Social Shorts provide interpretative frames encouraging specific understandings of The Walt Disney Company and the series, movies, franchises, stars, and channel brands in its entertainment arsenal. The content is part of a strategy that marketers call "brand signaling," or the exploitation of implicit forms of communication embedded in the actions a brand takes and the designs it chooses for its self-representation. As articulated by Peter Buckley: "It's what brands don't say that matters."[11]

3.4 The Obstinate Optimist and "In-Betweener" Content

An analysis of the engagement strategies of these shorts brings to light the cultural aspirations and anxieties on which they draw and the subjectivities they generate for the tween cohort they address and construct. As already noted, the shorts showcase the "brandcaster" as what Holt and Cameron would call the "cultural expression" of Disney Channel's "ideological counterpoint" to anxieties about neoliberal labor conditions, economic recession, downsizing, and outsourcing. The brandcaster appears in various short series such as *Make Your Mark*, *[This is] Who I Am*, *The CopperTop Flop*, and *Leo Little's Big Show*. In creating Disney's content about content, 7ate9, Riverstreet, and B2+ capitalize on "an ideological opportunity born of a massive demographic shift," in which Holt and Cameron would say, a "new cohort emerged."[12] In this case it is a cohort of those who were 8 to 13 years old at the start of Obama's first presidency. Rejecting the preceding Grunge era's defeatist mindset about the probability of a bleak future, the brandcasting paradigm appeals, I argue, because it breaks away from the "cultural orthodoxy" about the impossibility of making an impact and effecting change.[13] This cohort's philosophy is conveyed in the title of Disney's *Friends for Change* eco-responsibility campaign and its anthem, "We Can [Change the World]."

The "We Can" music video/channel brand campaign, along with most other short-form content created for Disney Channel, showcases the "obstinate optimists" who display optimistic determination despite setbacks. They are convinced they can make an impact in their local communities or in a creative industry. They challenge naysayers: those who view them as too young, too small, or too unseasoned to succeed. While 7ate9, B+, and Riverstreet bring a particular design signature and interpretation to their profiles of "obstinate optimists," they all follow Holt and Cameron's implied blueprint for innovation:

1) Take a cultural orthodoxy (competitors' dominant cultural expressions)
   —Grunge and Alternative Rock philosophy of 1990s
   —Nickelodeon's "Us vs. Them" messaging
2) Seize the opportunity to offer a more compelling ideology
   —Disney Channel's "We Can [Change the World]"

3) Borrow from subculture, media myth, and brand assets as source material
—Disney's legacy of "we can"-style obstinate optimism, with origins in the post-*Snow White* brand personality of Walt Disney himself
4) Update it through a current "cultural disruption"
—Obama's 2008 election as a triumph of another obstinate optimist and the culmination of the hope-filled, forward-looking mantra, "Yes We Can"
5) De-politicize and transform it into a more general generational anthem
—Disney's Friends for Change: We Can (Change the World).
We believe in ourselves. Our dreams can come true.

With this formula, Disney Channel appeals to its target audience's sense of identity by tapping into a desire for agency, acknowledgment and independence. It has been so successful because these boutique production firms used Social Shorts to transform the "brandcaster" into a compelling embodiment of the channel brand. This collection of video shorts tells the brand story and personalizes it. Although we could categorize the shorts as interstitials, I think of them as "in-betweeners," as the term references how *in-betweenness* functions as an implicit organizing principle for the channel brand:

- In-between boundaries of form—vacillates among Social Short/Personal Profile Video, Parent Company PR, and Branding
- In-between function—falls between entertainment content and branding for Disney Channel, series, stars, movies, soundtracks, singles, and/or Radio Disney
- In-between scheduling—airs between segments of sitcoms and other longer-form programming
- In-between viewing as user practice—viewers watching media content as they move between destinations, or take breaks in their normal daily routines
- In-between as a cultural state—being in limbo between life stages; or between imagining and achieving grand plans
- In-betweener as an animation term—creating intermediate frames between two images to give the appearance that the first image evolves smoothly into the second.

Through these "inbetweeners," Disney Channel addresses its viewers as if they were merely occupying a life stage between articulating and achieving their aspirations. Many of the *Make Your Mark* and *The Time I . . . (TTI)* episodes, for instance, model how viewers are (or at least could be) as articulate and self-actualizing as the young people profiled. In one episode of *TTI* produced by Riverstreet, a seven-year-old describes how she organized a shoe donation drive for a Guatemalan orphanage and as a six-year-old made presentations at local religious and civic organizations to solicit donations and asked for shoes instead of toys for her seventh birthday. In the end she collected 322 shoes for 166 boys and girls. In framing her story, the editors emphasize the girl's all-American surroundings, focusing on a picture in which her dad and brother wear cowboy hats. In several parts of the segment she wears cowboy boots and has her hair in braids, which gives her a vaguely cowgirl-like appearance. The shots of the family reinforce the sense that she is from a family of plucky ranchers. The shot composition emphasizing the open tailgate of the family truck reinforces this reading. The framing of her modest home and West Texas location share an image register with light truck advertisements. Recent commercials from the Detroit automakers, such as Dodge's "God Made a Farmer" spots, have focused on this kind of "obstinate optimist" Westerner as the embodiment of what has come to be thought of as the indomitable American spirit.

FIGURE 3.3 Riverstreet Productions created an American Dream-themed profile of a representative obstinate optimist for Disney's *The Time I . . .* short series.

Other *TTIs* profile similar obstinate optimists, young people who believe they can make a difference through local action. The philosophy also translates to career aspirations as depicted on Disney Channel. The seven-year old in the *TTI* profile aspires to be a future fashion designer, which is the career choice of Raven from *That's So Raven* (January 2003–November 2007) and Stella from *Jonas/Jonas LA* (November 2009–October 2010). More often, the characters' aspirations lean toward more overt entertainment industry professions. This is certainly the case with *Austin & Ally*, Disney's quintessential brandcaster sitcom. Premiering in December 2011, *Austin & Ally* follows four best friends who embrace brandcasting to pursue careers in the media industries. Their quick success is attributed to their access to DIY production and promotion technologies and platforms. The sitcom taps into collective yearning to engage in enjoyable, meaningful, but lucrative labor. *Austin & Ally* dramatizes anxieties and aspirations about attaining professional success without sacrificing a fulfilling work life or foundational friendships.

3.5   Brandcasters and Boutique Content-about-Content Firms

An *Entourage* for the "clean tween" set, *Austin & Ally* is initially focused on Austin, a budding pop star, and his team of good friends. The first step in this type of star-in-the-making story is to have a friend help you post performance videos to YouTube. Dez helps Austin do just that in the pilot episode and the video goes viral. Within the first season more videos are posted and Austin gets a recording contract by episode 18. The ease with which all this happens is not believable, especially given that his management team is comprised of his high school friends. Its appeal is because it is exactly the stuff of middle school fantasy. *Austin & Ally* makes brandcasting not only a desirable future, but also an achievable one, with a little help from your friends. The sitcom reinforces the friendship narrative common to all Disney programming about stars and stars-in-the-making. Not only is it plausible that one could achieve fame without sacrificing friendships, according to *Austin & Ally*, but it is necessary to maintain foundational friendships if one wants to succeed as a star. This friendship emphasis is thematic and economic. Sitcoms like *Austin & Ally* win over viewers through their dramatization of anxieties and aspirations about attaining professional success without sacrificing a fulfilling work life or foundational friendships. They also tap into anxieties and aspirations about whether the love of your youth can be the love of your life or whether you can make friends in childhood that stay friends for life.

As the "Can't Do it Without You" theme song informs us, Austin knows his success depends on the continuing emotional support of Ally, Trish, and Dez and on their respective skills as songwriter, publicist, and filmmaker. Austin becomes a YouTube sensation through Dez's music video for "Double Take," a song written by Ally. After she gets over her stage fright in season two, Ally evolves into a confident singer–songwriter–musician who later lands her own recording contract, and her pal Trish has success as a publicist and social content strategist. The videos Dez makes continue to go viral, signaling to the audience that he is on his way to a future in filmmaking.

Reflecting the channel's brandcentric structure, this sitcom embeds performances by Austin (Ross Lynch) into episodes. These performances promote the Disney recording division and Radio Disney and contribute to the rollout of Ross Lynch as one of its latest actor–singer–musician–dancer brands. He sings the sitcom theme song, releases singles, and contributes songs to compilation discs. He appears in music videos for his own band, R5, as well as solo videos for his singles and in shorts promoting him or his upcoming roles (e.g., as co-star of *Teen Beach Movie*).

Lynch is given a full profile in the Social Short, *Who I Am*. It shows him at home having fun with his R5 bandmates/siblings (two brothers, a sister, and an honorary brother named Ratcliff). The short functions on some level as promotion for R5. Yet, the *Who I Am* profile centers on Ross Lynch and makes the rest of the family supporting players in his story. His parents recall how Ross always was a performer and had picked up guitar quite early in life. As is typical of the *Who I Am* series, the short has an earnest tone and taps into the brandcaster paradigm of turning a youthful hobby into an adult profession. In 2013, Lynch's *Who I Am* short would often air within the same primetime flow as the parallel profile of his costar Laura Marano (Ally) and of Maia Mitchell, his *Teen Beach Movie* costar. Mitchell, an Australian singer–songwriter (and surfer like Lynch), is also the star of Disney–ABC Family's *The Fosters*, a drama about a foster child's desires and fears when she has the chance to join a blended family headed by two moms.

Who I Am is the current incarnation of the original Backstage at Radio Disney webisodes like the one produced about Demi Lovato by M3 Creative called, *I am . . . (Demi Lovato)*. These original profiles were chattier and offered fan magazine-style random information on Demi Lovato, the Jonas Brothers, and Miley Cyrus, among other singers. The newer incarnation of the Social Short has much more implicit profiling and feels more like documentary than staged interview.

As a supporting cast member, Calum Worthy, who plays Austin's best friend Dez, does not appear in one of these explicit profiles. Instead, Worthy parlayed his "wacky redhead" persona into comedy short series, *The Coppertop Flop*. Launched in 2013, *The Coppertop Flop* represents a creative way to reinforce Worthy's brand personality and does so in an even more indirect way than the *Who I Am* videos of his cast mates. The goofy approach of profiling through comedy sketches contrasts to the earnest tone of the "about us" social profiles. Disney Channel promotes *The Coppertop Flop* as if Worthy created it to share "his own unique and creative take on the world." The promotions don't mention that the shorts are co-written and produced as well as directed by Derek Baynham, a 34-year-old sketch comedy writer and videographer. Baynham has the hip credibility associated with having a channel on *Funny or Die*, the comedy video-hosting site, and from appearing as an actor on *Parks and Recreation* and other sitcoms. Baynham describes himself as a Digital Content Creator/Social Content

FIGURE 3.4 *Austin & Ally*'s credit sequence showcases each individual brandcaster/ best friend, using the cards to signify the career aspiration of each character (upper). Filmmaker Calum Worthy brandcasts himself through his side project, *The Coppertop Flop* sketch comedy shorts (lower).

Strategist whose skill is "adding humor to brands." Of course, Worthy has the target demo appeal and may yet get his own *Who I Am* episode, especially as he does recount in interviews how he and his friends "were always trying to make features and TV movies in our backyards and bedrooms." Understanding the short-shelf-life stardom built into the Disney Channel model, Worthy is wisely also preparing for a future of non-Disney co-productions with Baynham.

The boutique firms hired by Disney Channel employ people like Derek Baynham and other "entrepreneurial mavericks" who represent the fulfillment of brandcaster aspirations. B2+, for example, is a 16-person entertainment advertising, marketing, and production company founded by Brian Briskman in 2006. The team of designers, writers, and visual artists conceive, shoot, and assemble promotional material, webisodes, interview segments, and brand integration content for networks and cable channels.[14] In true brandcaster fashion, Briskman calls it "gratifying" work and reinforces the mythology about the creative think tank atmosphere in boutique firms. They claim to have efficient workflows that are superior to the media company's large divisions, which can "hamper creativity." In such environments "conflicts can arise" and so to avoid such internal tensions and bypass bureaucracy, media company executives turn to these firms.[15] "Internal management believes in doing things in one way," whereas people from the outside tend to bring a vision that is "eye opening sometimes," or so says Brian Dollenmayer, Fox's senior vice president of drama.[16] He buys the brand claims of small firms, who say they bring passion, innovation, and focus to a content-about-content project that might be done half-heartedly or be put on a back burner by an in-house division. Dollenmayer says that the "Let's try this" risk-taking philosophy is a major appeal of hiring independent firms like B2+. Boutique firms represent the alignment of organizational design and competitive strategy. In essence, their value proposition is that they have innovative institutional logic. Disney Channel's Ron Pomerantz credits Briskman's success to the fact that he is "a natural born storyteller"[17] who understands his own brand so well that he knows "how to best project the brands of his clients."[18]

The website for 7ate9 Entertainment, another hybrid production firm, uses self-descriptions that are similar to B2+. Unlike its emphasis on a whole staff of entrepreneurial mavericks, 7ate9 offers no compelling brandcaster backstory on its founder Art Spigel.[19] It could easily have done so given his American Dream trajectory from four-year-old Russian immigrant who first learned English in school to his 1996 establishment of his own boutique production company.[20] American Dream stories do inflect the content he creates for Disney Channel, although they tend more toward the new YouTube-to-Hollywood version.

3.6 Disney's Sunny Outlook on Stardom: YouTube to Hollywood

Brandcaster ideology is overt in the *Make Your Mark* installment 7ate9 created to profile singer–dancer–musician Austin Mahone leading up to his first huge New

York City concert. As he shares the story of his rise to fame after his best friend helps him with YouTube brandcasting, Mahone vacillates between attributing success to hard work and lucky breaks. It is the kind of ambivalence that Richard Dyer says characterizes most star stories. 7ate9 edits the video so that Mahone's account of his career trajectory aligns with the brandcasting profile: "We made some videos . . . We were so excited [to get] 10 views in one day. Now it's like . . . unreal." While Mahone details all the time he spends sharpening his skills as a musician, the video editing implies that Mahone has transformed a hobby into a profession: "The more I practice the more it felt true to me that this is what I wanted to do." He also codes his story in relation to the "regular guy" American Dream mythology: "I came from a family of cowboys and ranchers to selling out this huge theater in Times Square in New York City. I can't believe that I'm here." 7ate9 also uses the video profile to position Mahone as a role model for viewers whose hobbies or future aspirations align with his. It also reinforces the centrality of the recording division to Disney Channels Worldwide. Reminding them to be Radio Disney listeners, Mahone directly addresses viewers: "Music can change your life. It can change the way you look at things. It changed me. It changed me from being insecure and quiet, to putting myself out there and trying different things." The prosocial phrasing implicitly links Mahone's profile to Disney Channel's *The Magic of Healthy Living* campaign, which includes *Try It!* and the *Pass the Plate* shorts, some of which 7ate9 created. Mahone's final words of advice, "You never want to give up on yourself. Ever!" segue into the short's theme song, "Make your mark on the world."

Designed to appeal to viewers fascinated with the idea of making your mark and becoming a star, the brandcaster series cycle narrativizes the new media fantasy that "broadcasting yourself" on some new media-enabled platform could be the first step in your star trajectory. Disney Channel first capitalized on the fantasy in 2009's *Sonny with a Chance*, the sitcom that launched the career of Demi Lovato.[21] Then, as noted earlier, Disney Channel put the premise front and center in its 2011 sitcom *Austin & Ally*.[22] By 2009, Disney Channel had started thematizing and monetizing the concept of broadcasting yourself. In *Sonny with a Chance*, producers created a series character whose backstory includes broadcasting her talent for sketch comedy through video posts to YouTube. It is significant that the character's discovery by a Hollywood producer (head of the fictional Condor Studios) draws on Andy Samberg's backstory given that the sketch comedy show within the series fashions itself as a teen version of *Saturday Night Live* mixed with a *30 Rock*-style behind-the-scenes at the show sitcom.

The series spends less time on sketches and more on Sonny's negotiation of small-time Hollywood fame, and it places even more emphasis on her attempts to be a true friend to her often shallow and untrustworthy fellow Condor Studio actors, especially Tawni Hart and Chad Dylan Cooper. Through contact with Sonny, Tawni and Chad are gradually transformed by this obstinate optimist and new arrival who manages to stay refreshingly ordinary after she arrives in Hollywood. It is a typical dynamic, not only in Disney stardom-related sitcoms, but in star sitcoms in general. As we saw in Chapter 1, the "star as ordinary, the star as special" dynamic as articulated by Dyer is a central facet of the way audiences relate with stars.

The actual backstory of Demi Lovato is more traditional. She was a child actor on the kids' show *Barney*, where she met fellow castmate Selena Gomez. Whether or not the story about how they became best friends is just part of their management of their star brands, Demi Lovato and Selena Gomez did both arrive at Disney around the same time and were promoted as BFFs (Best Friends Forever). In a behind-the-scenes short about filming Gomez's guest spot on Lovato's sitcom, they both talk about being best friends and what a difference having each other has made in their Hollywood experiences. Of course, the short was also promoting *Princess Protection Program*, their DCOM about how an American tomboy and a European princess became unlikely, but fast friends. In the movie Gomez stars as tomboy Carter Mason who coaches a princess-in-hiding on how to look and act like an ordinary girl. In turn, of course, the princess (Demi Lovato) gives Carter lessons on being a princess and a makeover.

Assertions about Disney stars as friends are intended as a form of brand differentiation from the stereotype of the self-obsessed Hollywood star. In every star-in-the-making sitcom (and in the star sitcoms like *Hannah Montana*) there is a badly behaved star positioned as the foil for the refreshingly down-to-earth main character. I will return to the important role assertions about stars as friends and friendship between the series stars have for the Disney Channel brand. First, we need to consider the uniqueness of stardom on Disney Channel.

As is commonly recognized, Disney Channel is in the business of creating multiplatform stars with television, film, and recording careers. The usual assertion is that television programs produce a kind of stardom, but because of the intimacy created by a weekly series broadcast directly into domestic settings, television stardom is at odds with the classical Hollywood notion of star power as aura. Disney intervenes in this discourse of televisual stardom, which typically distinguishes between television personalities (who are constructed to seem like approachable every day people) and stars (who have an aura that makes them seem glamorous and unapproachable). Disney's contract players are both recognized for their television personas and viewed as distinct from them. Their real names are constantly placed as on screen captions and loyal viewers know them as much, if not more, by those real names, even as the actors became associated with specific series personas. Disney's tween stars function as conglomerate contract players of sorts, especially given the way these multitalented performers are launched in and circulate through different properties. In the channel identifiers and bumpers, the stars wield Disney's signature magic wand and state their full names.

These individualized channel and series identifiers are inserted into the flow to indicate the start of a new episode or segment of a DCOM. Prior to the first story segment of a Friday night episode of *Wizards of Waverly Place*, for instance, the

Disney star directly addresses the viewer: "Hi, I'm Selena Gomez from *Wizards of Waverly Place* and you're watching the Disney Channel." As she makes the identification, Gomez "taps" the mouse graphic with her graphically inserted wand and that signals the start of an episode of *Wizards of Waverly Place*, the series on which Selena Gomez plays Alex Russo, one of three sibling wizards-in-training. Alex is the sarcastic, slacker sister of Justin, her studious older brother, and Max, her dim-witted younger brother. Gomez's Disney Channel identifier reflects the sassiness and the bohemian style associated with her Alex Russo persona and the Greenwich Village setting of the sitcom.

When *Wizards of Waverly Place* began airing in 2007 such an identifier served to remind viewers about the title of the new sitcom and the name of its emerging star. When Gomez was later launched as a recording artist for Hollywood Records, her less famous *Wizards of Waverly Place* costars were more likely to do the identifiers. By then, Gomez was starring in music videos and in Social Shorts that used behind-the-scenes and performance footage from her first world tour to convey that she was both a star and still a relatable person navigating newfound stardom. The short-form content did sometimes create a slippage between Gomez's continuing role as Alex Russo her new position as Selena Gomez.

This disconnect became most evident when Disney Channel began airing the music video for her single "Love You Like a Love Song" from her band's 2011 album, *When the Sun Goes Down*. This music video established a glamorous pop star image through her many costume changes. All the different glamorous-looking Selenas in the video made for a stark contrast to the more casual appearance of Alex Russo. A similar slippage between television persona and star aura occurred in relation to the lyrics to "Who Says," the platinum single from the 2011 album. In some performances of the song, the lyrics, "I'm no beauty queen/I'm just beautiful me," were at odds with the glammed up Selena Gomez who looked a lot like a beauty queen. The lyrics leave open the possibility that the reference is to racialized categories of beauty. As a mixed-race performer, Gomez might be asserting the widely accepted but largely unsupported assumption that in a post-Obama America racial conceptions of beauty or achievement are obstacles young people can individually push past, especially if they maintain the obstinate optimist worldview.

In any case, her commentary about not wanting to be anybody but herself is ironic in that a good number of her listeners would like to be Selena Gomez, whether in attitude or in appearance. The message of the song is that people can leverage talent to make it to the top of a profession if they challenge naysayers and continue to believe in themselves. The bridge to the song addressed that desire and offered an "obstinate optimist" viewpoint. The song's lyrics underscored the appeal of this philosophy, which is also at the heart of the brandcaster sitcoms. The song, about believing in yourself despite the opinions of naysayers, is the perfect brandcaster anthem. It references fantasy futures in Hollywood and in the White House. It calls viewers to listen only to Selena's voice, as she assures them that success comes when you listen to an internal voice not to the naysayers around you. The song's success is due in part to its catchy hook and an aspirational message, but it developed extratextual appeal when the news broke that Selena Gomez was dating pop idol, Justin Bieber. With a YouTube-to-Hollywood backstory, Bieber also had a "just an ordinary guy" appeal at the time. The Bieber relationship catapulted Gomez to a new level of fame as she became a hot ticket for chat shows where television personalities like Ellen DeGeneres and Robin Roberts of ABC's *Good Morning America* were eager to discuss the relationship.

Prior to all the broadcast media attention, Selena Gomez had received the standard star rollout for new Disney Channel arrivals. They first circulate among sitcoms, DCOMs, music videos, and Radio Disney appearances and then go on to star in feature films and release solo albums, typically after contributing a single to a Disney-related compilation or movie soundtrack. If they achieve star status before their series run comes to an end (all Disney series typically run for approximately four seasons), their stardom typically starts to disrupt the relatable teen dynamic on which the series had been premised. As we saw with Gomez's recording career persona, residual stardom remains when they return to television after doing work on other platforms (features, recording, radio, and Social Shorts).

3.7 Brand Managing Themselves: Miley Cyrus and The Jonas Brothers

Gomez's sitcom *Wizards of Waverly Place* technically came on air as part of Disney Channel's series cycle about secret lives of seemingly ordinary teens. The cash cow in this cycle is *Hannah Montana* (March 2006–January 2011), the sitcom in which Miley Cyrus plays Miley Stewart, a seemingly ordinary teen with a secret life as a pop superstar. *Hannah Montana* is emblematic of how Disney creates television personas for its performers that are compatible with their construction as stars, and often they are given character arcs that comment on that star construction process. As the series progresses, the actors develop a recognizable star image that must coexist (not always easily) with the characterization of the well-known television persona.

Television series that retain some elements of the off-screen life of the lead actor cannot help but complicate the operative distinctions between the actor and the television persona. In both *Hannah Montana* and *Jonas/Jonas LA*, the characters share a first name with the actors, respectively, Miley Cyrus and Joe, Nick, and Kevin Jonas. After the four actors became superstars in the teen recording industry, their wider Disney stardom sometimes conflicted with their status as television personas.

The appeal of *Hannah Montana* and *Jonas* depends upon the double promise: the star is like us (because of the television personality's everydayness and the commonality of our anxieties and experiences) and on some level we want to be like the star (and attain a glamorous look and lifestyle associated with film or music industry stardom). Cyrus' and Jonas' sitcoms share an emphasis on best of both worlds balance (e.g., intimacy of real friends and proximity to a Hollywood social circle). In the final seasons of their respective sitcoms they played out their own fantasies about their successful negotiation of the space between both worlds, and their comfort with a star's hybrid ordinary/special status. Yet, these star sitcoms make evident that the sitcom persona and public personality are both constructed for consumption by Disney audiences.

The Jonas Brothers' sitcom only ran for two seasons because it was derailed by the fact that the band had reached superstar status too early in the usual Disney rollout process. The main problem was that the sitcom was originally slated for production in 2007, following the Jonas Brothers' guest appearance on *Hannah Montana*. Even though production of the sitcom was halted by the Writer's Strike, the rest of the franchise elements had already been set in motion. The Jonas Brothers were already recording artists who had been on several tours during a few years with Columbia Records and then, starting in 2007, with Hollywood Records. Disney Channel already had begun filming a behind-the-music concert footage-based short series called *Jonas Brothers: Living the Dream* (May 2008). *Camp Rock*, their first DCOM, aired in June 2008, but their sitcom *Jonas* did not start until May 2009.

The original concept for a Jonas sitcom was to be part of the Disney Channel "teens with a secret life" series cycle. When they became pop stars before they became television stars, the sitcom concept morphed into a "stars balancing fame with ordinary life" series. Appearing in a star sitcom enabled the Jonas Brothers to embed music videos within regular sitcom episodes. Within the flow between story segments, they also appeared in actual music videos for singles from their records.

The Jonas Brothers had accrued enough star power as recording artists for Hollywood Records to request a rewrite for season two of their sitcom. The retooled series moved away from the original conception of a surreal and slapstick sitcom in the style of *The Monkees* (the 1966–8 sitcom). In *Jonas LA* the Jonas Brothers reimagined themselves as negotiating the shallowness of the Hollywood scene with the help of Stella and Macey, two female best friends who evolve into love interests for Nick and Joe. These relationships are presented as authentic in contrast to the shallowness of Hollywood relationships. While the series itself is forgettable, it is fascinating that even though they were already stars, the brothers still imagined themselves as bigger stars-in-the-making. Each brother character in the sitcom represented a different brandcasting aspiration: Joe wanted to be leading man/singer, his goofier older brother Kevin wanted to be a producer, and Nick, the youngest, moodiest, and most talented brother, wanted to be the solo singer–songwriter.

The new *Jonas* sitcom concept aligned not only with the actual aspirations of each Jonas, but also with what was happening on *Hannah Montana* and with series star Miley Cyrus in 2009. Episodes revolved around Miley Stewart getting a role in a big budget film, fake dating an actor for publicity, and later reconnecting with a teen idol love interest she had met in an earlier season. Miley Cyrus recognized that the final season of her sitcom could become a platform for the initial phase of her desired brand refashioning. The fourth and final season, which ran from July 2010 to January 2011, was distinguished from earlier seasons by its own special title, *Hannah Montana: Forever.*

From its first season in 2006, *Hannah Montana* offered self-reflexive commentary on the construction of a recording star at the same time it worked to construct Miley Cyrus as a Disney star with both a Hannah Montana and a Miley Cyrus recording career. It was a brand management sitcom in that it initially launched and maintained a new star brand. *Hannah Montana* kept its grounding in subsequent seasons through the peer-ent child relationship between Miley and her dad Robbie Ray (the role was played by Billy Ray Cyrus, her real life dad and country music star, adding to the blurred line between the star and the television persona). There were some *Ozzie & Harriet* elements to the series, as it had a musician from another decade helping to launch a sitcom that would quickly turn his tween into a teen idol. Miley Cyrus would spend her teen years enjoying popular music stardom, but then look to change her image by transitioning to dance club music with adult themes. This transition already was underway in her sitcom's final season.

The series had always privileged Miley's point of view and had at its center the friendship between Miley and Lily, her "best friend forever." Through this "BFF" relationship, the series grounded itself in the friend-com formula that has long been a successful broadcast television sitcom format. By this point, Miley Stewart was experiencing more tensions between maintaining an ordinary life and a star lifestyle, so episodes were less about a secret life than about how maintaining long-term friendships was the secret to having a balanced life.

The degree of the pull between friendship and fame that the character experiences in *Hannah Montana: Forever* spoke to the anxiety Cyrus had about making a transition to Hollywood's more broad-based stardom. Cyrus clearly did not want to be forever associated with her Hannah Montana persona. Yet, she also benefitted from the way the sitcom offered her a platform from which to manage her desired self-representation. Cyrus found ways within the final season's episodes to talk back to off-screen commentary about her image. In one episode, for example, Miley Stewart records a duet with Caribbean singer Iyaz called "Gonna Get This" and comments on how fans of Hannah Montana have to get used to changes in her musical style, her look, and her brand evolution more generally. The in-series Miley also reflects on how difficult it is to be almost 18 years old, and to still have some young tween fans. The disconnect is part of why Disney Channel assumes a short shelf life to its star sitcoms and its stars, who usually age out of their original roles. While some like Selena Gomez, do this gracefully, others like Miley Cyrus employ a wrecking ball to sever ties completely.

In the final season of *Hannah Montana*, one can find seeds of Cyrus' infamous 2013 dramatic post-Disney change. When Cyrus was filming the season, Disney could not completely contain the moments when her off-screen behavior was at odds with the series focus on (and her own publicity about) a teen star who remains grounded and unaffected by the seductive and destructive sides of stardom. *Hannah Montana: Forever* fetishizes the best friends forever (BFF) relationship between Miley Stewart and Lily Truscott. In the series finale, Miley decides to go to college with Lily as the two BFFs originally planned (rather than pursue a new opportunity for fame). Miley chooses to maintain her lifelong friendship over making a career move that could help her maintain lifelong fame. Yet, as Adrienne McLean notes, a star who puts anything before stardom is unlikely to become a star in the first place. In Cyrus' real life, she did not attend college and is unlikely to have friends from middle school because she was already acting at age ten and started *Hannah Montana* in 2006 at 13. She quickly became famous for the role, winning the Teen Choice: TV Actress Award for the role of Miley Stewart in 2007, 2008, and 2009.

3.8   From BFF Sitcoms to Disney's *Friends for Change*

With all the recent attention to Miley Cyrus' rejection of the pop star persona constructed by Disney's "best of both worlds" marketing, it is easy to forget that at its center *Hannah Montana* was a sitcom about BFFs. The core characterization of a star as having and being a best friend and privileging the bonds of friendship over all else was central to the way in which Disney Channel used the series as a brandcasting platform back in 2010. As established earlier, the quartet of friends in the more recent sitcom, *Austin & Ally* is the ultimate expression of the brand identity of Disney Channel, which relies on the friendly advice giver and friendship rhetoric in general to communicate a collective understanding of its brand.[23] Many Disney Channel sitcoms and DCOMs have at their core a best buddy pairing or a close-knit ensemble of friends, which is hardly surprising on a channel with a core audience of tweens (9–14) and a secondary audience of kids (6–11). Disney Channel's earlier sitcom hits like *Lizzie McGuire* and *That's So Raven* tended to parallel the dynamics of popular broadcast sitcoms such as ABC's trio-of-besties sitcoms, *The Wonder Years* or *Boy Meets World*. Disney Channel continues to specialize in the friend-com of the style that has long been popular at sister channel ABC, the broadcast network which aired *Laverne & Shirley*, *The Odd Couple*, *Bosom Buddies*, *Perfect Strangers*, *Gidget*, and a host of other sitcoms centered on a core friendship duo or trio. Yet, Disney Channel moved to the top of the ratings when it aired sitcoms that combined a core friendship dynamic with the stars-in-the-making or star sitcom fantasy lifestyle. The dynamic was modified a bit for Disney XD, the cable channel microcast to tween males. Some of its live-action series follow the Disney Channel formula of having best friends as the central characters, as is the case in *Zeke and Luther* and *Kickin' It*, but the fantasy futures involve stardom in the martial arts, skateboarding, or another arena assumed to appeal to tween males.

This returns us to the larger investigative purpose of this book's analyses, which is directed to the ultimate goal of understanding how peer-to-peer recommendations came to be so central to the audience address of networks, channels, and corporations. In Disney Channel's case, friendship is not only central to sitcom thematics, but also to the entire channel's infrastructure. An analysis of the peer-to-peer address that structures some of Disney Channel's short-form programming creates the impression that the channel's young actors are depicted as an ensemble of friends sharing their enthusiasm for all things Disney. When channel stars appear in short-form series, the entertainment aspects efface the fact that the stars are really paid endorsers. After its mid-2000s channel rebranding, friendship on Disney Channel went beyond thematics and characterization. Brand managers leverage the reliable friend and advice giver in its sitcom promotions and channel brand promotions as well as its sitcoms and DCOMs. The Walt Disney Company also puts friendship at the center of its company voice messaging and its corporate social responsibility initiatives. Both are showcased on Disney Channel in the short-form content related to Disney's *Friends for Change* campaign.

Short-form "content about content" positions its subjects as fantasy friends of viewers and trusted advice givers. These kinds of direct address shorts are part of the materialization of the Disney brand. Modifying Carolin Gerlitz and Anne Helmond's theories about the impact of Facebook's Like economy on consumer address, we can say that Disney Channel has developed a web-and social-media enabled Friend economy. Disney's customized Friend economy offers an infrastructure for the *materialization, measurement,* and *multiplication* of the Disney brand. To put this in the terms Gerlitz and Helmond use to describe Facebook's infrastructure, Disney Channel's Friend economy enables:

A. *materialization* of the Disney brand in its affiliated star personas through
    a. their characterization in sitcoms that privilege the bonds of friendship
    b. on-air and online modes of direct address that position them as fantasy friends of viewers and as trusted advice givers

B. *measurement* of brand reach through
    a. ratings
    b. downloads
    c. Like button analytics
    d. other new media metrics

C. *multiplication* of specific brands through
    a. their share-ability
    b. transmedia extensions of their story worlds
    c. transmedia marketing across Disney divisions.

In short, Disney's infrastructure enables *materialization* through star/television persona endorsers and product integration; *measurement* through new media metrics based more on engagement and expressions than on impressions (i.e., number of eyeballs on content and commercials); and *multiplication*, the broadened reach a multiplatform corporate structure can offer sponsors and advertisers.

Yet, all of this makes it clear that friendship on Disney Channel goes beyond buddy pairings in promotions and programs. Friendship is integral to the channel's economic structure in terms of its "friends of Disney Channel sponsorship paradigm." Procter and Gamble, Birds Eye, Lysol, and Nintendo, among others, are embraced as friendly entities. With specialized shorts that air on Disney Channel, they make friendly recommendations for lifestyle changes and offer products that help people feel as if they are contributing to a cause or a lifestyle change. In on-air and online edutainment shorts and in the press and PR coverage that accompanies the spots, sponsors like P&G depict their brands as "education platforms" about healthy lifestyles or "future-friendly" consumer behaviors. The integrated brands or sponsoring companies are represented as corporate partners not vendors. The dynamic is explicit because of customized product lines like Lego Friends, but also because the channel announcer constantly reminds viewers that companies are "proud sponsors of Disney Channel." The custom spots also use language that tries (not that successfully) to seem like friendly advice, rather than a product pitch. This language carries over to press releases and journalistic coverage. In short, the sponsor segments ostensibly "educate and inform" viewers about social behavior or practices (e.g., getting active or avoiding the spread of germs), but they do more to educate and inform them about brands. In the process the companies imply that consuming their products can be the solution to social or environmental problems.[24] Other sponsors of toys make for easier continuity as they can take a toys-as-buddies approach. In one for Build-A-Bear Workshop, the announcer says, "making friends makes every day more fun. The best way to make new friends is to do everything with heart" (at which point a bear building workshop is depicted).

In its most successful period between 2009–12, Disney Channel brought together its star friends from Disney Channel and Disney XD in Disney's *Friends for Change* cause marketing shorts. The multitasking shorts combine channel branding, promotion for sitcoms, movies, and music videos, and messaging about earth-friendly, green initiatives underway at The Walt Disney Company in partnership with nonprofit organizations. The campaign exemplifies how a brand can become a facilitator for organizing action related to a social cause. Disney's *Friends for Change* calls for the kind of commodity activism Mukherjee and Banet-Weiser analyze in their work. In this kind of cause marketing campaign, the brand is made to seem like the logical mechanism through which one can become active politically. A closer analysis of Disney's *Friends for Change* helps to illuminate "the contemporary logics connecting merchandising, political ideologies, and consumer citizenship."[25]

Disney's *Friends for Change* (*FFC*) is a tween "empowerment initiative" linked to green causes supported by The Walt Disney Company. The related cause marketing prompts viewers to adopt earth-friendly behaviors and a "Project Green" perspective. The *FFC* campaign highlights viewers who gather a network of friends to put their initiatives into action and thereby model the kinds of behavior which Disney is advocating. In the "Reg and Pledge" call-to-action, Disney Channel stars prompt viewers to register on the affiliated website and simply click to pledge to be a friend for change. Disney Channel constitutes its community through friendship rhetoric.

In its first phase, *FFC* played like a hybrid between edutainment and channel branding (featuring Disney's *circle of stars*). The segments featured an ensemble of stars from Disney Channel and Disney XD, offering recommendations and tips for saving energy and water and reducing waste. According to Michael Wilmott, such brand shepherds help brands resonate for people. The channel stars become the embodiment of the brand's social experiences, lifestyle values, and civic aspirations. Speaking through these friendly advice givers, The Walt Disney Company hoped to communicate a core vision to a target audience of tweens and a secondary audience of parents or caregivers and slightly older or younger siblings. The interactions depicted in the shorts also suggest that the group of channel stars enjoy a generally friendly relationship, and that duos and trios of stars have formed intimate friendships with each other. The intention here seems to be to equalize the positions of Disney stars and viewers and represent them as all part of the same social circle.

Disney Channel encourages viewers to identify not only with the friendly stars but also with the friend for change, the new populist type the brand offers to engage a generation anxious about the sustainability of the earth's resources during their lifetimes. The shorts offer simple, everyday lifestyle changes to ease those anxieties, but encourage those who imagine themselves as exemplary friends for change to take a community action, such as organizing a coastal cleanup crew. The *Friends for Change* (*FFC*) initiative contributes to what Mukherjee and Banet-Weiser describe as the commodification of social activism. As Banet-Weiser explains, "Rather than inserting brands into culture, brand managers seek to build culture around brands through emotive relationships."[26] *FFC* establishes emotive relationships between "Disney friends" and then uses them to build a culture around *FFC*.

To support and recognize local implementation by viewers, Disney Channel hired Riverstreet Productions to film some of the initiatives, thereby adding layers to the campaign. *FFC* monetary grants were also offered to middle school and grade school classes willing to take on larger projects. Some of these classes and individual viewers were profiled in Riverstreet Productions' *FFC Real Kids* spots. Those profiled got the chance to demonstrate their earth-friendly initiatives in action and to do so alongside an ensemble of Disney star friends. The early installments of the ongoing series of shorts showcased not only the actions

FIGURE 3.5 *Friends for Change* and Disney Channel star trios, including Joe, Nick, and Kevin Jonas (upper) and Selena Gomez, Demi Lovato, and Miley Cyrus (middle). The title card image is from the *FFC* music video, "Make a Wave" with Joe Jonas and Demi Lovato (lower).

of featured friends for change, but also the interactions among Disney stars and viewers. They were represented as part of a circle of friends brought together by Disney for a cause rather than as an ensemble of brand advocates.

The effectiveness of the *FFC* shorts comes from the entwinement of the usual viewer calls-to-action with calls-to-affiliation. While ostensibly directed toward gathering advocates for an environmental cause, the primary goal of *FFC* is to transform Disney Channel viewers into a network of brand advocates who create value for Disney through their willingness to share their affective investment in the brand, whether they put in the effort to lead a *FFC* initiative in a local school or community or just click to pledge to adopt behavior changes for the cause or to share elements of the campaign (and its company messaging) through social media. Yet, this content becomes something viewers and users willingly share only if the initiative engages them by making them feel as if Disney values what they value.

In its third phase it morphed into a short-form eco-competition series, Disney's *Friends for Change Games*, which was segmented into three parts and a finale special during the summer of 2011. In the segments, each team accepted an eco-challenge and competed for money that Disney would donate to conservation organizations (e.g., The World Wildlife Fund and The Ocean Conservancy). Produced by 7ate9 Entertainment, the games phase put more emphasis on entertainment and called more attention to the way in which Disney Channel and Disney XD have amassed this large ensemble of "brand shepherds" who help the brand resonate for viewers.[27] The ensemble even went global with the addition of Disney Channel stars from Argentina, Brazil, Italy, and Belgium, among other Disney Channel locations.

Also about expanding market reach, the 2011 *Friends for Change Games* introduced U.S. viewsers to the channel stars in other markets, including Argentina, Belgium, Brazil, France, Italy, Mexico, and Spain. Once they became familiar faces, it also became apparent that the supposedly "regular kids" from around the world represented in the previous year's *Pass the Plate* channel brand/PSA hybrids were often actually Disney Channel stars from international Disney channels.

Making *FFC* a global campaign is indicative of the increased importance of international market for Disney and ABC television programming, and Disney's expansion of its branded channels across the world. The latter development is particularly important in terms of company voice advertising. Having an international network of branded television channels allows for the dissemination of The Walt Disney Company's desired corporate image and its corresponding purchaser-citizen ideal. While each international channel has content customized for its particular market, and air several British or Australian co-productions, they all program a consistent core schedule of signature U.S. sitcoms. With its own channels, Disney can control the brand surround for its series and that of other Disney divisions' products (e.g., feature films, games, DVDs, consumer products, etc.), while also disseminating its desired corporate identity.

3.9 *Friends for Change* Music Videos

Although *FFC* has been retooled each season since its launch in 2009, the summer 2010 campaign exemplifies most clearly the Disney circulation strategy. It enhanced the star brands of Demi Lovato, the Jonas Brothers, and Miley Cyrus, among others, who were reaching ever more audiences in their careers as recording artists for labels within Disney's recording division. Disney even had a few new stars on deck, including Selena Gomez and some potential star newcomers from the live-action sitcoms airing on Disney XD, the basic cable channel microcast for tween males and launched in February 2009.

While technically a cause marketing campaign, *FFC* also functions as channel branding, which makes it seem like all of the actors who star in the channel's sitcoms comprise an off-screen social circle. Some of these Disney star friends appeared in two campaign-related music videos, "Send It On" and "Make a Wave." The music video for the pop ballad "Send it On" aired on Disney Channel in August 2009. It featured Disney Channel stars and singers Selena Gomez, Demi Lovato, the Jonas Brothers, and Miley Cyrus, all interacting as if they were friends. The lyrics are technically about the impact of adopting simple "green living" behavioral changes in everyday life. It is a message-heavy song with lines including: "imagine all we can do if we send it on" and "with one little action, the chain reaction will never stop." In the song as well as in the direct address PSA elements of the *Send It On* segments, Disney Channel stars remind viewers to help the earth in whatever way they can. They recommend everyday changes such as unplugging electronic devices and turning off lights and faucets as quickly as possible. Of course, the language calling for forward-thinking social action can also apply to forwarding as a social media action. As viewers spread the PSA/music video hybrid, they are also participating in viral marketing for Walt Disney and its channel brand. Jenkins, Green, and Ford might call it a spreadable campaign, as it encourages user circulation of content, prompted through top down releases of content, promotion, and hybrids of the two.

Send It On segued well into Disney Channel's May 2010 *It's On!* summer schedule presentation/music video/brand campaign hybrid. The dramatized channel campaign is set on the Santa Monica Pier and is hosted by the titular stepbrother inventors from the animated series *Phineas and Ferb*. (See Figure 3.1.) The theme song for the series includes the lyrics: "There's 104 days of summer vacation/and school comes along just to end it/So the annual problem for our generation/is finding a good way to spend it." While Phineas and Ferb are future MIT students who concoct an array of amazing inventions, the channel brand campaign encourages viewers to spend a good deal of their vacation watching Disney Channel, learning the songs and dances from the latest DCOM, and watching and re-watching the channel's sitcom episodes. Sitcom seasons often had their first run in the summer months to attract the attention of the vacationing school-age viewers that Disney Channel typically courts.

It's On! also doubles as branding for *Camp Rock 2*, the summer 2010 DCOM about a the final performance "battle round" in which the singing–dancing team from the well-heeled Camp Star face off against the underdogs at Camp Rock. The song was included on the soundtrack, which was released one month before the Labor Day weekend premiere of *Camp Rock 2*. The competitive tone of the *It's On!* channel brand campaign also reflects the fact that it aired after the break-through success of the *High School Musical* franchise (2006–9). Through its movies and signature sitcoms, Disney Channel finally succeeded in competing with and eventually besting Nickelodeon in the ratings in 2012.

It helped that Disney Channel of these years had a stable of teen idols, including Joe Jonas and Demi Lovato. The duo headlined in the *Camp Rock* film franchise. They starred in the second *FFC-related* campaign video, "Make a Wave," which complemented the summer of fun fantasy on display in *It's On!*. "Make a Wave" had an advantage over "Send It On" because it played more like a standard pop love song, rather than a simple PSA set to music. The "Make a Wave" video dramatizes a romantic afternoon beach date, made all the more plausible given that Joe Jonas and Demi Lovato were dating at the time. The video also acted as a promotion leading up to the Labor Day weekend premiere of *Camp Rock 2*. The DCOM's soundtrack, which included "Make a Wave," was released in August 2010 (see Figure 3.5). In the *Camp Rock* franchise Demi Lovato plays the romantic lead Mitchie Torres (an ordinary girl with a great voice) opposite Joe Jonas as Shane Gray (the lead singer and pop idol from the band Connect 3). The "Make a Wave" video leverages the popularity of their coupling and the extratextual information about Joe and Demi's off-screen romance fed into the spreadability of the video. Unfortunately, the relationship had a summer-romance longevity and it was over within a few months. Later, Lovato's widely publicized emotional breakdown during her appearance on the Jonas Brothers' fall 2010 world tour, her stint in rehab for an eating disorder and cutting behavior, and her eventual decision to quit her Disney Channel sitcom *Sonny with a Chance* contradicted the several months in which Disney Channel had crafted an "'exes' who remain friends" narrative into which the changed status of the Joe and Demi relationship could be contained. Lovato's openness about her recovery and her later release of personal empowerment rock anthems, first as singles and then on albums, helped her segue into a successful career as a solo artist.

While Lovato's solo singles would be big hits, and "Make a Wave" was successful as a download, the song was not as impactful in relation to the Disney campaign as the third *FFC* video, "We Can (Change the World)." This song had the most longevity in relation to *FFC* because it most encapsulated the messaging of the campaign and of Disney Channel more broadly. Debuting in June 2011, "We Can (Change the World)" was both the anthem for the *FFC* Games and the bridge to the roll out of the new-media-and social-media-savvy brandcaster type, which Disney Channel offered as its newest cultural expression. "We Can" was first released as a music video, put in the rotation on Radio Disney, and offered as a digital download. The anthem is sung by Disney Channel star Bridgit Mendler, but she has help from a chorus comprised of a global cohort of representative viewers and stars from various outlets of Disney Channels Worldwide. In the video, Mendler holds a smart phone and other portable devices. The implication is that she is reaching out to her global social media network and spreading the word, technically about this inspiring generational message, but also about Disney Channel. As Mendler's "We Can" video is circulated by real viewers watching it online, it then becomes a circulation platform not only for Disney Channel, but also for Mendler as a recording artist.

Mendler was already the star in the family sitcom *Good Luck Charlie* and had a recurring guest spot as Julia, the vampire girlfriend of Justin Russo (David Henrie), on *Wizards of Waverly Place*. Those roles led to April 2011's *Lemonade Mouth*, a DCOM in which she played lead singer in a before-they-were-stars backstory about a band that meets in high school and later makes it big. In addition to garnering 5.7 million viewers, *Lemonade Mouth* also had a successful tie-in soundtrack released by Walt Disney Records three days prior to the premiere, as part of the typical Disney Channel rollout strategy. Its hit single, "Determinate," features the lyrics, *Be Heard. Be Strong. Be Proud*, which could easily be another Disney Channel anthem/channel branding initiative.

The three music videos along with the summer 2010 campaign continue to have an afterlife on YouTube, where Disney posted content as part of its dedicated channel. Today, new elements of the campaign are posted simultaneously there and on Disney's website, where *FFC* was originally co-launched as a simultaneous on-air and online campaign. In its Summer 2010 iteration, *FFC* existed not only as a series of interstitials that aired on Disney Channel, but also as short snippets of the interstitials uploaded to Disney's YouTube Channel and Disney Channel's website. These official uploads, along with others provided by fans, give the older campaign an afterlife on YouTube. The campaign continues to evolve through on-air interstitials, with some changes in the roster given the changes in sitcoms and stars.

The various interlocking elements of *FFC* indicate that it is the kind of multiplatform cause marketing made possible by the available combination of legacy media and new media platforms. The Disney website is the central hub for all information related to the campaign. Yet snippets of the campaign and music videos circulate on YouTube. Viewers can encourage their friends on Facebook or other social networking sites to join the movement. The simultaneity of these elements and the use of television to launch recording artists point to the change in the way television platform functions in tandem with other platforms. Today's multiplatform television industry makes this happen at lightning speed, but it is not actually a new practice, as Chapter 1's discussion of Ricky Nelson indicates.

The *FFC* campaign exemplifies how new media-enabled behaviors impact the ways in which people interact with television content. As part of this campaign, The Walt Disney Company began not only collecting friends on Facebook and followers on Twitter, but also amassing pledges on its *FFC* web portal. More generally, the campaigns referenced new media behaviors of forwarding videos and messaging (*Send it On*) and friending corporate entities and television stars/personas. *FFC* also points to changes in the conceptualization of the public sphere as a space made of friends and families, not citizens.

The cause marketing campaign combines both a call to community action and a purchaser call-to-action. It advocates certain Disney-approved individual behavior modifications and community action. It also embeds typical media conglomerate television calls to action—tuning-in to channel series; awareness of upcoming schedule of premieres and specials as well as everyday episodes; downloading and purchasing songs or soundtracks; and accessing affiliated web content. Beyond the immediate goal of promoting its original programming, stars, and other Disney divisions, Disney Channel uses the multitasking messaging to disseminate its parent company's desired self-representation as a good corporate citizen concerned with socio-political issues. Through *Friends for Change* The Walt Disney Company attempts to demonstrate its commitment to creating value for families and tweens, partner corporations, and community groups, all while enhancing shareholder value and loyalty to brands across Disney divisions. When television viewers and site users become Disney brand advocates, they create value for Disney through their willingness to share their affective investment in the brand. The most valued viewers and users are those willing to offer visual and verbal evidence of their investment in Disney and its friendship paradigm.

3.10   Purchaser Citizens and Parent Company Sustainability

It would be a mistake to read *FFC* through a simplistic binary of political agency versus consumption. Instead, *FFC* registers the complex appeals of commodity activism and cause marketing and the paradoxes inherent in both. As is typical of this kind of cause marketing, *FFC* gives people easy ways to feel like contributors, such as by reducing water and electricity use. It privileges personal and local changes, while effacing the fact that impactful change requires legislative support, overhauls of company practices (not just new brand campaigns), and global adoption of sustainable living practices. Clearly, the long-term effects in which Disney is most interested are not related to global sustainability, but rather to brand sustainability. The company needs to make sure that it is growing the next generation of Disney advocates. To do so, it needs to keep its brand relevant by offering its experiences and its content as myth stories that address new desires and anxieties. Whether theirs are social or entertainment needs, Walt Disney messaging tries to persuade viewers that it is the company that is best able to assist them.

Through its skillful interweaving of its channel branding and its corporate responsibility campaigns, Disney Channel seeks to reinforce the notion that The Walt Disney Company is the ultimate family company, one that is better positioned than its competitors to combine caretaking and profit-making. Within its image campaigns as well as in its television programming Disney positions its viewers as purchaser citizens, who are, problematically, encouraged to see their entertainment and style choices as political and their political activism in consumer terms.

Corporate press releases carefully position *FFC* and other shorts which include a PSA element as representative of individual action initiatives rather than advocacy campaigns, as the latter are directed toward effecting political agitation with a goal of policy change. The hybrid programming forms reinforce neoliberal worldviews, but they also reveal the ruptures in the philosophy that individuals and communities should take responsibility for themselves and rely on outside help not from the government, but corporate, community, and sometimes Disney star friends.

Whatever you think of the cultural implications of its approach, you can't help but marvel at the genius of the Disney system, which is less a studio system in the terms established by Thomas Schatz, than a parent company brand circulation system. Why and how does it work so effectively? How does it command such loyalty from its viewers and consumers? On Disney Channel tweens are treated as and called to be contributors to society. For a relatively powerless demographic, this can be a very compelling form of address.

As the anthem for the games indicates, Disney Channel invites an increasingly global cohort of viewers to envision themselves as part of a generation of friends and brandcasters poised to "change the world," both through their commitment to global ecological causes and their new entertainment habits and leisure practices. Disney Channel takes this invitation to tweens even further in its variety of short-form programs, which seamlessly flow out of and into story segments of the sitcoms.

Chapter 4 continues to track the innovative ways in which today's Walt Disney Company continues to create innovative "content about content" shorts, and to blur boundaries between content and promotion. More generally, this chapter and the next demonstrate that new dynamics of distribution and reception have conditioned the forms that creative output takes. In recent years, there has emerged long-term strategic development interest in short-form series. In this chapter I take shorts seriously as a site of study because I believe that such content plays an ever more important role in the business of television when more content–promotion hybrids are created in response to alternate platform distribution and the need for innovative approaches to capture attention of multitasking viewers.

Notes

1 Holt and Cameron 2010, 5, 6, 7, 6, 11, 65.
2 Rampell, June 6, 2012.
3 Sennett 2006, 3.
4 Holt 2004, 5–9. The phrasing is from Holt's solo theories about iconic brands.

5 See Grainge and Johnson "TV and Digital Promotion Research Project" www.not
  tingham.ac.uk/cfm/research/projects/tvanddigitalpromotion.aspx.

6 See Catherine Johnson, July 20, 2012.

7 Bilton 2010, 34, 39, 31.

8 See Lauren DeVillier, *Cable FAX's 15 to Watch*, May 21, 2012. Available: www.cable
  fax.com/archives/cablefax-nbsp-15-to-watch-br-lauren-devillier-disney-channel-
  digital-media.

9 See Sara Bibel, "DisneyChannel.com Launches New Short Form Video Series, 'The
  CopperTop Flop Show'"(reprint of Disney Channel press release), August 8, 2013.
  Available: http://tvbythenumbers.zap2it.com.

10 Dennis 2004, 121.

11 Buckley 2012.

12 Holt and Cameron 2010, 12, 85.

13 Holt and Cameron 2010, 12.

14 B2+ website. Available: www.b2plus.tv/.

15 Brian Briskman is quoted in Mark R. Madler, "Best of Show: Broadcast and Cable
   Networks Turn to B2 Creative Studios," *San Fernando Valley Business Journal* 5 (December
   2011). Available: www.morrisanderson.com/resource-center/entry/Best-of-show-broad
   cast-and-cable-networks-turn-to-B2-creative-studios-for-p/.

16 Brian Dollenmayer quoted in Madler 2011.

17 Ron Pomerantz quoted in Madler 2011.

18 Madler's (2011) paraphrasing of Pomerantz's comments.

19 7ate9 website. Available http://7ate9.com/.

20 See Jesse McKinley, "Melissa Raney and Art Spigel (Profile)," *New York Times*, December 28, 2008. ST11. New York Edition.

21 *Sonny with a Chance* premiered February 8, 2009.

22 *Austin & Ally* premiered December 2, 2011.

23 Holt 2004, 3.

24 For its part, Disney Channel persuades companies that sponsor its programming that it
   can address their need to disseminate messaging as widely as possible. Trade press and
   journalistic sources reveal that Disney sponsors are attracted to the cross-platform efficiency of Disney's media approach. Messaging can travel across a self-described "family
   of brands": Disney Channel, Radio Disney, Disney Family Fun Magazine, disney.com,
   kaboose.com, disneyfamily.com, and familyfun.com.

25 Banet-Weiser's own chapter in 2012.

26 Ibid. 52.

27 The phrase is Wilmott's (2001).

Bibliography

Aaker, David. "Beyond Functional Benefits." *Marketing News*, September 30, 2009: 23.

Aaker, David and Enrich Joachimsthaler. "The Brand Relationship Spectrum: The Key to
  the Brand Architecture Challenge." *California Management Review* 42, no. 4 (Summer
  2000): 8–23.

Anderson, Christopher. *Hollywood TV: The Studio System in the Fifties*. Austin, TX: University of Texas Press, 1994.

Banet-Weiser, Sarah. *Authentic™: The Politics of Ambivalence in a Brand Culture*. New York,
  NY: New York University Press, 2012.

——. "'Free Self-Esteem Tools?': Brand Culture, Gender, and the Dove Real Beauty Campaign." In Mukherjee and Banet-Weiser 2012, 39–56.

——. *Kids Rule!: Nickelodeon and Consumer Citizenship*. Durham, NC: Duke University Press, 2007.

——. "'We Pledge Allegiance to Kids': Nickelodeon and Citizenship." In *Nickelodeon Nation: The History, Politics, and Economics of America's Only TV Channel for Kids*, ed. Heather Hendershot, 209–37. New York, NY: New York University Press, 2004.

Bennet, James. *Television Personalities: Stardom and the Small Screen*. New York, NY: Routledge, 2011.

Bickford, Tyler. "The New 'Tween' Music Industry: The Disney Channel, Kidz Bop and an Emerging Childhood Counterpublic." *Popular Music* 31, no. 3 (2012): 417–36.

Bierbaum, Tom. "The WB's Getting the Girls." *Variety*, November 2–8, 1998: 30.

Bilton, Chris. "Managing the Creative Industries: From Content to Context." In *Managing Media Work*, ed. Mark Deuze, 31–42. London, UK: Sage, 2010.

Bodroghkozy, Aniko."Make it Relevant: How Youth Rebellion Captured Prime Time in 1970 and 1971." In *Groove Tube: Sixties Television and the Youth Rebellion*, 199–235. Durham: Duke University Press, 2001.

Bolter, Jay David and Richard Grusin. *Remediation: Understanding New Media*. Cambridge, MA: MIT Press, 1999.

Boyd, Dana. "Why Youth Heart Social Network Sites: The Role of Networked Publics in Teenage Social Life." In *Youth, Identity, and Digital Media*, ed. David Buckingham, 119–42. Cambridge, MA: MIT Press, 2008.

Broadcasting & Cable. "A Strategy for Stemming the Slide." *Broadcasting & Cable*, May 20, 2002: 21.

Brown, Stephen, Robert V. Kozinets, and John F. Sherry Jr. "Teaching Old Brands New Tricks: Retro Branding and the Revival of Brand Meaning." *Journal of Marketing* 67, no. 3 (2003): 19–33.

Bruzzi, Stella. *New Documentary: A Critical Introduction*. London, UK: Routledge, 2000.

Buckley, Peter. "Exploiting the Implicit." *Campaign*, November 16, 2012. 6–12.

Burgess, Jean and Joshua Green. *YouTube: Online Video and Participatory Culture*. Cambridge, UK: Polity Press, 2009.

Caldwell, John Thornton. "Convergence Television: Aggregating Form and Repurposing Content in the Culture of Conglomeration." In Spigel and Olsson 2004, 41–74.

——. "Critical Industrial Practice: Branding, Repurposing, and the Migratory Patterns of Industrial Texts." *Television & New Media* 7, no. 2 (May 2006): 99–134.

——. "Cultures of Production: Studying Industry's Deep Texts, Reflexive Rituals, and Managed Self-Disclosures." In *Media Industries: History, Theory and Method*, eds. Jennifer Holt and Alisa Perren, 199–212. Malden, MA: Blackwell, 2009.

——. "Para-Industry: Researching Hollywood's Backwaters." *Cinema Journal* 53, no. 3 (2013): 157–65;

——. *Production Culture: Industrial Reflexivity and Critical Practice in Film and Television*. Durham, NC: Duke University Press, 2008.

——. *Televisuality: Style, Crisis, and Authority in American Television*. New Brunswick, NJ: Rutgers University Press, 1995.

——. "Welcome to the Viral Future of Cinema (Television)." *Cinema Journal* 45, no. 1 (Fall 2006): 90–7.

Caves, Richard E. *Creative Industries: Contracts between Art and Commerce*. Cambridge, MA: Harvard University Press, 2000.

Coontz, Stephanie. *The Way We Never Were: American Families and the Nostalgia Trap*. New York, NY: Basic Books, 1992.

Cotter, Bill. *The Wonderful World of Disney Television: A Complete History*. New York, NY: Hyperion, 1997.

Curtin, Michael. "Media Capitals: Cultural Geographies of Global TV." In Spigel and Olsson 2004, 270–302.

——. "On Edge: The Culture Industries in the Neo-Network Era." In *Making and Selling Culture*, ed. Richard Ohmann (with Gage Averill, Michael Curtin, David Shumway, and Elizabeth Traube), 181–202. Hanover, NH: Wesleyan University Press, 1996.

Davis, Aeron. *Promotional Cultures: The Rise and Spread of Advertising, Public Relations, Marketing and Branding*. Cambridge, UK: Polity Press, 2013.

Dawson, Max. "Television Abridged: Ephemeral Texts, Monumental Seriality and TV-Digital Media Convergence." In Grainge 2011, 37–56.

——. "Television's Aesthetic of Efficiency: Convergence Television and the Digital Short." In *Television as Digital Media* eds. James Bennett and Niki Strange, 204–29, Durham, NC: Duke University Press, 2011.

Deery, June. "Reality TV as Advertainment." *Popular Communication* 2, no. 1 (2004): 1–19.

Denis, Christopher Paul and Michael Denis. *Favorite Families of TV*. New York, NY: Citadel Press, 1992.

Dennis, Saul. "Brands Begin by Believing." *Promo Magazine*, June 2004: 121.

Deuze, Mark. "Convergence Culture in the Creative Industries." *International Journal of Cultural Studies* 10, no. 2 (2007): 243–263.

——. *Media Work*. Cambridge, UK: Polity, 2007.

Doherty, Thomas. *Teenagers and Teenpics*, Philadelphia, PA: Temple University Press, 2002.

Donaton, Scott. *Madison and Vine: Why the Entertainment and Advertising Industries Must Converge to Survive*. New York, NY: McGraw Hill, 2005.

Douglas, Susan J. *Where the Girls Are: Growing Up Female with the Mass Media*. New York, NY: Times, 1995.

Dyer, Richard. *Stars*. London, UK: BFI Publishing, 1986.

Ellis, John. "Interstitials: How the 'Bits in Between' Define the Programmes." In Grainge 2011, 59–69.

——. "Scheduling: the Last Creative Act in Television?" *Media, Culture and Society* 22, no. 1 (2000): 25–38.

Finkle, Jim. "New Shows, New Marketing." *Broadcasting & Cable*, February 21, 2005: 8.

Fiske, John. "The Cultural Economy of Fandom." In *The Adoring Audience: Fan Culture and Popular Culture*, ed. Lisa A. Lewis, 30–49. London, UK: Routledge, 1992.

Gabler, Neal. *Walt Disney: The Triumph of the American Imagination*. New York, NY: Knopf, 2006.

Gaines, Jane. "Costume and Narrative: How Dress Tells the Woman's Story." In *Fabrications: Costume and the Female Body*, eds. Jane Gaines and Charlotte Herzog, 180–211. New York, NY: Routledge, 1990.

Gerlitz, Carolin and Anne Helmond, "The Like Economy: Social Web in Transition." Conference Presentation at *MiT7: Unstable Platforms*. May 14, 2011.

Gillan, Jennifer. "*Extreme Makeover: Home* (land Security) *Edition*." In *The Great American Makeover: Television, History, Nation*, ed. Dana Heller, 191–207. New York, NY: Palgrave, 2006.

——. *Television and New Media: Must-Click TV*. New York, NY: Routledge, 2010.

Gitlin, Todd. *Inside Prime Time*. New York, NY: Routledge, 1985.

Gobé, Marc. *Brandjam: Humanizing Brands Through Emotional Design*. New York, NY: Allworth Press, 2007.

Goetzi, David. "How Networks Follow The Tweens." *Broadcasting & Cable*, March 26, 2007.

Grainge, Paul. *Brand Hollywood: Selling Entertainment in a Global Media Age*. New York, NY: Routledge, 2008.

——, ed. *Ephemeral Media: Transitory Screen Culture from Television to YouTube*. London, UK: BFI Publishing, 2011.

——. "TV Promotion and Broadcast Design: An Interview with Charlie Mawer, Red Bee Media." In Grainge 2011, 87–101.

Gray, Herman. *Cultural Moves: African Americans and the Politics of Representation*. Berkeley, CA: University of California Press, 2005.

Gray, Jonathan. *Show Sold Separately: Promos, Spoilers, and Other Media Paratexts*. New York, NY: New York University Press, 2010.

——. "Television Pre-views and the Meaning of Hype." *International Journal of Cultural Studies* 11, no. 1 (2008): 33–49.

——. *Watching with The Simpsons*. London, UK: Routledge, 2006.

Hacker, Jacob. *The Great Risk Shift: The New Economic Insecurity and the Decline of the American Dream*. Oxford, UK: Oxford University Press, 2006.

Haggins, Bambi. *Laughing Mad: The Black Comic Persona in Post-Soul America*. New Brunswick, NJ: Rutgers University Press, 2007.

Haley, Kathy. "Winning By Design." *Multichannel News Supplement*, April 14, 2003.

Hargadon, Andrew. *How Breakthroughs Happen: The Surprising Truth About How Companies Innovate*. Boston, MA: Harvard Business School Press, 2003.

Harries, Dan, ed. *The New Media Book*. London, UK: BFI Publishing, 2002.

——. "Watching the Internet." In Harries 2002, 171–82.

Hartley, John, ed. *Creative Industries*. Malden, MA: Blackwell, 2005.

——. *The Uses of Television*. New York, NY: Routledge, 1999.

Havens, Timothy. *Global Television Marketplace*. London, UK: BFI Publishing, 2006.

Hellekson, Karen and Kristina Busse, eds. *Fan Fiction and Fan Communities in the Age of the Internet: New Essays*. Jefferson, NC: McFarland, 2006.

Hogan, Lindsay. "The Mouse House of Cards: Disney Tween Stars and the Questions of Institutional Authority." In *A Companion to Media Authorship*, eds. Jonathan Gray and Derek Johnson, 296–313. Malden, MA: Wiley Blackwell, 2013.

Holliss, Richard and Brian Sibley. *The Disney Studio Story*. London, UK: Octopus Books Limited, 1988.

Holmes, Su. "'But this Time You Choose!': Approaching the Interactive Audience in Reality TV." *International Journal of Culture Studies* 7, no. 2 (2004): 213–31.

——. "Reality Goes Pop! Reality TV, Popular Music, and Narratives of Stardom in *Pop Idol*." *Television & New Media* 5, no. 2 (2004): 147–72.

Holmes, Su and Deborah Jermyn, eds. "Introduction: Understanding Reality TV." In *Understanding Reality Television*, eds. Holmes and Jermyn, 1–32. London, UK: Routledge, 2004.

Holt, Douglas B. *How Brands Become Icons: Principles of Cultural Branding*. Boston, MA: Harvard Business School Press, 2004.

Holt, Douglas B. and Douglas Cameron. *Cultural Strategy: Using Innovative Ideologies to Build Breakthrough Brands*. Oxford, UK: Oxford University Press, 2010.

Holt, Jennifer. "Vertical Vision: Deregulation, Industrial Economy and Prime-time Design." In Jancovich and Lyons 2003, 11–31.

Ito, Mizuko. *Hanging Out, Messing Around, and Geeking Out: Kids Living and Learning with New Media*. Cambridge, MA: The MIT Press, 2010.

Jackall, Robert and Janice M. Hirota. *Image Makers: Advertising, Public Relations and the Ethos of Advocacy*. Chicago, IL: University of Chicago Press, 2003.

Jancovich, Mark and James Lyons, eds. *Quality Popular Television*. London, UK: BFI Publishing, 2003.

Jenkins, Henry. *Convergence Culture: Where Old and New Media Collide.* New York, NY: New York University Press, 2006.

Jenkins, Henry and David Thornburn, eds. *Democracy and New Media.* Cambridge, MA: MIT Press, 2003.

Jenkins, Henry, Sam Ford, and Joshua Green, *Spreadable Media: Creating Value and Meaning in a Networked Culture.* New York, NY: New York University Press, 2013.

Johnson, Catherine. "The Art of Promotion: Planet Earth Live." *Critical Studies in Television Online,* July 20, 2012. Available: http://cstonline.tv/planet-earth-live.

——. *Branding Television.* New York, NY: Routledge, 2012.

——. "Tele-branding in TVIII: the Network as Brand and the Programme as Brand." *New Review of Film and Television Studies* 5, no. 1 (2007): 5–24.

Johnson, Derek. "Inviting Audiences In: The Spatial Reorganization of Production and Consumption in 'TV III.'" *New Review of Film and Television Studies.* 5, no.1 (April 2007): 61–80.

——. *Media Franchising: Creative License and Collaboration in the Culture Industries.* New York, NY: New York University Press, 2013.

Johnson, Victoria E. *Heartland TV: Primetime Television and the Struggle for U.S. Identity.* New York, NY: New York University Press, 2008.

Kozinets, Robert V. "E-tribalized Marketing?: The Strategic Implications of Virtual Communities of Consumption." *European Management Journal* 17, no. 3 (June 1999): 252–64.

——. "How Online Communities Are Growing in Power." *Financial Times,* November 9, 1998.

Kunz, William. *Culture Conglomerates: Consolidation in the Motion Picture and Television Industries.* Lanham, MD: Rowman and Littlefield, 1997.

Levine, Elana. *Wallowing in Sex: The New Sexual Culture of 1970s American Television.* Durham, NC: Duke University Press, 2007.

Lotz, Amanda. *The Television Will Be Revolutionized.* New York, NY: New York University Press, 2007.

Luscombe, Belinda. "How Disney Builds Stars." *Time,* November 9, 2009: 49–51.

Mann, Denise. "The Spectacularization of Everyday Life: Recycling Hollywood Stars and Fans in Early Television Variety Shows." In *Private Screenings: Television and the Female Consumer,* eds. Lynn Spigel and Denise Mann, 41–69. Minneapolis, MN: University of Minnesota Press, 1992.

McAllister, Matthew. *The Commercialization of American Culture: New Advertising, Control, and Democracy.* Thousand Oaks, CA: Sage, 1996.

McCarthy, Anna. *Citizen Machine: Governing By Television in 1950s America.* Durham, NC: Duke University Press, 2009.

McChesney, Robert W. *The Political Economy of Media: Enduring Issues, Emerging Dilemmas.* New York, NY: Monthly Review Press, 2008.

McCracken, Grant. *Culture and Consumption II: Markets, Meaning, and Brand Management.* Bloomington, IN: Indiana University Press, 2005.

McDonald, Paul. *The Star System: Hollywood's Production of Popular Identities.* London, UK: Wallflower, 2000.

McLean, Adrienne. *Being Rita Hayworth: Labor, Identity, and Hollywood Stardom.* New Brunswick, NJ: Rutgers University Press, 2004.

Meehan, Eileen. *Why Television is Not Our Fault: Television Programming, Viewers, and Who's Really in Control.* Lanham, MD: Rowman and Littlefield, 2005.

——. "Why We Don't Count: The Commodity Audience." In *Logics of Television: Essays in Cultural Criticism*, ed. Patricia Mellencamp, 117–37. Bloomington, IN: Indiana University Press, 1990.

Mittell, Jason. "The Cultural Power of an Anti-Television Metaphor: Questioning the 'Plug-in Drug' and a TV-Free America." *Television and New Media* 1, no. 2 (2000): 215–38.

——. "Generic Cycles: Innovation, Imitation, and Saturation." In *The Television History Book*, eds. Michele Hilmes and Jason Jacobs, 44–9. London, UK: BFI Publishing, 2004.

Moran, Albert. *Copycat TV: Globalisation, Programme Formats and Cultural Identity*. Luton, UK: Luton University Press, 1998.

Mosley, Leonard. *Disney's World*. New York, NY: Stein and Day, 1985.

Mossberger, Karen, Caroline J. Tolbert, and Ramona S. McNeal, *Digital Citizenship: The Internet Society, and Participation*. Cambridge, MA: MIT, 2008.

Mukherjee, Roopali and Sarah Banet-Weiser, eds. *Commodity Activism: Cultural Resistance in Neoliberal Times*. New York, NY: New York University Press, 2012.

Mullen, Megan. *Television in the Multichannel Age*. Oxford, UK: Blackwell, 2007.

Murray, Simone. "Brand Loyalties: Rethinking Content within Global Corporate Media." *Media, Culture, Society* 27, no. 3 (2005): 415–35.

Murray, Susan. *Hitch Your Antenna to the Stars: Early Television and Broadcast Stardom*. New York, NY: Routledge, 2005.

Murray, Susan and Laurie Ouellette, eds. *Reality TV: Remaking Television Culture*. New York, NY: New York University Press, 2004.

Napoli, Philip M. *Audience Economics: Media Institutions and the Audience Marketplace*. New York, NY: Columbia University Press, 2003.

Negra, Diane. "Re-Made for Television: Hedy Lamarr's Post-War Star Textuality." In *Small Screens, Big Ideas: Television in the 1950s*, ed. Janet Thumim, 105–17. London, UK: I.B. Tauris, 2002.

Negus, Keith. *Music Genres and Corporate Cultures*. London, UK: Routledge, 1999.

Nilsen, Sarah. "All-American Girl? Annette Funicello and Suburban Ethnicity." In *Mediated Girlhoods: New Explorations of Girls' Media Culture*, ed. Mary Celeste Kearney, 35–53. New York, NY: Peter Lang, 2011.

Nilsen, Sarah and Sarah E. Turner. *The Colorblind Screen: Television in Post-Racial America*. New York, NY: New York University Press, 2014.

Osgerby, Bill. "'So Who's Got Time for Adults!': Femininity, Consumption and the Development of Teen TV—from *Gidget* to *Buffy*." In *Teen TV: Genre, Consumption and Identity*, eds. Glyn Davis and Kay Dickinson, 71–98. London, UK: BFI Publishing, 2004.

Oswald, Laura R. *Marketing Semiotics: Signs, Strategies, and Brand Value*. Oxford, UK: Oxford University Press, 2012.

Ouellette, Laurie. "Take Responsibility for Yourself: *Judge Judy* and the Neoliberal Citizen." In Murray and Ouellette 2004, 231–50.

Ouellette, Laurie and James Hay, *Better Living Through Reality TV: Television and Post-Welfare Citizenship*. Malden, MA: Blackwell, 2008.

Rampell, Catherine. "More Young Americans Out of High School Are Also Out of Work." *New York Times*, June 6, 2012. B1, B6.

Reid, Michael D. "From Austin & Ally to CopperTop: Calum Worthy's On a Roll." *Times-Columnist* [Victoria, BC], August 22, 2013. Available: www.timescolonist. com/entertainment/television/from-austin-ally-to-coppertop-calum-worthy-s-on-a-roll-1.598271.

Romano, Allison. "Can Disney Attract Boys?" *Broadcasting & Cable*, July 14, 2003.

Ross, Sharon Marie. *Beyond the Box: Television and the Internet*. Malden, MA: Blackwell, 2008.

Sammond, Nicholas. *Babes in Tomorrowland: Walt Disney and the Making of the American Child, 1930–1960*. Durham, NC: Duke University Press, 2005.

Samuel, Lawrence R. *Brought to You By: Postwar Television Advertising and The American Dream*. Austin, TX: University of Texas Press, 2001.

Sandler, Kevin. "Life Without *Friends*: NBC's Programming Strategies in an Age of Media Clutter." In *NBC: America's Network*, ed. Michele Hilmes, 291–307. Berkeley, CA: University of California Press, 2007.

Seiter, Ellen. *Sold Separately: Parents & Children in Consumer Culture*. New Brunswick, NJ: Rutgers University Press, 1993.

——. *Television and New Media Audiences*. Oxford, UK: Oxford University Press, 1999.

Schatz, Thomas. *The Genius of the System: Hollywood Filmmaking in the Studio Era*. New York, NY: Pantheon Books, 1988.

——. "The New Hollywood." In *Film Theory Goes to the Movies*, eds. Jim Collins, Hilary Radner and Ava Preacher Collins, 8–36. London, UK: Routledge, 1993.

Sennett, Richard. *The Culture of The New Capitalism*. New Haven, CT: Yale University Press, 2006.

Shore, Nick. "No Collar" *Media Daily* [blog], March 15, 2012.

Shrum, L.J. *The Psychology of Entertainment Media: Blurring the Lines Between Entertainment and Persuasion*. New York, NY: Routledge, 2012.

Spigel, Lynn. *Make Room for TV: Television and the Family Ideal in Postwar America*. Chicago, IL: University of Chicago Press, 1992.

Spigel, Lynn and Jan Olsson, eds., *Television After TV: Essays on a Medium in Transition*. Durham, NC: Duke University Press, 2004.

Stanley, T.L. "Disney Channel: A Fresh-Face Factory." *Advertising Age*, December 11, 2006.

Staid, Gitte. "Mobile Identity: Youth, Identity, and Mobile Communication Media." In *Youth, Identity, and Digital Media*, ed. David Buckingham, 143–64. Cambridge, MA: MIT Press, 2008.

Stein, Louisa. "Pushing at the Margins: Teenage Angst in Teen TV and Audience Response." In *Teen Television: Essays on Programming and Fandom*, eds. Sharon Ross and Louisa Ellen Stein, 224–43.

——. "'This Dratted Thing': Fannish Storytelling Through New Media." In Hellekson and Busse 2006, 245–60.

Tapscott, Don. *Growing up Digital: The Rise of the Net Generation*. New York, NY: McGraw-Hill, 1999.

Tasker, Yvonne and Diane Negra."In Focus: Postfeminism and Contemporary Media Studies." *Cinema Journal* 44, no. 2 (2005): 107–10.

Taylor, Timothy D. *The Sounds of Capitalism: Advertising, Music, and the Conquest of Culture*. Chicago, IL: The University of Chicago Press, 2012.

Telotte, J.P. *Disney TV*. Detroit, MI: Wayne State University Press, 2005.

Thomas, Bob. *Walt Disney: An American Original*. New York, NY: Simon and Schuster, 1976.

Turner, Sarah E. "BBFFs: Interracial Friendships in a Post-Racial World." In Nilsen and Turner 2014, 237–57.

——. "Disney Does Race: Black BFFs in the New Racial Moment." *Networking Knowledge* 5, no. 1 (February 2012): 125–40.

Turow, Joseph. *Breaking Up America: Advertisers and the New Media World*. Chicago, IL: University of Chicago Press, 1997.

——. *Niche Envy: Marketing Discrimination in the Digital Age*. Cambridge, MA: MIT Press, 2006.

Ulin, Jeffery C. *The Business of Media Distribution: Monetizing Film, TV, and Video Content in an Online World*. 2nd edition. New York, NY: Focal Press, 2014.

Uricchio, William. "Historicizing Media in Transition." In *Rethinking Media Change: The Aesthetics of Transition*, eds. David Thornburn and Henry Jenkins, 23–38. Cambridge, MA: MIT Press, 2004.

——. "Old Media and New Media: Television." In Harries 2002, 219–30.

Valdivia, A.N. "Mixed Race on the Disney Channel: From *Johnnie Tsunami* through *Lizzie McGuire* and Ending with *The Cheetah Girls*." In *Mixed Race Hollywood*, eds. Mary Beltrán and Camilla Fojas, 269–89. New York, NY: New York University Press, 2008.

Van Riper, A. Bowdoin, ed. *Learning from Mickey, Donald, and Walt: Essays on Disney's Edutainment Film*. Jefferson, NC: McFarland, 2011.

Vogel, Harold. *Entertainment Industry Economics: A Guide for Financial Analysts*. 7th edition. New York, NY: Cambridge University Press, 2007.

Waisbord, Silvio. "Understanding the Global Popularity of Television Formats." *Television and New Media* 5 no. 4 (2004): 359–83.

Wasko, Janet. *Understanding Disney: The Manufacture of Fantasy*. Malden, MA: Polity Press, 2001.

Watts, Steven. *The Magic Kingdom: Walt Disney and the American Way of Life*. New York, NY: Houghton Mifflin, 1997.

Wee, Valerie. "Selling Teen Culture: How American Multimedia Conglomeration Shaped Teen Television in the 1990s." In Davis and Dickinson 2004, 87–98.

——. "Teen Television and the WB Network." In Ross and Stein 2008, 43–60.

Williams, Raymond. *Television, Technology and Cultural Forms*. London, UK: Fontana, 1974.

Wilmott, Michael. *Citizen Brands: Putting Society at the Heart of Your Business*. Chichester, UK: Wiley, 2001.

Wyatt, Justin. *High Concept: Movies and Marketing in Hollywood*. Austin, TX: University of Texas Press, 1994.

4

DISNEY STUDIOS' BRAND MANAGEMENT ON TV AND BLU-RAY/DVD

4.1 Parent Company Brandcasting

Brand management at millennial and midcentury Disney has some basic similarities despite the difference between today's Disney media conglomerate and Disney, the minor studio of the late 1950s and early 1960s. Both Disneys explored how legacy properties could be leveraged to promote current properties, especially through new distribution platforms, including broadcast television, cable television, and Blu-ray/DVD/Digital combo packs. They coordinated theatrical and television production and made sure to create television programming that doubled as promotion for Disney Studios output (and sometimes tripled as promotion for a Disney recording division).

7ate9 Entertainment, one of the boutique firms profiled in Chapter 3, proved particularly adept at the conceptualization of this content, which also contributed to branding Disney Channel as a tween destination. Building on some of its earlier shorts, 7ate9 perfected the form in *Leo Little's Big Show*. This content–promotion hybrid explicitly showcased Disney Studio and Disney/Pixar output, while functioning as entertainment in its own right. Aware of the appeal of YouTube and the direct-to-consumer brandcasting it encourages, 7ate9 structured *Leo Little's Big Show* to feel like a hybrid of a viewer vodcast/celebrity chat show/"on the set" interview series produced by an older tween and his big ham of a little sister. The conceit is that the fictional Leo and Amy Little host an interactive vodcast to share their enthusiasm for *Toy Story 3*, *Snow White*, *Pinocchio*, *Prince of Persia*, and *Tangled*, among other Disney and Disney/Pixar films. *Leo Little's Big Show* proved to be an inventive way to air a content-about-content short about films being released in the Blu-ray/DVD Combo pack format (prior to the addition of digital copies for a true multiplatform combination).

When Leo and Amy talk about the 2009–10 Blu-ray/DVD combo packs for the classic releases, such as *Snow White and the Seven Dwarfs, Diamond Edition*, they mention the variety of special features. While the millennial combo packs showcase Disney's embrace of new distribution formats, they would have been impossible to produce without the material ABC filmed for *Disneyland/Walt Disney Presents* or *The Mickey Mouse Club*. The producers of those programs found creative ways to repackage repurposed footage from Disney's films and to integrate that footage with new content. The brandcasting function of the millennial combo packs and the midcentury Disney television series is evident in the abundance of content–promotion segments created for each.

The Walt Disney Company is a particularly useful lens for a consideration of content–promotion hybrids because it has long been committed to a brand-centric approach to television. Indeed, it can even be credited with originating some of television's now-familiar paratextual forms, including the hosted lead-in during which a host offers a framing context for a film screening. The phrasing hosted "lead-in" appears in the studio's late-1950s in-house documents about its dual platform production schedule. From the time of its first regularly scheduled 1950s programming, Disney recognized television's potential as a cross-company promotional space. Commenting on Disney's "total merchandising" approach, Christopher Anderson describes how viewers of *Disneyland* were "propelled by a centrifugal force" from television outward. The program drew their attention to the television platform "only to disperse it outward, toward other Disney products."[1] Anderson is most interested in theme park promotion, which is significant in the first two years of *Disneyland*,[2] while the park was being built and to attract visitors in the first year. As theme park promotion continued, it was often framed within special episodes of the series. The more typical episodes repurposed studio content, and used it to frame a forthcoming release. The structure of the hosted lead-ins promoted films in ways that parallel strategies for the framing of trailers within today's on-air, web, and Blu-ray/DVD special features. Content-about-content shorts function in the way Jonathan Gray says paratexts do; they are the "texts before the text" that try to pre-create meanings in the minds of viewers.[3] *The Mickey Mouse Club*, for example, featured trailers for Disney films, a practice it utilized with more frequency in later seasons. The trailers were framed by lead-ins and lead-outs. In them, film excerpts would be introduced in a segmented fashion interspersed with commentary by (and implied endorsement from) a Mouseketeer, a star of one of the *Mickey Mouse Club* serials, a star of a Disney feature film, senior Mouseketeer and series host Jimmy Dodd, or a grouping of any of these studio spokespeople. Although ephemeral content in its own time, these segments are repurposed on today's Blu-ray/DVD sets and used to reinforce Walt Disney's desired framing of the films.

Disney is and always has been an infamous brandcaster. The reputation prompted some of the erroneous assertions about the studio's use of the 2013 film *Saving Mr. Banks* as a brand management platform. This chapter begins with an assessment of the validity of such claims in light of historical facts about the workings of Disney Studios circa 1961 and the role that brandcasting played in *Frozen*,

FIGURE 4.1   In the hosted lead-in to *Walt Disney Presents*, Walt often used an episode topic to remind viewers about earlier Disney output, often from the classic cartoon shorts and animated features.

Disney's 2013 megahit. The body of the chapter examines Disney brandcasting in the 1950s and early 1960s, especially through the studio's television series *Disneyland/Walt Disney Presents*. Of particular interest is the brand development of Walt Disney himself into Uncle Walt, as tracked through content–promotion hybrids related to Disney's *Snow White and the Seven Dwarfs*, *Alice in Wonderland*, *Peter Pan*, *20,000 Leagues Under the Sea*, and even 1961's *The Parent Trap*. The discussion turns to the repurposing of that television content on Disney's DVDs and its signature Blu-ray/DVD combo packs for its animated classics. This leads to an analysis of Disney Channel's *Leo Little's Big Show*, a short structured to feel like a viewer vodcast about new Disney Blu-ray/DVD releases. The dynamics of this series are examined alongside those of Disney Channel's other promotionally oriented shorts, especially *Disney 365*. The chapter concludes with an analysis of parent company promotional strategies, within the Disney-related episodes of the ABC sitcoms *The Middle* and *Modern Family*.

4.2   Disney Brand Management Films? *Saving Mr. Banks* and *Frozen*

While commentators rightly categorize Disney as particularly attuned to brand building, the description of Walt Disney Studios' release of *Saving Mr. Banks* as an exercise in brand management betrays a lack of understanding both of how brand-building works at the studio and why the film is a poor example of the usual Disney Studios strategy. If *Saving Mr. Banks* were a true brandcasting film, The Walt Disney Company would have done a better job of using the film for layers of cross promotion.

Headline-grabbing reviews depict 2013's *Saving Mr. Banks* as a Disney "info-mercial" and "disingenuous marketing exercise." The film generates drama out of the accommodations that a determined Walt Disney (Tom Hanks) was willing to make in order to secure the film rights to *Mary Poppins* from its recalcitrant author P. L. Travers (Emma Thompson). Gaining those rights proved no easy feat as Travers was cagey, demanding, and often rude. Although the claim makes for a good blog post topic and shareable online film review, *Saving Mr. Banks* is not a Disney Studios history that sugarcoats the behavior of Walt Disney in his Burbank and London negotiations with P. L. Travers. The first problem with this reading is that all of the film's drama over the negotiations is fabrication, as is Travers' humorously hostile side trip to Disneyland and her reaction to a hotel room stuffed with Mickey Mouses and other plush toys.

The most important overlooked detail is that a BBC-affiliated U.K. studio developed *Saving Mr. Banks* and The Walt Disney Company played no role in its scripting process. When the script was brought to Disney executives, they recognized it as "a damned if you do, damned if you don't" situation. They knew no one but Disney Studios could make the film given intellectual property rights considerations, especially related to the use of the songs from the film *Mary Poppins*. If the studio did not make *Saving Mr. Banks*, however, the headline would read that Disney Studios was shutting down the project because the behind-the-scenes story would damage its brand identity and its founder's legacy.

There is no room here to address all of the inaccuracies and half-truths circulating about Disney Studios' involvement in the making of *Saving Mr. Banks*. I will establish some of the known facts not depicted in the film as a way into clarifying what kind of studio Disney was in 1961 when the film is set and when the Disney television series was airing actual brand management content, as discussed later in this chapter.

Walt Disney and P. L. Travers had tea in London some time in the 1950s while he was there overseeing a film. It is unclear, however, if there were any official in-person rights negotiations. Those represented in *Saving Mr. Banks* definitely did not happen because the rights were already secured in 1960. The process actually began two decades earlier when Roy Disney made an unsuccessful negotiation trip to New York some time in the early 1940s when Travers was living there. No one knows the specifics of Roy's meeting with Travers. While it is fun to speculate about the level of hostility in such meetings, that is all director John Lee Hancock and screenwriter Kelly Marcel can do in their story "inspired by true events."

The film has the main negotiations occur over two weeks in April 1961. The real Travers did attend meetings with *Mary Poppins*' creative team at that time, but only in her contractual position as story consultant. The Disney Archives provided Marcel access to 39 hours of audiotapes chronicling those meetings. The tapes, made at Travers' request, helped Marcel capture the dynamics between Travers and screenwriter Don DaGradi (Bradley Whitford) and songwriters Richard and Robert Sherman (Jason Schwartzman and B.J. Novak). Travers had a litany of objections to their ideas for characterization, set design, dialogue, and song lyrics. Despite some reviewers' suspicions, Marcel insists she was not required to whitewash Disney and demonize Travers. It is tempting, if inaccurate, to recast her as a feminist hell-raiser whose bad behavior arose solely from her fierce protectiveness of her art. Marcel did have to soften Travers as the tapes reveal her to be so abrasive, rude, and shrill that an exact impersonation would not allow for the audience's eventual empathy.

The tapes offer nothing about Disney because he's not on them. In fact, he was away from the studio for the whole of Travers' 1961 visit. As some accounts put him at his Palm Springs house, it is plausible that he was avoiding her; whether it was because she was an abrasive *woman* or just because she was abrasive is impossible to say. Her documented tendency to denigrate Disney's work and her general distaste for all things American make it likely that Disney would not be eager to meet with her. He didn't need to because he already had secured the film rights and could leave the story details to the team. Travers' visit did coincide with a very busy and pivotal spring at the studio.

Consider only the major theatrical output between December 1960 and 1961: *Swiss Family Robinson*; *101 Dalmatians*; *The Absent-Minded Professor*; *The Parent Trap;* and *Babes in Toyland*. Add in the full television schedule for *Walt Disney Presents*, for which Walt Disney had to film the hosted lead-ins and lead-outs framing the episodes. Skip ahead to *Mary Poppins'* August 27 premiere and Disney's attention would turn to the debut of *Disney's Wonderful World of Color*, the renamed anthology series which moved from ABC (where Disney felt creatively stifled) to NBC. On the horizon was the work for some sponsors of the 1964 World's Fair. Marcel's script even makes subtle reference to General Electric, an allusion to Disney's "The Carousel of Progress" fair exhibit. Eventually, the various fair projects would help the studio perfect Audio-Animatronics, a term coined in 1961 to describe its robotics animation technology (and used by Harriet Burns to create the robin for *Mary Poppins'* "Spoonful of Sugar" sequence).

The studio-set storyline is only one part of *Saving Mr. Banks*; over 40 minutes of the film are scenes set in 1906 Australia. Marcel uses this structure to hint at how Helen Goff, daughter of two unreliable parents and witness to some severe childhood trauma, transforms herself into Pamela Lyndon Travers, the creator of the quintessentially English Mary Poppins. As if also privy to the extensive flashback sequences, Marcel's Disney finally convinces Travers to give over the rights when he flies to London after an epiphany about their parallel childhood traumas. She is won over after he talks about his troubled relationship with his father and his later idealization of his childhood. While she fabricates the meeting, Marcel culls the psychological motivations from the existing biographical accounts of their childhoods. She bypasses the personal traumas that Travers was facing in 1961. Viewers are allowed to assume that she is a lonely spinster, but Travers was a single mother. At the time, her son Camillus was in jail for drunk driving without a license. He was also angry with his mother because a few years before he learned of his Irish twin brother from whom Travers separated him when she refused to adopt both. The twins first met in a bar, which sounds like the family melodrama version of the summer camp meeting that takes place in 1961's *The Parent Trap.*

Sue Smith included these kinds of surprising details in her original screenplay. Helen left home to become an actress and dabbled in erotica. Later, Helen traveled in modernist literary circles, studied mysticism, had a long-term relationship with a married older man, and lived with a female romantic partner. Smith was following the outline provided by Ian Collie. He had hired Smith after he completed production of *The Shadow of Mary Poppins*, a 2002 Australian television documentary. When he sent the script to Alison Owen at the BBC-affiliated Ruby Films, she suggested the move away from the original concept and brought on Marcel who compressed Travers' biography. The only hints about her adult personal relationships come in a subplot about the bond an American chauffeur forges with Travers. It bears repeating that the story sequencing and characterizations are Marcel's. To her surprise, when Disney signed on as co-producer, it did not ask for changes and even allowed Walt a scotch, as was his custom. The real Walt Disney also chain-smoked, but Hancock notes that the film's Disney could only stub out a cigarette because the studio now has a nonsmoking policy for all its films.

Variously described as a "making of" film, a behind-the-scenes at Disney Studios story, and a biopic, *Saving Mr. Banks* has proven a bit of a lightning rod, likely tied to its use of what television scholar Annette Hill calls "staged authenticity" and dramatizations of interactions that never happened to convey psychological realism. The facts about Travers' actual life and attitude have not deterred those who see the film as evidence of the studio's bulldozing of everyone else's intellectual property rights, while vigilantly safeguarding its own. Fixating on the fact that the film is distributed by Disney Studios without knowing any facts about the studio's involvement, they assume that Marcel was forced to depict events in a way that flatters Walt Disney and Disney Studios. Such readings may stem from the fact that the screenplay does position Disney as more self-aware than Travers, but it also implies that he's just had more practice in honing his "presentation of the self." Travers signs off on the deal, the screenplay postulates, after Disney takes the time to understand her desire to use art to contain unresolved childhood trauma by giving it a more satisfying ending.

In the end, *Saving Mr. Banks* moved me, although I was disappointed that it is less about Disney Studios than about the legacy of fathers. I have a taste for such fare, but others may find the film more emotionally manipulative. *Mr. Banks's*

Disney advises Mrs. Travers to channel ambivalence about a father's legacy into creative production. It is a lesson also learned by Salman Rushdie, who has shared his bittersweet recollections of a father who was "a magical parent of young children," but one prone as much to puffs of dragon smoke as flights of fancy. Given all the impassioned reactions from those who have been moved or annoyed by *Saving Mr. Banks*, it is intriguing to recall Rushdie's acknowledgment that his reading of *The Wizard of Oz* as "a film whose driving force is the inadequacy of adults, even of good adults" is read through his own early childhood experiences. I suspect Kelly Marcel, the Walt Disney she wrote into being, and the creative team behind Disney's *Oz, the Great and Powerful* (2013) would appreciate Rushdie's assertion that the 1939 film dramatizes "how the weakness of grown-ups forces children to take control of their own destinies, and so, ironically, grow up themselves."[4]

If The Walt Disney Company wanted to make a movie about Disney Studios circa 1961, it would have made a better movie than 2013's *Saving Mr. Banks*.[5] A true Disney version of the behind-the-scenes drama of the making of *Mary Poppins* would have featured an original song, perhaps one written by Richard Sherman, the surviving member of the Sherman Brothers songwriting duo. The brothers wrote the songs for *Mary Poppins*, *Chitty Chitty Bang Bang*, and the *It's a Small World* attraction at Disneyland. The hypothetical original song for *Saving Mr. Banks* would have to be calculated to chart on Billboard and compete with U2's "Ordinary Love" (written for the Nelson Mandela biopic). To sing a cover version of the song, the studio would likely pick one of its in-house Hollywood Records artists. The logical choice would be former Disney Channel star Demi Lovato, as she performed the cover of "Let it Go" from *Frozen*. Disney's billion-dollar baby, *Frozen* not only dominated the box office to become the top-grossing animated feature of all time, but it also won the 2013 Academy Award for Best Animated Feature and Best Original Song.

With lines like, "I know I left a life behind but I'm too relieved to grieve," the song is fitting for Lovato who left behind her Disney Channel stardom. She did so after a public meltdown during a Jonas Brothers concert in South America led to her revelation of very personal struggles with cutting and eating disorders. She said she wanted to let go of her starring role in the hit sitcom *Sonny with a Chance* because being on television negatively impacted her body image and self-perception. The rest of the song suits Lovato's recent image makeover, which has also been premised on similar message of letting go of other people's perceptions of you and feeling the freedom of being who you are.

To guarantee an Academy Award, a Broadway powerhouse such as *Frozen*'s Idina Menzel (Elsa) would sing the in-film version of the song for the hypothetical *Banks* film (which would have had a better title, perhaps *Thawed!*). If this film were a more accurate biopic of P. L. Travers, producers could choose Maia Mitchell to sing the cover song. The Australian teen costars in the Disney Channel original musical *Teen Beach Movie* and in ABC Family's *The Fosters*, playing one of several foster kids adopted by a lesbian couple. The melodrama surrounding that television family would actually align well with the personal history of P. L. Travers. She was a woman with lovers of both sexes not the prim British spinster depicted in *Saving Mr. Banks*. The story about her strained relationship with her adopted son after he learned the truth about his background and his twin brother would be just the kind of melodramatic backstory that would fuel several seasons of one of ABC Family's angst-ridden, young adult domestic melodramas.

Surprisingly, there is quite a bit of family melodrama in *Frozen*, Disney's actual 2013 brand management success story. Heralded as the number one animated film of all time, *Frozen* has earned over a billion dollars at the box office as of May 2014. According to *The Hollywood Reporter*, Disney sold 3.2 million *Frozen* Blu-ray/DVDs on its first day of release March 18, 2014, which was preceded by a record number of downloads two weeks earlier when Disney made the digital copy available. The film's single "Let It Go" sold 1.7 million copies and reached #4 on Billboard's digital songs chart, #9 on the Billboard 100, and #5 on iTunes.

In true Disney brand management style, *Frozen* maintains the branded princess character type, but offers a story about an heroic journey and a message that prioritizes sisterly love and the bonds of friendship over romance. The unreliable parents theme surprisingly finds its way into the film as well. *Frozen* begins with parents whose inability to navigate crises traumatizes and isolates one of their daughters (Elsa). The film's arc follows the journey of Anna, Elsa's sister, who is forced to grow up and find a way to fix the mess caused by her parents' poor decision-making. Anna takes control of her destiny, helps Elsa, sacrifices herself in her sister's place, and saves the kingdom, with a little help from her friends.

Disney Channel has been busy updating the princess type not only in its recent animated films, but also in its self-reliant and spunky sitcom characters who value "sisterly" bonds and friendship above all. The messaging carries through to the Disney Junior preschool series, *Sofia the First*, and in shorts such as *I am a Princess*, which celebrates girls who are "Brave and determined. Compassionate and kind. Smart and strong."[6] Of course, Disney also continues to promote the legacy princesses and perpetuate princess fantasies for each new generation. This strategy of keeping legacy characters in circulation makes it certain that each new princess movie opens strong at the box office, and ideally, as in the case of *Frozen*, eventually performs over a billion dollars strong. In the 2000s, the merchandising division had already begun selling the princesses as an ensemble of friends. Then it created a line called the Disney Fairies and replicated the process in the "B-film" series on Disney's Fairies. The Fairies were a boon to the merchandising division, especially in relation to the inhabitable elements of the story world called Pixie Hollow. As the Disney website tells us, today's princess "still believes in magic, but this time the magic of her own design. The magic she believes in is herself," and, of course, in her friends from Pixie Hollow. Once again, we see how central friendship has been to materializing and monetizing the millennial Disney brand.

As if it were also made for reimagining as an ABC Family teen melodrama, *Frozen* even has the angst ridden teen type in the character of Elsa who actually sings "Let It Go" in the film. The main character is Anna, the obstinate optimist. It is a character type that Walt Disney also embodies in the accounts of production team dynamics conveyed through the shorts included on Disney Blu-ray/DVD combo packs. He also would have made an anthology episode about the adaptation of *Frozen* from Hans Christian Andersen's *The Snow Queen*.

4.3   Authorizing Walt Disney

Clearly, it is fun to speculate about all these "what ifs," especially those related to the idea of *Saving Mr. Banks* as a true Disney brand management film. Although some Internet commentators have taken it as history, *Saving Mr. Banks* spends much more time in "what if" speculation about the personality dynamics of the in-person negotiations between Walt Disney and P.L. Travers. Those viewers looking for backstory on "what was" would be better off watching the variety of featurettes sprinkled across several of Walt Disney's Blu-ray/DVD/Digital combo packs. They provide quite a bit of insight into how Walt Disney's personal dynamics impacted production teams working on what have since become the Disney film classics. The production this kind of content about content was a part of Disney's earliest business strategies, as is evident from the following discussions of Disney's classic films.

One way that the special features provide evidence for their claims is through various iterations of "Walt in his own words." Most often, Walt's commentary from the television series is edited into the featurettes, but sometimes, there are stand-alone special features. On *Snow White*, Blu-ray/DVD the "in his own words" source is a radio interview; on *Peter Pan*, the source is a magazine article; and on *101 Dalmatians*, Walt's words come from a dramatization of his written correspondence with author Dodie Smith about her original book and her feelings about the changes for the film adaptation.

The magazine article related to *Peter Pan* reveals Walt's attraction to characters with the capacity to fly. He relates a story about spending his savings to go see the famous actress Maude Adams as Peter Pan in a stage production. Then he recounts how he later played Peter Pan in a school play and rigged a way to fly into the audience (and crash). These experiences stayed with him and fueled his determination to create a better *Peter Pan*. Animation would help him bypass the limitations inherent in a stage play. Conversely, he would move beyond the limitations of animation when he figured out how to mix in live action (the very mixture that won the studio some Academy Awards, but irked Mrs. Travers). Read through the psychological point of view favored by *Saving Mr. Banks*, Walt's creative output was forever impacted by his flight from his memories of childhood drudgery as a ten-year-old newsboy working on the newspaper route his father managed when he failed at farming and moved the family to Kansas

City. It required Walt to work in all kinds of weather before school, starting at 4:30 a.m., and again after school, all for no pay for his hard-driving father. Prior to these difficult tween years, Walt lived with his family on a farm in Marceline, Missouri. Given his age during the farm years and the nostalgia for that time once he was uprooted to Kansas City and put to work, Walt idealized Marceline. He also associated the life there with his grandmother, who read him the fairy tales he later adapted into films.

Whatever the truth of his actual experiences on the farm and in Kansas City, the details have become part of Disney's self-mythologizing. The intriguing element of the *Peter Pan* special features is that they rely on a common narrative: Walt Disney was always personally motivated to adapt the stories he did. Special features across the Blu-ray/DVD sets for Disney Studios' classics circulate the idea that Walt was explicitly adapting classic stories to which he was exposed in childhood and other works which he happened upon as an adult. This personalizing is both an appealing hook to draw viewers into the special features and a way to move the output of the studio away from economic production and toward a mode of personal expression. Sharing such personal details can be read as a form of brand management, finding the "use value" in illustrative scenes from his biography. The verifiable details of this origin story are difficult for even Disney's most careful biographers to separate from the brand story that began to be crafted by the early 1950s. In any case, the significance of the inclusion of this special feature on the *Peter Pan* Blu-ray/DVD is that it feels like access to Walt himself. Of course, the "in his own words" iterations are forms of mediated communication, part of Walt's careful "presentation of self."

The more typical special features are content-about-content shorts created out of the integration of film scenes, still images, storyboards and other archival material into existing and new interviews with production workers and historians. Given the variety of shorts on offer, Disney's Blu-ray/DVD releases of its classic films play a significant role in circulating Disney's own self-assessment. The shorts highlight the significance of specific films and frame the history of Walt Disney, the man and the studio, in flattering ways. Analyzing several sets reveals that the same archival footage and interview snippets are repurposed and reframed.

4.4 Interpretive Frames on Blu-ray/DVD

The special features enable the studio to shape the meaning of the film at the site of its exhibition. As Robert Alan Brookey and Robert Westerfelhaus explain, the format "collapses exposure to promotional material into the experience of viewing the film by bringing the film and its makers' commentary about it in close proximity, temporally and spatially." The relationship between film and special features becomes intratextual. As such it has the advantage of increasing "the chances that promotional tactics will reach their target audience." This proximity makes the film "viewing and commentary" feel like a continuous experience.[7]

The Blu-ray/DVD combo packs register a change in the function of the platform, signaling a move from convenience (at home and repeat viewing) and collectability to audience immersion (in-depth viewing) and textual expansion (film as it exists in context of multiple industrial and cultural factors chosen by the studio and/or production team). Commenting on this change, John Caldwell says that the recent proliferation of "making of" commentaries are ways for a studio or a production culture to mediate "knowledge about itself." He compares DVDs to electronic press kits used in the official studio publicity distributed to the press.[8]

Across the special features from different Blu-ray/DVD sets, there is a degree of consistency in messaging and format. The special features encourage viewers to read Disney Studios through a set of interconnected interpretive frames: immersion, insights, innovation, inspiration, artistry, imagination, and commemoration (see below). Through their commemorative designations (e.g., the 25th anniversary edition, the Diamond edition) special Blu-ray/DVD sets position Disney films as legacy texts, as foundational for the studio, the brand, and sometimes for animation as an art form.

Disney has a vested interest in affirming the studio's desired self-representation as an innovator and as a purveyor of classic entertainment properties, which can be enjoyed for generations to come. The special features encourage a long-view on each film, depicting its contributions as important to advancements in the industry. As Brookey and Westerfelhaus put it, special "features can direct the viewer toward preferred interpretations of the primary text while undermining unfavorable interpretations, especially those that might hurt the product's success."[9] In this way, they have a rhetorical function, making a case for specific interpretations.

Framing Motif	Message
Immersion	Immersion in the universe of the film and its storyworld
Insights	Insights into studio and production history from "eyewitnesses"
Innovation	Innovations in production processes, or animation, or sound
Inspiration	Inspiring source material and problems adapting it; the problems then inspire solutions
Artistry	Working together as a studio of skilled artisans who create classics
Imagination	Engaging audiences through the ability to distill complexity into digestible form
	Entertaining by extracting central elements and simplifying them to convey to a popular audience
	Captivating audiences while educating and informing
Commemoration	Re-releasing as part of an anniversary celebration
	Signifying a milestone work in cinematic and brand history
	Honoring Walt Disney: the man, the studio, the craftspeople
	Archiving and preserving cinematic (and brand) history

The special features on Disney's Blu-ray/DVDs have a particular tendency to encourage viewers to read films as emblematic of Disney Studio's "firsts." They might be:

Storytelling innovations:

1. advances in endowing animated human figures with personality and motivation in *Snow White and the Seven Dwarfs*
2. innovative use of music in *Snow White* to move the story forward through musical numbers as indirect sound over visual storytelling sequences (rather than as breaks in action)
3. stereophonic sound to enhance storytelling in *Sleeping Beauty* conveyed through a special television radio simulcast.

Technical innovations:

1. multiplane camera for creating natural-looking depth in the animated landscape for *Snow White and the Seven Dwarfs*
2. Xerox process to eliminate the expensive hand inking process and aid in animation on *101 Dalmatians*
3. underwater cameras and diving suits for filming *20,000 Leagues Under the Sea*.

FIGURE 4.2   Walt Disney explains how stereophonic sound enhances storytelling in *Sleeping Beauty* and tells viewers of *Walt Disney Presents* that they can watch a special television radio simulcast.

The "making of" stories about specific films recalled by their production teams reinforce a myth story about a group of craftspeople working together to make the best film their combined talents would allow. These insights offered directly from the creative teams encourage viewers to appreciate the artistry of the challenges. Both elements structure the 90-minute feature, "Making of *20,000 Leagues Under the Sea*." It is so detailed because its producers had an hour-long *Disneyland* episode on the film from which to take content. As part of the build-up to the film's theatrical release, "Operation Undersea" ran as the December 8, 1954 episode of the first season of *Disneyland*, which led to the studio's first Emmys: Best Individual Program of the Year and Best Television Film Editing. *Disneyland* also won Best Variety Series that year. "Operation Undersea" is an early example of the practice at the studio of filming "making of" content– promotion hybrids, which would become standard features on special edition home media releases.[10]

The *Disneyland* episode and the DVD special features highlight elements that support why the film brought home Academy Awards. Standing in for those awards and scattered around the set in the hosted lead-in to the "Operation Undersea" episode are models of key elements of the film. There is no licensed merchandise in the shots, but third party licensees did sell tie-in merchandise such as the Sutcliffe Submarine scale model toy. Shot composition encourages the preferred mode of reading the film's production in terms of creativity and personal affinity rather than economics and marketplace trends. Immediately behind Walt Disney is a large painting of author Jules Verne. The framing and shot composition imply an equivalence between Walt Disney and Jules Verne. Beyond a slight physical resemblance, they are similar in that they both share a fascination with "tomorrowland" stories. By positing himself in this way, Walt is associating himself with the visionary author, but also with personal motivations for adapting his book and telling the story in a different medium. This aligns with the persona Walt was testing out in this early television episode. He was positioning himself as someone who loved the classics and wanted to share his take on them with the world. The Jules Verne book Walt holds is quite fantastical looking, which suits the literary theme and the science-fantasy thematics. The motif is used again when Walt shows the audience an oversized book on the giant squid. While the genre is fantasy, Walt uses the giant book to suggest that this story leans more to a story "inspired by" scientifically studied undersea worlds.

Both the television and DVD iterations of the "making of" showcase the studio innovations for the film, including the undersea camera work and in the development of costume designs that would accommodate the needs both of those behind the camera and in front of it. The Production Art section, which includes a collection of stills on costume design, represents the tendency of current special features to highlight the contributions of below-the-line production workers. The DVD also calculates its special features to offer evidence of why the film won Academy Awards for Special Effects and Art Direction and highlights

FIGURE 4.3 The framing and shot composition implies an equivalence between Walt Disney and Jules Verne, the author of *20,000 Leagues Under the Sea*. The film and "Operation Undersea," the "making of" feature on the adaptation, contributed to the studio's growing award tally and its self-mythologizing.

FIGURE 4.4 "Operation Undersea," the first behind-the-scenes television feature, "captures" Kirk Douglas and Peter Lorre as the friends goof around on the set of *20,000 Leagues Under the Sea*. This kind of behind-the-scenes segment is now common on Blu-ray/DVD special edition sets.

the work of those who contributed to those wins. John Hench makes for a particularly compelling subject not only because he was largely responsible for the film's infamous giant hydraulic squid, but also because of his later work on theme park attractions. Hench is framed within a narrative that calls attention to his long tenure at Disney and his rise up the ranks from a lowly position. Similar to that of other long-time Disney production workers in other special features, this profiling aligns with American Dream mythology about upward mobility. Obviously, any of the rumors about the frustrations and limitations of working for the studio do not make it into these kinds of special features. Those commentators who mention any difficulties of the working environment or the weight of Walt Disney's expectation that everyone give 110 percent are balanced by their sense of admiration for Disney's skill at marshaling the troops and overseeing every production.

As a television episode airing about ten days prior to the films initial release, "Operation Undersea" also had to build anticipation for the film's upcoming release. It functioned as a call-to-action for television viewers to plan a December 1954 holiday outing to the movie theater. *20,000 Leagues Under the Sea* stands out in Disney Studios history as its first live-action adventure film to use Hollywood A-list stars and to be released when *Disneyland* was already on the air.[11] "Operation Undersea" tapped into the appeal of watching A-level movie stars behind the scenes. Kirk Douglas is established as a good sport when he directly addresses viewers. He has his guitar casually slung around his neck, referencing the musical sequence in which he performs the novelty song, "A Whale of a Tale." This is an early version of the well-known Disney strategy of releasing a single to add revenue while promoting the film. The more interesting segments come later when Douglas searches out his costar Peter Lorre. They converse in front of the storyboards for the film. This shot composition reminds viewers about the artistry of the film and implies that they are getting a rare glimpse at all the work behind the filming. Douglas and Lorre are also depicted as two friends just palling around on the set between filming. The segment offers the fantasy that such behind-the-scenes footage gives us a glimpse of "actors as-they-really-are" when they are "off the clock." "Operation Undersea," the first behind-the-scene television episode, "captures" Kirk Douglas and Peter Lorre as they goof around on the set of *20,000 Leagues Under the Sea.*

4.5   Hosted Lead-ins and Studio History as Creative Nonfiction

The larger fantasy, of course, of every *Disneyland* episode is that viewers were seeing Walt Disney as he really was, an impression conveyed by a decade's worth of hosted lead-ins, especially in the ABC years where the series began in 1954 as *Disneyland* and was renamed *Walt Disney Presents* in 1958. The anthology series was a brand management platform. It provided viewers with the frames through which to interpret the particular content profiled in the episode and the broader range of Disney Studios entertainment that was or would be on offer elsewhere. Episodes were literally framed by Walt Disney's introductory and concluding appearances. Through these lead-ins and lead-outs Walt Disney became entrenched as the embodiment of the company's brand. The framing segments were typically filmed in Walt's "office" and that set became the one most synonymous with him and his "Uncle Walt" persona.

In brand terms, the office set for the anthology series utilizes the motifs detailed in the explanatory chart below. The framing lead-ins and lead-outs, especially in *Walt Disney Presents*, dramatize the idea of Walt Disney presenting entertainment material directly to viewers for their enjoyment. They typically begin with viewers "meeting" Walt in his office where he is often standing by his wall of bookshelves. Walt's interest in classics to adapt into films is eventually referenced in the fact that the shelves are filled with hard cover books, many bound in rich leather. Within this library conceit, Walt calls attention to the creators behind iconic characters or classic stories. In doing so, he further entrenches his position as a creator and an iconic American character in his own right. In some lead-ins, Walt acts as if he was interrupted while casually reading a favorite book. This idea is conveyed when Walt keeps the book open or places his finger in it while he speaks to the audience, as if he will continue to read it when he is done talking. Sometimes it feels as if he is reading a bedtime story, which may be part of his public persona as "Uncle Walt." Tweens in the audience might actually be watching right before bedtime. This element also aligns with Walt's personal history. As already noted, Walt fondly recalled how his grandmother read him bedtime stories, many of them the fairy tales that he would later adapt for the

Motif	Signification
Office	Disney as a major industry figure and visionary granting the audience access to his inner sanctum
	Disney as Uncle Walt, who happens to be a famous CEO, inviting the audience for casual day at the office
Library	Disney as the host of a book club
	Disney as the storyteller (in a visual medium)
	Studio as the adapter of classic source material
	Studio adaptation as distinct from the original version by an author, who is nonetheless revered and credited by name
Awards	Accolades from the film and television industries
	Recognition from peers
	Legitimation in the profession
Family Pictures	Disney as a family man rather than a businessman
	Studio as interested in whole family entertainment
Storyboards	Disney as a tour guide through the studio archive
	Studio as a collection of artists and craftsmen
	Studio archiving as ingrained in Disney production culture
	Studio repurposing as business strategy

screen. These different kinds of lead-ins effectively position the studio's adaptation choices as if they are motivated by personal values rather than economic values, as will be evident in the discussion of Disney's *Alice in Wonderland* later in this chapter.

Other lead-ins focus more on the artistic challenges the animators and production teams faced on different projects. Often, Walt stands in front of storyboards and uses them to explain the history of some strategy, or to convey some complexity the studio encountered and the innovative solution the production team found. The discussion of the topic at hand can be used to remind viewers about earlier Disney output, whether in the classic cartoon cycle or feature animation (see Figure 4.1 for this dynamic). Walt's commentary is often about creativity and artistry, and is never about business decisions. The cumulative impression conveyed by these kinds of lead-ins or in similarly themed special features is that Walt was always willing to spend whatever it took to do the best artistic work, without much attention to the bottom line. Walt often sheepishly admits that it worked out in the studio's favor in the end, usually only because of some scrambling on the part of his long-suffering brother Roy Disney (who handled the financial side of the business). Whatever the truth of the brothers' dynamic, this version of their partnership is part of the larger Disney mythology reinforced by the television episodes (and later by the Blu-ray/DVD special features).

The lead-ins and the behind-the-scenes footage used in episodes play like creative nonfiction, which is a literary genre that mixes essay and memoir with a teaching component. Disney clearly intends to enthrall people with facts as much as fantasy. The anthology episodes are stories that communicate information as they entertain. The creative nonfiction label is often applied to personal yet informative stories about a field or a technique. Crafting a "factually accurate" story "about real people and events, in a compelling, vivid, dramatic manner" is the essence of creative nonfiction, according to Lee Gutkind.[12] For the shorts, the various long-time studio production workers shape technical explanations into stories that feel like memoirs about a certain era at the studio. There is a variation on this theme when the commentary comes from children of production workers, because it feels like they grew up with Disney in a very personal way. They also shared the general experience that many viewers had of growing up watching various Disney movies, entwining memories of watching films with their childhood experiences.

These first-hand accounts coupled with the literary framing of the hosted lead-ins contribute to the creative nonfiction tone of the shorts. Clearly, they are the product of exhaustive research, and so are marked by a documentable subject matter with credible and verifiable details. As with creative nonfiction, the finished creative work has a narrative form and structure that leans more toward entertainment than technical instruction. Barbara Lounsberry describes the technique as "revivifying" the scene rather than reporting on it.[13] Of course, the literary framing is also part of the effacement of the fact that a studio story is being crafted through these kinds of shorts.

According to animator Paul Carlson, Walt filmed several lead-ins at a time and they would "rotate sets so he could film a bunch of lead-ins in different settings." Carlson recalled that Walt "was very self-conscious and he made a lot of mistakes" when he filmed the mid-1950s segments. Carlson speculated that Walt liked doing them by the end: "as he went on he became acclimated to his task and he became much better." Walt Disney knew power of TV brandcasting—but he took a bit of time to perfect his pitch and tone. The evolution is apparent in the modifications in Walt's body language and phrasing in the lead-ins to *Disneyland*'s *Alice in Wonderland* episodes in 1954 and 1964. In the November 3, 1954 lead-in to the film screening, Walt Disney is still just a businessman selling a product. By 1964, he inhabits his Uncle Walt persona, which has at its foundation an American Dream story about his own success and about his belief that he could do the impossible.

The 1954 episode is only the second of the series and so it makes sense that Walt is still getting comfortable in the on-screen hosting role he only reluctantly accepted. Walt holds one of the licensed merchandise tie-ins, *The Big Golden Book: Alice in Wonderland*. He sits at his desk, looking stiff, which makes it feel as if he is pitching a product, rather than reading from a story. It is as if Disney is saying to viewers, "Don't forget that we offer large tie-in picture books for our animated versions of classics, too!" The differences between this early performance and the later one signal the evolution of the more carefully managed persona Walt was developing and the cultural narrative he was circulating. By the 1964 episode, he had developed his familiar "Uncle Walt" persona and the licensed tie-in book has been replaced by a beautiful *Alice in Wonderland* storybook, which a true reader would cherish in his or her library. The 1964 version makes it seem as if Walt is sharing a personal favorite from his childhood. A slight variation in phrasing between the two episodes is also telling because in 1964 he adds a class distinction when he describes Lewis Carroll's work at "the Oxford University." The misidentification implies that Uncle Walt takes "classy" British books and inflects them with a simple American perspective. This usually meant taking out the dark elements and making the stories more whimsical. Of course, these kinds of changes are the sort that Mrs. Travers was right to worry about in relation to the Disney version of *Mary Poppins*. As *Saving Mr. Banks* accurately recounts, Walt did make everything over in an upbeat tone and he relied on personalized logic to justify adaptation choices. In the case of *Mary Poppins*, he claimed he doggedly pursued the rights because it was his daughters' favorite bedtime reading.

By the 1960s, Walt Disney had become comfortable in a role he had played for a decade. In episodes in this later period Walt was more likely to lean casually on his desk than to sit behind it. Often, when the segment starts, Walt was across the room by the bookshelves, which were filled with an impressive collection of hardcover books; when he took one out, the action signified Walt's personal

FIGURE 4.5 Brand evolution is registered in the differences between Walt Disney's 1954 lead-in to the *Alice in Wonderland* screening on *Disneyland* and his 1964 lead-in for the screening on *Walt Disney Presents*. Note the change from Disney overtly selling tie-in merchandise like the picture book to a more subtle positioning of Disney as storyteller and preserver of classic literature.

selection process for the adaptations. The transformation of an industrial logic into a personal one is a narrative reinforced by the behind-the-picture feaurettes. They usually explain some childhood connection or other personal link to the classic book being adapted. Again, this facilitates the effacement of profitable production logics into a form of self-expression and social exchange. It is as if Disney was saying, "I adapted this because I thought you would enjoy it as much as I did." Typically, the shorts reinforce the idea that the adaptation is motivated by a desire to share his interest in a story he learned to love in childhood. He wants to make a literary work come alive for new generations, and to offer children a version of a story they would find appealing.

4.6   Coca-Cola and Custom Character-Based Commercials

Disney Studios tested out a dramatized lead-in format before it even had its own television series. In the 1940s Disney had done some institutionalized advertising work for corporate clients. Consequently, in 1950, Coca-Cola hired the studio to produce its holiday special. The result was *One Hour in Wonderland*, which aired the December prior to the summer 1951 release of Disney's animated feature, *Alice in Wonderland*. The conceit is that Walt Disney has invited Edgar Bergen and Charlie McCarthy (Bergen's ventriloquist's dummy) to a tea party at the studio. Bergen and McCarthy feel like the stars of the CBS special both because they are film stars and they are also Coca-Cola spokespeople (via their CBS radio show airing from 1949–52). The special had some trouble finding a tone as it had to promote Coca-Cola as an ideal holiday party drink, and it had to accommodate the snarky delivery of Bergen and Charlie McCarthy.

Disney also structured the special to be a blatant promotion for *Alice in Wonderland* along with work from the Disney back catalogue. As a reminder of *Snow White* iconography, the slave in the magic mirror actually screens the clips. In addition to promoting earlier studio work, the special works as a paratext for Disney's animated *Alice in Wonderland*. It gave viewers the chance to become familiar with Kathryn Beaumont, the 12-year-old girl who would voice Disney's Alice. The special's more famous tween was Bobby Driscoll, who was already the well-known star of several Disney films. In 1950, he would have been promoting *Treasure Island*, Disney's first all live-action feature film, but he would go on to be the voice of Peter Pan in Disney's 1953 animated version (with Beaumont voicing Wendy Darling). All in all, the holiday party set-up is more an extended lead-in to screening clips of studio content. The idea was innovative because people did not really see trailers outside of theaters. With this move, Disney set in motion some standards of his later style: the hosted lead-in to clips, a studio cohost (later it would be Tinker Bell), special appearances by actors, and a creative framing of repurposed studio content.

Walt Disney is paired mostly with Beaumont, who is dressed in an Alice costume. She has the job of "requesting" to see clips from Disney films and helping

FIGURE 4.6 Ostensibly a Coca-Cola promotion, Disney leveraged his client's *One Hour in Wonderland* 1950 TV special to familiarize viewers with the voice actor for Disney's upcoming *Alice in Wonderland*. In this multitasking paratext, she has the job of "requesting" that the magic mirror (from *Snow White*) screen Disney Studio's clips.

to beg the magic mirror to screen her favorites, such as a *Snow White* scene and a Mickey Mouse cartoon. The final offering is the sneak peek screening of *Alice in Wonderland*. This mixture of clips from the classic features and shorts with sneak peeks of a forthcoming film became a template for the kind of content included in a typical episode of *Disneyland*, which would debut on ABC on October 27, 1954. To make the repurposed content feel new, clips were framed with lead-ins by Walt Disney and intercut with new material. In the case of this special, some of the new material is an excuse for the product integration of Coca-Cola bottles and shots of Beaumont and others holding or drinking Coca-Cola.

The special feels a bit forced, which is something Disney tried to avoid once he had his own television program. It helped that the primetime anthology series was structured to have participating sponsors airing commercial spots in magazine format, which was not yet the norm. According to Carlson, a separate

FIGURE 4.7   Brands like Ipana deepened their connection with *The Mickey Mouse Club* and its tween audience by offering gifts and special offers, often marketed on product packages.

commercial production studio, housed on the Disney lot and headed by Walt's niece Phyllis Hurrell, produced customized animated commercials. The familiar characters made the commercials feel more continuous with the story segments. Mickey Mouse and family drive Nash Automobiles ("Live a Little, Drive a Rambler!"), *Alice in Wonderland* characters "entertain with Jell-O," and *Peter Pan*'s Captain Hook, Tinker Bell, Peter Pan, and the Crocodile fight over Derby Food's Peter Pan Peanut Butter ("the favorite with people and crocodiles too"). It was not hard to find sponsors who wanted to entwine their brands and messaging with *Disneyland*. It was even easier to find sponsors for *The Mickey Mouse Club*, which enabled narrowcasting to kids. Its sponsors included General Mills (Cheerios, Sugar Jets, and Trix), Welch's Juices and Jellies, and Ipana toothpaste (Bristol-Meyers). Bucky Beaver's "Brusha, Brusha, Brusha" jingle for Ipana was written by Jimmie Dodd, the adult Mouseketeer "troop" leader (see images in the Introduction and in Fig. 4.7). Brands like Ipana deepened their connection with *The Mickey Mouse Club* and its tween audience by offering kid-centric premiums (i.e., gifts and special offers, often marketed on product packages) in exchange for proof of purchase and/or a small fee.

Recollections of his work on the anthology series' custom commercials led Carlson to explain the production process of the hosted lead-ins to anthology episodes segments in which Walt took on the role of subtle (and sometimes not-so-subtle) pitchperson for Disney Studio content. Carlson claimed that the studio had some trouble with regulators questioning the balance between storytelling and promotion. Carlson said, "If you look at [the typical episode of the anthology program], you see it was an hour commercial . . . But it was so good, and it was entertaining, that somehow they got by with it." The original content always included (and was sometimes limited only to) Walt Disney's hosted lead-in segments that provided a frame for the episode.

4.7 Television "Trailerizing" and *The Parent Trap*

As much as Walt and the studio tried to shape perceptions of its intentions in the program, the trade press was critical of the strategies. In September 1957 *Variety* complained about Disney's blatant "trailerizing," although it was a term the entertainment-trade magazine applied to all the movie studios' anthology programs, especially when an episode's studio promotion was not effectively counterbalanced by original entertainment content. The next month in its review of *The Mickey Mouse Club*, *Variety* called it Disney's "'trailerizing' kick, wherein he uses the initial program to run off snippets of what's coming up next in later programs." The review referenced how the 1957 season of *The Mickey Mouse Club* would be airing a new *Hardy Boys* serial, building on the success of the first *Hardy Boys* serial from 1956. *The Mickey Mouse Club* also ran a variety of other serials in this segmented format, but its most popular was *Spin and Marty*, which had three series (1955, 1956, and 1957). Segmenting these serials over the course of several weeks was an effective cliffhanger strategy to get viewers to continue to tune in on a regular basis to the late-afternoon series, which ran every weekday in the mostly un-programmed afternoon dead zone. The serials typically included several key actors from the stable of tween stars Disney was then amassing. Tim Considine, Annette Funicello, and Kevin Corcoran were particularly popular. All three went on to feature film success and Corcoran continued to play the *Spin and Marty* character Moochie for his Disney anthology series appearances. The success of his 1959 and 1960 episodes of *Walt Disney Presents*—*Moochie of the Little League* and *Moochie of Pop Warner Football*—suggest that Disney had begun to understand that tween stars might be an even bigger draw than teen stars. Unfortunately, Walt Disney lost his tween-address series when the studio got out of its ABC contract at the end of 1960–61 season and moved the anthology series to NBC, where it would air in color and under better terms as *Walt Disney's Wonderful World of Color*. It would take until the turn of the next century for Disney Channel to assemble another stable of bankable tween stars to circulate through its television series and movies as well as to headline its "Tween B" feature films and recording division.

If you wanted to demonstrate that Disney was a self-promoter, the April 9, 1958 episode, "An Adventure in the Magic Kingdom" would certainly help make your case. In it, Walt shares hosting duties with Tinker Bell, the animated fairy from *Peter Pan*, and "interacts" with her throughout his opening lead-in. She already technically presided over the anthology series each week, activating each episode with a sprinkle of pixie dust in the opening credits. Walt and Tinker Bell are stand-ins for the Disney Studio brand. Walt asks "Tink" if she would act as episode hostess because she could "take the audience along" on an aerial tour of Disneyland and fly down to various new attractions in the park's four realms: Fantasyland, Tomorrowland, Adventureland, and Frontierland. Walt and Tink's interactions in the episode remind the audience of key elements from Disney's *Peter Pan*: sprinkling with fairy dust enables humans to fly, and fairies can hear at a different register than humans (so the bell Disney holds does not ring). As Tink cannot speak, Walt calls on familiar *Disneyland* narrator Dick Wesson to be her voice and to narrate the episode. After the introductory interaction, the episode spends most of the hour showing Tink flying through footage that promotes some new attractions at the theme park; while Dick Wesson narrates the aerial tour over the park, the episode also mixes in footage from the 1956 theatrical release *Disneyland, USA*. Such repurposing is a key practice in relation to the anthology series, and the segment is indicative of the studio strategy of combining legacy footage with more recent material.

When the anthology series moved to NBC for September 1961 it was renamed as *Disney's Wonderful World of Color* and opened with an original song by the Sherman brothers. Tinker Bell was still the cohost, but now she used her fairy dust to fill the screen with a kaleidoscope of color. This color would complement the colored feathers of NBC's peacock logo. It was also the year supposedly dramatized in *Saving Mr. Banks*. The episode with the Tinker Bell tour of Disneyland is also the one Mrs. Travers watches in her hotel room in *Saving Mr. Banks*. Although historically inaccurate, the snippet from the 1958 episode was chosen for its mixture of live action and animation. This kind of mixture was emblematic of what Travers initially disliked about Disney films and later about Disney's *Mary Poppins*, even though the film's live action/animation mix was much more impressive than this early television effort. *Saving Mr. Banks* includes the anthology series footage in a scene in which Travers is overwhelmed by the plush toys and other Disney merchandise filling her room at the Beverly Hills Hotel when she watches with disdain as Walt Disney interacts with an animated Tinker Bell.

The episodes of *Walt Disney Presents* that Travers could actually have watched in April 1961 are different from the April 1958 episode recreated for *Saving Mr. Banks*. They were installments of the serials, and during her visit in April 1961 *Texas John Slaughter* would have been airing. The winter–spring 1961 programming slate also included episodes of *Daniel Boone*, *The Swamp Fox*, and the rebroadcast of the 1956 film, *Westward Ho! The Wagons*. This list hints at Disney's frustration with ABC, which led to the move to NBC for September 1961. Disney felt that ABC just wanted to copycat itself each time it had a hit. The success of the *Davy Crockett* franchise back in the mid-1950s led to a call for more

FIGURE 4.8 Disney's cohost Tinker Bell appears during the lead-in to the episode P.L. Travers (the creator of Mary Poppins) supposedly watched during the 1961 visit depicted in 2013's *Saving Mr. Banks*.

westerns and other stories that mixed "tall tales and true." Walt had other ideas. He pitched the concept of *The Shaggy Dog*, for instance, but ABC rejected it. Walt went ahead and made it into a feature film in 1959 and it was a surprise box office hit that spawned a film franchise and established a lucrative studio relationship with Hollywood star Fred MacMurray that lasted through the late 1960s. It also signaled Disney's movement toward the embrace of tween-inclusive live-action family comedy. It found a second lucrative partnership with Hayley Mills, who played Pollyanna in Disney's 1960 film of the same name and then became a big star through *The Parent Trap* in a dual role as tween twins separated at birth who reconnect at summer camp. The trailerizing of the film occurs in "The Titlemakers," a June 1961 episode of *Walt Disney Presents*.

"The Titlemakers" episode is an example of a creative way that Disney Studios used the anthology series episodes as long-form trailers embedded within some original content of the kind that might appear on today's Blu-ray/DVDs. "The Titlemakers" is a content–promotion hybrid that is positioned as 1) a television episode; 2) an "educational/informational" short on creating title sequences; 3) a "company voice" advertisement for Walt Disney; 4) a grouping of behind-the-scenes interstitials about Disney television and film studios and its production workers; and, most predominantly; 5) a hosted lead-in to the trailer for *The Parent Trap*, with a bonus preview of the song for the film *Babes in Toyland*. The segments related to the film have the deeper purpose of circulating brand messaging about Walt Disney Studios and its stars. The existence of such a complex paratext in 1961 is not as surprising as the remarkable consistency of the ideological messaging about "togetherness" in midcentury and millennial Disney programming. A comparison of this text to several recent Walt Disney Company paratexts makes this consistency apparent.

Contrary to the kind of "look how far we've come since the *Father Knows Best* era" framing of snippets from midcentury television posted to YouTube, Disney's "The Titlemakers" features several elements that are socially critical of, or at least ambivalent about, the 1950s ideology of nuclear family togetherness and the social formation's supposedly positive impact on children. In place of the unstable nuclear family, which, even in 1961, was depicted as something that could be easily dissolved through divorce, Disney offers the lasting bonds of sisterhood and close friendship, both between its studio stars and the characters in its films and televisions series.

"The Titlemakers" calls attention to the friendship between Annette Funicello and Tommy Sands, who sing the title song for *The Parent Trap* and do the work of the hosted lead-in to the trailers. Funicello was the most famous star of Disney's *The Mickey Mouse Club* and a major Disney/Hollywood Records artist. Tommy Sands, her costar in *Babes in Toyland*, became a teen idol after a 1957 television movie, *The Singing Idol*. "The Titlemakers" doubles as promotion for the young stars and their upcoming film, *Babes in Toyland* (December 14, 1961), but their primary role here is as peer endorsers of *The Parent Trap* (June, 19, 1961). Speaking to the coordination of television episode air dates and the theatrical release dates, "The Titlemakers" aired on June 11th, creating awareness of the film and giving ten days of buzz building before the general release of the film.[14] When they are first introduced as the singers of the title song, a pull back dolly shot reveals that viewers are watching "behind-the-scenes" footage of Funicello and Sands singing to a live orchestra at the title song recording session. All this staging of a supposedly live event acts as part of the dramatization leading in to clips from *The Parent Trap*. Funicello, who also sings the film's signature teen tune, "Let's Get Together," would have been familiar with the lead-in strategy. She was often featured in such segments integrated into *The Mickey Mouse Club* (see cover image and Fig. 4.9). Midcentury Disney used *The Mickey Mouse Club* to launch tween stars and *Disneyland/Walt Disney Presents* to promote the feature films in which they appeared, as is evident in Funicello's role in "The Titlemakers."

FIGURE 4.9   *The Mickey Mouse Club* promoted albums for Annette, the singing idol who had a serial named after her. The album also promoted other serials like *Spin and Marty* and *The Hardy Boys*. Those two serials made Tim Considine a tween star before he graduated to his role as the eldest of *My Three Sons*.

Promotions for singles and compilation albums were built into the structure of late-1950s episodes of *The Mickey Mouse Club*, just as they are built into today's multitasking Disney Channel paratexts. "The Titlemakers" also contains within it music videos promoting Disney-related soundtracks and singles, which are connected through resonant myth stories about togetherness. The *Toyland* song references togetherness in romantic terms in relation to a couple on the night before their wedding, but *The Parent Trap* lyrics undercut the messaging by openly talking about the prevalence of divorce. Reinforcing this point, the film depicts immature and unreliable parents. *The Parent Trap* film works to contain this social criticism by embedding within it a remarriage plot. Yet, Funicello and Sands contradict what might be assumed to be the film's cultural orthodoxy about the nuclear family as the optimal social unit. The hosted lead-in to the film trailer and its songs acknowledge that the film's remarriage conclusion is an unlikely fulfillment of a childhood fantasy. Whatever the outcome of the parents' relationship, the song is quite clear that kids are often left dealing with problems caused by their parents. As the lyrics put it, parental failures often force kids to—"Straighten up their mess/with togetherness"—a reading that Funicello and Sands emphasize when they comment on the film's plot. Contrary to its reputation for reinforcing cultural orthodoxies, Disney Studios offers a paratext here that is moving toward cultural commentary, if not critique.

Douglas Holt and Douglas Cameron would say that the emphasis in *The Parent Trap* on friendship as the most significant form of togetherness takes advantage of the cultural disruption caused by divorce rates and dissatisfaction with the suburban nuclear family ideal and offers an even more appealing myth story—a togetherness that is more generationally focused in the way that we saw *Friends for Change* was in Chapter 3. "The Titlemakers" episode is representative of Disney's content–promotion hybrids that register mutually reinforcing textual and commercial goals, or, in Holt's terms, that offer *identity value* and brand value.[15] In my analysis of content about content, I am interested in Walt Disney's current and historical uses of "togetherness" as a trope that can apply to matters of form, industry, and cultural messaging of various kinds. Holt would say that the *identity value* that consumers associate with stories about togetherness enables Disney to accrue brand equity.[16] Togetherness is flexible enough to reference the standard cultural orthodoxy about nuclear family togetherness and a new myth story about friendship as a mode of togetherness with more longevity.

This reading of "The Titlemakers" is supported by the fact that the majority of *The Parent Trap* does not depict the appeal of family togetherness, but emphasizes instead the sustaining ideology at the core of Disney's teen- and tween-address content: the desirability of a lasting friendship that begins in adolescence and helps carry one through the upheavals likely to occur in one's family life. As I noted at the outset of this chapter, *Frozen* conveys a version of this messaging about sisterly bonds but the concept is more overtly at the center of today's "best-friends-forever" Disney Channel content about content. While it is a dynamic

FIGURE 4.10 Rocky and CeCe are Best Friend Brandcasters. The *Shake It Up* costars are the millennial parallels to ABC's 1970s odd couple best friends, just with "mad" dance skills that they showcase on their show-within-a-show.

in most of the sitcoms, it is especially apparent in *Shake It Up*'s focus on "odd couple" best friends Rocky and CeCe.

The most overt parallel between "The Titlemakers" and *Shake It Up* comes within "The Parent Trap It Up" episode. It follows Rocky's misguided attempt to reunite CeCe's divorced parents. Rocky has been reading about the transformation of hostilities into romantic attraction in *Pride and Prejudice*. She becomes convinced that CeCe's divorced parents are still in love and should reunite. CeCe and her brother Finn recount how horrible it was when their mismatched parents were married. At first Rocky does not accept the couple's history of constant antagonism as indicative of their mismatch. By the end of the episode she agrees that neither the parents nor children would be better off if the parents were to remarry. The ideological messaging here is not reinforcing cultural orthodoxy, as might be expected given the public perception of Disney as a family company. The episode leaves viewers with the lesson that it is foolish to invest in the mismatched couple in a romantic sense, but wise to develop an odd couple friendship in adolescence like Rocky and CeCe do, because such a relationship can last a lifetime.

Chapter 3 established that the best friend pairing or a coalition of friends is the "family" more often referenced on Disney Channel. Friendship is clearly at the center of its sitcom credit sequences for *Shake It Up*. The credits depict how Rocky (the academic superstar) and CeCe (the slacker) meet as equals on the dance floor. After school, they perform together a teen dance show, "Shake It Up Chicago," and specialize in hip hop dance routines similar to those on MTV's *America's Best Dance Crew* (a connection made through the appearance of *ABDC* guest stars on the show within a show).

In addition to the performance elements, the sitcom focuses on the screwball antics of Rocky and Cece. The characters were conceived by Chris Thompson, who worked on ABC's *Laverne and Shirley* and who created *Bosom Buddies* (starring Tom Hanks). As an update of the wacky BFFs subgenre, *Shake It Up* covers familiar tween-address sitcom territory, but the best friend dynamic is also part of the characters' role in materializing a marketable brand for Disney Channel. CeCe is the wacky half-Cuban redhead who manages to get rule-following Rocky into screwball situations. Although it is well established that Rocky's dream is to be a doctor like her dad, a flashback episode about a possible future has both Rocky and CeCe ending up as superstars in the entertainment industry. This projected future places the sitcom alongside *Austin & Ally* as one of Disney Channel's before-they-were-stars sitcoms.

This thematic focus distinguishes *Shake It Up* from the earlier Disney Channel best friends sitcom cycle, which included *That's So Raven*. In that series the wacky redhead is the reluctant accomplice to her Lucille Ball-style best friend Raven.[17] *That's So Raven* and *Lizzie McGuire* also added a male friend to expand the demographic appeal. In doing so, they mirrored broadcast television's popular tween and young teen trios of two boys and a girl from *The Wonder Years* and *Boy Meets World*. With the coupling of the BFF thematics with a performance element and an in-series performance venue (e.g., the "Shake It Up Chicago" stage), more recent sitcoms like *Shake It Up* become literal platforms from which to market new Disney Channel "triple threat" stars. Short-form series playing in the flow between episode segments create continuity between the in-series and off-series appearances of their dancer/singers. As Disney Channel has expanded to ever more international television markets, the BFF branding has also been used as in channel identifiers and content-about-content shorts airing in Germany, Italy, and the UK, among other markets. Some shorts air on Disney Channel, and then air internationally in dubbed versions (e.g., on Disney Channel France and Disney Channel Germany). In one, Zendaya Coleman and Bella Thorne talk about their off camera friendship and put it in context of their respective characterizations of Rocky and CeCe. Viewers are invited to go along with the BFFs as they do press tours in the UK, France, and other stops in Europe. The duo goof around and pose for selfies and seem very much like best friends off camera as well as on camera. Of course, playing best friends seems to be part of the current contract for Disney Channel stars, so it is hard to say where the acting stops and the real friendship might begin. Off-camera friendships are part of the economics of a channel with flow built around multiplatform invitations to viewers to participate in a social network that includes other Disney Channel viewers and its "circle of stars." The circle is increasingly diverse.

Just as "Laverne and Shirley" had male counterparts in "Lenny and Squiggy," Zendaya Coleman and Bella Thorne have Roshon Fegan and Adam Irigoyan. The male duo might be thought of as representative of what I call Disney Channel's "ethnicity without specificity" casting strategy. Their presence complements

FIGURE 4.11 *Shake It Up*'s Zendaya (Rocky) and Bella (CeCe) appear "as themselves" goofing around in a short series set in Germany. The BFF branding was used in international markets on Disney Channels Worldwide.

the lead duo's embodiment of the television's trope of the black and white best friend as symbolic of an "already-achieved diversity" post-racial worldview. Of course, Thorne is actually part Cuban and part Italian, which is typical of Disney's penchant for mixed-race casting. This kind of "ethnicity without specificity" also helps the show's circulation in the world market, as the characters have the potential to be read as inflected with different ethnicities in different markets.

On the U.S. channel the series stars also appear in music videos and other short-form content that registers the role that hip hop music and dance might play in upward mobility fantasies in the United States. Although it is usually just Zendaya and Bella in the shorts, the foursome appears in an odd content–promotion hybrid technically promoting *Cars 2*, a Disney Pixar feature film. It is also just a showcase of the friendly interactions among the sitcom ensemble, all of whom wear "street preppy" hybrid fashions as they wash a Mini Cooper parked in a suburban driveway.

4.8 Disney Channel's Decision Engines

Shake It Up is one of several Disney Channel programs playing on the fantasy of becoming a star alongside your best friend. Disney's *Stars on the Set* plays instead on the more typical fantasy of becoming friendly with stars. The short-form series is a hosted-lead in/interview hybrid in which a teen host, sometimes a sitcom star like Calum Worthy, conducts an interview on the set of a current or upcoming feature film release. The shorts depict a friendly interaction between channel star and film star (e.g., Jake Gyllenhaal of *Prince of Persia* or Robert Downey Jr. of *Iron Man*) and sometimes extend that dynamic to show a friendly relationship between film costars (e.g., Chris Hemsworth and Tom Hiddleston of *Thor*). While *Stars on the Set* is obviously intended to screen snippets from promotional trailers for Disney and Marvel films, it is structured as if it is a behind-the-scenes featurette in which channel stars and a film's stars introduce and comment on trailer snippets from a forthcoming film.

Prior to *Stars on the Set*, Disney Channel had a more creative way of embedding film promotion into content. Its promotional short-form series for those home media releases was its hosted lead-in series, *Leo Little's Big Show* (2009–10). It offered kids and tweens "peer reviews" of a variety of new Disney home media releases. 7ate9 Entertainment created *Leo Little's Big Show* as a short-form series structured to feel like a hybrid of a viewer vodcast/celebrity chat show/"on the set" interview series produced by an older tween and his big ham of a little sister. Although ostensibly a way for Leo and Amy to share their enthusiasm for films, including *Toy Story 3* and *Prince of Persia*, *Leo Little's Big Show's* is created by 7ate9 to promote films being released on Disney's signature Blu-ray/DVD combo pack format. As a Disney Channel series, it aligns with other shorts discussed in Chapter 3 in that it dramatizes fantasies about in-home brandcasting, and about translating fandom into amateur production and then into a professional future. The shorts mix existing film trailer footage or other film-related snippets with new elements, such as star interviews conducted on the set, via laptop, or as a "chat show" on the Littles' family-room couch. Other episodes mix existing footage with new play-acting segments (often with costumes and sets with a school play aesthetic). A *Tangled* episode is staged as if it is a satellite interview with voice actors, Zach Levi and Mandy Moore. Yet, it is also a game show involving a paper princess tower set and the frying pan that Rapunzel uses to defend herself. In other episodes Leo and Amy create a new dance or song, which is characterized by gentle mocking of their skills, each other, and often the form itself. For *Toy*

FIGURE 4.12 *Leo Little's Big Show*, a faux vodcasting series, creatively showcases Disney's signature Blu-ray/DVD combo pack format. Amy Little play acts as Rapunzel (lower), while her older brother Leo asks his "online viewers" trivia questions in the *Tangled* episode (middle). In another, Amy is thrilled to play act alongside the "Hollywood teen divas" from *Sonny with a Chance*, Disney Channel's version of NBC's *30 Rock* (upper).

Story 3, for instance, Leo and Amy film a hip-hop video set on the playground and in a faux Barbie dream house. Their performance affectionately mimics hip-hop style and plot elements from the film.

The interplay between Leo and Amy feels authentic given their age and gender dynamics. They mock each other when they try to play at being adult (posing as a serious on-location correspondent or as a serious potential romantic interest to a star). Showing his life stage between kid and adult, Leo also devolves into goofy behavior and purposely irritates his sister, especially when curtailing her one-on-one time with the stars and character actors. Segments tap into anxieties and aspirations about whether friendship can transcend differences in age or status, and gesture toward the fantasies of friendship with older siblings, teens, and even stars. This dynamic is evident in the way Amy treats the female teen stars from Disney Channel sitcoms when they come to the Littles' family-room set. Amy is slightly starstruck to play act alongside Tiffany Thornton and Sterling Knight from *Sonny with a Chance*, and thrilled to sit next to *The Suite Life On Deck*'s Debby Ryan, but it is clear that she also enjoys the fantasy that older teens like Tiffany and Debby would really want to be friends with her. The friends with an older teen fantasy carries over into *Dog With a Blog*, the sitcom on which G. Hannelius (Amy) now plays Avery, who becomes close friends with the girlfriend of her older stepbrother Tyler.

On *Leo Little's Big Show* Amy and Leo are representative Disney Channel characters negotiating the spaces among kid, tween, teen, and adult worlds. They copycat adult activities, fantasize about future activities, but still enjoy the goofiness of being a kid. Often they are just having fun, mugging for the camera, upstaging each other, acting out roles, dancing around, singing off key, and dressing up in costumes. Yet, as the older brother, Leo has clearly been conditioned to tolerate his younger sister, even when Amy tries to upstage him or acts silly when he is being a serious host or interviewer. In addition to displaying assumed target audience behaviors such as co-viewing, flirting with adult identities, identifying up to the next age bracket, or displaying tech savvy and entrepreneurial spirit, *Leo Little's Big Show* also models brand advocacy for viewers, encouraging them to communicate love of brand to others.

Although much more innovative than *Stars on the Set*, *Leo Little's Big Show* ended when the faux siblings graduated to starring roles in sitcoms. G. Hannelius (Amy Little) plays an important role in the transition because her memorable performance as Amy Little dancing with an ensemble of Disney Fairies from Pixie Hollow at Disneyland is paralleled by her return trip as some hybrid of herself/Avery Jennings, the sitcom character she plays on *Dog with a Blog*. She visits Disneyland with her television family in an episode of *Disney's 365*, which is tied to a Disney Parks campaign, *Family Time Resolutions*. The actress is once again positioned as the younger sister since most of the shots pair her with her sitcom stepbrother Tyler, played Blake Michael who was known as a costar of the brandcasting DCOM, *Lemonade Mouth*. The teens are joined by Francesa Capaldi, who plays their almost-a-tween sibling Chloe. She closely resembles Merida from Disney Pixar's *Brave*, so it is easy for her to have an "Amy Little moment" when she gets to practice archery alongside a Merida character actor during the park visit. She also clearly enjoys getting to hang out with her teen costars, which also was the fantasy played out by Amy in relation to Disney Channel's teen stars who took a seat on the Littles' family-room couch. G. Hannelius even exclaims, "I especially love hanging out with Francesca!" Francesa says, "We love to do nails," and then a short shows us their brightly colored manicures. Later, we see them all have an exciting time on the Mad Tea Party Ride. From the standpoint of parks promotion, the money shots are the responses of the trio. These shots pick up on the dynamic of most *Disney 365* shorts, which promote a specific Disney Channel series as they highlight the reactions of its costars to rides and attractions at the parks (see Fig. 4.13).

The *Dog with a Blog* episode also adds in a family element given the *Family Time Resolutions* New Year's campaign tie in. Regan Burns, who plays the dad in the blended family sitcom, points to the reality behind the fantasy: "Normally in TV world when you have a make believe family you don't get to actually do things like this with them." Then he reinforces the idea that the cast is his surrogate family and says that they all "get to bond not only on camera, but off." Although there is irony here because he has no time to bond with his actual family because of his job playing at family bonding on TV, Burns' comment is contextualized more in relation to the usual *Disney 365* messaging about castmates as friends with each other.

Disney 365 is created by M3, and the boutique firm builds many episodes around footage of Disney Channel's tween and teen stars enjoying some aspect of a Disney park. In a typical segment a teen correspondent interviews channel stars, often a duo from a relatively new Disney Channel or Disney XD series that could benefit from some increased brand exposure.[18] Typically, the appearances are made by costars, which was the case in the early days of *Wizards of Waverly Place* when Selena Gomez and Jennifer Stone experienced *Summer Night-tastic* electrical light parade together at Disney's California Adventure and shared their enthusiasm with *Disney 365* viewers. The pairs can also come from different shows like Ross Lynch of *Austin & Ally* and Olivia Holt of Disney XD's *Kickin' It*. This doubles the promotional potential for Disney series and implies that they are friends off camera and spend leisure time together.[19] Episodes can also feature one star promoting a less established star, as Lynch did for Maia Mitchell from *Teen Beach Movie*. No matter the format, the duos in the shorts reinforce my point from Chapter 3 that friendship is integral to Disney Channel's economic structure.

Disney 365 plays a central role in Disney Channel's function as a decision engine for viewers searching for entertainment content and experiences. It provides a platform through which to position Disney Channel stars as peer-to-peer advice givers and endorsers of channel and parent company entertainment

BLAKE MICHAEL   G. HANNELIUS

FIGURE 4.13   Three actors who play stepsiblings on a Disney Channel sitcom enjoy the Mad Tea Party Ride. Appearing in this *Disney 365* short, they endorse the ride, Disney parks, their sitcom, their star brands, and the fantasy that teens want to hang out with tweens.

experiences and content. The short-form series obviously parallels the episodes of *Disneyland* set in the theme park like "Disneyland 4th Anniversary Show" (September 11, 1957) and "Disneyland 10th Anniversary Show" (January 3, 1965). In the summer of 1959 ABC even aired *Kodak Presents Disneyland 1959*, a 90-minute special, which included dramatized advertisements of Ozzie and Harriet using their Kodak cameras at Disneyland. One important function of such programming was to bring potential attendees inside the park, and encourage return visits by those viewers who had already been there. For this reason these special shows previewed new rides, such as 1965's Matterhorn Bobsleds, Submarine Voyage, and Swiss Family Robinson Treehouse, or showcased future attractions, including Pirates of the Caribbean, The Haunted Mansion, and It's a Small World.

While the midcentury shows feel like tours similar to the one Tinker Bell gives of Disneyland, the *Disney 365* shorts have a more personalized feeling and they are short snippets. The shorts are a good length for YouTube circulation, and they embed trailer footage and teasers for the featured stars' upcoming roles. Beyond star and park promotion, *Disney 365* covers company-wide entertainment on offer from "Disney Destinations," such as its Broadway theater, Hawaiian resort, and cruise ship fleet (*Disney Wonder, Magic,* and *Fantasy*). One episode, for example, takes viewers on board the *Disney Magic* with the actors who play siblings on Disney's *Liv & Maddie*. While the two teens ride the Aquaduck, "a watercoaster at sea," the tween visits Marvel's Avengers Academy, an entertainment space filled with branded elements from the Marvel Universe story worlds (see Figure 3.2 for the Marvel image). The reaction shots register his enjoyment of the brand-related interactive experiences, including a simulation game that allows the player to undertake "a high tech training mission" in the persona of Iron Man. The attraction is located within "The Oceaneer Club" section of the ship, and there "kids 3–12" can experience Disney "worlds" as literally inhabitable. Others include Andy's Room from *Toy Story* and Pixie Hollow, the story world from the Disney's *Fairies* franchise.

The new branded elements on the other cruise ships have gotten similar endorsements from other cast members on *Austin & Ally*, *Jonas*, and *Suite Life on Deck*. The direct address of these shorts reflects the assumption that Disney Channel's tween viewers have the potential to be influencers of household spending and lobbyists for the Disney entertainment content and experiences or leisure-time activities and vacations available across divisions.

4.9   Disney Parks on *Modern Family* and *The Middle*

In the case of park-set episodes of *Disney 365*, channel stars are there to entice repeat visitors as well as new ones because they ride new rides, such as when China Anne McClain and Sierra McCormick, tween costars from the then-new sitcom *A.N.T. Farm*, showed their enthusiasm in 2011 for California Adventure's new *The Little Mermaid: Ariel's Undersea Adventure*. Toward the end of the series run of *A.N.T. Farm*, a now mature teen China Anne was filmed in 2013 at Walt Disney World with the rest of the McClains. The short follows the African American family of six as they go to different parts of the Florida resort beyond the traditional theme park. This episode with the McClains parallels the focus on African American park-goers in some more recent Disney Parks' commercials. The *Disney Memories* advertising campaign, for instance, expanded the representational spectrum to include more diverse families.

The park visit of the blended TV family from *Dog with a Blog* has its parallel in the "Disneyland" (3.22) episode of *Modern Family*, which depicts a blended family within a larger extended family. Both families are framed in front of iconic elements at Disneyland, including the *Mickey Mouse* shaped green space. *Modern Family* has three generations of Pritchetts, and in the *Disney 365* short G. Hannelius says she plans to take her grandparents on the Pirates of the Caribbean Ride, which is featured in the short along with Mater's Junkyard Jamboree (from *Cars*) and California Screaming Roller Coaster. The final sequence is about the funny picture taken of the Jennings/James kids as they come down the final chute of the water ride Splash Mountain. Being sure to *save good times in pictures* on this Disney ride is also one of the calls-to-action in the park visits of the families in ABC's *The Middle* and *Modern Family*.

In *Modern Family*'s "Disneyland" episode, Gloria Delgado-Pritchett and Manny Delgado are the ones who ride Splash Mountain, which aligns with the emphasis in some recent Disney parks promotions on Latino parkgoers. In the sitcom the souvenir photograph becomes part of the storyline as Gloria's husband Jay uses it to prove that Gloria regrets her choice of stiletto heels as appropriate theme park footwear. Although she won't admit it to Jay, he sees in the picture that she rides Splash Mountain holding her stiletto heels. Instead of picking on her, Jay just goes off to purchase her some oversized, pillow-like Minnie Mouse shoes, much to the later disapproval of his fashion-conscious stepson Manny Delgado-Pritchett. Manny notices the new shoes when he is riding Dumbo the Flying Elephant with Gloria, who disapproves of the fact that Manny has spent the whole day on his smart phone trying to manage a hypothetical stock market portfolio for a Wall Street investment strategies assignment for school. Manny's comic beats in the episode are connected to his continuing characterization as a middle-aged man trapped in the body of a young teen.

FIGURE 14   Manny Delgado-Pritchett is at Disneyland riding Dumbo the Flying Elephant with his mother Gloria. She disapproves of the fact that he spends the day mobile-managing a hypothetical stock portfolio, even while riding Splash Mountain.

While Manny always plans ahead for his future, this new characterization of him as a striver who plans to make a killing in the stock market seems influenced by his new cushy life as the stepson of a self-made businessman. From an earlier episode about Jay's attitude toward a fancy private school he and Manny visit, we know that monetary success was Jay's life goal too, and one he fulfilled. Of course, in a consumer culture, Jay's success is also broadcast through his second marriage to a young and sexy Latina. Earlier episodes try to contain negative readings of their relationship by directly taking on and complicating a characterization of Jay as a rich older man in the market for "a trophy wife" and Gloria as a broke but beautiful younger woman in need of "a sugar daddy." The "Disneyland" episode provides some backstory to reinforce this preferred reading: Jay and Gloria are attracted to each for more complex personality dynamics involving their negative experiences in first marriages to flaky narcissists. We also learn a bit more about the connection between a late-1970s trip to Disneyland and Jay's "happily divorced" backstory. One especially Disney-centric shot with the iconic castle in the background positions Gloria as the princess and Jay as the prince when he kneels down to put comfy Minnie Mouse slippers on her feet, taking off the stiletto heels she wore against his advice. She is grateful to him. Yet, Jay makes it clear that Gloria is his rescuer too, thereby aligning the depiction of their relationship dynamics with the revisions of the princess storylines more generally at Walt Disney.

The episode also plays with the princess-related characterization of Jay's granddaughter Lily, who was adopted from Vietnam by his son Mitchell and his life

FIGURE 4.15 In a *Modern Family* episode, Jay puts a comfy Minnie Mouse plush shoe on the aching foot of his grateful wife Gloria, as she rests on a bench in front of the *Sleeping Beauty* Castle.

partner Cameron Tucker. Several seasons of episodes have established that Lily is obsessed with princesses. We learn that it began in earnest when her dad Mitchell implied one night while he was sleepily reading her a bedtime story that her birth mother was a princess. Lily dresses as a princess for Halloween, chooses a princess costume as her flower girl dress for her dads' wedding, and has a princess party (an episode—2.15—in which her dad Cam has an altercation with the Princess character actor). In "Old Wagon" (2.1) Jay helps Cam put together Lily's life-size princess castle playhouse in the backyard and they both try to exclude Mitchell from the process because of his track record of home improvement disasters. The princess house becomes a source of comedy not only for the power tool dangers Mitchell poses to everyone during its construction, but also because Mitchell gets trapped inside the house several times.

This episode and other episodes (like 2.11) gesture toward a more subversive gender positioning, first when the dads reference their own princess fantasies and later when a hot drifter decides to take up residence inside the princess castle and Cam and Mitch enjoy keeping him around. For the most part, the episodes tend toward making the gay couple safe for straight suburban consumption by depicting them as "just like you and me." Mitchell gets emotional in one of the direct-to-camera interviews, which are a signature of the series, and says that every dad wants to build his daughter a princess castle. The line feels more like it is part of a parent company brand integration arc and an endorsement of consumer modes of happiness than actual characterization of Mitchell. Still, the comedy does work to

FIGURE 4.16 On *Modern Family* Mitchell Pritchett gets trapped in his daughter Lily's princess castle two months prior to the release of *Tangled*. The title change from *Rapunzel* signaled that the animated film was Disney's "gender-neutral" reimagining of the fairy tale, according to press releases.

efface the overtness of parent company integration in the princess castle episode, even though its art has a Rapunzel theme. Of course, the episode was the season two premiere airing in September 2010, which made it a paratext of sorts for the November 24, 2010 release of *Tangled*, Disney's animated Rapunzel reimagining.

All of these details provide some context for Lily's enthusiasm for the princess shoes she gets from her Grandpa Jay in the "Disneyland" episode. He buys them because they prevent Lily from running and give her two dads a break from chasing her around the park. In recent years, Disney consumer products has made doubly sure that little girls know about playing dress up in princess dresses even if they don't go to Bibbidy Bobbidy Boutique, the *Cinderella-inspired* boutique in the park or the "enchanted beauty salon." It is intriguing that the costuming and shot composition in this episode links two naturalized Americans, Lily from Vietnam and Gloria from Colombia, with Disney princesses. The choice aligns well with recent Disney Parks' marketing, which have ethnic Americans as representative of typical families in its commercials.

As is the case with the filtering of the two dads storylines through universal parenting issues, Gloria is also depicted in "Disneyland" as a typical American mother just trying to enjoy her leisure time with her son before he is too old to go on family vacations. The humor of the Gloria–Manny conversations is that Manny is already too old, even though he dons the mouse ears and rides a flying Dumbo and Splash Mountain with his mom. The parallel story to Gloria's focuses on Phil Dunphy and his continuing characterization as a peer-ent who bonds with his son Luke over their shared enjoyment of the same leisure time activities, especially a mutual love of roller coasters. The *Disney Memories* campaign played on this dynamic in spots with a "make memories while you can" messaging about how fast kids grow up.

The sentimentality of some of the Disney Parks campaigns seems to have affected Frankie Heck, the mother in ABC's *The Middle*, as she gets very upset in "The Wonderful World of Hecks" (5.24) when her family cannot have the kind of *Disney Memories* experiences depicted in the commercials. Earlier episodes let viewers know that the family has been "saving money" in their Disney vacation jar for years, and it is still mostly empty. As the Hecks are lower-middle class at best and are always in danger of slipping further down the class ladder, they don't have enough money for basics, let alone an expensive trip to the Walt Disney Resort. They finally make it to Disney through a contest won by Sue, the series' obstinate optimist high schooler. The family drives from Orson, Indiana to Orlando for a meager two-day park visit, including one free overnight stay at a Disney hotel.

Picking up the running series theme about her desire to look like a perfect family, Frankie has a meltdown after a failed attempt to get a holiday card-style family picture with the *Cinderella* Castle in the background. Up until that point, a series of mishaps prevent the family from actually enjoying the park or getting on any rides. Consequently, the Hecks are too busy blaming each other to pose long

FIGURE 4.17   "Hecking Up" a *Disney Memories* photo opportunity in front of the *Cinderella* Castle and Walt Disney statue during a free trip to Walt Disney World Resort on *The Middle*.

enough to get a good shot. Their disappointment comes from their high expectations for how great the trip would be for "making memories." Frankie measures her family in terms of their inability to look like one of those happy families wearing matching t-shirts monogramed with their surnames. Frankie likely got this image from the *Disney Memories* campaign. One particularly notable spot depicted the Rodriguez Family, all wearing matching yellow t-shirts with their surnames emblazoned on them (a "personalizing your Disney vacation experience," feature apparently available at the park itself). It is also a significant spot, as it signals the attempt to court a diversity of potential parkgoers. While still targeting upper-middle-class families who can afford all Disney has to offer, it is also courting future consumers from among those aspiring to middle-class status. They might take that first-time Disney Parks' vacation or vow to do so when they grow up. The company is interested in nurturing lifelong consumers and Disney brand advocates and planting the desire to become future consumers in those who do not currently have the financial or technological access to *all things Disney*, to borrow the tagline from *Disney 365*.

"The Rodriguez Family" spot offers a dramatization of what seems to be an extended Latino family in an implied narrative in which an adult son treats both his father and his nuclear family to a long-awaited Disney vacation. The grandparents are particularly proud and look as if they feel rewarded for sacrificing so much to make the American Dream of upward mobility a reality for their son. It is a consumer culture fantasy in which the ultimate reward is the branded vacation experience. In consumer culture worldview the ultimate sign of success is fulfilling the consumer dreams of family members and being recognized by society as a generous big spender. Gloria Delgado-Pritchett can occupy this position when in "Hawaii" (1.23) she secretly uses Jay's money to "give" her husband an (unwelcome) surprise "birthday present" of taking the whole 11-person extended family on vacation to the Four Seasons Resort in Maui. In contrast, Mike Heck has no hopes of even bringing his immediate family on a simple weekend at Disney World, let alone his wife's fantasy trip to Paris. He is thrilled when his daughter wins the overnight at a Disney hotel because he sees it as a way to get his wife to Epcot's version of Paris. We learn of this desire during the frustrating picture-taking attempt, and it becomes a very effective promotion for the faux-European vacation aspect of the Disney experience that has been particularly mocked by shows with "quality television audiences" goals. Yet, even *Modern Family* does some mocking of those Ron Becker calls the slumpy class (socially liberal, urban-minded, professionals) when it plays along with the self-mocking Mitch engages in when he tells Cam to stop calling it "Downton Disney," a reference to the fact that they watch the PBS series, *Downton Abbey*. It is just a day trip to Anaheim for the Tucker-Pritchetts and it looks as if it might be another excursion financed by Jay Pritchett. Mitch and Cam would be much more likely to spend their money on an actual overnight fantasy vacation in a place like the Four Seasons Maui. Viewers who have more in common economically with more middle-class characters are likely to be the target of the Disney Parks' advertising campaigns. The spots implied that making it to the middle class should be celebrated by a Disney vacation, whereas making it to the upper-middle class should translate to annual Disney vacations.

The majority of Disney Parks' commercials depict potential parkgoers, whatever their ethnicity, as families on the upper end of the middle-class spectrum, although some spots also highlight sale packages. Sale or no sale, the Heck family could not afford a Disney Resort vacation. In keeping with the product integration episodes producers found ways to integrate one even though the Hecks are barely scraping by financially. Getting the Hecks to Walt Disney World for the season five finale took some doing, and the in-episode struggles of the family to get there make its promotional elements all the more effective. As Neil Flynn, the actor who plays father Mike Heck, puts it, "I think, like for a lot of families, this is a special trip." Atticus Shaffer, the actor who plays tween Brick Heck, gets to the heart of the promotional function of the episode: "It's a wonderful commercial for Disney World. There's only going to be a lot of kids going, 'I want to go to Disney World like the Hecks.'" In the episode "Axl," Sue, and Brick Heck spend more time bickering than enjoying the rides, but just like China Anne McClain did on *Disney 365*, they do finally enjoy The Little Mermaid and Test Track. The money shot is of the three siblings bonding and getting their souvenir picture of their "happy times together" on Splash Mountain.

The second money shot comes in the whole family's joyous response to an unexpected upgrade to a hotel suite, their one stroke of good luck on the mostly disastrous trip. The spacious suite is a consumer goods paradise, with shiny, new stainless steel appliances in the kitchen, large flat screen televisions in the living area and the bedrooms, plush bedding on the over-sized mattresses, and even pillow soft toilet paper and spa quality toiletries. Most of these items are memory triggers for viewers to earlier episodes revolving around the Heck's appliances, their shabby bedrooms, and their attachment to their television and their cable package. All of the details reinforce the long-arc characterization of the class level of the Hecks as signaled through the fact that they can't fix their broken appliances or even buy name brand household items. The Hecks almost never look relaxed and happy, except when they get consumer goods (which is rare). In this episode, it is really the hotel room that gives them to most pleasure and their reaction shots to the various consumer pleasures the suite has to offer are the most joyous. As a content–promotion hybrid aligning with the particular emphasis in recent Disney Parks' commercial spots about the benefits of staying in a hotel within the resort, the episode works well and is notable for the way it manages to retain the family's usual characterization. While capturing happy moments in pictures, for instance, is part of all the Disney Parks' spots, the Hecks cannot manage to take one good family photograph in front of Walt Disney World's castle.

★★★

"The Wonderful World of Hecks" registers how Disney Park promotions continue to inculcate in viewers a desire to visit the park and expectations about what they would find once they entered. The weight of these expectations, it seems, even causes Sue Heck to faint at the first sight of the *Cinderella* Castle after the Heck family finally gains entrance to Walt Disney World. As she explains, "It's more beautiful than I've ever imagined. I've dreamed of this my whole life." In *Hollywood TV*, Chris Anderson offered a comprehensive analysis of the role the anthology series played in promoting the theme park to 1950s viewers, both as it was being built and as it continued to expand. In *Disney TV*, Telotte also covered these earliest promotional episodes, but he looked beyond the use of the initial seasons of the series to promote the park. While he offered some astute analysis of later episodes, I want to go further and argue that the anthology series of the 1950s and the many creative forms of The Walt Disney Company self promotion in the present not only brandcast images of the park, but also circulate preferred readings. The sitcoms and the various Disney Channel shorts analyzed above became paratexts for an experiential relationship to the park, which would begin when television viewers became site visitors. Borrowing from Gray's paratextual theory, I think of all of these television programs as "entryway" texts in that they provide narratives through which Walt Disney desired viewers to experience the park. They shape viewers' perceptions of what they would see at the park when they did make a site visit (which was the ultimate call-to-action of these television programs).

The sitcom episodes parallel the anthology series episodes like "The Titlemakers." The existence of this remarkably multifaceted hybrid of narrative and promotion in 1961 indicates that such forms are not unique to the contemporary television industry. This short-form content reflects the framing ideological narrative of the Disney brand and is especially relevant to this discussion in light of something Walt Disney himself says in his portion of the hosted lead-in to *The Parent Trap* trailer within "The Titlemakers." In the dramatization, Annette and Tommy figure out that Walt Disney himself is disguising his voice and using the PA system to ask them questions about the picture, when he really is just having them promote it. They sneak backstage and see Disney working a bunch of levers and using a voice machine. At that moment, he is the Great Oz and the puppet master. Annette affectionately chastises him, "Mr. Disney!" When Tommy gently mocks him saying, "And I always heard he was a modest man," Disney responds with a defense of brandcasting: "Tommy, my father used to tell me, 'Never be too proud to toot your own horn if you've done something worthwhile. You can depend on the others to make the noise if you've done something wrong.' " After the young stars go back to the soundstage, Walt Disney directly addresses the camera and says in winking manner, "I think we got the message through!" Earlier in the segment he also directly addressed viewers when he self-reflexively pointed out that title sequences: "help to get the audience in the proper frame of mind." The use of the word *frame* is significant, of course, as it is the same language Gray uses to discuss contemporary paratexts. The content-about-content shorts on Disney Channel and on Blu-ray/DVD combo packs work as frames for specific channel content, but they also point to the larger framing narratives Disney Studios utilizes to try to disseminate its desired brand messaging. Such frames encourage a specific interpretation of studio output. When Walt Disney introduces viewers to production workers, his comments encourage audiences to characterize Disney Studios less as a corporation and more as a coalition of craftsmen. While this observation is one that is commonly asserted in analyses of Disney Studio's self-representation, scholars do not typically consider the role that paratexts play in circulating this messaging.

Through the analyses in this chapter, I join other scholars in making the case for taking current and historical forms of promotional surround seriously as sites of study. Doing so requires us to look at elements of the on-air and off-TV promotional surround not only as creative texts, but also as sensitive registers of the industry logic and brand messaging of the media companies that produce them. The readings of various shorts have illustrated the ways in which paratexts are framing devices which function as content in their own right, as promotional surround for other texts, and as "parent company voice" messaging related to a desired brand identity.

Notes

1 Anderson 1994, 155.
2 The series was initially titled *Disneyland* (ABC 1954–8), and later *Walt Disney Presents* (ABC 1958–61). When it moved from ABC to NBC network for 1961, it was rebranded *The Wonderful World of Color*. ABC also aired Disney's *Zorro* (ABC, 1957–9), and *The Mickey Mouse Club* (1955–9).

3 Gray 2008, 33.

4 Rushdie 2001, 10.

5 Brad Bird (of Pixar's *The Incredibles*) and Damon Lindelof (of ABC's *Lost*) wanted to make a film about Disney Studios circa 1952, but the studio wisely retitled it *Tomorrowland*, which references one of the segments of the theme park and one of the episode cycles on *Disneyland/Walt Disney Presents*. The film pairs a journey involving a jaded older person with an obstinate optimist young person, which is a very on-brand dynamic for Disney. Add in the fact that the older guy is an inventor played by George Clooney and the film seems calculated to replicate the success of *Back to the Future*, although it's plausible it goes the way of Disney's moderately successful *Oz, the Great and Powerful*.

6 On Disney princesses, see www.disney.com.au/iamaprincess/index.php.

7 Brookey and Westerfelhaus 2002, 24, 23.

8 Caldwell 2006, 2008.

9 Brookey and Westerfelhaus 2002, 24.

10 Some of the later live-action films such as *Swiss Family Robinson*, *The Parent Trap*, and *Pollyanna*, got the "Vault Disney Collection" treatment, which translated to an abundance of production shorts and features included with the DVD release.

11 *Treasure Island* (1950), Disney's first all live-action film, was shot in England and used some big name British actors alongside Disney's first contract tween, Bobby Driscoll.

12 Lee Gutkind, founder of the journal *Creative Nonfiction*; see www.creativenonfiction.org/what-is-creative-nonfiction.

13 Lounsberry 1990, xiv–xv.

14 The second half of the June 11, 1961 episode of *Walt Disney Presents* rescreened the 1951 film "Nature's Half-Acre" from the studio's *True-Life Adventure* documentary/entertainment film series.

15 Holt 2004, 3.

16 Holt 2004, 3.

17 Raven is played by Raven-Symoné who became famous in the early 1990s as Denise Huxtable's four-year old stepdaughter on *The Cosby Show*.

18 Disney XD is the channel Disney created to microcast to tween boys when research found that many boys thought of Disney Channel as for girls. To offset the claim that Disney Channel is for babies, Disney also launched a stand-alone channel called Disney Junior, which had been the brand name given to blocks of preschool programming.

19 As Chapter 3 demonstrates, Disney Channel stars are depicted as part of an ensemble of friends in Disney Channel's cause marketing short series.

Bibliography

"ABC-TV's 'Get 'em Young': Major Payoff in Kid Accent." *Variety*, March 23, 1955: 21, 38.

Alvey, Mark. "The Independents: Rethinking the Television Studio System." In *The Revolution Wasn't Televised: Sixties Television and Social Conflict*, eds. Lynn Spigel and Michael Curtin, 139–58. New York, NY: Routledge, 1997.

Anderson, Christopher. *Hollywood TV: The Studio System in the Fifties*. Austin, TX: University of Texas Press, 1994.

Banet-Weiser, Sarah. *Authentic™: The Politics of Ambivalence in a Brand Culture*. New York, NY: New York University Press, 2012.

Barnes, Brooks. "Forget the Spoonful of Sugar It's Uncle Walt, Uncensored." *New York Times*, October 17, 2013. C1

Barnouw, Erik. *The Sponsor: Notes on a Modern Potentate*. New York, NY: Oxford University Press, 1979.

Baughman, James L. *Same Time, Same Station: Creating American Television, 1948–1961*. Baltimore, MD: The John Hopkins University Press, 2007.

Bennett, James. *Television Personalities: Stardom and the Small Screen*. New York, NY: Routledge, 2011.

Bennett, James and Tom Brown, eds. *Film and Television After DVD*. London, UK: Routledge, 2008.

Bickford, Tyler. "The New 'Tween' Music Industry: The Disney Channel, Kidz Bop and an Emerging Childhood Counterpublic." *Popular Music* 31, no. 3 (2012): 417–36.

Bilton, Chris. "Managing the Creative Industries: From Content to Context." In *Managing Media Work*, ed. Mark Deuze, 31–42. London, UK: Sage, 2010.

Bjarkman, Kim. "To Have and To Hold: The Video Collector's Relationship with an Ethereal Medium. "*Television and the New Media* 5, 3 (2004): 217–46.

Boddy, William. *Fifties Television: The Industry and its Critics*. Urbana and Chicago, IL: University of Illinois Press, 1993.

——. "Interactive Television and Advertising Form in Contemporary U.S. Television." In Spigel and Olsson 2004, 113–32.

——. "New Media as Old Media: Television." In *The New Media Book*, Dan Harries, 242–53. London, UK: BFI Publishing, 2002.

——. *New Media and Popular Imagination: Launching Radio, Television, and Digital Media in the United States*. Oxford, UK: Oxford University Press, 2004.

Boedeker, Hal. "Disney World Welcomes Fighting 'Middle' Clan." *Orlando Sentinel*, May 20, 2014. Available: http://articles.orlandosentinel.com/2014–05–20/entertainment/os-middle-season-finale-disney-20140516_1_walt-disney-world-new-fantasyland-modern-family.

Bolter, Jay David and Richard Grusin. *Remediation: Understanding New Media*. Cambridge, MA: MIT Press, 1999.

Borys, Kit. "*Frozen* Sold 3.2 million Blu-ray, DVD Units in First Day." *Hollywood Reporter*, March 9, 2014. Available: www.hollywoodreporter.com/news/frozen-sells-32-million-blu-689770.

Brookey, Robert Alan and Robert Westerfelhaus. "Hiding Homoeroticism in Plain View: The Fight Club DVD as Digital Closet." *Critical Studies in Media Communication* 19, no. 1 (2002): 21–43.

Brooks, Tim and Earle Marsh. *The Complete Directory to Primetime Network and Cable TV Shows: 1946–Present*. 8th edition. New York, NY: Ballantine, 2003.

Brown, Les. *Television the Business behind the Box*. New York, NY: Harcourt Brace Jovanovitch, 1971.

Brown, Stephen, Robert V. Kozinets, and John F. Sherry Jr. "Teaching Old Brands New Tricks: Retro Branding and the Revival of Brand Meaning." *Journal of Marketing* 67 (2003): 19–33.

Brown, Tom. "The DVD of Attractions? *The Lion King* and the Digital Theme Park." *Convergence* 13, no. 2 (May 2007): 169–83.

"Bruns, George" (Interview with David Tietyen). In Ghez (Vol. 11) 2011, 306–11.

Bruzzi, Stella. *New Documentary: A Critical Introduction*. London, UK: Routledge, 2000.

Buckley, Peter. "Exploiting the Implicit." *Campaign*, November 16, 2012. 6–12.

Burr, Ty. "How Disney Came to Own Mary Poppins." *The Boston Globe*, December 12, 2013.

Caldwell, John Thornton. "Convergence Television: Aggregating Form and Repurposing Content in the Culture of Conglomeration." In Spigel and Olsson 2004, 41–74.

——. "Critical Industrial Practice: Branding, Repurposing, and the Migratory Patterns of Industrial Texts." *Television & New Media* 7, no. 2 (May 2006): 99–134.

——. "Para-Industry: Researching Hollywood's Backwaters." *Cinema Journal* 53, no. 3 (2013): 157–65;

——. "Prefiguring DVD Bonus Tracks: Making-ofs and Behind-the-Scenes as Historic Television Programming Strategies Prototypes." In Bennett and Brown 2008,149–71.

——. *Production Culture: Industrial Reflexivity and Critical Practice in Film and Television.* Durham, NC: Duke University Press, 2008.

——. "Second-Shift Media Aesthetics: Programing, Interactivity, and User Flows." In *New Media: Theories and Practices of Digitextuality*, eds. Anna Everett and John Caldwell, 127–44. New York, NY: Routledge, 2003.

——. *Televisuality: Style, Crisis, and Authority in American Television.* New Brunswick, NJ: Rutgers University Press, 1995.

"Carlson, Paul" (Interview). In Ghez (Vol. 9) 2008, 222–34.

Castleman, Harry and Walter J. Podrazik. *Harry and Wally's Favorite TV Shows.* New York, NY: Prentice Hall, 1989.

——. *The TV Schedule Book.* New York, NY: McGraw-Hill, 1984.

Caves, Richard E. *Creative Industries: Contracts between Art and Commerce.* Cambridge, MA: Harvard University Press, 2000.

Coontz, Stephanie. *The Way We Never Were: American Families and the Nostalgia Trap.* New York, NY: Basic Books, 1992.

Cotter, Bill. *The Wonderful World of Disney Television: A Complete History.* New York, NY: Hyperion, 1997.

Davis, Aeron. *Promotional Cultures: The Rise and Spread of Advertising, Public Relations, Marketing and Branding.* Cambridge, UK: Polity Press, 2013.

Dawson, Max. "Television Abridged: Ephemeral Texts, Monumental Seriality and TV-Digital Media Convergence." In Grainge 2011, 37–56.

Denis, Christopher Paul and Michael Denis. *Favorite Families of TV.* New York, NY: Citadel Press, 1992.

Deuze, Mark. "Convergence Culture in the Creative Industries." *International Journal of Cultural Studies* 10, no. 2 (2007): 243–63.

——. *Media Work.* Cambridge, UK: Polity, 2007.

Doherty, Thomas. *Teenagers and Teenpics: The Juvenilization of American Movies in the 1950s.* Philadelphia, PA: Temple University Press, 2002.

Donaton, Scott. *Madison and Vine: Why the Entertainment and Advertising Industries Must Converge to Survive.* New York, NY: McGraw-Hill, 2005.

Douglas, Susan J. *Where the Girls Are: Growing Up Female with the Mass Media.* New York, NY: Times, 1995.

Dyer, Richard. *Stars.* London, UK: BFI Publishing, 1986.

Ellis, John. "Interstitials: How the 'Bits in Between' Define the Programmes." In Grainge 2011, 59–69.

——. "Scheduling: the Last Creative Act in Television?" *Media, Culture and Society* 22, no. 1 (2000): 25–38.

Feuer, Jane. "The Concept of Live Television: Ontology as Ideology." In *Regarding Television: Critical Approaches—An Anthology*, ed. E. Ann Kaplan, 12–21. Los Angeles, CA: The American Film Institute, 1983.

Fiske, John. *Television Culture*. London, UK: Routledge, 1989.

Flanagan, Caitlin. "Becoming Mary Poppins, P. L. Travers, Walt Disney, and the Making of a Myth." *New Yorker*, October 12, 2005.

Friedberg, Anne. "The Virtual Window." In *Rethinking Media Change: The Aesthetics of Transition*, eds. David Thornburn and Henry Jenkins, 337–53. Cambridge, MA: MIT Press, 2004.

Gabler, Neal. *Walt Disney: The Triumph of the American Imagination*. New York, NY: Knopf, 2006.

Gaines, Jane. "Costume and Narrative: How Dress Tells the Woman's Story." In *Fabrications: Costume and the Female Body*, eds. Jane Gaines and Charlotte Herzog, 180–211. New York, NY: Routledge, 1990.

Genette, Gerard. *Paratexts: Thresholds of Interpretation*. New York, NY: Cambridge University Press, 1997.

Ghez, Didier, ed. *Walt's People: Talking with the Artists Who Knew Him*. Bloomington, IN: Xlibris, 2008 (Vol. 9) and 2011 (Vol. 11).

Gillan, Jennifer. *Television and New Media: Must Click TV*. New York, NY: Routledge, 2010.

Gitelman, Lisa. *Always Already New: Media, History and the Data of Culture*. Cambridge, MA: MIT Press, 2006.

Gitlin, Todd. *Inside Prime Time*. New York, NY: Routledge, 1985.

Goetzl, David. "How Networks Follow The Tweens." *Broadcasting & Cable*, March 26, 2007.

Gomery, Douglas. *A History of Broadcasting in the United States*. London, UK: Blackwell, 2008.

———. "Talent Raids and Package Deals: NBC Loses Its Leadership in the 1950s." In Hilmes 2007, 153–68.

Grainge, Paul. *Brand Hollywood: Selling Entertainment in a Global Media Age*. New York, NY: Routledge, 2008.

———, ed. *Ephemeral Media: Transitory Screen Culture from Television to YouTube*. London, UK: BFI Publishing, 2011.

Gray, Jonathan. *Show Sold Separately: Promos, Spoilers, and Other Media Paratexts*. New York, NY: New York University Press, 2010.

———. "Television Pre-views and the Meaning of Hype." *International Journal of Cultural Studies*, 11, no. 1 (2008): 33–49.

Halberstam, David. *The Fifties*. New York, NY: Villard, 1993.

Hamamoto, Darrell Y. *Nervous Laughter: Television Situation Comedy and Liberal Democratic Ideology*. New York, NY: Praeger, 1991.

Haralovich, Mary Beth. "Sit-coms and Suburbs: Positioning the 1950's Homemaker." In *Private Screenings: Television and the Female Consumer*, eds. Lynn Spigel and Denise Mann, 111–41. Minneapolis, MN: University of Minnesota Press, 1992.

Hargadon, Andrew. *How Breakthroughs Happen: The Surprising Truth About How Companies Innovate*. Boston, MA: Harvard Business School Press, 2003.

Hesmondhalgh, David. *The Cultural Industries*. Thousand Oaks, CA: Sage, 2002.

Hilmes, Michele. *Hollywood and Broadcasting: From Radio to Cable*. Urbana, IL: University of Illinois Press, 1990.

———, ed. *NBC: America's Network*. Berkeley, CA: University of California Press, 2007.

———. *Only Connect: A Cultural History of Broadcasting in the US*. 2nd edition. Belmont, CA: Wadsworth, 2006.

Holliss, Richard and Brian Sibley. *The Disney Studio Story*. London, UK: Octopus Books Limited, 1988.

Holt, Douglas B. *How Brands Become Icons: Principles of Cultural Branding*. Boston, MA: Harvard Business School Press, 2004.

Holt, Doulgas B. and Douglas Cameron. *Cultural Strategy: Using Innovative Ideologies to Build Breakthrough Brands*. Oxford, UK: Oxford University Press, 2010.

Holt, Jennifer. "Vertical Vision: Deregulation, Industrial Economy and Prime-time Design." In Jancovich and Lyons 2003, 11–31.

Holt, Jennifer and Alisa Perren, eds. *Media Industries: History, Theory, and Method*. Malden, MA: Wiley-Blackwell, 2009.

Ito, Mizuko. *Hanging Out, Messing Around, and Geeking Out: Kids Living and Learning with New Media*. Cambridge, MA: The MIT Press, 2010.

Jancovich, Mark and James Lyons, eds. *Quality Popular Television*. London, UK: BFI Publishing, 2003.

Jaramillo, Deborah L. "The Family Racket: AOL-Time Warner, HBO, *The Sopranos*, and the Construction of a Quality Brand." *Journal of Communication Inquiry* 26, no. 1 (2002): 59–75.

Jenkins, Henry. *Convergence Culture: Where Old and New Media Collide*. New York, NY: New York University Press, 2006.

Jenkins, Henry and David Thornburn, eds. *Democracy and New Media*. Cambridge, MA: MIT Press, 2003.

Johnson, Catherine. *Branding Television*. New York, NY: Routledge, 2012.

———. "Tele-branding in TVIII: the Network as Brand and the Programme as Brand." *New Review of Film and Television Studies* 5, no. 1(2007): 5–24.

Johnson, Derek. "Inviting Audiences In: The Spatial Reorganization of Production and Consumption in 'TV III.'" *New Review of Film and Television Studies*. 5, no.1 (April 2007): 61–80.

Johnson, Victoria E. *Heartland TV: Primetime Television and the Struggle for U.S. Identity*. New York, NY: New York University Press, 2008.

Kernan, Lisa. *Coming Attractions: Reading American Movie Trailers*. Austin, TX: University of Texas Press, 2004.

Klinger, Barbara. *Beyond the Multiplex: Cinema, New Technologies, and the Home*. Berkeley, CA: University of California Press, 2006.

———. "Digressions at the Cinema: Reception and Mass Culture." *Cinema Journal* 28, no. 4 (1989): 3–19.

Kompare, Derek. "Publishing Flow: DVD Box Sets and the Reconception of Television." *Television and New Media* 7, no. 4 (2006): 335–60.

Korkis, Jim. "The Secret Walt Disney Commercials." In Ghez (Vol. 9) 2008, 218–21. Also in *Animation World Magazine*, August 25, 2006. Available: www.awn.com/animationworld/secret-walt-disney-commercials.

Kozinets, Robert V. "E-tribalized Marketing?: The Strategic Implications of Virtual Communities of Consumption." *European Management Journal* 17, no. 3 (June 1999): 252–64.

———. "How Online Communities Are Growing in Power." *Financial Times*, November 9, 1998.

Kunz, William. *Culture Conglomerates: Consolidation in the Motion Picture and Television Industries*. Lanham, MD: Rowman and Littlefield, 1997.

Lawson, Valerie. *Mary Poppins, She Wrote: The Life of P.L. Travers*. New York, NY: Simon & Schuster, 2006.

———. *Out of the Sky She Came: The Life of P.L. Travers, Creator of Mary Poppins.* Sydney, AU: Hodder Headline Australia, 1999.

Leibman, Nina C. *Living Room Lectures: The Fifties Family in Film & Television.* Austin, TX: University of Texas Press, 1995.

Lounsberry, Barbara. *The Art of Fact: Contemporary Artists of Nonfiction.* Westport, CT: Greenwood Press, 1990. xiv–xv.

Lumenick, Lou. "Saving Mr. Banks More Like 'Selling Mary Poppins,'" *The New York Post*, December 10, 2013.

Luscombe, Belinda. "How Disney Builds Stars." *Time*, November 9, 2009: 49–51.

Macnab, Geoffrey. "Saving Mr. Banks Film Review: A Sugar Coated, Disingenuous Marketing Exercise for Disney." *The Independent* (London), November 28, 2013.

Mandese, Joe. "DVR Threat Gets Downgraded." *Broadcasting & Cable*, September 12, 2005. 20.

Marling, Karal Ann. *As Seen On TV: The Visual of Everyday Life in the 1950s.* Cambridge, MA: Harvard University Press, 1994.

Mashon, Mike. "NBC, J. Walter Thompson, and the Struggle for Control of Television Programming, 1946–58." In Hilmes 2007, 135–52.

Mayer, Vicki, John Thornton Caldwell, and Miranda J. Banks, eds. *Production Studies: Cultural Studies of Media Industries.* New York, NY: Routledge, 2009.

McCarthy, Ellen. "Making Queer Television History." *GLQ: A Journal of Lesbian and Gay Studies* (2001): 593–620.

McClintock, Pamela. "Box Office Milestone: 'Frozen' Becomes #1 Animated Film of All Time." *Hollywood Reporter*, March 30, 2014.

Meehan, Eileen. "Why We Don't Count: The Commodity Audience." In *Logics of Television: Essays in Cultural Criticism*, ed. Patricia Mellencamp, 117–37. Bloomington, IN: Indiana University Press, 1990.

Murray, Simone. "Brand Loyalties: Rethinking Content within Global Corporate Media." *Media, Culture, Society* 27, no. 3 (2005): 415–35.

Murray, Susan. *Hitch Your Antenna to the Stars: Early Television and Broadcast Stardom.* New York, NY: Routledge, 2005.

Napoli, Philip M. *Audience Economics: Media Institutions and the Audience Marketplace.* New York, NY: Columbia University Press, 2003.

Newcomb, Horace M. and Robert S. Alley. *The Producer's Medium.* New York, NY: Oxford University Press, 1983.

Nilsen, Sarah. "All-American Girl? Annette Funicello and Suburban Ethnicity." In *Mediated Girlhoods: New Explorations of Girls' Media Culture*, ed. Mary Celeste Kearney, 35–53. New York, NY: Peter Lang, 2011.

"Performer or Pitchman?" *Variety*, November 11, 1953: 31.

Rochlin, Margy. "Not Quite All Spoonfuls of Sugar." *New York Times*, January 5, 2014. AR 22.

———. "A Spoonful of Sugar For a Sourpuss." *New York Times*, December 8, 2013. AR 16.

Rushdie, Salman. *The Wizard of Oz (BFI Film Classics).* London, UK: BFI Publishing, 2001.

Sammond, Nicholas. *Babes in Tomorrowland: Walt Disney and the Making of the American Child, 1930–1960.* Durham, NC: Duke University Press, 2005.

Samuel, Lawrence R. *Brought to You By: Postwar Television Advertising and The American Dream.* Austin, TX: University of Texas Press, 2001.

Schatz, Thomas. "The New Hollywood." In *Film Theory Goes to the Movies*, eds. Jim Collins, Hilary Radner, and Ava Preacher Collins, 8–36. London, UK: Routledge, 1993.

Scott, A.O. "An Unbeliever in Disney World: [Review of *Saving Mr. Banks*]."*New York Times*, December 13, 2013. C8.

Sexton, David. "Saving Mr. Banks [Review]." *Evening Standard*, November 29, 2013.

Shrum, L.J. *The Psychology of Entertainment Media: Blurring the Lines Between Entertainment and Persuasion*. New York, NY: Routledge, 2012.

Skopal, Pavel. "'The Adventure Continues on DVD': Franchise Movies as Home Video." *Convergence: The International Journal of Research into New Media Technologies* 13, no. 2 (2007): 185–98.

Spigel, Lynn. *Make Room for TV: Television and the Family Ideal in Postwar America*. Chicago, IL: University of Chicago Press, 1992.

Spigel, Lynn and Jan Olsson, eds., *Television After TV: Essays on a Medium in Transition*. Durham, NC: Duke University Press, 2004.

Sporich, Brett. "DVD is Crowned Sell-Through King." *Hollywood Reporter*, January 9, 2002.

Stanley, T.L. "Disney Channel: A Fresh-Face Factory." *Advertising Age*, December 11, 2006.

Staid, Gitte. "Mobile Identity: Youth, Identity, and Mobile Communication Media." In *Youth, Identity, and Digital Media*, ed. David Buckingham, 143–64. Cambridge, MA: MIT Press, 2008.

Stedman, Alex. "'Frozen' Becomes the Highest-Grossing Animated Film Ever." *Variety*, March 30, 2014. Available: http://variety.com/2014/film/news/frozen-becomes-the-highest-grossing-animated-film-ever-1201150128/.

Taylor, Timothy D. *The Sounds of Capitalism: Advertising, Music, and the Conquest of Culture*. Chicago, IL: The University of Chicago Press, 2012.

Telotte, J.P. *Disney TV*. Detroit, MI: Wayne State University Press, 2005.

——. *The Mouse Machine: Disney and Technology* Champaign, IL: University of Illinois Press, 2008.

Thomas, Bob. *Walt Disney: An American Original*. New York, NY: Simon and Schuster, 1976.

Tryon, Chuck. *Reinventing Cinema: Movies in the Age of Media Convergence*. New Brunswick, NJ: Rutgers University Press, 2010.

Tunstall, Jeremy. *The Media Were American: U.S. Mass Media in Decline*. New York, NY: Oxford University Press, 2007.

Turner, Sarah E. "BBFFs: Interracial Friendships in a Post-Racial World." In *The Colorblind Screen: Television in Post-Racial America*, eds. Sarah Nilsen and Sarah E. Turner, 237–57. New York, NY: New York University Press, 2014.

——. "Disney Does Race: Black BFFs in the New Racial Moment." *Networking Knowledge* 5, no. 1 (February 2012): 125–40.

Turow, Joseph. *Breaking Up America: Advertisers and the New Media World*. Chicago, IL: University of Chicago Press, 1997.

——. *Niche Envy: Marketing Discrimination in the Digital Age*. Cambridge, MA: MIT Press, 2006.

Ulin, Jeffery C. *The Business of Media Distribution: Monetizing Film, TV, and Video Content in an Online World*. 2nd edition. New York, NY: Focal Press, 2014.

Uricchio, William. "Historicizing Media in Transition." In *Rethinking Media Change: The Aesthetics of Transition*, eds. David Thronburn and Henry Jenkins, 23–38. Cambridge, MA: MIT Press, 2004.

——. "Old Media and New Media: Television." In *The New Media Book*, ed. Dan Harries, 219–30. London, UK: BFI Publishing, 2002.

Valdivia, A.N. "Mixed Race on the Disney Channel: From *Johnnie Tsunami* through *Lizzie McGuire* and Ending with *The Cheetah Girls*." In *Mixed Race Hollywood*, eds. Mary Beltrán and Camilla Fojas, 269–89. New York, NY: New York University Press.

Van Riper, A. Bowdoin, ed. *Learning from Mickey, Donald, and Walt: Essays on Disney's Edutainment Film*. Jefferson, NC: McFarland, 2011.

Variety. "*Disneyland* [Review]." *Variety*, September 12, 1957.

Variety. "*The Mickey Mouse Club* [Review]." *Variety*, October 1, 1957.

Vogel, Harold. *Entertainment Industry Economics: A Guide for Financial Analysts*. 7th edition. New York, NY: Cambridge University Press, 2007.

Wasko, Janet. The Future of Film Distribution and Exhibition." In Harries 2002, 195–206.

———. *How Hollywood Works*. Thousand Oaks, CA: Sage, 2003.

———. *Understanding Disney: The Manufacture of Fantasy*. Malden, MA: Polity Press, 2001.

Watts, Steven. *The Magic Kingdom: Walt Disney and the American Way of Life*. New York, NY: Houghton Mifflin, 1997.

Wee, Valerie. "Selling Teen Culture: How American Multimedia Conglomeration Shaped Teen Television in the 1990s." In *Teen TV: Genre, Consumption and Identity*, eds. Glyn Davis and Kay Dickinson, 87–98. London, UK: BFI Publishing, 2004.

Williams, Raymond. *Television, Technology and Cultural Forms*. London, UK: Fontana, 1974.

Wilmott, Michael. *Citizen Brands: Putting Society at the Heart of Your Business*. Chichester, UK: Wiley, 2001.

Wyatt, Justin. *High Concept: Movies and Marketing in Hollywood*. Austin, TX: University of Texas Press, 1994.

EPILOGUE

Twitter Multitasking, *Mad*-vertising, and Sustainable TV

E.1   Disney *Re-Micks*

Television Brandcasting begins with the premise that U.S. television has a long history as a "recommendation engine." Chris Anderson, editor of *Wired* magazine, employs the term as part of his theory about "the long tail" to refer to the infrastructure of sites for e-commerce and digital distribution. They entice potential purchasers of digital files, Blu-rays, DVDs or multi-format combo packs through the recommendations of "customers like you." The sites also generate customized "recommendations to drive demand down the long tail," leveraging an established star or brand to sell the lesser known to potential consumers based on their prior purchases.[1] A reader of Anderson's general theory or other commentaries like it might assume that converting recommendations into a form of marketing is a recent phenomenon made possible by the World Wide Web. With the emergence of "viewsers"—television viewers who are also users of a variety of mobile devices and social networking utilities—recommendations certainly circulate quickly and efficiently. Now that television content is distributed and accessed via digital delivery, websites, mobile devices, and Blu-rays and DVDs, viewers are recruited—along with television stars, television characters, and production workers—to keep the recommendation engine generating ever more immediate direct-to-viewer endorsements on as many platforms as possible. As this book has detailed, the basic function of television as a brandcasting platform and the creation of content to recommend other content was already a component of the audience address of the mid-1950s and 1960s U.S. television industry.

Offering a comparative analysis of the current period of transition with the 1950s–60s—the chapters of *Television Brandcasting* have examined the kinds of content–promotion hybrids that have been employed in each era and the continuities between the two. It has considered how both periods saw the emergence of new ways to position television characters and stars as brand emissaries and endorsers. New media has made these recommendations more effective and all pervasive. Endorsements now cross platforms and are delivered through many kinds of content and promotion.

A largely invisible production sector of boutique production houses now specializes in the creation of content–promotion hybrids. The content created for Disney stands out in part because so much can be created for such an established media company brand. More to the point of this book, Disney needs to fill its dedicated brandcasting channel with attention-generating hybrids that feel more like content than promotion. My interest in these shorts came out of my viewing of *Disney's Re-Micks*, a short-form series first produced in 2009 for Disney by 7ate9 Entertainment. Art Spigel and his team took footage from Disney's classic cartoons, including *Steamboat Willie* and *The Barn Dance*, and digitally remastered the snippets to sync them to contemporary music such as The Black Eyed Peas, "I Got A Feeling," Bruno Mars, "Just the Way You Are," and Ne-Yo, "Miss Independent." This synching of classic cartoons to the lyrics and beat of contemporary music reflects the current logic of bringing together legacy brands (in this case, Mickey and Minnie Mouse, Donald and Daisy Duck, Goofy, and Pluto) with contemporary fare. The logic of these hybrids is to attract people who like one form of content and encourage them to sample another kind of content (classic Disney shorts or contemporary music).

The opening visuals reference different distribution technologies: gramophones, radios, console televisions, portable televisions, digital televisions, home theater systems, and portable media devices. This variety is indicative of Disney's self-proclaimed "platform agnostic" approach to distribution and changing technologies. As the *Re-Micks* arrow zips around the screen, it charts the evolution of television from the era of large family consoles to the smaller, individual-sized dial televisions. While some of these small televisions are technically portable, a red, kid-sized television seems to be included as a visual segue into the more recent handheld media players. The cumulative effect of this fast-paced opener reinforces the perception that the iconic brand and its legacy character have always adapted to changing technologies and distribution platforms or reception practices and cultural changes.

The opening sequence for *Disney's Re-Micks* registers the long history of Disney circulating its legacy brands, especially Mickey Mouse, among different platforms. While we associate this kind of media convergence and multiplatform circulation policy with today's industry, Walt Disney of the 1950s was embracing elements of it. The *Re-Mick's* graphics tell of Disney Studios' long-term relationship with television. They also make a case for Disney's historical agility when it came to finding ways to use new platforms to recirculate (and repurpose) legacy properties, introduce new versions of familiar brands, or remix them in new ways. Finally, the *Re-Micks* also reference how Disney excels at leveraging one

FIGURE E.1 The opening sequence for *Disney's Re-Micks* registers the long history of Disney circulating its legacy brands among different platforms.

kind of platform to promote content on another platform. With the launch of Walt Disney Records, for instance, midcentury Disney reimagined its films as content that could then be shaped in different ways for different platforms. It already screened feature films in theaters, and then condensed versions of studio films on its television program. It added to that some different iterations of the content for its signature storyteller LPs, along with other recording division output (e.g., soundtracks). Such agility is necessary for survival in the current U.S. television industry. Creative brand building and circulation requires promotion that doesn't feel like promotion and content with already embedded promotion.

As content–promotion hybrids, the *Re-Micks* have several functions beyond entertainment in their own right. They act as brand identification for Disney Channel and promotion for Walt Disney Studios. They are easily scheduled interstitial content to air between episode segments. They attract audience attention and entice those who like the songs to pay attention to the content. *Re-Micks* are structured to be an ideal duration and form for shareability on YouTube. They also promote the new slate of Mickey Mouse cartoon shorts, conceptualized by 7ate9 to combine 1930s design with contemporary pacing.

Re-Micks aired on Disney Channel and its web and mobile platforms and circulated on YouTube at a time when The Walt Disney Company was publicizing its forward-thinking embrace of new distribution platforms and its nimbleness in reimagining its content in relation to the parameters of those platforms. The opening sequence references the alternate entryways approach; one can access content through linear media or one can have an extended experience with the content as it appears across platforms.

It was not until later that I learned the production history behind these content–promotion hybrids. At first, I was simply fascinated by the opening segment's visualization of Jenkins' convergence culture theories and of my theories about Must-Click TV. In my 2010 book I used the phrasing to describe an approach that utilizes standard notions of televisual flow between a broadcast network's programs and across its scheduling grid and capitalizes on new media-enabled content circulation on new platforms and devices. The Must-Click TV programming model assumes that the television content available through different platforms and devices must click together seamlessly to form interlocking pieces of a whole branded experience, one that is structured to encourage viewers to make emotional investments that will ideally lead to economic investments. This kind of transmedia storytelling approach, as Henry Jenkins points out, replaces franchise models based on "urtexts and ancillary products."[2] Savvy producers realize that all the divisions of the franchise need to be created simultaneously and click together in an interlocking gear model; in this way, the on-air, online, and on-mobile content make the product move (as well as "move" sponsor products and encourage viewers to move across the divisions of a media conglomerate). The key is to keep content always in circulation and the audience always interacting with it. Disney's *Re-Micks* register the impact of such circulation paradigms. Whether first encountered on a new media site or a television channel, the *Re-Micks* are structured to attract the attention of viewers, and then drive them to other branded spaces in the Disney entertainment universe.

E.2   Complementary Storytelling: The Influence of the *Lost* Model

Some production teams at ABC and ABC Family have embraced other creative strategies, becoming trendsetters in innovative content–promotion creation and circulation. The use of Twitter by ABC Family's *Pretty Little Liars* stands out as effective "off-television" brandcasting. Even before its premiere in June 2010, *Pretty Little Liars* generated buzz for its online and mobile campaigns promoting its serial mystery structure about popular high school girls terrorized by threatening text messages after their friend is missing and presumed dead. As the series developed, its producers tapped into the tendency of smart phone users to multitask and then redirected that potentially distracted viewing behavior toward focused engagement with the series through text messaging and Twitter micro-blogging. The strategies employed by its production and marketing teams are representative templates for addressing some of the industry challenges of the last decade, including:

* maintaining an on-air audience in an era when viewers can access episodes via alternate platforms for delivery (e.g., digital downloading)
* capturing the attention of viewers with smart phones and tablet computers, which give them instant access to web browsing, social networking, emailing, text messaging, video streaming/sharing, and micro-blogging capabilities, and
* transforming distracted viewing into "multitasking television" by redirecting new media-enabled behaviors toward the consumption of branded content related to television series.

Premiering in 2010 when a multiplatform television model and marketplace were already established, and after ABC's *Lost* had already pioneered both the long-arc serial mystery and multiplatform engagement strategies, *Pretty Little Liars* aired on multiple platforms from the outset. ABC Family, the Disney–ABC Television Group cable channel that airs *Pretty Little Liars*, is governed by the Must-Click TV model. For Must-Click TV to work, transmedia producers and channel brand managers have to attract and maintain the attention of loyal viewers who act as brand advocates. Their web-commentary and engagement and their contributions to social media sites can then be leveraged to sustain and spread awareness for a particular program brand. Television series no longer simply contribute to a programming slate intended to make a channel desirable to the viewers of interest to advertisers. A series now functions as a stand-alone brand, a product that circulates on multiple platforms (e.g., Blu-ray, DVD, and smart phone), with all contributing to the revenue stream produced by the series and to its capability for self-promotion. Fan-generated circulation of content and commentary about the series bolsters the profit potential of the program brand and that of the channel or platform on which it can be watched, streamed, downloaded, or purchased. As Anne Sweeney, president of Disney–ABC Television Group, explains: "every new opportunity we create for viewers creates new revenue streams."[3] The marketing department shares these conversations and the data they mine with advertisers. In creating opportunities for fans, they are also offering opportunities for advertisers and channel brands to make contact with potential consumers.

This model would not have emerged without the October 2005 deal that Disney made with Apple. Showing a willingness to take risks, Disney broke with the standard practice of preserving the exclusivity of the on-air television window and distributed its programming directly to viewers through the iTunes Store, and later the abc.com episode player. As I discussed in *Television and New Media*, these changes were promoted in part by concerns about illegal download in relation to Disney content, including ABC's *Lost*. Series producers quickly realized that they would need to leverage new media platforms to sustain viewers for their complex serial mystery, which began as an attempt to use a plane crash storyline to fictionalize the strangers-stranded-on-an-island premise made infamous by the reality series *Survivor. Lost* producers structured the episodes and online extensions so that viewers would feel compelled to watch on-air and then speculate online as they had in relation to *Survivor*.

When *Lost* first aired in the U.S. in 2004, broadcast networks were worrying over the new web-enabled behaviors of audiences, particularly their ability to download episodes illegally. Rather than watching episodes as they aired, audiences were developing the habit of downloading multiple episodes or whole seasons. Assuming illegal downloading would diminish if content providers offered online access to episodes, Disney partnered with Apple to turn iTunes into an alternate distribution platform for television and film. The April–June 2006 trial run of ad-sponsored episodes available on abc.com as streaming Video-On-Demand (VOD) soon followed and led to the upgrade to a HD player.[4] Such players were embedded in branded websites packed with exclusive content to entice site visitors to stick around and to make advertisers see the web as a viable space for attracting audience attention. Sweeney explained, "We've leveraged technology to create new ways to give viewers what they want, while protecting our content from piracy and generating additional revenue."[5]

While initially intended to address piracy concerns, the media player had a significant role in sustaining audiences for *Lost*, which could have been canceled if there were no alternative ways for lapsed viewers to keep up with this long-arc serial mystery. Between the online episodes and the DVD releases, the series was also able to gather new viewers at different points during the first three seasons. Then it trended toward consistently losing viewers, in part because of the complex storytelling structure. Each episode of *Lost* draws on details from a discontinuous set of episodes over the course of the series as a whole, which makes it particularly ill suited to broadcast television. It is much easier to remember all these narrative details and not become so frustrated that you stop watching if you are screening multiple episodes or even seasons in one block of time. The problem with *Lost* was that it could not continue to attract casual viewers and had a hard time getting its current viewers to watch episodes on-air as they aired. It also failed to act as an effective lead-in for other series, most of which were canceled, even in the first four years when it was generating high ratings in the top 20 shows and doing very well for its genre category. (See schedule E.1.)

Viewers of *Lost* were less likely to "go with the flow" of the schedule and watch other shows, several of which had long-arc storylines that ABC programmers clearly assumed would have appeal for *Lost* viewers. Viewers seemed to already be thinking of *Lost* as a stand-alone brand rather than a part of the ABC schedule, which meant that they were most interested in consuming more content from *Lost* or related to *Lost*. The standard scheduling model of getting viewers interested in watching blocks of new television programming is becoming much less feasible in an era in which people watch series in delayed viewing modes.

As one of the series most likely to be illegally downloaded, *Lost* helped prompt the change toward multiplatform distribution and the broad embrace of

SCHEDULE E.1 The ABC schedule grid for the series run of *Lost*, which changed in 2007–8 to a compressed "no repeats" winter/fall schedule in an attempt to retain audience attention.

ABC Network	Day of Week	8:00 p.m.	8.30 p.m.	9:00 p.m.	10:00 p.m.
2004–5	Wednesday Fall	Lost		Bachelor	Wife Swap
	Wednesday Spring	Lost		Alias	Eyes
2005–6	Wednesday Fall	G. Lopez	Freddie	Lost	Invasion
	Wednesday Spring	Alias		Lost	The Evidence / Invasion
2006–7	Wednesday	Dancing with the Stars		Lost	The Nine
2007–8	Thursday Winter	Lost (Reruns)		Lost	Eli Stone
	Thursday Follow-up	Ugly Betty		Grey's Anatomy	Lost
2008–9	Wednesday Winter	Lost (Reruns)		Lost	Life on Mars
	Wednesday Follow-up	Scrubs	Better off Ted	Lost	The Unusuals
2009–10	Wednesday Spring	Dancing with the Stars (Results)		Lost	V

technological advances that enabled it. *Lost* has also been credited with sparking a serial mystery boom during the 2006–8 seasons, and was a model for the kind of long-arc mystery used in *Pretty Little Liars*. With all of the later attention paid to its role in opening the door for complex scripted dramas on network television, it is easy to forget that *Lost* got on the schedule in the first place because ABC executives wanted to counter the reality television dominance of CBS' *Big Brother*, *Amazing Race*, and *Survivor* franchises. It is surprising to see that ABC first scheduled *Lost* alongside *The Bachelor* and *Wife Swap*. With its love triangle and two shirtless hunks, *Lost*'s pairing with *The Bachelor* and later with *Dancing with the Stars* makes some sense. It is important to remember that *Lost* emerged during the period in which ABC was searching for a scripted drama that would have the addictive appeal of *Survivor* and similar reality television programs. Recalling these origins helps illuminate the way *Lost* parallels *Survivor*: its stranding of strangers on an island premise; casting for conflict; embedded challenges that test ordinary people's capacity to navigate extraordinary circumstances; and its generation of suspense through the cultivation of uncertainty about which characters could be trusted and which would survive to appear in another episode. Borrowing audience engagement elements and storytelling techniques from *Survivor*, *Lost* purposefully prompted online speculation about outcomes and character motivations. In its initial seasons, *Lost* also dramatized the distrust among the survivors and encouraged viewers to share those suspicions, especially online.

The web presence of *Lost* was certainly central to its sustainability as a broadcast network series. As co-showrunner Carlton Cuse said, "I think that 'Lost' would never succeed in the pre-Internet era. It's the fact that the show is complicated and intentionally ambiguous; it allows the fans to become involved in its analysis."[6] *BusinessWeek* also attributed *Lost*'s original success to its paratextual existence on the web via official sites and fan sites.[7] The summer between seasons one and two was a period of intense fan activity fed by the production team's release of in-mythology web sites and fan postings of user-generated content related to the circulation of official clues and content.[8] A space for interaction and debate, the web offers a variety of sites for sharing, finding, and circulating information.

The cultural innovation of the *Lost* producers was that they understood, ahead of the many others in the television industry, that fans were worth courting. Their awareness that a primary fan practice is to speculate about outcomes and test out theories led the producers of *Lost* to host their own fan board site called The Fuselage. To transform this site into a hub for online activities, they offered podcasts and interacted on message boards. It was a space in which they could elaborate on controversial content decisions, provide updates, breaking news, and teasers, and keep an eye on viewer response, while providing more in-depth content that could not find a place in the on-air series. The existence of this producer-generated fan site in the mid-2000s was a testament to the changed attitude toward fans and the fact that the cultural penetration of broadband Internet made fans desirable audience members. Producers also tried to entice the fan amplifiers through "The *Lost* Experience," the Alternate Reality Game (ARG) that had at its core a series of interlinked hidden websites associated with the fictional organizations referenced in the on-air series and the actual corporations that were sponsoring the ARG. TV tie-in ARGs are intriguing because they rely on click-based consent by which viewers click on a sponsor's site to find clues for the game. Once there, they have to give their attention to the marketing site in exchange for accessing the series content they desire. It is a new media version of the television paradigm in which viewers exchange attention to advertising in return for entertainment content. Given their anxieties about the impact of DVR use on the ability of advertiser-supported broadcast television to deliver as much audience attention as they once promised in the past, advertisers are shoring up their on-air investments by sponsoring such web content or co-creating hybrid advertising content.

In relation to television brandcasting, the TV tie-in ARG is marketing that does not register at first as marketing because it blurs the lines between content and promotion. In this paradigm viewers' opportunities for interaction (with content) are also opportunities for interaction of consumers with products and for product makers with potential consumers. As Henrik Örenbring says, ARGs exemplify new forms of hybrid promotion that involve "creating opportunities to market texts through other texts." It is easy to see how tie-in ARGs, "fit well with cultural industry goals and strategies of brand building and creating a loyal consumer base."[9]

Lost's ARG and its other new media content encouraged viewers to embark on a circulatory "path of further investigation" that leads "away from" and "back to" the core media text. In this immersive model, the relationship of television series and website is a circulatory one in that the objective is to keep a series alive by keeping viewers ever moving from show to site and back again, all the while keeping the buzz in circulation on the Internet. In the buzz marketing paradigm "encouraging the consumer to purchase is seen as secondary to generating talk about and recognition of the advertised brand."[10] In addition to the usual on-air marketing and popular press advertising, Senior Vice President Mike Benson and his marketing team at ABC turned to other platforms, all to keep people engaged by *Lost* content circulating through the loop of platforms and back to the series: "we thought, 'What about TiVo, DVDs, the iPod, and the Internet?' They are all huge opportunities to drive people back to TV."[11] Fast-forward and the new challenge is to drive smart phone users back to on-air television through incentives to watch episodes on live television.

E.3   Must-Tweet TV: #*Pretty Little Liars*

Echoing Benson's remarks, Danielle Mullin, ABC Family's Vice President of Marketing, concluded, "Buzz-worthy shows come from expert storytelling with jaw-dropping cliffhangers and unanswered questions that leave fans dying to find out what happens next." According to Mullin, the pacing of the social media content rollout for *Pretty Little Liars* was intended to sustain this level of anticipation for new episodes and seasons: "Our team develops creative assets—videos, games, blogs—that incorporate mini-cliffhangers and tantalizing teases, which we then use in the social media space to amplify the conversation."[12]

Mullin made her commentary in May 2012, two years after the season finale of *Lost*, and the platforms and devices on which to engage viewers clearly had proliferated. Television executives and producers now had to worry about viewers distracted from the television set by 4G iPhones and next generation iPads, among other video-enabled smart phones and tablet computers that could be used for quick access to entertainment content and social media utilities. The challenge was to leverage smart phone and tablet computer multitasking in order to sustain live television audiences and continue to sell the promise of their attention to advertisers. This led to "connected viewing" initiatives, which were facilitated by the cultural penetration of text messaging, by the popularity of social networking utilities, and sometimes by the interactive possibilities of tablet computing. *Pretty Little Liars* addressed these audience behaviors first by positioning the use (and abuse) of new media at the center of its storylines and then by organizing its marketing strategies around audience engagement through new media devices and utilities. In this way, *Pretty Little Liars* not only reflected, but also capitalized on the use of social media by its target demographic of 12- to 24-year-olds, particularly their habit of accessing their networks from mobile phones. Cell phones appear in every single scene, not only making them seem like a must-have accessory for every viewer, but also enabling the series to find sponsors among mobile phone manufacturers and service providers.

Other series had relied on such sponsorships and represented the ubiquity of text messaging, but the practice had not yet been at the center of a program's audience engagement strategy. For instance, the title character of *Veronica Mars* carried around a *T-Mobile Sidekick* smart phone and spent a good deal of time text messaging in relation to the private investigation cases she handled for her high school peers.[13] Flying under the radar on two mini-networks (UPN, 2004–6; CW, 2006–7), *Veronica Mars* combined the case-based procedural structure with a long-arc mystery about the upheaval in the wake of the murder of Lilly Kane, Veronica's best friend. Episodes dramatized the reverberations caused by the secrets and mysteries surrounding the circumstances of Lilly's murder. As Veronica investigates that case and others, often aided by her *Sidekick*, the audience learns surprising details about the rest of the community and their secrets. These details suggest parallels between *Veronica Mars* and *Pretty Little Liars*, especially the way they naturalize smart phone use and texting, but some key differences make the latter program much more melodramatic. In *Pretty Little Liars* Alison, the best friend, might not even be dead. If she is indeed alive, it is possible that she is "A," the mysterious cyber terrorizer, especially given that she often was more "frenemy" than friend.

Producers did not link Veronica's phone to their audience engagement strategies. It was less a missed opportunity than a reflection of the limitations of the smart phone technology at the time, the minimal budget for the series, and the relative obscurity of the network on which it initially aired.[14] *Pretty Little Liars* leveraged its characters' smart phones in a more effective way than had been possible in 2004 because newer models have more speed and functionality, including video, sharing, and synching capabilities. They can be connected to social networking sites or Twitter and, thereby, broadly and instantly disseminate information (as well as incriminating photographs and videos). These features were integrated thematically into the program, but they also proved useful in its promotion.

From the outset *Pretty Little Liars* relied on an innovative and extensive Social TV strategy and its smart phone-optimized mobile site. Producers engaged viewers as participants alongside characters in the investigation into those responsible for the cyber stalking. The production team tapped into new communications technologies to offer a simultaneous audience experience for those watching the series on broadcast television. The in-episode text messages had their parallels in the actual texts sent to viewers' phones. On-air prompts reminded viewers that they could sign up to receive such texts from "A," which often included exclusive videos. Contributing to the sense that new media users were getting special access and insider information, series creator Marlene King tweeted every day from the set and she and the other producers actively worked to generate conversations in the social space.[15] As Mullin put it, the interactions on social media create "a tremendous amount of excitement among our fans. They're also a marketing dream come true—always reminding fans to tune-in and actively supporting all our marketing activities."[16] King and others from the production team and cast embraced all these activities and often participated in live tweeting or Twitter Q & A sessions. She declared, "We love Twitter; we love Facebook . . . You're talking to people in Brazil, in China. Gosh, if I were 14 years old and I could've tweeted the creator of a TV show while sitting in my bedroom—and they're tweeting back—I'd be delighted."[17] Judging by the number of Twitter followers each has, some of the actors are an even bigger draw on these platforms. Dalia Ganz, the program's social-media manager, calls attention to the appeal of the offer of this kind of access to the stars. She requires them to stay on Twitter during episodes and then posts pictures of them while they are tweeting.[18] The most active star is Ashley Benson (Hanna) with over 14,200 tweets and 2.99 million followers. Although Lucy Hale (Aria) is only in the range of 10,000 tweets, she had gathered over 3.73 million followers by 2014.

A quick read through the promotional tweets within their feeds is indicative of how Twitter became the most significant part of the Social TV strategy for *Pretty Little Liars*. By 2011 the series had landed in Twitter's top trending television series. The series website provided a list of the Twitter handles of the characters and actors, so new viewers could easily track and join the conversation. The on-air series promoted its Twitter topics when *#PLL* and other hashtags such as *#WhoIsA?*, #tobyisback, and #thebetrAyal appeared on the bottom of the screen, prompting viewers to use mobile devices to tweet as they watched. In this same manner special events like the Twitter countdown to the Halloween Special or the season finales were particularly promoted. Participating on Twitter provided viewers with access to content that would not be available from merely watching an episode.

As evidence that the strategy worked, producers cited the fact that the hashtags were top trending topics on Twitter, a status achieved in part because of their practice of generating specific clickable hashtagged topics around which viewers could engage and circulate content. Their success was evident in June 2012 when the show dominated eight of the ten top trending topics on Twitter.[19] According to Socialbakers analytics, *Pretty Little Liars* reached one million Twitter followers by 2013 and was adding new ones at a rate of almost 5,000 a day (reaching 22.1 million by May 2014).[20] A big milestone came on August 28, 2012 when *Pretty Little Liars* achieved 1.6 million social media comments on Twitter and Facebook combined for the season finale episode, "The Lady Killer" (3.12), thereby displacing the number one status of the May 2012 *American Idol* season 11 finale, which had garnered 1.4 million social media comments.[21] At the time, *Pretty Little Liars* held spots three through five for other episodes in June 2012, March 2012, and January 2012.

These records were set with the help of multiplatform engagement strategies like "The BetrayAyal Suspect Tracker." In this summer 2012 second-screen initiative, created by Mass Relevance, each of the twelve characters got a dedicated Twitter stream and viewers were asked to speculate about which one was "guilty of the ultimate betrayal."[22] Site visitors were invited to "click on the photo to see what fans are saying" about each suspect. Speculations were tabulated through dedicated hashtag voting. To measure the accuracy of their predictions, players had to watch each episode after the experience was launched midseason. "By clicking on each character's photo, fans can get immersed in social conversations."[23] To find the answers, they had to then "watch the summer finale Tuesday, August 28" because it promised to expose the betrAyer and answer some of the questions. In the meantime, they could click on the character thumbnails and track how many votes a suspect was accumulating.

An online scavenger hunt game called "Pretty Little Puzzle Hunt," was also launched to generate excitement for the 2012 summer season. The rebus puzzle had pieces scattered across fifteen websites. Putting the pieces together in the right order created a riddle that players needed to answer in order to unlock the exclusive sneak peek. This feature had the added appeal of being initiated by the cyber terrorizer known as "A," described by the marketing team as "the voice" of online engagement activities.[24]

Building up to the January 2013 premiere, producers created a real-time, Twitter-based scavenger hunt. This time the person now revealed to be "A" tweeted the clues that would take players around the web until they found the way to unlock the secret video. Once again, the goal of the content–promotion hybrid was to sustain the anticipation and drive tune-in to the season premiere. With this strategy, ABC Family producers were trying to control sequencing because this extra content would have to be viewed in order, and thereby build anticipation in the days prior to the on-air premiere. The same motivation prompted the "Interactive Countdown Calendar" feature on the series website and the creation of a fake Twitter account for one of the villains who then live-tweeted clues that led a secret video. In the process the account amassed 54,000 followers within four days.[25] Such content–promotion rollouts are intended to put viewers in the right frame of mind for watching the new episode. Leading the audience in a series of well-paced rounds of speculation generated excitement for the premiere. Their speculation would then become part of the hype preceding the new season, and even those not directly participating were likely to hear the buzz and hopefully tune-in live.

The team found many other innovative ways to deliver clues to hungry viewers. As ABC Family's Michelle Walenz, said, "We know that our viewers devour any new clues about the incredible mystery and heightened suspense."[26] The marketers scattered those clues across platforms with the intention of sustaining audience engagement with the series and heightening interest in the new season. Leveraging yet another platform, they released a music video: Z. Z. Ward's "When the Casket Drops." The video had an embedded hashtag (#Agame) to promote the summer 2012 season. The duality of this video as content and promotion is clear from a glance at the resulting social conversations about the music and the series. Music was also promoted on the website through its "Celebrity Playlists" (i.e., the top five songs in each actor's playlist). It was just one of many special topics links (e.g., "Style Files" videos) now common on program sites offering an array of content–promotion hybrids.[27] These elements also reflect how the website functioned as a consumer space where one could find products and purchase information about the fashions, accessories, and music showcased on television series. As with *Lost*'s websites, those for *Pretty Little Liars* were also spaces in which to extend storytelling by developing backstories, alternative points of view, and minor characters, as well as to transform fans into brand amplifiers as well as information gatherers.

The series website continued the emphasis on social media interaction. For the hiatus after the summer 2012 season and before the Halloween Special, the team launched *Pretty Dirty Secrets*, 2- to 3-minute webisodes that ran in the series' usual timeslot for eight consecutive Tuesday nights.[28] The uploaded content was part of the strategy for sustaining a desired level of excitement, for enabling the program to retain viewers in its designated timeslot, and for attaining social buzz. Walenz knew her team could count on fans circulating commentary about the series around the web: "we really wanted to highlight new clues for them that we think will generate posts, tweets, and blogs." This strategy is most effective when it taps into what viewers are talking about in the social media space and when it also serves to remind viewers of the details from the story arcs that help them interpret upcoming episodes. There is a circularity to the approach because fans will always be "speculating about what happens next" when the producers and the social media team give them a good deal to speculate about. Mullin uses the sustainability rhetoric to explain the strategy of keeping the momentum going between seasons "by not letting a day go by without giving fans more content to be excited about." For instance, when the summer 2012 finale offered a resolution to one part of the mystery, it opened a new layer to the story because the episode also revealed that the mystery about what happened to Alison was always more complex than it appeared. Mullin explains the post-finale strategy to maintain the series' infinitely delayed resolution and hence to hold viewer interest: "we've been actively messaging via ABCFamily.com, Twitter and Facebook that the reveal of 'A' was just the beginning and that the mystery runs much deeper than this one person."[29]

In addition to driving and sustaining tune-in to episodes as they aired, the social media activities also provided an actual record of viewer investment and reaction in real time. In addition to tossing "virtual goodies to fans," Ganz "tracks who's watching, and what they are saying." Such audience attention had value in negotiating deals with advertisers. As Ganz remarked about the Twitter data, "commercials often trend" and the team tracks for that and "we share that information with advertisers."[30] Rick Haskins, of marketing and brand strategy at CW network, likens sending out program information to Facebook friends and Twitter followers to a media buy. Channeling messaging through social media and reaching millions of fans instantly is "the most efficient, effective media buy you can do. And by the way, it's free."[31] By March 2013 *Pretty Little Liars* would reach over ten million on Facebook and one million on Twitter (#ABCFpll). Mullin attributed the success of the *Pretty Little Liars* strategy to the ways the team used social media spaces as a friend would, and "friends don't only talk to you between 9 and 5." She explains, "We act like a friend to our fans," adding "friends don't use a corporate tone of voice when they talk to you." Mullin explains that *Pretty Little Liars*' Twitter followers, Facebook friends, and the like "actually do think they're speaking to their friend. And that's a really incredible opportunity for marketers."[32]

Social media has certainly expanded the reach of messaging and made it all feel more intimate, but addressing viewers as virtual friends had been a strategy already in use when the high school-set series *Dawson's Creek* aired on the WB, the early-2000s equivalent of the CW network. Will Brooker details how the website for the fictional town in the series offers links to the "handwritten personal journals of Dawson and his crew, invites the visitor to catch up with 'your friends on Capeside', rather than admitting their status as fictional characters." With the many in-character features on these sites (such as receiving emails from a character), they permit "the illusion that the characters have ongoing lives between episodes." Coining the term "overflow," Brooker analyzes how the site visitor is "invited to extend the show's pleasures, to allow the show into her everyday life beyond the scheduling framework." In the overflow model the viewer is offered the place of "confidante, knowing the character intimately and immersing herself in the protagonist's life."[33] Twitter takes this to another level and allows viewers to feel as if they are part of the everyday lives of the actors playing their favorite characters. Ruth Page would say that the key phrase here is "feel as if," because celebrity tweets often take the form of promotional blasts that position followers as a "fanbase to be managed rather than as individual peers."[34]

E.4   From *"Mad*-vertising" *Mad Men* to Mad Predictions

Of course all of the brandcasting strategies discussed in this book and the endorsements they imply do not necessarily create new viewers or consumers. The U.S. television industry's recent attempt to leverage viewers is an implicit acknowledgment that programmers, promoters, and schedulers have very little control over audience behavior and engage in a good deal of speculation about audience tastes and values. The good news for them is that the advertiser-supported television industry model continues to rely on the clearly flawed practice of selling advertisers the *idea* that certain programs and promotions can attract *"effective* audiences," those that, as Philip Napoli puts it, "can be efficiently integrated into the economics of media institutions."[35] In the television brandcasting model, *effective* television audiences are those that have the potential to be engaged and mobilized to answer calls-to-action that involve both consuming related content or products and proselytizing for brands.

Reception behaviors are notoriously hard to predict. As a result, programmers and schedulers are often the victims of their false assumptions about what television viewers will and will not do. Even the much vaunted purveyor of quality drama HBO falls victim to miscalculations about audience behavior. It famously passed on *Mad Men*, even though it had first look at the series because of the work creator Matt Weiner had done on HBO's *The Sopranos*. The success of *Mad Men* launched AMC as a quality television channel brand. This new brand identity, in turn, led to pitches for other quality drama series, including *Breaking Bad*. AMC started winning Emmy Awards, and in doing so chipped away at HBO's self-representation as THE place on the channel spectrum for quality dramas. The added bonus for AMC as a basic cable channel still partially funded by advertising was that advertisers wanted to be associated with quality dramas, especially *Mad Men* because its advertising industry subject matter enabled them to engage in some innovative custom campaigns.

The underwriting deal Jack Daniel's whiskey made for *Mad Men* represents a return to 1950s style branded entertainment. An executive from Universal McCann that helped set up the Jack Daniel's underwriting explains that *Mad Men*'s branded entertainment and its coordination of its commercial spots is representative of a new kind of television sponsorship, "one that capitalizes on subject matter," by calibrating the flow between story segments to reflect it.[36] Jack Daniel's underwrote the interstitial spots featuring "legendary advertising execs who share their stories of what it was like to work in the business at that time." A particularly effective tie-in to the show was the one was about George Lois, the self-described "Greek big mouth" Korean War vet who branded Xerox and created Doyle Dane Bernbach's "Think Small" and "Lemon" Volkswagen print ads on which Don Draper's creative team comment in episode 1.3.[37] While the fictional team is resistant to adapting its strategy to a changing media landscape, often underestimating the impact of new media (e.g., television), new products (e.g., imported small cars) and demographics (e.g., youth culture) on the advertising industry, AMC took a risk when it acquired *Mad Men*. It was its first original drama series from Lionsgate, newly launched as an independent willing to embrace new media approaches to content distribution and advertising and offering a features approach to marketing its TV productions. Together they opted for multiplatform advertising, incorporated a social networking presence (e.g., Facebook and Twitter accounts), created a content-immersive faux *Advertising Age* insert, hired flash mobs to attract attention in Grand Central Terminal, where *Mad Men* billboards had a large presence near subway entrances, and developed the unique *Mad*-vertising interstitial and commercial pod pairings obviously designed to discourage the fast-forwarding through commercials that is made possible by DVR viewing.

In addition to on-air buys, *Mad Men* offers companies the opportunity to split time buys between television and alternate content delivery platforms (such as Jack Daniel's sponsorship of the series' website and the Zippo lighter collaboration on the Zippo-style DVD case).[38] A company could distribute its purchase time across multiple media platforms or it could be the single sponsor of one off-air platform or some aspect of special content on offer there. Of course, any kind of deal can be tailored to whatever is the company's desired percentage of branded entertainment sponsorship or spot-oriented magazine sponsorship. Such variety, advertising executive Benjamin Palmer notes, is indicative of how today's producers and advertisers are not that different from those in the *Mad Men* era: "Even before the internet, advertising has always had to come up with a point of view that would work well in a magazine, on a sign, along the side of a bus, or on TV, all at the same time."[39] Don Draper is adept at such flexibility.

Mad Men also adopted a strategy to drive tune-in to the on-air series. It coordinated relevant commercial pods within the usual magazine-style TV advertising. The pods were made more memorable with its *Mad*-vertising, which paired advertising for pharmaceuticals such as Viagra with interstitials offering factoids about the drug. For example one title card read: "Prescription drugs could not be advertised on television in the United States until 1997" and preceded a commercial for Caduet, anti-hypertension medication that Don might have benefitted from taking.[40] Creator Matt Weiner opined that it would have been easier to have a single sponsor "during the whole show and tie them into the show." He applauds the *Mad*-vertising concept, however, saying "It looks like something Don Draper would have thought of."[41] It is doubtful that Weiner would actually want to enter into a traditional single sponsorship deal given his comments about the restrictions associated with the multi-episode presence of Jack Daniel's. The biggest complaint about single sponsorship in the 1950s was loss of creative control.[42] After interviewing 1950s and 1960s TV producers, Nina Liebman concluded: "The constant and vocal presence of the sponsor's or the agency's representative on the set steered programs toward the sponsor's perspective. The look of a program was often altered after a script was written as the sponsor and producer cooperated to portray the product (nameless but visible) in the best possible light."[43] In contrast, Weiner wants to use products to create texture to his story, not to sell the products. That worked fine when he was a production worker on premium subscription cable, but it is not completely practical on AMC as it is a basic cable channel, that is, at least in part, advertiser-supported. Whether he likes it or not, Weiner (and every showrunner today) is in the advertising business as well as the business of entertainment.[44]

As *Television Brandcasting* has shown, U.S. television has always been a brand platform, but the brands have typically been thought of as advertisers' products, television channels, and sometimes star brands. With series becoming brands in their own right and sold to individual consumers sometimes on an episode-by-episode basis and sometimes on a season pass basis, it makes sense that many cable providers' interfaces have become more brandcentric. In an era marked by simultaneity of models, the classic network era's familiar grid schedule has not disappeared, but in the on-air arena it must coexist with the content menu concept utilized by off-television content providers like Netflix. To try to match the appeal of the position of television series as stand-alone brands available on alternate distribution platforms, digital cable providers offer their viewers access both to a standard grid (now interactive and informational), and alternative modes of searching for scheduled and on-demand programs. Accommodating the multitasking viewer, the grid and the alternative content menus can be accessed in full screen or as a split between viewing panes. With the grid open in a column format next to the viewing pane as a list of current programming for the current time slot, the viewer can watch and channel surf. With the content window minimized alongside a reading pane open to the full primetime schedule grid, the viewer can watch, while organizing later content choices.

Of course, viewers have to be willing to watch television on television in the first place for this brandcentric recommendation menuing to matter. Since the late 2000s the story has been that young viewers will not watch television on television. Yet, smart producers have found ways to leverage the position of television programs as standalone brands as a way to create branded new media spaces around individual programs and then utilize the buzz built through web and mobile content to bring viewers back to television. Of particular interest are the producers who counter the challenge of new media technologies and platforms for the attention of potential viewers by engaging the smart phone "multitasker" through connected viewing initiatives like "live tweeting" or through special content designed for in-the-moment interactivity between iPad tablets and television series. I am an obstinate optimist about the future of the Must-Click TV model enabling on-air television to continue to exist. I am betting on some current Disney Channel viewers and future entrepreneurs to find a way to brandcast themselves into a power broker position, and then create some new kind of content–promotion hybrid to keep people tuning in to television. Maybe they will even be best friends who manage not to let success come before friendship. Or maybe at this point I have just seen too many Disney Channel Original Movies.

Notes

1 Anderson 2006, 55, 107–10.
2 Jenkins 2006, 293 and chapter 3 "Searching for the Origami Unicorn: The Matrix and Transmedia Storytelling," 93–130.
3 Adler 2011.
4 Disney–ABC Television Group 2006.
5 Adler 2011.
6 Marikar 2007.
7 Gray 2008 considers the way a TV series now exists within a pre-release flow of hype that shapes the text's meaning on other platforms before it ever exists as an on-air show.
8 Lowry 2006.
9 Örnebring 2007, 448, 450.
10 Örnebring 2007, both quotations from p. 35.
11 Lowry 2006. ABC Press Release 2006.
12 Edelsburg 2012.
13 I address these elements in *Television and New Media*, 55–65.
14 *Veronica Mars* (2004–7) is fascinating for the way the fanbase for the cult television series remained active enough online that it could be leveraged for a Kickstarter campaign that became the foundational financing for a feature film released in March 2014.
15 Edelsburg 2012.
16 Ibid.
17 Villarreal 2011.
18 Ulaby 2012.
19 Dowling 2012.
20 See Socialbakers posts on current Facebook statistics at, www.socialbakers.com/facebook-pages/291824160232-pretty-little-liars and those for Twitter at, www.socialbakers.com/twitter/abcfpll.
21 Dowling 2012. *Pretty Little Liars* was soon displaced from the top spot by *The X-Factor*, which came in at 1.9 million in December 2012. Then the big "event television" programming of winter 2013 took all the top spots. The Super Bowl XLVII on February 3, 2013 topped the list with a likely unbeatable 30.6 million social media comments. See http://bostinno.streetwise.co/channels/pretty-little-liars-summer-finale-breaks-social-tv-record/ and www.ooyala.com/es/videomind/archive/key-trends-2012-social-tv-season-infographic.

22 The Suspect Tracker won a 2013 SHORTY industry award for Best Use of Social Media for Television. The campaign rationale and home page are featured at: http://industry. shortyawards.com/nominee/5th_annual/Tz/pretty-little-liars-thebetrayal-campaign.
23 Ibid.
24 Both quotations from Edelsburg 2012.
25 Seles 2013.
26 Edelsburg 2012.
27 ABC Family often posts insider fashion videos, among other features. See, for example, http://abcfamily.go.com/news/listing/pretty-little-liars/get-the-look-pretty-little-liars-halloween-special\.
28 For a discussion of the webisodes, see http://mashable.com/2012/08/29/pretty-dirty-secrets-web-series-pretty-little-liars/. The webisodes are available as of August 2014 at www.youtube.com/watch?v=2wTe6abCjx8.
29 All the quotations are from Edelsburg 2012.
30 Both quotations are from Ulaby 2012.
31 Villarreal 2011.
32 All the these quotations are from Ulaby 2012.
33 All the quotations are from Brooker 2001, 460, 461.
34 Page 2012, 195.
35 Napoli 2003, 3.
36 Jaffee 2007.
37 Witchel 2008.
38 Elliot 2007.
39 Hitt 2008.
40 Flaherty 2008.
41 Benton 2008.
42 Boddy 1993, 160–3.
43 Liebman 1995, 110
44 Jaffee 2007.

Bibliography

ABC Press Release. "'Lost' Game Lets Fans Hunt for Clues." abcnews.go.com, April 24, 2006. Available: http://abcnews.go.com/Entertainment/story?id=1881142.

Adler, Tim. "MIPCOM: Disney–ABC TV Boss Anne Sweeney Says Television Will Get Even More Personal." [Transcript of Sweeney's MIPCOM Keynote Speech]. Deadline/Hollywood [Blog], October 5, 2011. Available: www.deadline.com/2011/10/mipcom-disney-abc-tv-boss-anne-sweeney-says-television-will-get-even-more-personal/.

Anderson, Chris. *The Long Tail: Why the Future of Business is Selling Less of More*. New York, NY: Hyperion, 2006.

Aslinger, Ben. "Rocking Prime Time: Gender, the WB, and Teen Culture." In Ross and Stein 2008, 78–91.

Benkler, Yochai. *The Wealth of Networks: How Social Production Transforms Markets and Freedom*. New Haven, CT: Yale University Press, 2007.

Benton, Joshua. "'Mad Men' Ads Keep You On Your Couch." Nieman Journalism Lab at Harvard. [Blogs]. October 3, 2008. Available: www.niemanlab.org/2008/10/mad-men-ads-keep-you-on-your-couch/.

Boddy, William. *Fifties Television: The Industry and its Critics.* Urbana and Chicago, IL: University of Illinois Press, 1993.

Bolter, Jay David and Richard Grusin. *Remediation: Understanding New Media.* Cambridge, MA: MIT Press, 1999.

Boyd, Dana. "Why Youth Heart Social Network Sites: The Role of Networked Publics in Teenage Social Life." In *Youth, Identity, and Digital Media*, ed. David Buckingham, 119–42. Cambridge, MA: MIT Press, 2008.

Brooker, Will. "Living on Dawson's Creek: Teen Viewers, Cultural Convergence, and Television Overflow." *International Journal of Cultural Studies* 4, no. 4 (2001): 456–72.

Caldwell, John Thornton. "Convergence Television: Aggregating Form and Repurposing Content in the Culture of Conglomeration." In Spigel and Olsson 2004, 41–74.

——. "Critical Industrial Practice: Branding, Repurposing, and the Migratory Patterns of Industrial Texts." *Television & New Media* 7, no. 2 (May 2006): 99–134.

——. "Cultures of Production: Studying Industry's Deep Texts, Reflexive Rituals, and Managed Self-Disclosures." In *Media Industries: History, Theory and Method*, eds. Jennifer Holt and Alisa Perren, 199–212. Malden, MA: Blackwell, 2009.

——. "Para-Industry: Researching Hollywood's Backwaters." *Cinema Journal* 53, no. 3 (2013): 157–65.

——. *Production Culture: Industrial Reflexivity and Critical Practice in Film and Television.* Durham, NC: Duke University Press, 2008.

——. *Televisuality: Style, Crisis, and Authority in American Television.* New Brunswick, NJ: Rutgers University Press, 1995.

——. "Welcome to the Viral Future of Cinema (Television)." *Cinema Journal* 45, no. 1 (Fall 2006): 90–7.

Caves, Richard E. *Creative Industries: Contracts between Art and Commerce.* Cambridge, MA: Harvard University Press, 2000.

Disney–ABC Television Group. "Disney–ABC Television Group Takes ABC Primetime Online." Press Release, corporatedisney.go.com, April 10, 2006. Available: http://thewaltdisneycompany.com/disney-news/press-releases/2006/04/disney-abc-television-group-takes-abc-primetime-online-offering.

Dowling, Eleanor. "Pretty Little Liars Summer Finale Breaks Social TV Record." Bluefin Labs [Blog], August 29, 2012. Available: http://bostinno.streetwise.co/channels/pretty-little-liars-summer-finale-breaks-social-tv-record/ and www.ooyala.com/es/videomind/archive/key-trends-2012-social-tv-season-infographic.

Edelsburg, Natan. "How ABC Family is Using Social Media to Launch the New Season of 'Pretty Little Liars.'" *LostRemote: The Home of Social TV* [Blog], May 31, 2012. Available: http://lostremote.com/abc-familys-social-tv-strategy-for-the-new-season-of-pretty-little-liars_b29988.

Elliot, Stuart. "What Was Old is New as TV Revisits Branding." *New York Times*, June 13, 2007.

Flaherty, Mike. "AMC introduces 'Mad-vertising': Blurbs reference products and theme of 'Men.'" *Variety*, August 22, 2008.

Foster, Derek. "'Jump in the Pool,' The Competitive Culture of Survivor Fan Networks." In *Understanding Reality Television*, eds. Su Holmes and Deborah Jermyn, 270–89. London, UK: Routledge, 2004.

Gillan, Jennifer. "Fashion Sleuths and Aerie Girls: *Veronica Mars*' Fan Forums and Network Strategies of Fan Address." In Ross and Stein 2008, 185–206.

——. "Kodak, Jack and Coke: Advertising and *Mad-vertising* on *Mad Men*." In *Analyzing Mad Men: Critical Essays on the Series*, ed. Scott F. Stoddart, 95–116. Jefferson, NC and London, UK: McFarland, 2011.

———. *Television and New Media: Must-Click TV.* New York, NY: Routledge, 2010.

Grainge, Paul. *Brand Hollywood: Selling Entertainment in a Global Media Age.* New York, NY: Routledge, 2008.

Gray, Jonathan. *Show Sold Separately: Promos, Spoilers, and Other Media Paratexts.* New York, NY: New York University Press, 2010.

———. "Television Pre-views and the Meaning of Hype." *International Journal of Cultural Studies* 11, no. 1 (March 2008): 33–49.

Gray, Jonathan and Jason Mittell. "Speculation on Spoilers: *Lost* Fandom, Narrative Consumption, and Rethinking Textuality." *Particip@tions: Journal of Audience and Reception Studies* 4, no.1 (2007). Available: www.participations.org/Volume%204/Issue%20 1/4_01_graymittell.htm.

Gripsrud, Jostein. "Broadcast Television: The Chances of Its Survival in a Digital Age." In Spigel and Olsson 2004, 210–23.

Gwenllian-Jones, Sara and Roberta E. Pearson, eds. *Cult Television.* Minneapolis, MN: Minnesota University Press, 2004.

Haralovich, Mary Beth and Michael W. Trosset. "'Expect the Unexpected': Narrative Pleasure and Uncertainty Due to Chance in *Survivor.*" In Murray and Ouellette 2004, 75–96.

Harries, Dan. ed. "Watching the Internet." *The New Media Book.* 171–82. London, UK: BFI Publishing, 2002.

Hartley, John. "From the Consciousness Industries to the Creative Industries: Consumer-Created Content, Social Network Markets, and the Growth of Knowledge." In *Media Industries: History, Theory, and Method*, eds. Jennifer Holt and Alisa Perren, 231–45. Malden, MA: Wiley-Blackwell, 2009.

Hill, Annette. "Big Brother, the Real Audience." *Television & New Media* 3, no. 3 (August 2002): 323–40.

———. *Reality TV: Audiences and Popular Factual Television.* London, UK: Routledge, 2005.

Hills, Matt. "*Dawson's Creek*: 'Quality Teen TV' and 'Mainstream Cult?'" In *Teen TV: Genre, Consumption and Identity*, eds. Glyn Davis and Kay Dickinson, 54–67. London, UK: BFI Publishing, 2004.

———. *Fan Cultures.* New York, NY: Routledge, 2002.

Hitt, Jack, moderator. "Multiscreen Mad Men." *New York Times Magazine*, November 23, 2008.

Holt, Jennifer and Kevin Sanson, eds. *Connected Viewing: Selling, Streaming, and Sharing Media in the Digital Age.* New York, NY: Routledge, 2013.

Jaffee, Larry. "All the Mad Men." *Promo Magazine* 20, no. 8, August 1, 2007. 28.

Jancovich, Mark and Nathan Hunt. "The Mainstream, Distinction, and Cult TV." In Gwenllian-Jones and Pearson 2004, 27–44.

Jancovich, Mark and James Lyons, eds. *Quality Popular Television.* London, UK: BFI Publishing, 2003.

Jaramillo, Deborah L. "The Family Racket: AOL-Time Warner, HBO, *The Sopranos*, and the Construction of a Quality Brand." *Journal of Communication Inquiry* 26, no. 1 (2002): 59–75.

Jenkins, Henry. *Convergence Culture: Where Old and New Media Collide.* New York, NY: New York University Press, 2006.

Jenkins, Henry and David Thornburn, eds. *Democracy and New Media.* Cambridge, MA: MIT Press, 2003.

Jenkins, Henry, Sam Ford, and Joshua Green, *Spreadable Media: Creating Value and Meaning in a Networked Culture.* New York, NY: New York University Press, 2013.

Johnson, Catherine. *Branding Television*. New York, NY: Routledge, 2012.

Johnson, Derek. "The Fictional Institutions of *Lost*: World Building, Reality and the Economic Possibilities of Narrative Divergence." In Pearson 2009, 27–49.

——. "Inviting Audiences In: The Spatial Reorganization of Production and Consumption in 'TV III.'" *New Review of Film and Television Studies*. 5, no. 1 (April 2007): 61–80.

Kelly, Liz and Jen Chaney. "Pre-Season 5 Lost Finale: Q & A With Showrunners Carlton Cuse and Damon Lindelof." *The Washington Post*, May 13, 2009.

Kirby, Justin and Paul Marsden, eds. *Connected Marketing: The Viral, Buzz, and Word of Mouth Revolution*. Oxford, UK: Butterworth-Heinemann, 2005.

Liebman, Nina. *Living Room Lectures: The Fifties Family in Film & Television*. Austin, TX: University of Texas Press, 1995.

Leverette, Marc, Brian L. Ott, and Cara Louise Buckley, eds. *It's Not TV: Watching HBO in the Post-television Era*. New York, NY: Routledge, 2008.

Lévy, Pierre. *Collective Intelligence: Mankind's Emerging World in Cyberspace*, trans. Robert Bononno. Cambridge, MA: Perseus, 1997.

——. *Cyberculture*, trans. Robert Bononno. Minneapolis, MN: University of Minnesota Press, 2001.

Lotz, Amanda. *The Television Will Be Revolutionized*. New York, NY: New York University Press, 2007.

Lowry, Tom. "Network Finds a Marketing Paradise with 'Lost': Using Podcast, Interactive Games, Web sites, and Good Old-fashioned Hype, ABC Has Turned a Cult-Style Show into a Cross-media Sensation." *BusinessWeek*, July 24, 2006.

Marikar, Shelia. "'Lost' Producers Promise a Showdown Now, Answers Later." abc.news. com. May 21, 2007. Available: http://abcnews.go.com/Entertainment/story?id=3197096.

Mittell, Jason. "Lost in An Alternate Reality." *FlowTV* 4, no. 7, June 16, 2006. Available: http://flowtv.org/2006/06/lost-in-an-alternate-reality/.

Murray, Simone. "'Celebrating the Story as the Way It Is': Cultural Studies, Corporate Media, and the Contested Utility of Fandom." *Continuum: The Journal of Media and Cultural Studies* 18, no.1 (2004): 7–25.

Murray, Susan and Laurie Ouellette, eds. *Reality TV: Remaking Television Culture*. New York, NY: New York University Press, 2004.

Napoli, Philip M. *Audience Economics: Media Institutions and The Audience Marketplace*. New York, NY: Columbia, 2003.

Örnebring, Henrik. "Alternate Reality Gaming and Convergence Culture: The Case of *Alias*." *International Journal of Cultural Studies* 10, no. 4 (2007): 445–62.

Page, Ruth. "The Linguistics of Self-branding and Micro-celebrity in Twitter: The Role of Hashtags." *Discourse and Communication* 6, no. 2 (2012): 181–201.

Parks, Lisa. "Flexible Microcasting: Gender, Generation, and Television-Internet Convergence." In Spigel and Olsson 2004,133–56.

Pearson, Roberta, ed. *Reading Lost: Perspectives on a Hit Television Show*. London, UK: I.B. Tauris, 2009.

Peitzman, Louis. "Eight Reasons You Should Be Watching ABC Family." Buzz Feed Entertainment, Feb 26, 2013. Available: http://www.buzzfeed.com/louispeitzman/reasons-you-should-be-watching-abc-family.

Rogers, Mark C., Michael Epstein, and Jimmie L. Reeves. "*The Sopranos* as HBO Brand Equity: The Arts and Commerce in the Age of Digital Reproduction." In *This Thing of Ours: Investigating The Sopranos*, ed. David Lavery, 42–57. New York, NY: Columbia University Press, 2002.

Ross, Sharon Marie. *Beyond the Box: Television and the Internet*. Malden, MA: Blackwell, 2008.

Ross, Sharon Marie and Louisa Ellen Stein, eds. *Teen Television: Essays on Programming and Fandom*. Jefferson, NC and London, UK: McFarland, 2008.

Seiter, Ellen. *Television and New Media Audiences*. Oxford, UK: Oxford University Press, 1999.

Seles, Sheila. "The Transmedia Genius of Pretty Little Liars." Bluefin Labs [Blog], January 9, 2013. Available: www.scoop.it/t/transmedia-storytelling-for-the-digital-age/p/3994801721/2013/01/10/the-transmedia-genius-of-pretty-little-liars.

Spigel, Lynn and Jan Olsson, eds. *Television After TV: Essays on a Medium in Transition*. Durham, NC: Duke University Press, 2004.

Staid, Gitte. "Mobile Identity: Youth, Identity, and Mobile Communication Media." In *Youth, Identity, and Digital Media*, ed. David Buckingham, 143–64. Cambridge, MA: MIT Press, 2008.

Stein, Louisa. *Millennial/Fandom: Television Audiences in the Transmedia Age*. Iowa City, IA: University of Iowa Press, 2015.

——. "Pushing at the Margins: Teenage Angst in Teen TV and Audience Response." In Ross and Stein 2008, 224–43.

——. "'This Dratted Thing': Fannish Storytelling Through New Media." In *Fan Fiction and Fan Communities in the Age of the Internet: New Essays*, eds. Karen Hellekson and Kristina Busse, 245–60. Jefferson, NC: McFarland, 2006.

Tapscott, Don. *Growing up Digital: The Rise of the Net Generation*. New York, NY: McGraw-Hill, 1999.

Tryon, Chuck. *Reinventing Cinema: Movies in the Age of Media Convergence*. New Brunswick, NJ: Rutgers University Press, 2010.

Ulaby, Neda. "Ratings Success? It's All in the (ABC) Family." National Public Radio (NPR), October 22, 2012. Available: www.wbur.org/npr/163252267.

Ulin, Jeffery C. *The Business of Media Distribution: Monetizing Film, TV, and Video Content in an Online World*. 2nd edition. New York, NY: Focal Press, 2014.

Uricchio, William. "Old Media and New Media: Television." In Harries 2002, 219–30.

——. "Television's Next Generation: Technology/Interface Culture/Flow." In Spigel and Olsson 2004, 163–82.

van Dijck, José. *The Culture of Connectivity: A Critical History of Social Media*. Oxford, UK: Oxford University Press, 2013.

Vance, Ashlee. "Netflix, Reed Hastings Survive Missteps to Join Silicon Valley's Elite." *Bloomberg Businessweek*, May 9, 2013.

Villarreal, Yvonne. "'Pretty Little Liars' Finds and Keeps Fans on Social Media." *Los Angeles Times*, February 9, 2011.

Witchel, Alex "'Mad Men' Has its Moment." *New York Times Magazine*. June 22, 2008. Available: www.nytimes.com/2008/06/22/magazine/22madmen-t.html?partner=permalink&exprod=permalink.

INDEX

Page numbers in *italics* denote illustrations

ABC 10, 18, 20, 37, 67–8, 71, 73, 93, 94–114, 172, 249; aspirational programming 94–5, 96; cancelling of *Gidget* 121; "connected viewing" initiatives 254; and Disney 12, 95, 96, 216; and *Lost* 94, 249–53; mid-1970s ratings dominance 134–8; as middlecaster 95–7; movement toward teen-centric series 118; programs and scheduling 96–139; suburban sitcoms 95; *TGIF* programming block 138–9; *Thursday's Girls* schedule promotions 127–32; Tween Fridays 132–4, *133*; Tween Tuesdays 135, *135*, *137; see also* individual programs
ABC Family 12, 95, 139, 249, 257; social media/Twitter and *Pretty Little Liars* 255–9
ABC Silver Anniversary Special 135–6
Adventures of Ozzie & Harriet, The 19, 34, 37, 38, 65, 97, 100–2, *104*, 112, 117; and Coca Cola 52–4, *53*; dramatized advertisements 50–2, 56–60, 61; embedded music video structure 100, 101; and Hotpoint 58, 60–1, *61*; and Kodak 8–9, 36, 54–6, *55*, *57*, *58*; pairings with other programs 103; parallels with *My Three Sons* 107; and the peer-ent 97, 99, 101; and product integration and endorsement 35–6, 49–61, *51*, *53*, *55*, *61*; programs airing alongside *98*, 100; promotion of Ricky Nelson 100–3, *102*, *105*
Adventures of Rin Tin Tin, The 99
advertising/advertisements 3; dramatized *see* dramatized advertising; and *Mad Men* 259–61; participating 35, 73, 74; skipping of 3, 9; spot 1, 35, 93, 153
Alice in Wonderland 208, 209, *210*, 211
All in the Family 108
Alternate Reality Games (ARGs) 253
AMC: and *Mad Men* 259–61
America in Primetime 90
American Bandstand 100
American Dairy Association 52
American Dream 39, 43, 92, 94, *165*, 206
American Tobacco Company 43
Anderson, Chris (*Wired*) 245
Anderson, Christopher 192, 235, 245; *Hollywood TV* 15–16
A.N.T. Farm 10, 139, 228
Apple 32; and Disney 10, 18, 250
Arnaz, Desi 38–9
Arvidsson, Adam 11, 12
Austin & Ally 10, 154, 162–3, *164*, 166, 172

B2+ 157, 158, 159, 165
Ball, Alan 91
Ball, Lucille 38, 43, 44
Banet-Weiser, Sarah 20, 157, 174, 175
Baynham, Derek 163, 165

beach culture 132; and *Gidget* 120–1, *122*; *see also Teen Beach Movie*
beach musicals 114, 117
beach party films 114, *116*, 118, 153
Beaumont, Kathryn 211, *212*
Becker, Ron 234
Berg, Gertrude 63
Best Friends Forever (BFF) genre 167, 171, 172–3, 221, *222*
Bewitched 65, 95, 118, 123, 124–5, *126*, 127, 130, *131*
Bieber, Justin 169
Big C, The 87–9, *88*, 91, 92
Big Three networks 3, 19, 86, 94
Bilton, Chris 158
Bing (search engine) 2, 5
bleak comedies 19–20, 86, 87–92; Showtime's pairing of 87–92
Boyce & Hart 130
boutique production firms 21, 160, 162–5
Brady Bunch, The 132, 133–4
brand equity 8, 219
brandcaster type 149–52, 156–7, 159, 160, 162–3
branded credit sequences 7, 10, 35–7, 47
branding theories 8, 11, 12, 13, 149, 150, 152, 159, 219
Briskman, Brian 165
Brooker, Will 258–9
Brookey, Robert Alan 200, 201
Buckley, Peter 159
Bucky Beaver (Ipana toothpaste) 1, *213*, 214
buying: assimilation with being American 61–5
Byrnes, Edd 103, 106

Caldwell, John 12, 37, 201
Californication 89, 90, 91
call-to-affiliation: and television endorsements 8–12
Cameron, Douglas 20, 150, 152, 159, 219; *Cultural Strategy* 150
Camp Rock 2 179
Capaldi, Francesca 225–6, *227*
car sponsorships 47–8; and *Leave It to Beaver* 65–6; *see also* Chevrolet and Dodge
Carlson, Paul (animator) 209, 213–14
Cassidy, David 132, 133
CBS 3, 73, 94, 97
channel branding 11, 13–14, 149–51, 158–60, 173–5, 179; *see also* individual channels and campaigns

channel bugs 37
Charlie's Angels 138
Chevrolet: and *My Three Sons* 47–8
classic network era 3–4, 9, 18, 35, 36, 94, 261
Coca-Cola 36, 50; and *Adventures of Ozzie & Harriet* 52–4, *53*; and Disney 211–13, *212*
Coleman, Zendaya (Rocky) 155, *220*, 220–1, *222*, 222–3
Collette, Toni 92
commodity activism 156–7; *see also* Disney Channel's *Friends for Change*.
company voice advertising 2, 6, 8, 149, 173, 177, 217; and parent company voice 149, 160, 181–2, 191, 226, 236.
Considine, Tim *46*, 108, *109*
content–promotion hybrids 2, 3–4, 8, 10, 21, 38, 192; *see also Disney 365, Disney Re-Micks, Disneyland*, DVD special features
Coontz, Stephanie 71
Coppertop Flop, The 163, *164*, 165
Corcoran, Kevin (Moochie) 215
Cosby Show, The 110
cultural expression theory 159–60
Cuse, Carlton 252
Cyrus, Billy Ray 171
Cyrus, Miley 169, 171–2, *176*, 178

Danny Thomas Show, The 65, 71, 73, 97; *see also Make Room for Daddy*
Dawson's Creek 258–9
Dennis, Saul 149
DeVillier, Lauren 158
Dexter 91
Disney 365 153–4, *154*, 225, 226, *227* 227–8, 234
Disney Channel 10, 12, 17–18, 20–1, 95, 139, 149–82; and Best Friends Forever (BFF) genre 167, 171, 172–3, 221, *222*; and boutique content-about-content firms 163–5; as brandcaster 149–52; brandcasting through myth stories 20, 156–9; broadcast yourself imperative 156; decision engines 223–8; disassociation from/by stars 171; *Friends for Change* (FFC) campaign 21, 159, 173–7, *176*, 180–1; *Friends for Change* music videos 178–81; friendship theme 21, 172–4, 220; obstinate optimist and "in-betweener" content 159–62, 168; as premium/basic cable hybrid 152–6; princess type 198; purchaser citizens and

parent company sustainability 181–2; and Radio Disney 153, 159, 168–9, 179, 180; rerun schedule 155; and short-form content/Social Shorts 149–50, 153–4, 157–9, 160, 163; special event programming 155; sponsors and product integration 174; stable of stars 167; sunny outlook on stardom 21, 165–9
Disney Channels Worldwide 13–14, 18
Disney Fairies 198; and Pixie Hollow 198, 225, 228
Disney Junior 12
Disney Parks: on *Modern Family* and *The Middle* 228–35; and *Disney Memories* 232–4
Disney Princesses 167, 198–9; 223–4, 226, 228, 230–2
Disney, Roy 194, 208
Disney Studios 14–18, 21–2, 191–236; and ABC 12, 95, 96, 216; and Apple 10, 18, 250; Blu-ray/DVD combo packs 11, 15, 21, 191–2, 199–206; and brandcasting 191–3; Coca-Cola and custom character-based commercials 211–14, *212*; content-about-content shorts 21, 192; and *Frozen* 15, 197–9, 219; and hosted lead-ins 21, 192, 206–11, *212*; interpretive frames on Blu-ray/DVDs 200–6; peer-to-peer marketing 15, 16–18; and product integration 174, 213, 234; and *Saving Mr. Banks* 15, 22, 192, 193–7, 199, 209, 216; sponsors of films 214; television "trailerizing" 214–23; and "The Titlemakers" 217–19, 235–6; uses of "togetherness" 219–20; *see also* individual programs
Disney, Walt 193–5, *193*, 199–200, *202*, 203, *204*, 206, 207–12, *210*, *212*, 215, 216–17, *216*, 236; as "author" and interpretive authority 199–200; and office set *202*, *204*, 207–11, 209, *210*, 215, *216*, 217; and self-mythologizing *204*, 205–9; *210*, 211, 215; *see also* hosted lead-ins
Disney XD 12, 172–3
Disney–ABC Television Group 12
Disneyland (ABC-TV) 2, 12, 16, 21–2, 96, 99, 192, 203, 206, 213, 215, 227
Disneyland *154*, 215, *227*, 227–8; in *Modern Family* and *The Middle* 228–35, *229*, *230*, *233*
Disney's Friends for Change 139
Disney's Re-Micks 246–9, *247*
Disney's Wonderful World of Color 215

Dodd, Jimmie 1, 214
Dodge: and *Make Room for Daddy* 39, *40*, *41*, 42
Dog with a Blog 225–6
Donna Reed Show, The 9, 35, 47, *48*, 61, 62–3, 100, 112, 114–17, *115*, *116*; linking with *My Three Sons* 106, *106*
Donny and Marie 138
Douglas, Kirk *204*, 205
Douglas, Susan 106
dramatized advertisements/advertising 10, 35, 38–9, 62; *The Adventures of Ozzie & Harriet* 50–2, 56–60, 61; and Kodak 54–6
Driscoll, Bobby 211
Duchovny, David 90, 91
DVD special features 200–6
Duff, Howard 44
Duke, Patty 117–18, *119*
Dyer, Richard 43, 166

Eight is Enough 134–5, 138
Ellis, John 14, 20, 87, 149
embedded music video 9, 19, 100, *105*
ethnic issues 62, 63, 71, 228–32; and *Bewitched* 125, *126*; and ethnic striver type on *Make Room for Daddy* 39–40, 42, 65
ethnic sitcoms 63, 64, 65, 71
"ethnicity without specificity" (on Disney Channel) 221–2

Fabares, Shelley 9, 114, *115*, *116*, 117
Facebook 4–6; Like function 4, 5, 173; partnership with Bing 5
family: branding the modern 32–5
Father Knows Best 61, 62–3, 65, 99, 111
Field, Sally 96, 118, 120, 121, 132
Flying Nun, The 121, 123, 132
Ford, Sam 178
Fosters, The 197–8
FOX 94
Frawley, William 45, 108, *109*
"friend and recommend" paradigm 5, 6–7
Friends for Change (FFC) campaign: Disney Channel 21, 139, 159, 173–7, *176*, 180–1
Friends for Change Games 177
Friends for Change music videos 178–81
friendship theme, and Disney Channel 21, 172–4, 220
Frozen 15, 197–9, 219
Funicello, Annette 215, 217, 218, *218*, 219, 235–6

Gaines, Jane 114
generational accord programs 9, 19; and *My Three Sons* 106–10
George Burns and Gracie Allen Show, The 1
Gerlitz, Carolin 4
Gidget 9, 110, 118, 119–21, *122*, 132
Giggey, Lindsay 103
Gillan, Jennifer: *Television and New Media* 13, 35, 250
Girl Meets World 139
Goldbergs, The 63–5
Gomez, Selena 167, 168–9, 171, *176*, 178, 226
Grady, Don *46*, 107, 108, *109*
Grainge, Paul 13, 14, 157, 158, *Brand Hollywood* 13; *Ephemeral Media* 13, 14
Gray, Jonathan 12, 14, 158, 192, 235–6; *Show Sold Separately* 12; *see also* paratexts
Green, Joshua 178
Gutkind, Lee 208

Hannelius, G. (Amy Little) 223–6; *227*, 229
Hawaiian Eye 103, 106
Halberstam, David 66, 72
Hannah Montana 18, 155, 169–72
Happy Days 110, 135
Hartley, John 62, 95
Hay, James 20
HBO 91, 92
Helmond, Anne 4
Hench, John 206
Hine, Thomas 38
Holt, Douglas 8, 12, 20, 150, 152, 157, 159–60, 219, 237; *How Brands Become Icons* 150; *Cultural Strategy* 150
Homeland 92
Honey West 118
Honeymooners, The 63
hosted lead-ins: and Disney 21, 192, 206–11, *212*
Hotpoint: and *Adventures of Ozzie & Harriet* 58, 60–1, *61*
Howard, Leo (Leo Little) 223–6; *227*, 229

I Love Lucy 39, 42–4, 97
identity value 8, 219
implicit communication 152, 158–9
iPad 10, 18, 32
It's On! (Disney Channel) 178, 179
iTunes 250

Jack Daniel's 259–60, 261
Jenkins, Henry 178, 248
Jobs, Steve 18
Johnson, Catherine 13, 157–8; *Branding Television* 13
Jonas 169–70; *Jonas LA* 169, 170–1
Jonas Brothers 169–70, *176*, 178
Jonas, Joe *102*, *176*, 179
Jones, Shirley 132

King, Marlene 255
Knight, Sterling *224*, 225
Kodak 36; and *Adventures of Ozzie & Harriet* 8–9, 36, 54–6, *55*, *57*, *58*
Kompare, Derek 64

Laverne & Shirley 135, 136, *136*, 221
Leave It to Beaver 35, 38, 65–7, 73, 97, 110–14, *113*
Lemonade Mouth 180
Leo Little's Big Show 191–2, 193, 223–6, *224*
"Like economy" 4–5
Lipsitz, George 64
Livingston, Stanley *46*, 108 *109*
Lizzie McGuire 221
Lorre, Peter *205*, 206
Lost 94, 249–53
Lounsberry, Barbara 208
Lovato, Demi *102*, 167, *176*, 178, 179, 197
Love on a Rooftop 127, 130
Lucy–Desi Comedy Hour, The 44
Lupino, Ida 44
Lury, Celia 12
Lynch, Ross 153–4, *154*, 163

M3 Creative 163, 226
McClain, China Anne 139, 228
McCormick, Maureen 133
MacMurray, Fred 44–5, *46*, 107, 108, 110, 217
McNichol, Kristy 136
Mad Men 22, 259–61
Mad-vertising concept 260–1
magazine-concept commercial spots 73, 74
magic sitcoms 118, 125
Mahone, Austin 165–6
Make Room for Daddy 39–42, *40–1*, 43, 65, 97, *126*
Make Your Mark 160, 165–6
Malibu U 118
Mama 64
Mann, Denise 437

Marcel, Kelly 194–6
Marshall, Gary 135
Mary Poppins 194, 197, 209, 216
Mendler, Bridgit 180
Michael, Blake 225, *227*
Mickey Mouse Club, The 7, 12, 16–17, *17*, 96, 100, 192, 214; sponsors for 214
Mickey Mouse 193, 214, 246–9, *247*
Middle, The 10, 19, 67–71, *70*, 93; Disney Parks on 232–5, *233*
Mills, Hayley 217
mind share model 8
Mitchell, Maia 163
Modern Family 9, 10, 19, 32–4, *33*, 58, 67, 68, 93, 94; Disney Parks on 228–32, *229*, *230*, *231*; Phil Dunphy and peer-enting on 10, 32–4,*33*; and product integration 34–5, 68
Monkees, The 107
Montgomery, Elizabeth 96, 118, 125, 127, 130, *131*
Moor, Liz 12
Moore, Mary Tyler 60
Mukherjee, Roopali 20, 157, 174, 175
Mullin, Danielle 253–4, 255, 258
Murray, Susan 37
Must-Click TV model 248, 249, 262
My Three Sons 9, 35, 44–8, *46*, *57*, 63, 65, 97, 106–10, *109*; and Generational Accord sitcom cycle 106–10; linking of with *Donna Reed Show* 106, *106*
myth stories 8–9, 92, 139; Disney Channel and brandcasting through 20, 156–9

Nanny and the Professor 134
Napoli, Philip 12, 90, 259
narrowcast broadcasting 86–7
NBC 3, 35, 86, 94, 96
Negra, Diane 43, 44
Nelson, Harriet 36, 49
Nelson, Ozzie 9, 19, 34, 36, 49, 58, 100, 101
Nelson, Ricky 49, 56, 58, 100–3, 101, *102*, *105*
Netflix 261
Nickelodeon 139, 153
Nielsen ratings 5
Nurse Jackie 89, 91–2

obstinate optimist type *136*, 157, 159–62; *see also* Walt Disney
Odd Couple, The 134
One Hour in Wonderland 211, *212*

101 Dalmatians 199, 202
Osmond, Donny and Marie 138
Ouellette, Laurie 20
Ozzie & Harriet see The Adventures of Ozzie & Harriet

P&G 62
Page, Ruth 259
Palmer, Benjamin 260
paratexts 10, 12, 14, 158, 192, 211–12, 217–19, 235–6
Parent Trap, The 217, 218, 219
participating advertising 35, 73, 74
Partridge Family, The 132–3
Patty Duke Show 117–18, *119*
peer-ent 9, 19, 96, 101, 110, 135; and *Adventures of Ozzie & Harriet* 97, 99, 101; and *Modern Family* 33
peer-to-peer recommendation/marketing 6, 9, 11, 19, 173; and Disney 15, 16–18
Pepsi 52
Pepsi Generation campaigns 58
Pepsi-Cola Playhouse, The 99
Peter Pan 199–200, 215; and Peter Pan Peanut Butter 1, 213–14
Phineas and Ferb 151, 152, 178
Pomerantz, Ron 165
Porter, Don (Russ Lawrence) 110, 120
presentation of the self 200
Presley, Elvis 117
Pretty Little Liars 249, 252, 254–6
Prime-Time Access Rule (PTAR) 93
Princess Protection Program 167
product integration 19, 62; and *The Adventures of Ozzie & Harriet* 35–6, 49–61, *51*, *53*, *55*, *61*; and Disney Channel/Studios 174, 213, 234; and *Father Knows Best* 62–3; and *Leave It to Beaver* 111; and *The Middle* 34, 67–71; and *Modern Family* 32, 34–5, 68; and sitcoms 37, 50; and sponsored credit sequences 35–7
promotional surround 8, 11, 12, 13–14, 18, 23, 236
pull model 4
push model 3–4, 100–6

Quaker Oats: and *Adventures of Ozzie & Harriet* 50, *51*

Ralston Purina 38
Ray Bolger Show, The 99

recommendation engine: US television as
a 245
Red Bee Media 13, 158
Reed, Donna 100; as Donna Stone 47,
48, 62
Riverstreet Productions 157, 158, 159, 160,
175
rock 'n' roll: on ABC 100–6; and *Gidget*
118, 119–20; and *Patty Duke Show*
117–18, *119*
Room 222 134
Rushdie, Salman 197

Sands, Tommy 217, 219
Saving Mr. Banks 15, 22, 192, 193–7, 199,
209, 216
schedule/scheduling 86–139; and ABC
96–139; classic network 94; definition
96; how it works on a broadcast
network 93–4; importance of as an
industry practice 96; Showtime's "bleak
comedies" pairing 87–92
Send It On Disney Channel campaign 178
Sennett, Richard 20, 157
7ate9 Entertainment 157, 158, 159, 165,
166, 177, 191, 246
Shaggy Dog, The 16
Shake It Up 220–1, *220*, 223
Sherman Brothers 197
Shindig! 117, 118
Shore, Nick 157
Showtime 86–7, 92; and American
Dream 92; bleak comedy pairings
87–92; and HBO 90–2; number of
subscribers 92
sitcoms 3, 10, 35, 37; ethnic 63, 64, 65, 71;
magic 118, 125; and product integration
37, 50; re-contextualizing 1950s
sponsored 71–4; star 36, 38, 42–8, 50,
117, 167, 170; suburban 36, 37, 62, 63,
65, 71–2, 73, 95; tween-inclusive 34, 68,
123, 125, 134–5, 136, 138–9; urban 65;
see also individual programs
smart phones 1, 2, 4, 180, 229, 249–50,
253–5, 262
Smith, Sue 196
Snow White and the Seven Dwarfs 199, 202
social media: and *Dawson's Creek* 258–9;
and *Pretty Little Liars* 255–8; *see also*
Facebook; Twitter
Social Shorts: and Disney 149–50, 153–4,
157–9, 160, 163

Sonny with a Chance 166–7
Sopranos, The 91
Spigel, Art 165
Spigel, Lynn 60
Spin and Marty 16, 214
sponsor messaging 9–10
sponsored credit sequences 35–7; and
Adventures of Ozzie & Harriet 52, 54–6,
56; and Kodak 54–6, *55*; and *My Three
Sons* 47–8
sponsorship model 73
spot advertising 1, 35, 93, 153
spreadable media 178
"stamps of ownership" 37, *57*
star sitcoms 36, 38, 42–8, 50, 117, 167, 170
stardom: Disney's sunny outlook on 165–9
Stars on the Set 223
Stevens, Connie 103, 106
Stu Erwin Show, The 99
suburban sitcoms 36, 37, 62, 63, 65, 71–2,
73, 95
suburbanality 62, 95
Survivor 252
Sweeney, Anne 153, 250

Tangled 223, *224*, *231*, 231–2
Teen Beach Movie (*TBM*) 153, 163, 197,
226
television endorsements: and call-to-
affiliation 8–12
Telotte, J.P.: *Disney TV* 15, 16, 235
text messaging 254
Thank God It's Friday/*Thank God It's
Funny* (*TGIF*) 138–9
That Girl 123–4, 127, 130, 132
That's So Raven 221
"think youngs" 20, 32, 33–4, 52, 58, 62,
95–6, 133
Thomas, Danny 38–9, *39*, 44, 65
Thomas, Marlo 123, 127, *129*
Thompson, Sada 136
Thorne, Bella 155, *220*, 220–1, *222*,
222–3
Thornton, Tiffany *224*, 225
Thursday's Girls *129*
time franchises 6, 36–7, 73, 100
Tinker Bell 215, 216, *216*
Time I…., The (*TTI* …) 160–1, *161*
Travers, P.L. 194–5, 198, 199, 216
True Blood 91
Turow, Joseph 12
Tween B movies 16, 180, 215

tween-inclusive programming 34, 68, 123, 125, 134–5, 136, 138–9, 160, 162, 175, 182, 214, 223
20,000 Leagues Under the Sea 202, 203–6, *204*, *205*
24 2
Twitter 249; and *Pretty Little Liars* 253–7

Ultimate Goldbergs, The (DVD) 72–3
United States of Tara, 89, 91

Veronica Mars 254
Video-On-Demand (VOD) 250
viewers: and their networks of friends 4–8
"viewsers" 4, 177, 182, 245
viral model 8

Walt Disney Company 10, 12, 13, 14–15, 152, 173, 177, 181; brand-centric approach to television 192; *see also* Disney Channel; Disney Studios

Walt Disney Presents 2, 16, 21–2, 192, 193, *193*, 195, *202*, 206–7, 215, 216, 217
Walt Disney Records 248
Wasko, Janet: *Understanding Disney* 15
Weeds 88, 89–92, *92*
Weiner, Matt 260–1
Welch's 7, 214
Welcome Back, Kotter 33–4
Wernick, Andrew 66
Westerfelhaus, Robert 200, 201
Who I Am 163
Wilmott, Michael 175
Wizard of Oz, The 197
Wizards of Waverly Place 167–8, 169
Worthy, Calum 163, 165
Wyatt, Jane 62

YouTube 156, 165–6, 180, 191

Zorro 12

Printed by PGSTL